Documentary Resistance

Documentary Resistance

SOCIAL CHANGE AND PARTICIPATORY MEDIA

ANGELA J. AGUAYO

OXFORD
UNIVERSITY PRESS

Oxford University Press is a department of the University of Oxford. It furthers
the University's objective of excellence in research, scholarship, and education
by publishing worldwide. Oxford is a registered trade mark of Oxford University
Press in the UK and certain other countries.

Published in the United States of America by Oxford University Press
198 Madison Avenue, New York, NY 10016, United States of America.

Library of Congress Cataloging-in-Publication Data
Names: Aguayo, Angela J., 1974– author.
Title: Documentary resistance : social change and participatory media /
Angela J. Aguayo.
Description: [New York, New York] : Oxford University Press, [2019] |
Includes bibliographical references and index.
Identifiers: LCCN 2018054422 (print) | LCCN 2019010774 (ebook) |
ISBN 9780190676230 (updf) | ISBN 9780190676247 (epub) |
ISBN 9780190676254 (oso) | ISBN 9780190676216 (cloth :alk. paper) |
ISBN 9780190676223 (paperback :alk. paper)
Subjects: LCSH: Documentary films—United States. |
Documentary films—Social aspects—United States. |
Social change—United States.
Classification: LCC PN1995.9.D6 (ebook) |
LCC PN1995.9.D6 A33 2019 (print) | DDC 070.1/8—dc23
LC record available at https://lccn.loc.gov/2018054422

This book is dedicated to my ancestors,
who dared to dream and sacrifice for who I could become.

And to my son Zachary,
whose energy and excitement about the future fuels my daily resolve for justice.

Contents

Preface   ix
About the Companion Website   xiii

1. Introduction: Documentary Resistance   1

2. A Critical History of Documentary and Participatory Media
   Cultures   27

3. Documentary Goes Popular: The Rise of Digital Media Cultures   61

4. Laboring under Documentary: Collective Identification and
   the Collapse of the American Working Class   103

5. Subjugated Histories and Affective Resistance: Abortion
   Documentaries as Botched Political Subjectivity   149

6. Street Tapes: The People's History of Unjustified Police Force   183

7. Conclusion: The Documentary Commons and Conditions of
   Resistance   227

Notes   241
References   255
Index   271

Preface

When I think of pivotal moments I experienced while writing this book, one particular memory comes to the surface. As I began researching documentary film in historical archives and poking around film collections in libraries and museums, I asked archivists, curators, and librarians how to search for political films. I asked this question without realizing how it violated hard disciplinary boundaries set in place precisely to hinder such an investigation. The reoccurring looks of bewilderment I received will long remain with me, a sign that I was clearly offroading in interdisciplinary history, moving away from the well-worn trails of the cinema archive. At the time, I was too naïve to realize that the question I was asking was unanswerable within the existing classification frameworks. Cinema history was organized to tell the story of auteurs and great films; cinema archives are arranged to preserve a "high art," above the base reaches of "low" politics.

I would like to be able to report that this is where my research trouble ended, but when I packed up my recording equipment and traveled across the country to ask filmmakers, activists, funders, and distributors about social change documentary, the look I received when I asked the question, "Do you make activist documentary?" was almost as uncomfortable as the look the archivists had given me when I asked about finding political films. The way media creators squirmed, talked around, and resisted the term *activist* was fascinating. It was as though the question forced them to decide between activist and artistic subjectivity. Some filmmakers went to great lengths to explain the incompatibility of these subjectivities, resisting the way an "activist" orientation could taint the creation of "art." Others gladly accepted the label and leaned into this mode of production thinking. The tension between the aesthetic and political hangs over documentary history, obscuring a dynamic capacity for documentary to exceed the cinema. Studying documentary's position at the intersection of other social formations, such as civic engagement and social protest, contributes to understanding the shifts of democratic practice. After discovering these obstacles to establishing a basic shared vocabulary for documentary and social change, you might think I would give up, but something kept pulling at me.

My involvement with documentary and social change was almost accidental. It started in the summer of 2000, when I found myself at the University of Texas working toward a PhD in Communication Studies, with a focus on rhetoric, media, and social movements. I began taking video production classes because the readings I did for my PhD course work did not always align with my activist production experiences. I was bringing my Hi8 video camera to protests and demonstrations in the area, recording things I had never seen on television, from the collective joys of mass mobilization to the unjust use of police force. Media production became a way for me to use the theories of communication and rhetoric I was studying in the actual process of political struggle. This meant experimenting with theories of identification while editing activist street tapes and crafting political images around points of stasis in my efforts to circulate grassroots narratives. This period in my life happened to coincide with one of the most significant technological shifts of our time, the movement from analog to digital. This shift radically transformed the process of making, manipulating, and circulating documentary discourse.

I found myself in a position where I had to confront the mounting tension I felt between my studies and my production practice. The story of documentary and social change begins before a film is made, exists on and off screen, and lingers long after it is shown, but the scholars I was reading viewed the screen as the dominant frame for meaning construction. There is a deep disparity between the way documentary and social change happens in the streets and the way it is (or is not) articulated in scholarship. This divide covers a rich terrain of social knowledge that has not yet been deeply explored in the study of documentary: the public capacities of documentary that exceed cinema. There are opportunities for social change at every point in the creative process, from the moment one starts asking questions through postproduction and circulation. This book is an attempt to step into this void of academic understanding and create space for different approaches to knowledge production, exposing intellectual pathways that could help us navigate the world as it evolves.

Documentary Resistance rereads documentary history with a focus on participatory media cultures, attempting to understand some of the more concrete ways documentary engages social change. Scholars have had periods of magical thinking about documentary's revolutionary potential, but they have not sufficiently investigated how the force of cinematic intervention might manifest in micro-interactions, local struggles, collective experiments, and in the stories of people who have direct experience with this engagement. Documentary circulation creates something new in politics, a space I call a *documentary commons*, which continually grows, takes shape, and expands its participatory capacities. I extend this idea of the documentary commons by focusing on the period of history when technology shifts from analog tools into a digital landscape.

Underlying the study of documentary and social change is a story about people's movements, the powerful interventions made possible through collaborative action with others. If collective identification around shared interests is the most powerful force we have to combat the institutional structures that contain our autonomy, there is a type of political agency that only manifests in collaboration with others. The histories of struggles, represented and channeled through documentary, continue in our contemporary environment. These book chapters are commitments to understanding the vital struggles around race, class, and gender that underpin our most pressing social problems. I am particularly grateful to the filmmakers, activists, curators, and critics who opened up their lives and shared their experiences to help us understand this shifting documentary landscape, including Barbara Abrash, Pat Aufderheide, Jennifer Baumgardner, Ronit Bezalel, Skip Blumberg, Mike Bonanno, Maria Juliana Byck, Sarah Chapman, Salome Chasnoff, Tony Chauncy, Antonino D'Ambrosio, Larry Daressa, Kirby Dick, Brian Drolet, Larry Duncun, Jill Friedberg, Josh Fox, Tami Gold, Stephen Gong, Pam Haldeman, Sue Harris, Judith Helfand, Judy Hoffman, Mary Kerr, Penny Lane, Wendy Levy, Anne Lewis, Linda Litowsky, Marty Lucas, Cornelius Moore, Jennifer Morris, Dee Mosbacher, Justine Nagan, Doug Norbert, Lourdes Portillo, DA Pennebaker, Gordon Quinn, Karen Ranucci, Stefan Ray, Brigid Reagan, Amy Richards, Jim Sommers, Lauren Sorenson, Ellen Spiro, George C. Stoney, Judy Tam, Dorothy Thigpen, Keiko Tsuno, Lois Vossen, Martha Wallner, Tom Weinberg, Garry Wilkison, Denise Zaccardi, Steve Zelzer, and Debra Zimmerman.

This book would not be possible without the material and institutional support of Southern Illinois University, Carbondale. To support the field research and completion of this book project, I was awarded a Faculty Seed Grant and the Judge William Holmes Cook Professorship, as well as sabbatical release. This internal funding was critical to sustaining the scope of this project. My colleagues in the College of Mass Communication and Media Arts at Southern Illinois University have been incredible champions of this work. I deeply appreciate the support of Dean Deborah Tudor, Dean Dafna Lemish, Dean Gary Kolb, John D. H. Downing, Jyotsna Kapur, Cade Bursell, Howard Motyl, Jan Roddy, Lilly Boruszkowski, Jennida Chase, Wago Kreider, Lisa Brooten, and Sarah Lewison. Much of this research began at Eastern Illinois University, where I was awarded the Redden Funds Grant and the Council on Faculty Research Grant to complete preliminary research into this project. I am grateful for their willingness to support such an ambitious proposal.

I dearly appreciate Senior Editor Norm Hirschy and Oxford University Press for the dedicated support they have shown for *Documentary Resistance*. With the sustained help of assistant editor Lauralee Yeary, Norm has guided this project with precision and ease, allowing the book to develop beyond my expectations. One of my favorite books from Oxford University Press is Eric Barnouw's *Documentary: A History of the Non-Fiction Film*. This book shaped my thinking around documentary as a movement of people committed to creating social change with cinematic vision. His essential book trails off in an exciting part of the story, just as the digital landscape radically transforms the possibilities of the documentary impulse. This book is my contribution to documentary history, picking up where Barnouw leaves off and documenting the shifts into a burgeoning digital world of participatory engagement.

I am also tremendously grateful to the generous colleagues who provided constructive criticism on portions of this work, including Dana Cloud, Chris Robé, Lisa Foster, Julia Lesage, Chuck Kleinhans, Kristen Hoerl, Anne Demo, Sarah Projanski, and Sarah VanGundy. Many people, consciously or not, provided critical insights at conferences, passing in hallways, in collaborative meetings, and while working together in the process of organizing life. I am grateful to the following people who are a significant influence on this project: Rob Asen, Jennifer Asenas, Deirdre Boyle, Dan Brouwer, Karma Chavez, Richard Cherwitz, Cara Finnegan, Terri Fredrick, DeeDee Halleck, Melissa Hubbard, Kevin Johnson, Casey Kelly, Megan Lotts, Steve Macek, Shane Miller, Phaedra Pezzullo, B. Ruby Rich, Clemencia Rodriguez, Mehdi Semati, Tim Steffensmeier, Carrie Wilson-Brown, Rebecca Walker, Jaime Wright, Amy Young, and Patricia Zimmermann. There was a generous village that came together to help organize the research for this project. I am thankful for the graduate assistants who dedicated labor and care: Molly Brandonis, Katie Griffis, Abimbola Iyun, Joseph Valle, and Mark Walters. There are also a handful of people who have shaped my process, pushing me into productive spaces with an unwavering belief in my ability to figure it all out. Thank you for showing me a little light so that I could find my way: Matt Taylor, Liana Koeppel, Sharon Downey, Karen Rasmussen, Dana Cloud, Ellen Spiro, Rosa Eberly, Ronald Greene, Chuck Morris, Alex Juhasz, and Angharad Valdivia. To my glorious band of friends and family who keep me buoyant in rough and calm seas, thank you for your love and support: Larry and Sarah Aguayo, Alex Hivoltze-Jimenez, Caroline Rankin, Felicia Coco, Christopher DeSurra, Nicole Sieber, Angela Reinoehl, my parents, Florencio and Cheryl Aguayo as well as my extended family

Finally, I would like to thank my life partner, coconspirator, and project doula, Daniel Elgin. Dan lives his feminism every single day, placing energy and resources behind my ability to complete this project and many others like it. The Elgin family, Joan and Gary, provide invaluable support by stepping in to be our village at a moment's notice. Thank you for helping make this dream come true.

Angela J. Aguayo
Carbondale, IL
October 2018

About the Companion Website

www.oup.com/us/documentaryresistance

This companion website includes a small sample of the raw interview data generated in the research process. These extended interviews with filmmakers continue the conversation started by *Documentary Resistance: Social Change and Participatory Media*. You will find interview clips from eight featured filmmakers discussing historical context around specific productions, questions of ethics, descriptions of production culture, and experiences with documentary in the process of social change.

1

Introduction

Documentary Resistance

Cinema, with its status as both popular and "high" art and its ability to creatively reimagine linear depictions of time and causality, offers filmmakers and audiences new ways to visualize themselves and their futures. When communities are disenfranchised and marginalized or when injustice is buried by the news feed, motion picture storytelling can fill in what is elided from dominant media narratives. By drawing attention to the public imaginary's willful amnesia, cinematic representation creates empathetic pathways to a more inclusive public commons. Coming into its own during the Progressive Era, a period of widespread activism and political reform that spanned the years 1890–1920, motion picture technology attracted educators, activists, and moral leaders. As this technology progressed, the belief grew that movies could help solve society's problems. In the years before 1919, "social problem" or "thought films" were used to sway mass audiences. These films were sociological, addressing unsavory behavior or social delinquency as well as systemic problems such as poverty, capturing the attention of audiences seeking more than entertainment. Instead of providing escape, these motion pictures engaged audiences with the political power of novel representations, riveting viewers with reflections of daily life that could compel hearts, change minds, and give spectators a motivation to act. Historically, in moments of political and social crisis, the documentary impulse has intervened in the political process, challenging viewers to engage in the world around them.

The story of documentary and social change in the United States is one of self-determination. People—often of humble means—demanding recognition and dignity for themselves and their communities have used the documentary to find pathways into a better life. In 1909, fifty years after the end of slavery, Booker T. Washington commissioned his first documentary, projecting new images of a free and self-determining African American working class on community screens across the nation. In the 1930s, workers risked financial destitution and their own safety to document collective responses to abusive working conditions. Galvanized by technological ingenuity that made formerly cumbersome cameras mobile, people documented workers' struggles in the streets. The story of documentary is a story of people unwilling to give up on the dream of an inclusive democracy, harnessing the use of moving images, the form of film, and the mode of documentary to represent their demands for a better world. In the 1960s, for example, women were dying from dirty medical procedures in makeshift operating rooms. The horror of back-alley abortions and the lack of access to birth control led women to pick up film cameras and demand a new vision for women's health. This required an unwavering belief in the inclusivity and diversity of democracy as women were met with exploitation and marginalization. Lesbian, gay, bisexual, transgender (LGBT) workers in the 1990s, suffering widespread discrimination and at the risk of losing their jobs, picked up cameras to demand labor protections and adequate access to medical care. The evolution of documentary production has seen media makers attacked and arrested, including Lester Balog, who spent forty-five days in jail for screening a labor documentary for striking agricultural workers. In these acts of resistance, beginning with a refusal of consent and compliance, activists set limits on the authority of others by demonstrating "the failure to adapt one's behavior to the demands of the state, of the law and of capital."[1] Even when they were oppressed by the powerful, these filmmakers persisted, and their media practices proliferated and propagated new ideas and dreams. The story of documentary and social change in the United States is a story of self-determination and the long and treacherous roads of resistance we have traveled and continue to travel to achieve these ends. Documentary's potent collision with political struggle is deeply woven into every layer of the United States' social world.

In our contemporary media ecology, popular culture often demonstrates that truth is more compelling than fiction. The documentary genre, with audiences growing in leaps and bounds, has captured the mass imaginary in the past twenty years. There is a robust but selective commercial market for documentary, led by HBO, PBS, ESPN, Sundance, and Tribeca. Short-form documentary is increasingly present in public culture, with major media outlets like the *New York Times*, National Public Radio, and *The Atlantic* now investing in short-form production. Documentary moving image has advanced from the margins of the mediascape to inhabit the spaces of popular media and online circulation.[2] Political documentary is readily visible, accessible, and present in popular culture and sometimes proves tremendously influential. As many film critics suggest, documentary viewers are left with "the feeling that these are more than just movies."[3] Technological innovations at the turn of the century, including the standardization of the internet and developments in mobile recording, helped move the influence of documentary and its audience beyond the screen, creating the potential for cross-platform experiences and the emergence of digitally connected participatory media cultures.

Filmmakers at the inception of moving-image technology could never have imagined the unprecedented emphasis on media engagement in our current historical moment.[4] The evolution of mobile media technology, our social media habits, and the omnipresence of multiple media platforms have resulted in new and evolving ways of interacting with the media screen: "The defining narrative of our online moment concerns the decline of text, and the exploding reach and power of audio and video."[5] These conditions of digital culture coincide with significant contemporary political and social upheaval. This moment bears witness to multiple sectors of society experiencing a crippling economic crisis, growing dissatisfaction with representative government, and widespread disillusionment with state institutions. This combination of historical and technological conditions has given rise to emerging participatory media culture(s) that are engaged in recording life, addressing publics, exposing exploitation, facilitating media witnessing, and wresting back the means of media production and circulation from the hands of the powerful.

These intersecting documentary media cultures have produced a growing participatory commons that uses collective social practices of creating, remixing, and sharing documentary recordings as a means of engaging politics. The present volume responds to this charged contemporary reemergence of documentary moving-image culture(s), investigating the ways the genre is harnessed as a tool of political engagement and exhibiting protest functions such as witnessing, petitioning, solidification, polarization, and promulgation. This project explores how "antagonism opens the possibility not only for questioning ideologies and hegemonic discourse that sustain relations of oppression and marginalization but for beginning to articulate alternatives."[6] Antagonism in the form of open friction and opposition is critical; it fuels the social change process in a way that produces opportunities for collective conjuring. In addition to recognizing the protest function of documentary, it is important to ask practical questions about the everyday ways the genre engages and enacts the process of social change. The tempo of social transformation is slow, and the struggle is often incremental; where does documentary fit? As new media technologies emerge, altering who is speaking and to whom, documentary studies and practices rest on the precipice of history, an incredible vantage point from which to realize the long-theorized potential of the genre to support democracy and social transformation.

The contemporary documentary audience includes home media makers who can systematically recirculate documentary discourse and enter into conversation with existing, often activist, participatory media publics. As Jonathan Kahana explains, documentary makes "visible the invisible or 'phantom' realities that shape the experience of the ordinary Americans in whose name power is exercised and contested."[7] The evolving ties between documentary and digital innovation in a turbulent political moment has created promising new spaces of civic engagement. As Jane Gaines suggests, "The reason for using films instead of leaflets and pamphlets in the context of organizing is that films make their appeals through the senses . . . where the ideal viewer is poised to intervene in the world that so closely resembles the one represented on screen."[8] Although many are grappling with the question, little existing theoretical research attempts to understand documentary as a material force of social change.

Over the past century, documentary film and video have routinely intervened in social change processes, with mixed results. Although some documentaries have functioned as a significant political force, others have been nothing more than a small flicker on the cinematic landscape. We can see this in the contrast between Fredrick Wiseman's work, which resulted in significant social change—altering the privacy regulations for state mental institutions[9]—and the participatory media street tapes that emerged from video collectives in the 1970s. These collectives, such as the People's Video Theater and Video Freex, began to surface following the proliferation of lightweight, inexpensive, portable video technology, which provided the tools for representing absent voices in a troubled democracy. As Deidre Boyle[10] and DeeDee Halleck[11] noted, however, these tapes did little to improve civic participation or ignite systematic social change. In 1988, Errol Morris debuted *A Thin Blue Line*, which helped secure the release of Randall Adams, a falsely convicted death row inmate. During this same time, several historical documentaries about abortion history, such as *Back-Alley Detroit* and *From Danger to Dignity*, were released and functioned primarily to create cultural change through education, with little connection to the active political struggles around abortion. A surge in high-profile advocacy-oriented documentaries at the turn of the century, including *Fahrenheit 9/11* (2004), *Super Size Me* (2004), *Wal-Mart: The High Cost of Low Prices* (2005), and *An Inconvenient Truth* (2006), left news reporters, critics, educators, and politicians wondering how these documentary events might impact the contingent social and political landscape.[12]

Discussions of documentary and social change take place under a variety of conceptual labels: participatory media, solidarity documentary, advocacy documentary, committed documentary, agit-prop documentary, social justice documentary, and activist documentary. The media identified by these terms often share common concerns and an intention to participate in the struggle for social justice, but they are not equally engaged in the process of social change. As film critic A. O. Scott notes, "There may be more well-intentioned bad non-fiction movies than any other kind, films that satisfy the moral aspirations of their makers, but not much else."[13] This book investigates exactly what happens when documentary discourse succeeds or fails in intervening in the process of social change and how films made during specific moments of history reveal a new understanding of the status of the nonfiction image.

Documentary and social change is a broad and emerging area of research, conducted mostly by social scientists and critical scholars engaged in assessing the reception, learning, and collective processes facilitated by documentaries,[14] as well as the historical and political context of documentary circulation.[15] As David Whiteman notes, " investigations of the political impact of documentary film have typically been guided by a quite narrow 'individualistic model' of assessment that does not reflect the diverse and layered potential of the genre to intervene in the process of social transformation."[16] It is well established that documentary can function as a democratic tool with civic potential,[17] but little research has been done on the specific practices through which documentaries engage, call forth, and speak to media publics for social change.[18] The current scholarship lacks (1) a serious theoretical consideration of social change as it is facilitated by the documentary experience; (2) an understanding of social change documentary as an action, not a subgenre; (3) a broader historical account of influential but little known film communities (undocumented community screenings and practices, an account of influential underground filmmakers, and a framework for understanding rare but noteworthy activist works); (4) a bridging of documentary scholarship and practice that seeks a more holistic understanding of the social function of the field; and (5) an interpretation of the possibilities for social change documentary as technology shifts from an analog environment into a digital culture of participatory media publics. This book hopes to address these underdeveloped areas of research by building on established interdisciplinary work in documentary studies.

Most social change documentary manifests locally, with community-based organizing and coalition building with other struggles, coalescing in participatory media cultures invested in change. The scope of this study, which is focused on the U.S. documentary and historical context, is significantly determined by the very local character of the genre's enactment. The project acknowledges that documentary travels beyond the nation-state and that its global impacts are undeniable, but the local, grounded, and specific ways participatory media cultures coalesce around documentary within the borders of the nation-state are the primary focus. The flows of economic support for documentary production are partially determined by the commitments of specific nation-states to cultivate media production and its uses. In contrast to the United States, for example, Canada has historically shown strong government commitment to funding and cultivating the democratic possibilities of documentary.[19] These values and commitments shape how government resources are used to support the documentary field in terms of financial and cultural infrastructure. In other words, the possibilities of documentary culture are often constrained by the nation-state.

This project, focused on the documentary history of the United States, attempts to create a more solid foundation for discussions of documentary and social change by paying close attention to the kind of small-scale organizing that often gets lost in studies focused on global documentary. Tracing the genre's form and function over time, this study is an effort to distill important aspects of documentary, observing how the field has been shaped by national investments and constraints. Participatory media cultures, the "imagined communities" around which social change documentary is often built, construct a sense of affiliation that is bound up in national identity.[20] As Jeffrey Geiger suggests, "Films, with the discourses that surround them and the institutions that support them, are a central means through which the idea of the national is articulated and culturally determined."[21] In the case of U.S. documentary, this includes a strong tradition of resisting the "universal nation and its narrational strategies through its location within contestatory newly emerging identities and social collectives."[22] The focus on U.S. documentary acknowledges the political structures of the nation-state that often undergird social change processes, as well as the slippery way documentary can seep into a global audience. Documentary has the capacity to translate experience and make it available for interpretation[23] and to call attention to or facilitate conversation about problems that plague the national consciousness. It can also help audiences "imagine ideas and futures beyond its immediate framework and subject matter."[24] It is this capacity of imagining that translates into political potency.

This book proposes that the influence of social change documentary is primarily constitutive; it provides a sense of shared identification around which an audience can be oriented. Documentary offers a grid of intelligibility for audiences, creating structures for making sense of global reality and navigating which subjectivities to adopt in relation to the struggles on the screen.[25] Social change documentary is also about context, timing, and appropriate discourse. The rhetorical influence of documentary is not primarily determined by aesthetic articulation or moving content, although good art does require good content; what turns a documentary screening into a documentary event is the context. By shifting focus from a traditional understanding of social change documentary—as a series of intentions and aesthetics—to look more broadly at how documentary engages political structure(s), our understanding of the scope and function of documentary's transformative potential expands. This project is invested in defining social change documentary by its agency and the action, movement, and transformative potential in concrete historical contexts. Through the unpredictable pathways of circulation, documentaries live on beyond their initial moments of production and screening. Rather than propping up an approved canonical definition of what constitutes documentary based on academic tradition, this book asks how the documentary impulse is moving people into action. Sometimes we find that this impulse leads to traditional filmmaking, and other times it manifests in more vernacular inflections of moving-image production. Expanding the scope of the study to include vernacular documentary expression provides a broad framework to consider how the status of the documentary impulse might constitute a significant and evolving public commons.

Documentary travels along pathways that can create collective participatory cultures invested in political movement. We are seeing more and more examples of documentary discourse going beyond dissemination of ideas to facilitate the active exchange of political ideas. The intersections of multiple participatory media cultures around the documentary impulse form a growing public commons[26] united by media objects and events and defined by participation. By bringing groups together and moving collective action forward, this documentary commons creates spaces for diverse people to share in modes of deliberation and the work of establishing the infrastructure needed to sustain relational connection, as well as making possible the production of new discourses that generate political arenas of intervention. The origins of this commons can be traced through the collective social practices of documentary history, found in the articulated truth of vernacular voices forged through traditions of resistance.[27] Hardt and Negri suggest understanding the function of the commons as a way to confront power, "Revealing some of these really existing forms of the common is a first step toward establishing the bases for an exodus of the multitude from its relation with capital."[28] The documentary commons is a critical site of intervention where the underrepresented confront the structures of power. With all their optimism about the commons, however, Hardt and Negri remain uncertain about how communities are mobilized into an assemblage and connect with a "unit of action."[29] Documentary history is a series of these actions, with a growing force that is mapped on to the practices of political knowing in the United States.

This introductory chapter provides context for the book's analysis of social change documentary by addressing the ways the field of documentary and social change is shifting with the emergence of digital media technology. I begin by outlining the problems in the field and then link together the foundational concepts of this book: social change, agency, and collective identification.

The Trouble with Documentary and Social Change

> There is no easy ethical position once a filmmaker decides to become entangled with the life circumstances of the subjects he or she portrays.
> —Professor Linda Williams in *Collecting Visible Evidence*

While academic scholarship has been slow to address the possibilities of documentary engagement, commercial media and philanthropic institutions were quick to adopt approaches to "strategic outreach," "audience engagement," and "impact." With the unprecedented commercial boom of documentary at the turn of the 21st century, the collapse of arts funding, and the new distribution models made possible by digital technologies, by 2008 the "conceptual and practical architecture that comprises what we call 'documentary' began to unravel."[30] This revolution in socially responsible filmmaking ushered in new actors who began contributing to the documentary field. "Filmanthropists," who are often technology entrepreneurs, continue to make significant cash investments in documentary work, which they hope will produce financial returns and social impact, creating a "double bottom line." Some believed this approach would create more sustainable production practices by making the nonprofit world responsible for financial discipline.[31] The result, however, has been an uncritical and market-based approach to understanding documentary and social change.

The documentary industry celebrated and embraced the concept of "impact." Influenced by the "functionalist orientation" of social entrepreneurs, filmmakers are expected to demonstrate political influence through specific "performance criteria by which some change can be imagined and then assessed."[32] This uncritical, ahistorical approach to public engagement with documentary produced evaluation tools and metrics for assessing social change. In the new century, emerging documentaries received industry funding based on measurable impact, regardless of whether the actions serve the injustices on the screen. The results of this market-based approach to social change have included building nonprofit coalitions, ensuring that the documentary reaches target audiences, and tailoring documentary messaging to meet the perceived needs of activists.

The market approach to social change documentary is problematic, both conceptually and in practice. It flips the focus of the creative process from storytelling to campaign outcomes, leaving the creative team to negotiate with stakeholders who may or may not help in the production process or social change. The metrics model of assessment does not build on an understanding of social change documentary in its historical context; it elides the role of larger social and political currents to influence productive circulation for social change. It is an approach uncritical of institutions and their role in sustaining status quo power relationships, substituting contact with activist communities for real measures of social change. The connection between story, action, and material forces of change is still obscure. I would suggest that the corporate embrace of social change in the form of "impact" should be treated with some suspicion.

This book acknowledges that an account of social change documentary must address complex personhood[33] in the production process, both on the screen and in exchanges with the audience. Sociologist Avery Gordon suggests that complex personhood means that all people "remember and forget, are beset by contradiction, and recognize and misrecognize themselves and others." The condition of power in society in which some people matter and others do not, "even those called 'other' are never never that." Most importantly for this study: "Complex personhood means that the stories people tell about themselves, about their troubles, about their social worlds, about their society's problems are entangled and weaved between what is immediately available as a story and what their imaginations are reaching toward." Documentary intervenes to widen and diversify the stories available to our public imaginaries, providing the data for our own collective field of vision. These conditions generate a complex personhood, where "groups of people will act together, that they will vehemently disagree with and sometimes harm each other, and that they will do both at the same time." People act on their own interests and on behalf of the interests of others—often in unpredictable ways—working collectively and generously toward social change. We should not withdraw from this complex arena of social exchange because it defies our desire for stability and resists simple assessment through calculations and metrics. Rather, we need an energized, scholarly effort to map this terrain to produce insight into how documentary engages communities to productively move people into action in relation to specific historical context.

One potential pitfall for social change documentary in practice is the tendency to embrace activism for the sake of access or institutional support, only to replace the important and difficult work of social change with a simple curation of images representing social injustice. Researchers of all varieties often visit marginalized communities to study, collect data, record stories, and then disappear. This has led to what Gubrium and Harper identify as "research fatigue," or a general distrust of academic researchers and media makers in the communities being researched. There is often well-founded concern about researchers' motives for recording the historical memories and traumas of underserved communities, instilling a fear that this kind of documentation will lead to problematic political tourism.

Tourism is a fraught framework for thinking about public engagement. In her book, *Toxic Tourism*, Phaedra Pezzullo suggests that tourism in all its varied capacities—as a public practice, a counterexperience of everyday life, and an educational experience—involves an outsider in unfamiliar territory walking on precious ethical ground. We can resist the problems of tourism by first recognizing its "unpleasant, offensive, and harmful" consequences.[34] Pezzullo ultimately suggests that tours and tourism have political possibilities worth contemplating, but documentary as a field, industry, and practice has yet to seriously consider its own tourism problem. Production impulses that move toward political tourism demand further scrutiny, now more than ever.

A few years ago, along with a small production crew, I joined a delegation of teachers, community activists, students, and journalists on a trip to Juarez and Chihuahua, Mexico. We spent the week learning about the social, political, and economic collisions occurring on the U.S./Mexican border, specifically seeking to understand how and why these conditions contributed to systematic violence toward young women. The circumstances of this atrocious violence, which documentary filmmaker Lourdes Portillo highlights in *Senorita Extraviada* (2001), have evolved and exploded in recent decades. We discussed our intentions with the delegation before we arrived; we told them we wanted to learn about the situation and possibly use what we recorded to bring visibility and mobilize communities to demand justice for the missing women. To our surprise, American activists and scholars who had been working on the border for the last ten years met us with caution. Claiming to speak on behalf of the many families we would encounter during our trip, they expressed concern about a revolving door of media makers who have, as they put it, "[c]ome to Mexico to record the pain of these families for their own benefit, promising to bring visibility to the issue only to never be heard from again." Not only were we surprised by this caution, but it created a firm line between those who are experiencing this injustice and those who are on the outside. It did not feel good to be told we were on the outside. My family was from this region of Mexico; I shared the same last name of a few women on the missing list, and I had traveled there as a child. I felt connected, and I identified with the struggle to find justice for the disappeared women. What I had to confront is that I had enormous privileges that were invisible to me: I could travel back and forth across the border without consequence. I had the confidence that, as a doctoral candidate in the United States who would soon become a professor, my voice mattered. I could leave the danger around me and not leave everything I loved behind. I had the money and resources to leave this injustice behind. Our documentary production team needed to understand this dynamic in order to avoid speaking for the voiceless and move forward collaborating and speaking with them.

This scenario highlights a key problem for social change media: the potential for exploitation and armchair political tourism exists in the processes of both documentary production and consumption. The tourism metaphor refers to the connections between media production, audiences, and justice movements. It is important to ask in whose interests documentary images of social injustice are being created and circulated. In her book *Justice Interruptus*, Nancy Fraser reminds theorists to identify two types of injustice in the process of social change: (1) socioeconomic injustice, which is a result of the political economic structure, and (2) cultural or symbolic injustice, which is rooted in social patterns of representation, interpretation, and communication. Fraser warns that we must not conflate these types of injustice nor substitute one for the other.[35] In the realm of documentary, this prompts us to complicate our thinking about the relationship between the cultural recognition work of social change documentary and the real-world redistribution of resources in service of the injustices on the documentary screen. The process of social transformation is laborious and complex, and includes necessary bodies in motion.[36] Without collective bodies in motion to act on behalf of the cultural and economic injustices presented on the screen, cultural change can distract from necessary socioeconomic change. There are blurred lines between the creative teams working on documentaries and the people whose stories are being recorded, sometimes resulting in the prioritizing of aesthetic and production interests over those of the people whose story is being told. This point must be considered as we begin theorizing about social change in the documentary context.

Thirty years ago, Bill Nichols addressed these concerns as axiographics—how values and ethics of representations come to be understood within a space. This involves the nature of consent, codes of conduct, and ethical implications of production. Nichols explains: "An indexical bond exists between the image and the ethics that produced it. The image provides evidence not only on behalf of an argument but also gives evidence of the politics and ethics of its maker."[37] For Nichols, these ethical concerns are like fingerprints on the screen, available for the critic to discover. However, this is a rather indirect way to address this matter. The screen, the indexical bond, does indeed provide a residue of values and ethics, but how this shows up in the creative process, embedded in the process of invention in the form of shared interests, is not so clearly transparent.

Labor activist and documentary filmmaker Anne Lewis describes the tourism phenomenon of documentary exploitation as cultural rape; it represents the systematic documentation of social injustice motivated by a media maker's quest for success and personal gain, while the needs of the marginalized and exploited bodies on the screen play a supporting role.[38] It is invested in the recognition of the politics of documentary without concern for the redistribution of resources needed to actually solve the problem. This kind of disconnection between documentary filmmaking and social change action is a toxic exchange and is often reflected in the institutions that provide funding for such films. Larry Daressa of California Newsreel argues as follows:

> After thirty years, I've come to the conclusion that the conventional cycle of funding, producing and then distributing these projects in the hope they will meet some audience's needs must be reversed so that we start from those needs. . . . Perhaps we should declare a moratorium on social change filmmaking until we establish procedures which ensure productions will be accountable to organizing needs and can function as integrated parts of long-term strategies for social change. . . . I would insist that media projects which do justify themselves in terms of social objectives must be rigorously evaluated as to how efficiently they will contribute to those objectives. Otherwise we will continue to get banal art and puerile politics pretending to be a significant social service.[39]

In light of these issues, I suggest three considerations for approaching the study and production of social change documentary. First, social problems are a productive place to begin for filmmakers and scholars. As creative thinkers, we are encouraged to invest in research agendas and productions that satisfy our interests and curiosities. What if we started with social problems and sorted out our curiosities within that range? Second, the connections between the maker, the documentary, and the audience of the recorded social injustice should matter to those who study and practice social change documentary. Emerging methods of studying the genre can help us unpack the mechanisms of these critical connections that currently sit in the margins of documentary studies. Third, in a world in which documentary practitioners are often encouraged to make claims about serving communities as a condition for funding, scholars have an opportunity to critically engage the connection between documentary and social change to make it more apparent for intervention. Echoing the slippery issues of telling the stories of underserved communities, critical scholars Eve Tuck and K. Wayne Yang offer this meditation: "How do we learn from and respect the wisdom and desires in the stories that we (over)hear, while refusing to portray/betray them to the spectacle of the settler colonial gaze?"[40] This meditation is one we need to hold close, grow into, and collectively answer as a field of scholars, producers, and industry professionals.

Other challenges to understanding the field of social change documentary include the rapid evolution of a new digital culture with a history that is only partially archived. This means the study of documentary and social change is always on the brink of incompletion; the fragments of the history that exist rely heavily on oral traditions and memory. Social movements and their media, as John Downing suggests, "are often fluctuating and transitory and thus especially resistant to iron-clad theorizing."[41] One way to address this issue is to bring together the knowledge of scholars and practitioners to explore alternate ways of understanding the complexities of change on the screen before and beyond the viewing process. This is an exciting meeting, as theories of social change are often challenged by the dexterity of documentary circulation, especially as it travels along asynchronous and automated pathways.

I suggest that the study of documentary and social change should be concerned with how documentary facilitates material and cultural justice for the communities and issues represented on screen(s). This is a distinct move away from the traditional approach to social change based on the intentions of the filmmaker or historically constructed aesthetic choices, instead seeking an understanding of how documentary functions as a force of social influence. Although we should pay attention to the documentary object, we should also study the participatory publics that emerge around documentary media, asking how production and circulation of documentary discourse reveal the key players (individual, institutional, governmental) and historical networks shaping the influence of the films. Networks can take on many forms, connected through people and wired through automation. We are selected into networks and choose them ourselves, creating conditions for the kinds of information that circulates within our attention. The durability of networks varies, with some networks having stable institutional frameworks and others being more fragile or popping up for temporary use. The objective of this book is to provide a better understanding of the quickly evolving production and political culture of documentary in the context of emerging digital technology. This objective includes attention to the aural and visual aspects of documentary discourse that constitute collective identification and the genre's use of new technologies to mobilize participatory publics.

In this book, I connect the theoretical impulses of participatory media culture research with social movement theory to establish frameworks of social change. Locating the process of social change as a central question in the evaluation, assessment, and consideration of the documentary experience requires a focus on documentary as a material and experiential form of communication. This includes focus on textual, visual, and aural properties that recirculate across various platforms, while paying attention to the production process and the political cultures that determine and shape documentary. Documentary occupies a unique position in media history because of its ability to simultaneously reflect and critically oppose the social order. This project situates communication at the center of cinema and media studies, understanding the screen as an essential but insufficient site of investigation. Since the 1950s, film studies—the de facto home of documentary studies—has been dominated by the study of film itself.[42] The constellation of documentary discourse is much more tangled and expansive, however, especially in the new, digital environment. By methodically studying the screen in relation to participatory publics and other assemblages, scholars can come closer to understanding the civic, social, and political functions of documentary media.

In my own experience and based on the stories of other practitioners, I have observed that the power and residue of social change are found in the processes of documentary production, circulation, and the movement of publics around such media work. In practice, the social change documentary experience has a force before and beyond the screen, the interrogation of which requires rigorous attention to production culture and discrete sectors of the production community. In his book, *Production Culture*, John Caldwell argues that industry workers critically analyze and theorize their work, producing a kind of "indigenous cultural theory that operates outside of the academy."[43] Many documentary interventions manifest their social change potential in the processes of production and circulation. We see it again in the reception of documentary texts by the participatory culture(s) that emerge around them. These components of the documentary experience, if taken up, could collectively yield critical insights relevant to scholars as well as documentary practitioners. This project analyzes selected documentary works, interviews, and primary documents to answer the proposed research questions. It conducts a rigorous analysis of documentaries and their historical context, representation, and political uptake, including circulation in broadcast news, online sources (blogs, websites, networking sites), and other noncommercial channels of communication.

Documentary works that are created and circulated outside the canon and beyond the mainstream only sporadically receive proper archiving and historical recognition. This book seeks out the core of the tension between mainstream and lesser known works and asks how the archiving of documentary material is being transformed in the digital age. The fringe nature of social change documentary history and the ways it is often subjugated at the margins of cinema history have led me to reconsider archiving and records acquisition practices. In my research, I traveled to public archives, but I also visited the basements and storage closets of people who lived through the historical moments that have been the focus of this book. Archives give us access to the unknown world of others, but the apparatus is partial, selective, and representative. Archives are places where authority and social order are exercised, often to support the power relations of colonial subjugation.[44] Documentary history is archived similarly, according to canons of artistic advancement, with little attention paid to political engagement as a category of merit or value. Many of the documentary works selected for study in this book were not considered precious enough to formally archive; the primary papers and the conditions of their intervention into public life are lost or buried in storage closets or on tapes belonging to those who lived through this history. The news is not all hopeless, however, as the emergence of digital and participatory methodologies could bridge the chasm between formal and undocumented history.

The participatory turn in research methodologies is rapidly gaining ground in many fields, including sociology, anthropology, media studies, communication, and history. Digital and visual methodologies are emergent data-gathering processes that use frameworks of storytelling and archiving to conduct research. Social scientists and interpretive scholars are using digital-recording technologies to "open up new possibilities for participatory approaches that appeal to diverse audiences and reposition participants as co-producers of knowledge and potentially co-researchers."[45] This expansion in field methods helps scholars come to new "answers to methodological questions about text, context, audience, judgment and ethics."[46] Elusive and complex research inquiries require innovative data acquisition.

For us to understand how the genre functions in the larger social field, the focus on the documentary screen needs to shift. We must examine the routine and everyday practices that surround the media artifacts. Field-based research—participatory interviews, oral history, ethnographic participant observation, and performance—allow access to otherwise inaccessible discourse. This access can reveal ways of knowing grounded in production practice and material conditions of change. Fieldwork can challenge and expand the assumptions of documentary studies that privilege close reading of accessible texts over other kinds of experiences, especially those quotidian experiences that are often written "out of history."[47] Social change documentary history is on the verge of disappearing, lost in the people who lived through it and in the undiscovered storage closets containing the people's history outside perceived historical significance.

Toward this end, I conducted over sixty interviews with filmmakers, funders, distributors, collectives, critics, archivists, and activists. The interviews were collected through a snowball sampling: that is, each subject was asked to name other key practitioners who could contribute to the understanding of documentary and social change. I prioritized interviews according to the perceived influence of the media maker and/or organization. The sample was limited to those who responded to inquiries sent by email and postal mail. These interviews with practitioners fill in some of the blanks in formal archives by adding an oral history of independent and community-based media movements. I included transcripts of already published filmmaker interviews in the data collection. The discourse of practitioners is suffused with memories of history, but more importantly, the practitioners articulate what specific historical experiences meant to those who lived through them. This approach allows research to build connections through the screen, between bodies and across the divide between those who write about documentary and those who create it.

This project systematically attempts to bridge the practitioner/scholar divide in the development of documentary theory, grounding knowledge production in material practices. The study of documentary has long been open to the inclusion of practitioner–theorists who influenced canonical thinking about early documentary theory and history. John Grierson, Dziga Vertov, Sergei Eisenstein, and Emile de Antonio are some of many filmmakers who documented important observations, insights, and prescriptions for scholars to engage and theorize. Great books of media history have followed this path, connecting documentary practitioners to the development of academic thinking.[48] In this moment of massive change in digital culture, we need to consider the rapid pace at which our society is being (re) imagined and shaped by digital interactivity. These conditions mean the perspective of the practitioner–theorist is now needed more than ever.

Radical shifts are taking place in the ways documentary moving images are circulated and interpreted. We have come to a critical juncture at which connecting critical theory and practice is essential to understanding documentary in public culture. As Michael Chanan describes our current dilemma: "[T]he old canons of the institutional documentary are once again being thrown into question, and new methodologies and ways of working are emerging."[49] It is possible that the dynamics of documentary influence have changed and evolved—as Chanan put it—while "film theory wasn't looking." Critical and cultural studies approaches open spaces where scholars and media creators can come together for the purpose of addressing this unique media moment. In this project, I integrate and synthesize intellectual, creative, and political practices.

My initial training is in research and scholarship, but I am also a media maker with a focus on creating social change documentary. The ideas, questions, insights, and reasoning found in the pages of this book are informed by scholarship, but they also reflect my on-the-ground experience working with the process of documentary and social change. This experience includes standing in a crowded church basement during a hot summer day in July, patiently listening to community members talk about their experience with racism in a small town. Heart-wrenching stories were articulated for the first time in public, long and tense pauses filled the room between each emotional revealing. These production experiences include recording clashes with protestors and police in the streets—reckless violence that escalated as police weapons of control became more militarized over the years. The hair on the back of my neck still stands up when I think of the sound of full-body riot gear colliding as police organize into a shield wall, the sign that officers were ready to descend on the crowd. Or the tense moments of my nervously confronting security guards in another country, not protected by any rule of law and unsure whether my disturbance would threaten my own safety or harm those around me. I feel most honored when my experience includes waiting silently with someone reliving a long-buried trauma. To receive these stories and sit with someone through the vulnerability of memory can elicit a tremendous emotional release. To help create a space that is safe for that kind of excavation involves a contract of trust. This contract includes doing something good and productive with the pain, ensuring that this excavation will not be wasted but will instead be transformed into stories of healing and justice. My production experience also includes organizing community media workshops focused on training middle school, high school, college students, and older adults about the power of documentary storytelling for themselves and their communities. The most profound engagement and one that is most connected to this book involves many of the above experiences and then witnessing the magical process of a community's transformation into a participatory media public, taking on the interests presented on the screen and making them their own.

Perhaps one reason scholars have failed to notice the potential of social change media is that we have unconsciously and uncritically applied criteria designed for one purpose, commercial and aesthetic entertainment, to a dramatically different one, civic activism. This project intends to combine interpretation of documentary artistic expression with a dynamic understanding of political engagement. Social change, in practice and theory swirls around the documentary field, holding it in a hapless and sometimes messy embrace.

Theories of Social Change

In whose interests are social change documentaries produced? This is the key question theorists, historians, and filmmakers need to ask themselves in locating the creative process within relations of power. Answering this question yields insight into the processes of privilege, exploitation, and marginalization that are masked by an uncritical approach to documentary representation as social change. Theorizing about documentary and social change is a delicate and complicated matter. The data are challenging to gather, the fluctuating dimensions of this media resist rigid theorizing, and nearly invisible ethical boundaries abound. Owing attention to problems of documentary and political tourism, the focus of this book is on social change that produces contact with the political structure and alters material conditions. In their book, *What Democracy Looks Like*, Christina R. Foust, Amy Pason, and Kate Zittlow Rogness suggest that social change "exists as an interaction between various material and symbolic elements defined by and coordinated through communication, where change is about shifting power."[50] Documentary has traditionally traveled along varied pathways to help facilitate this political work. As a media practice, the genre does all sorts of cultural work, much of which is unconcerned with political engagement. Focusing on documentary's social change function, however, can yield insights into avenues of protest, resistance, and dissent for those in positions of subjugation with limited agency.

Social change is a broad concept studied across multiple fields that use a variety of different approaches with no uniform method and analysis. While there are many competing frameworks to understand social change,[51] I contend that social change is a process mediated by communication. The story of social change is not about progress in a linear way. Transformation works in a circle, moving back and forth, traveling a path that is open for intervention. Rhetoric facilitates the process of social change through key terms and shifts in meaning construction[52] that produce the conditions for action. Not all rhetorical gestures alter material conditions by making contact with the political structure. The symbolic is contingent on the limitations of the material conditions of its expression.[53] Given the specific circumstances of documentary and political engagement, the ethical problems that arise around the issue of whose interests are being served, together with the variable ability of documentary to make contact with the political structure, social change should be understood as actions that contribute to material change, negotiated through communication. This process is necessarily limited by material conditions. In attempting to assess social change in the production process, on the screen, and in circulation, we should consider both cultural "recognition" politics and the "redistribution" of resources to address the injustices unveiled on the screen, being careful to avoid substituting one for the other.

We need to carefully consider the social change politics surrounding the idea of recognition. The process of capturing knowledge is deeply, historically intertwined with colonial conquest.[54] The history of documentary is no exception; it carries a long legacy of collecting pain narratives and using these real stories of human suffering as a foundation for storytelling. Sometimes this history is approached with the best intentions. When telling stories about the significance of a project, either creatively or scholarly, "harm must be recorded or proven in order to convince an outside adjudicator that reparations are deserved."[55] These uncritical politics of recognition often demand that marginalized communities "only speak from that space in the margin that is a sign of deprivation, a wound, an unfulfilled longing."[56] This narrative requires that disenfranchised communities take on the subject position of being "defective and powerless to make change."[57] Telling and retelling pain narratives produce the problems of voyeurism, political tourism, and a type of "ventriloquism" through which the colonial voice appropriates vernacular discourse. This pattern becomes endemic when researchers conflate the work and struggle of the underserved with their own research and begin speaking for disenfranchised others in terms that are self-serving or that cater to colonial logics.[58] When media makers become aware of these conditions—marginalization masked with good intentions—their impulse might be to retreat back to the spaces we know. Maybe there are some stories that particular scholars or filmmakers do not have the requisite insight and experience to tell, but rather than dismissing the social change potential of documentary, we should embrace a process of thinking through limits and boundaries. It's a delicious bind to consider the ethics of speaking for and with others. As Linda Alcoff suggests, the consequences of retreat are too costly, and, ultimately, the safety in retreat is an illusion. We need to "design methods to decrease the dangers" of speaking for others, striving to "create wherever possible the conditions for dialogue and the practice of speaking with and to rather than speaking for others."[59] Documentary history provides plenty of opportunities to lean into the uncomfortableness and seek the conditions of ethical articulation.

The processes of social change include actions that alter material conditions and address the recognition needs of the most vulnerable intersectional interests in a given struggle. Rhetoric confronts power, while also shaping how "social relationships are constituted and coordinated."[60] Power and difference exist among communicators,[61] and I argue that our political identifications are fluid but must involve intervention.[62] As Thomas Waugh suggests in *Show Us Life*, social change documentaries "attempt to act, to intervene . . . as films made by activists speaking to specific publics to bring about specific political goals."[63] The term not only suggests the instrumentality of Waugh's committed documentary, but also assigns the work a function beyond representation. It is not enough for a documentary to "be" activist; we also need to pivot the question and ask how documentary can create a public space for social change. Like a skilled conversationalist, social change documentary integrates itself into broader public discourse, raising questions, reframing arguments, and suggesting new directions or additional resources—in short, providing a structuring frame for larger civic-sector conversations, collective action, and long- and short-term social organizing. Documentary provides a location for grasping and destabilizing knowledge, producing a discourse that creates "connections and commitments across and through bodies."[64] Annie Hill theorizes this as "transmaterial intra-actionality," a way "of grasping the intra-active materialization and movement through human and nonhuman bodies in specific contexts and the impacts they experience."[65] Corporeal solidarity connects, defines, positions, and casts what is already "comergent," aligning this project with the movements of people for social justice.

Rhetorical intervention can create transformational spaces opened by communication processes.[66] Documenting the ways marginalized communities resist dominant practices with this kind of intervention provides a robust site to study social change documentary. Film scholar Jane Gaines refers to bodily expressions of affect that prompt action,[67] but there are also deliberative functions at work in these spaces. Significantly, integrating the stories of the margins into broader social frameworks can challenge and change public imaginaries—especially when these stories prompt collective action directed at power structures. Practitioners have some of these same questions. Documentarians and members of political collectives I interviewed expressed concern over the reception and uptake of activist documentary, wanting to know more about modes of address that range from the very political act of witnessing—a term that implies political action—to spectatorship, a mode of address inferring distance between those who are on the screen and those who watch.

Theorists must be careful of uncritically celebrating radical images or representations of social change. This historical moment requires nuanced investigation into social change documentary practices that distinguish between armchair political tourism and viable pursuits of social change. Theoretical and social conceptions of social change documentary are based on a wide spectrum of approaches ranging from representing social change to actually intervening in the social change process. In this book, I seek to refine our articulations of the various functions of the genre. Mapping documentary and participatory engagement can provide insight into the empathetic pathways created by cinema in the untidy process of political struggle.

Agency as Rhetorical Performance

In many instances, documentary moving images have entered the realm of broad public influence. Investigating the ways publics engage documentary media artifacts requires careful consideration of the function of agency in media production and reception. Agency refers to the ability of individuals and collectives to bring about desired outcomes in the world. If rhetoric is the art of informing, persuading, and inspiring action in an audience through communication, agency is a key term signaling the presence, autonomy, and effects of the actors. Scholars consider agency a communal and participatory process that can involve a variety of acts, including "invention, strategies, authorship, institutional power, identity, practice, and subject positions."[68] In recent years, however, the concept of agency has been steadily questioned.[69]

There has been a turn toward understanding agency in "new materialist" terms, these efforts "generally sharing poststructuralist affinities" and aiming to "refigure meaning in less anthropocentric and more ecological terms." It is a call to understand a "contingently dynamic" agency that assumes that human discourses connect with "other-than-human creatures, critters, things, actants, objects," which have powers to "behave as meaningful agencies in their own right."[70] Developing theories from such philosophers as Jane Bennett, Karen Barad, and Bruno Latour, posthumanist theories of agency have revived interest in the interconnections of ecological relations, giving vitality to matter itself. As Jane Bennett suggests, there is a tendency to give priority to human bodies while overlooking *things* and what they can do.[71] This leads us to ask questions about how agency functions in contexts where public speech is mediated through documentary (a thing) and also works as art, the kind of art a viewer could experience over and over again. It is my intention to put these theoretical impulses into conversation with a materialist critique within the framework of production practice as a means of better understanding the circulation of documentary discourse as a political force. Even if only part of the world can be made intelligible because there is no outside of interconnected ecological relations, our political realities demand that we act with urgency—sometimes based on partial information—as a means of survival. I am interested in the language of engagement when we must make political decisions to act in the world.

At the end of any creative process, we are often left with a "thing." While the meaning of photos, films, books, and vinyl records transcend the physical matter that captures them, they are still objects. The significance and meaning of "thingness" form difficult theoretical terrain. Bennett suggests that the power of the "thing" is "the curious ability of inanimate things to animate, to act, to produce effects dramatic and subtle."[72] In other words, power exists not only at the symbolic level of communication; the medium and motion of delivery are also charged with potential. While I hesitate to follow Bennett down a path in which inanimate objects—a video file, DVD, or tape—have agency comparable to that of human intervention, I do acknowledge that we often undervalue the role of material objects in rhetorical interventions. For instance, we attribute rhetoric to human subjects rather than investigate the potential kinetic energy—the agency—of documentary objects on events, energy set in motion independently of creator and audience intention. Carolyn Miller contends that our preoccupation with traditional concepts of agency and the body move us away from exploring how "symbolic action confronts non-symbolic motion."[73] What is at stake in such confrontations is rhetorical agency.[74] The mechanical reproduction of images and sound includes a kind of automation. With easy access to editing and recording processes, participatory actors can produce media products that circulate in automated networks of information for decades, with fragments of the original "thing" living far beyond the context of its initial release. Documentary circulates on streaming outlets and social media platforms for years beyond the initial broadcast in networks of automation, picked up and given new meaning at different historical moments. Miller offers a concept of agency that considers symbolic and nonsymbolic action, emphasizing the potential set in motion by rhetorical actions such as a documentary. In this framework, agency is understood as "the kinetic energy of rhetorical performance . . . invoking the distinction that physics makes between potential and kinetic energy." Miller continues:

> I'm comparing agency not to the energy of a stone sitting at the top of the cliff but rather to the energy it has as it falls, the energy of motion. . . . As the kinetic energy of performance, agency resolves its doubleness, positioned exactly between the agent's capacity and the effect on an audience. Our task is to understand how the kinetic energy of performance works in writing as well as in speaking.[75]

I would add to this the task of exploring the kinetic energy of agency as it intersects with documentary. This project investigates the ways documentary agency, in all its symbolic and nonsymbolic "thingness," moves through analog and digital formats to make indelible impressions on the public life of people living in embattled communities.

Collective Identification

Documentary screenings can vary from routine events to electric moments pregnant with political movement. At this second type of event, something emerges that goes beyond the screening itself. The kinetic energy of documentary performance produces connection and prompts further investigation, investment, and/or collaboration. Audience members are constituted as a group, creating identifications with the sensory experiences of the screen. What motivates mobilization for social change after a screening? A swirl of logic, reason, and affective communication. Rhetorical invention is critical to mobilization; documentary must inspire a lasting sense of urgent investment in the issues on screen to produce embodied agency in the audience, compelling real-world action. When we become relationally engaged with others, we often develop a sense of responsibility and empathy. Collective identification is the glue that makes participatory media publics and social change possible.

Film theorists, many of them feminist scholars, have primarily constructed identification as a psychoanalytic process. In this way, identification is understood as a cultural process reinforcing the dominant forms of identity complicit in prescribing hegemonic values.[76] There is a conscious level of interaction and identity formation, where political documentary seeks to engage viewers within the world in which they live, a rhetorical process with material force. Social change documentary is subversive in its power to create an empathetic experience that allows people at the center to identify with the margins both "within oppressive communities and between different communities."[77] I would suggest that collective identification is defined as the discursive location around which citizens can orient themselves in the process of social change. More specifically, collective identity is an "individual's cognitive, moral, and emotional connection with a broader community, category, practice, or institution. It is a perception of a shared status or relations, which may be imagined rather than experienced directly, and it is distinct from personal identities, although it may form part of a personal identity."[78]

The construction of collective identity is rhetorical. Moving-image stories, especially in documentary contexts, have the potential to create discursive collective audience identifications on multiple sensory and cognitive levels. In her book, *AIDS TV: Identity, Community, and Alternative Video*, Alexandra Juhasz argues that "activist video is a site where the interrogation and even potential change of one's 'identity' can occur on both conscious and unconscious levels. . . . viewing alternative media that willing[ly] identifies its construction from a position of difference, opinion and politics can aid the spectator to challenge the stability of those positions."[79] Moving-image storytelling opens up the possibilities of integrating new narratives and realigning identifications that create substance with others. As literary philosopher Kenneth Burke suggests, when entities are united through common ideas, they share a substance of humanness; they are consubstantial in their shared values.[80]

The process of identification is how collective identity finds its substance. Social movements are sometimes born from shared conditions and counterhegemonic discourse, providing the social cement needed for a participatory media culture to develop.[81] These collective identifications can be fluid, "choosing participation in some publics over others."[82] Feminist Chela Sandoval posits a "differential consciousness" that is not fixed but flexible and is able to adapt to changing conditions and shifts in power. It is a kind of subjectivity forged while laboring under the conditions of multiple oppressions, recognizing alliances with others committed to egalitarian social justice. "Tactical subjectivity" is the idea that "coalitions of resistance" can be formed to utilize collective resources of power more efficiently.[83] Karma Chávez suggests that these relationships are forged as a means of "differential vision," the way activists position themselves in "coalitions of resistance" that share particular goals but may differ in their approach and systematic analysis. Collective identification is a state of "holding competing positions for the sake of building coalitions" and remaining flexible in political form and relationalities.[84]

A close relationship exists between collective identity and agency; groups must understand themselves as capable of acting in the world, demanding political recognition and consideration. Shared interests, conditions, and affect initially draw strangers together, creating an awareness of the potential to act as collective agents that share substance. We are relational beings, connected through social networks. When we become relationally engaged with others, we often develop our sense of responsibility, our affective care and concern for others. These connections become the scaffolding of social change as networks are held together with shared interests but also with love. Bodies are situated in space and time; as Sarah Ahmed suggests, they take shape as they move through the world.[85] Affective connections intervene by directing bodies toward and away from objects and others. It is through the creative actions of self-organizing, performing collective tasks, engaging in deliberative labor, and coming together in time and space, that more robust and long-lasting collective identifications are formed. It is through this participatory transformation from gathering to producing and acting together that movements solidify their collective identity.

Identification, organizing, and performing collective tasks can become a form of labor for autonomous production and survival. This participatory labor informs and solidifies collective identification through circulation. Rhetoric scholars theorize how symbolic and image-based discourse circulates in public culture, providing insight into how rhetoric forms, transforms, and travels through networks of influence. Circulation theory concerns the effort to understand how discourse, bodies, text, ideas, and emotion move through time and space, making up a constitutive force that has considerable influence in public life. Circulation is often described as a mode of delivery, but it also functions as a form of invention and memory. As Dustin Edwards suggests, we articulate "with, from and because of circulation."[86] Given documentary's capacity to endlessly circulate, in parts, remixed, and utilized by those who need it at the moment, theories of circulation should inform how we understand collective identification. The participatory labor of self-organizing and joining together for collective tasks frequently includes circulating and recirculating social movement discourse, producing more complex identifications in terms of a material force of change.

Conclusion

The study of social change documentary, which has become increasingly influential in public life, is especially timely in the current moment. Documentary moving-image discourse around political struggle has shifted over the last four decades, and there has not yet been a broad and productive study of social change documentary that systematically focuses on its civic and activist potential. Scholars, media makers, and activists have not clearly articulated how we imagine and theorize the ways that documentary intervenes, functions, and participates in the process of social change. Investigating how documentaries can make contact with social and political structures—either directly, in the form of witnessing, and/or through the creation of participatory media publics that are ready to pick up the political work foregrounded by a documentary event—is where I begin this project.

Chapter 2 begins with a broad historical framework for understanding opportunities for participatory media culture and social change that have emerged from documentary history. It is not inclusive of all social change documentary, but it does outline surges in participatory activity and collective agitation. This chapter assembles the most widely recognized documentaries, while subsequent chapters venture outside these more recognized moments to include important but rarely acknowledged people, events, films, and collaborations. I approach the following chapters by first asking, what is missing from this history? This inquiry has led me to engage with the silences and absences, reflecting on how inclusion of the missing pieces enriches the nuance of understanding power and agency. When we centralize marginality within the field of documentary studies, we gain understanding of other values and practices, providing insight into the institutional changes that must occur. As Michelle Holling suggests, perspectives from the margins "upend standards of what and who is central to society and, by extension, to the discipline" while "eschewing tokenizing moves that undermine centralizing efforts."[87]

The following chapters represent sections of the larger history of documentary and social change. Chapter 3 addresses the recent trend in popular social justice documentaries and the effects of widespread access to the internet in the past two decades. More specifically, I examine how this set of circumstances pushed the documentary experience beyond the screen and into global environments. Participatory media coalitions have emerged around these films, occasionally organizing into social justice formations. The emergence of popular activist documentary is a sign of the regular social practice of understanding documentary as a mechanism of political change that has now crossed over into commercial culture, magnifying the impact of an emerging documentary commons.

Labor documentary is one of the most robust themes in documentary history. Chapter 4 will address how these films document violent clashes over worker rights and decades of police brutality—establishing documentary's first experiments with participatory media cultures. Collectively, these documentaries encourage identification with a laboring subject that is confrontational toward capitalism and forced to contend with the collapse of the American working class under the strains of neoliberalism. This chapter will demonstrate the longstanding relationship between documentary and participatory media collectives, long before and after the emergence of the internet.

Chapter 5 will consider the complicated relationship between documentary practices and the shifting cultures around women's reproductive health in the United States. Within this struggle, documentary discourse pivots around affect and expression of voice as strategies of activism and resistance. This chapter will explore how the affective registers around abortion shape the political function of documentary representation, influencing agency and collective action for social change.

The proliferation of screen media and the saturation of everyday life with digital culture led to dramatic shifts in public communication, challenging our sense of what it means to be a citizen in the 21st century. Digital technologies have expanded our capacity to author and circulate information in unforeseeable ways. Chapter 6 focuses on the witnessing of police brutality and street-tape culture in the documentary commons, using examples ranging from the Passaic Textile Strike in 1926 to recordings of the Rodney King incident in the 1990s and beyond. The primary focus is on the ways images circulate in response to police brutality, resulting in accidental witnessing, and the formation of an unprecedented documentary commons for the intersections of race, power, and media. This chapter also addresses police brutality, and the participatory media cultures around the deaths of Michael Brown, Eric Gardner, and Philando Castile, as well as the implications of live streaming and vernacular street reporting.

It is tempting to broadly conceptualize the social change potential of documentary without theoretical clarity, while neglecting the varied ways the genre engages in the process of social change during preproduction, distribution, and uptake into the larger public discourse. One reason for this tendency may be the disconnection between theory and practice. The academy usually trains media theorists or producers; the two rarely come together, which has consequences for academic scholarship. As documentary theorist Bill Nichols notes:

> The very mention of the words 'theory' and 'practice' in close proximity tends to produce an ossification of the mind, at least for those who have seen the terms bandied about for a few decades. Their dyadic invocation implies that they belong together in some way yet our teaching institutions, from which this invocation most commonly comes, seldom integrate the two terms in any meaningful way.[88]

This book directly confronts the tension between theory and practice that Nichols articulates. The current heightened political climate means we cannot continue to ignore this divide; our work needs to begin with problems in the world. Scholars must provide analysis and theory that offer insight into action in the sociopolitical struggles we face. Understanding social change documentary requires challenging the practices of scholarship as usual, questioning canons, and creating new methods and ways of writing.

2

A Critical History of Documentary and Participatory Media Cultures

The 20th century kicked off with an increase in documentary film production, which led to new social and political spaces where communities could form. Since then, documentary film and video have produced and facilitated participatory publics. In the 1920s, cine-clubs provided a space for people to meet, talk about film, and screen experimental works.[1] Film collectives developed out of later manifestations of the documentary impulse. In the 1930s, for example, the Workers Film and Photo League organized to make activist newsreels and critical political films.[2] In the mid-1950s, collectives formed around producing documentaries, later called "black films," critical of the administrative shortcomings of socialism.[3] With further technological developments in the 1970s, media cultures formed with the goal of democratizing media by establishing a network of local production communities and a parallel broadcasting system that took advantage of community-operated cable stations in the United States.[4] In the last two decades, the standardization of the internet and the increased visibility of political documentary in mainstream commercial culture have transformed generally passive documentary viewers into agents of interactive activist engagement.[5]

Benedict Anderson theorized these kinds of public collectives as imagined communities in which members hold in their minds an image of affinity and solidarity created through shared interests and forged through identification independent of face-to-face communication in everyday life.[6] A social movement's success in creating instrumental social change depends on its ability to forge a collective identification by "transforming mere aggregates of people sharing the same condition into a social network, and thus into a more easily mobilizable group."[7] Social movements are sometimes born from shared conditions, and counterhegemonic discourse can provide the social cement for a participatory media culture.[8] Examining the dynamics of participatory media cultures allows us to study how groups with shared interests become a "historical bloc"[9] that is a complex, contradictory public agitating for recognition and redistribution of resources.

The participatory condition[10] is composed of practice, culture, and expectation. We are fundamentally motivated to act by the promise that participation will strengthen "social bonds, communities, systems of knowledge, and organizations, as well as politics and culture."[11] Our invitation and hailing into participation forms part of the foundation of society; it is how we become political subjects invested in the system. These impulses go back to the Athenian polis, where being political was defined by participating in public life and committing to speech as action.[12] Participatory acts of democratic expression generate power by moving opinions through critical-rational debate and other means, testing the legitimacy and authority of the status quo.[13] There is widespread optimism about the power of participation, but does more activity create a productive political process? Art historians and critics are pushing back on the magical thinking that surrounds the concept of participation, challenging what constitutes an effective intervention. What if dialogue, exchange, and connection don't yield political outcomes? For contemporary art historian Claire Bishop, antagonism must be present as part of the participatory intervention; otherwise the potential is lost, along with the capacity to challenge forms and confront power.[14] Agitation exists when people outside of the decision-making process advocate for social change and encounter significant resistance in the process, requiring more intentional and substantial intervention. For social movements, these interventions have established patterns and practices that include petition, presenting the social injustice to decision makers; promulgation, tactics used to win social support from outsiders; solidification, rhetoric that unites unlikely actors and builds connections between supporters; and polarization, presenting a forced choice to the audience.[15] Agitation is a sign that power is being confronted and that a request for change is being presented, demanding a response.

Participation is a fundamental principle of Western democratic culture, but "what is distinctive about the present conjuncture is the degree and extent" to which social, political, and economic activities are organized around participation.[16] The tendency toward participation is increasing, and the invitations to act are plentiful. While many scholars study facets of participation in social life, research into participatory media cultures focuses on specific community actions that respond to, with, and around media. Most of this research is bound up in the more recent capacities of digital culture to shift pathways of communication, with a focus on virality and spreadability of media communication.[17] Media and communication scholar Henry Jenkins led the field in investigating fan culture and other kinds of participatory media publics. In *Textual Poachers* (1992), he began sketching out the possibilities opened by these emerging public spaces. Over the next several decades, the idea of participatory media cultures evolved together with scholarship. In the last several years, Jenkins's new research has been grounded in educational technology, with special attention to youth production culture. In *Spreadable Media* (2013), Jenkins, Ford, and Green argue that participation replaced resistance. Jenkins clarifies this position in *Participatory Culture in a Networked Era* (2016): "There may no longer be a unified mainstream culture against which subcultures can define themselves."[18] While he acknowledges the value in the bottom-up, local participatory enterprise, Jenkins is skeptical about the radical political possibilities of this type of initiative. Instead, he places a premium on how communication travels through networks, gaining meaning and value. His focus is on the spreadability of communication and its ability to range and transform,[19] with the content generating value in attention and visibility as opposed to how it challenges power. Expressions that might have had a limited audience now have the potential to yield significant social consequences.[20] An interest in the ways documentary discourse travels through networks, gaining meaning and value, is central to the present study. In social change documentary, the circulation of discourse meets collective, material movements for change. It is a rhetorical engagement in which participation includes or translates into resistance, rather than one replacing the other.

I define participatory media culture historically, in terms of a trajectory of participatory networks across time.[21] This trajectory begins with early, nondigital communities and arcs into an exploration of how the documentary impulse is transformed in our digitally immersive contemporary culture. Some scholars studying digital networks assume that participatory culture began with social media. To correct for this assumption, Jenkins argues, "we need to place these practices in larger historical context".[22] This allows us to better understand the particular atmosphere created by the participatory environment in a digital culture as distinct from the primarily analog and face-to-face communities in previous historical moments. There is no mistake that digital culture has radically transformed participation, but the participatory impulse finds its roots in the human experience and the desire to transform the world for one's own pleasure or survival.

Documentary theory and history seldom address documentary and the participatory condition. Some of the earliest efforts to understand documentary as a material force with collective action are found in the research on social realism and radical filmmaking in the United States during the 1930s.[23] In privileging the relationship of film to reality and referring to a world outside the art object itself, this scholarship opened up the space to consider documentary as a material force of change. Thomas Waugh further contributed to this trajectory with his book, *Show Us Life: Toward a History and Aesthetics of the Committed Documentary*. He suggests, "[I]f films are to be instrumental in the process of social change, they must be made not only *about* people directly implicated in change, but *with* and *for* those people as well."[24] For Waugh, this research involved connections with the world outside the film and included conversations about documentary history and theory with filmmakers, programmers, distributors, and activists.

Attempting to use scholarship to shape the terrain of politics, Michael Chanan explores the capacity of documentary to create pathways for new attitudes to enter into wider circulation,[25] and Jonathan Kahana posits that documentary "makes us think about the world outside the sphere of media consumption," inviting "public subjectivity and civil interaction that transports viewers beyond the immediate context of viewing."[26] Alex Juhasz complicates the act of choosing what we include in the study of media, acknowledging the nuance of collective action in a documentary public sphere. Activist documentary, she states, is agitational in production, distribution, and exhibition, fragmented in coalition building, hostile to the mainstream, and built for vernacular expression.[27] Juhasz's intervention is important in that it insists on including alternative documentary media in the study of a larger canon of documentary work, providing a complicated assessment of social change. This fragmented research space does not clarify understanding among scholars about the ways documentaries can act as catalysts, propelling organized collectives with shared interests and investments into taking political action. As the editors of a recent forum on documentary functions and impacts suggest, "scholars need to consider more deeply the important dimensions that distinguish a film that engages and empowers publics."[28] It is especially crucial to examine how this field evolved from analog expressions into an expanding digital culture; documentary history provides robust ground for understanding participatory media culture from multiple dimensions and technological shifts. We need interpretations of the participatory condition that "require[s] us to think beyond accounts that would simply equate it with the rise of digital technologies."[29] This underscores the importance of illuminating networks whether they are built in analog culture or are circulating in digital life. Alongside participatory media culture research, scholars Rita Felski and Rosa Eberly passionately argue that cultural texts, through a variety of media and contexts, prompt the formation of publics.[30] Documentary history provides complex insight into participatory media culture, before and after the rise of the digital landscape. It is historical context that draws attention to the way people act in the world with media, circulation as a form of belonging to each other.

Documentary and participatory culture is a radical idea; it's a force of grassroots social change, involving cultural practices that make a difference in local and political struggles. The history of this culture is largely in opposition to the dominant culture, resisting government, mainstream institutions, news, and capitalism. Exploring participatory media cultures in documentary history may yield new assessments of the participatory condition and its possibilities for political intervention.

The documentary impulse and participatory culture are places where re-emerging publics construct shared identification that again coalesces around documentary media. This chapter focuses on how the participatory condition around documentary (1) confronts power in the form of agitation, (2) shares information, (3) creates new output, and, as a consequence, (4) experiences control and surveillance. I broadly map the terms of participation, identifying when different forms occur and emerge, and then I explore the ways documentary production has shaped and been shaped by technology, advancing from recrafted lightweight cameras and portapaks in the late 1960s to the explosion of inexpensive digital video and editing equipment in the 1990s and finally to the emergence of mobile media and online community building at the turn of the century. The imagined communities that form around documentary are diverse in composition and function, including fan cultures as well as communities formed through shared production interests, such as mobile recording and activism. The emergence of documentary participatory culture—the core interest of this book—is not a new phenomenon, but the new ways these publics engage with documentary are specific to this form of cultural production.

What function(s) does documentary have in the process of social change, especially in initiating and sustaining activist participatory media cultures? In her book *Reality Bites*, rhetoric scholar Dana L. Cloud argues that facts alone don't move people to action. What turns facts into beliefs and then into common sense, she says, are emotion, embodiment, narrative, myth, and spectacle. These rhetorical strategies create regimes of doxa (common sense) that organizes knowledge and creates priorities around what is true.[31] This mediation of information—which Cloud understands as primarily a process of language—can shift frameworks of understanding. This chapter traces the well-documented opportunities for participatory media culture and social change that have emerged from the documentary impulse since its beginnings, moving through the development of the portable sync-sound analog, video-recording equipment of the late 1960s, and a digital culture of mobile recording.

This chapter establishes a broad framework for rethinking documentary history in relationship to the participatory condition. It does not include all films or social change encounters, but it identifies significant waves of movement toward using documentary for collective agitation. This history is organized around three waves of documentary production in which political unrest, technological innovation, and artistic movements in documentary expression have collided to produce new patterns of documentary circulation and activist reception. Such a theoretical mapping process can help us gain more conceptual clarity about what formations of participatory media publics and documentary are conducive to social change. These include a consideration of documentary as a political platform, mirror, and vehicle to challenge representation, an axis of collaboration, a conduit for information exchange, a tool of political intervention, and an organizing agent. The remaining chapters in this book use this historical framework to address undocumented film communities that sit on the sidelines of this history as well as underrepresented topics and filmmakers that fall outside current scholarship. This organization of documentary history will allow us to consider documentary and the varying ramifications of these impulses for the process of social change. Finally, I outline a framework for understanding documentary as it engages the process of social change.

The portrait of documentary history that I offer is painted in broad brush strokes; the narrative is by no means complete or inclusive. Working with the partially archived history of a largely underground media culture means that access to the work itself is limited. The retelling of this history is also limited by the sparse documentation that exists in formal scholarship, archives, and oral history. My conversations with media professionals forced me into introspection and a rethinking of the ways academic scholarship typically organizes ideas, calling attention to some of the unquestioned intellectual frameworks about documentary that need to be reconsidered. As a result, I seek to blur the boundaries of traditional cinema scholarship in order to also consider how people are using the documentary moving image in their everyday lives. This telling of documentary history is the start to a conversation about the possibilities presented by participatory media cultures. I offer this book as an invitation to include and integrate more voices into the history of social change documentary, especially those stories that have rarely found proper documentation. Finally, this particular investigation of documentary history through the lens of social change does not negate the other capacities of documentary. This history shines an intentional light on the political dimensions of documentary capacity, so we can all take a closer look.

The First Wave of Social Change Documentary

In the world of silent film, before distinctions were made between documentary and narrative film, cinema production often intervened in political controversy. Melodrama that depicted life and ideological perspectives on sex, drugs, Prohibition, crime, political corruption, women's suffrage, prisons, poverty, immigration, and labor exploitation were projected on the screen, with reception ranging from tolerance to outright censorship and criminal arrest. Almost three-quarters of the film audience of the time was working class, and early films were seen as the "organ for revolt."[32] Despite not quite living up to the expectations of facilitating revolt, films did intervene to polarize, bring people together, and change the world outside the screen. These early "sociological films" contained precious historical evidence such as representations of slum districts in big cities and stories that featured real people, like Margaret Sanger, at the center of controversy. Beginning in 1905, there was a steadily growing working-class film culture—silent filmmakers creating representations of everyday life featuring real people and images of workers that met the demands of vaudeville houses, road shows, and the expansion of exhibition outlets.[33] This influenced the radical documentary cinema that emerged around the 1930s. Film critics played a significant role in redefining working-class cinema as it "flickered dangerously across a liminal zone of cheap amusement and the avant-garde, depravity and reform, American and foreign influences—and the introduction of sound further burst open its possibilities."[34] People were experimenting with cinema, and, from the beginning, political influence was more than a playful possibility.

In the early 1930s, economic collapse produced significant political tension and strife. As a result, media outlets were dominated by controversy over political ideology.[35] Documentary film technology had just acquired sound and was simultaneously celebrating the last moments of silent film. For the first time, words could be added to image. For many documentary film scholars, this historical moment initiates the genre's civil potential. This period was populated mainly by social-issue documentaries concerned with representations of marginalized communities. Yet the technology of documentary production remained nestled squarely in the hands of the elite.[36] Governments, scholars, and rich patrons controlled documentary production technology, which meant the form and content of the genre often reflected these interests and perspectives. Under these constraints, documentary was not radical in that it did not typically question political and state institutions, but films did sometimes engage the politics of representation. The early period of social change documentary film in the 1930s was primarily reformist in nature, while still situated left of dominant political conservatism and showing the influence of the emerging radical ideas of the time.[37]

The 1930s were a moment of abundance for reformist documentary, yet a radical working-class cinema existed before and throughout this profusion. For example, *The Passaic Textile Strike* (IWA 1926) documented the work stoppage of over 25,000 mostly foreign-born mill workers in New Jersey.[38] In this strike, organized by the Trade Union Education League of the Workers' Party, workers fought against dangerous working conditions, low wages, and their lack of recourse to address their circumstances. Directed by Samuel Russak and Alfred Wagenknecht, the film was part documentary footage and part melodrama. It begins with a reenacted prologue showing the events that led to the strike; the living conditions of workers are edited alongside villainous portrayals of the bosses, creating identification with the collective worker.[39] There is an emotional and heavy-handed crafting of identification as a form of polarization, and in this way power is confronted directly. The audience is with either the working class or the bosses; there is no middle ground. Footage from the rooftops shows police charging into lines of peaceful protestors and powerfully documents bloody attacks on the crowd. The framing of the strike actions is recorded at a distance, in wide shots with no close-up framing. The police are seen steadily and forcibly encroaching upon a sizeable crowd. Working-class identification is forged in opposition to the state, which is seen as the instigator of violence.[40] The footage was "straightforward," with "dramatic tension," created by "cutting back and forth between the hardships faced in the workplace and home," alongside parades and mass meetings.[41] The strike ended in November 1926 with the company agreeing to restore wages and grant union recognition.[42] *The Passaic Textile Strike* (IWA 1926) was an important radical documentary for many reasons: (1) it was a precursor of what was to come, functioning as a bridge between the melodramas of earlier workers' films and the social realism of radical films in the

1930s[43]; (2) it represents an ongoing labor struggle as it happened in real time; and (3) the representations led to social change. Documentary films of the 1930s form part of a larger body of cultural discourse focused on social critique, political representation, and grassroots social change through media production.

In his book *The Cultural Front*, Michael Denning addresses the cultural strategies of U.S. political movements in the 1930s: "The thirties became an icon, the brief moment when politics captured the arts, when writers went left, Hollywood turned Red, and painters, musicians and photographers were socially minded."[44] This cultural front

> reshaped American culture. Just as the radical movements of abolition, utopian socialism, and women's rights sparked the antebellum American Renaissance, so the communisms of the depression triggered a deep and lasting transformation of American modernism and mass culture—the laboring of American Culture.[45]

The social investments of documentary in the 1930s led directly to its later function as a political platform and mirror.

DOCUMENTARY AS A PLATFORM AND MIRROR

Many basic forms of social change documentary film were established during the time Denning identifies as "The Cultural Front,"[46] and by most accounts, British filmmaker John Grierson led the charge. While studying at the University of Chicago, Grierson traveled around the United States interviewing filmmakers, scholars, politicians, and journalists, observing the workings of the American melting pot. Like many of his contemporaries, he began to question what seemed like the illusory democracy of the United States. According to Grierson, social problems had grown beyond the comprehension of most citizens, and their political participation was nonexistent, apathetic, or performed out of a sense of obligation. Grierson believed that popular media could provide a solution, influencing ideas and actions historically shaped by churches and schools. He believed that the documentary genre had the potential to persuasively command the zeitgeist, turning benign cultural production into a political act. Grierson is widely recognized as the first to argue for the use of documentary film as a platform for political analysis; he sought to conceptualize the documentary as a mirror for political culture.

"Documentary as mirror" and "documentary as hammer" are two of the more robust metaphors used to describe the relationship between documentary images and the world. The concept of "documentary as mirror" foregrounds the revelatory aspects of seeing ourselves on the screen, highlighting the elastic power of identification and audience-centered reflexivity. The metaphor minimizes attention to how stories are selectively shaped and narrativized for viewing. The comparison insists on the indexical connection between the documentary image and reality. In this metaphor, recordings function as a copy of the world for others. Through this exposure to the lives of communities who are less visible, documentary helps us see ourselves and our connections with others. Given the rudimentary media technology of the time, the documentary form was one of the few mediums to visually and verbally reflect the immediate world around it. Documentary film could evoke a "hangover" effect, creating a lingering ideological impression on audiences.[47] It became Grierson's mission to produce films that dramatized issues and their implications in a meaningful way. He hoped that documentary could lead citizens through the political wilderness.[48]

Grierson's work laid the groundwork for social change documentary film in several ways. Overall, his approach to the production and distribution of documentary film was unique. Instead of viewing the documentary film as entertainment to be consumed, he believed it could be instrumental in transforming people and institutions. Specifically, documentary could inform a citizenry and improve a crumbling democracy. In his film *The Drifters* (1929), Grierson dramatized the work of herring fishermen that astonished audiences in packed theater houses. According to film historian Eric Barnouw, "There was nothing doctrinally radical about it, but the fact that British working men—virtually ignored by British cinema except as comedy material—were the heroes, gave the film an almost revolutionary impact."[49] The film gave the workingman a new public dignity, a new narrative. In Grierson's hands, the documentary camera functioned as a mirror, reflecting images that challenged normative notions of class and legitimacy. In vivid detail, Grierson edited together labor sequences, depicting the relationship between human and machine. His idea was to bring the image of the workingman away from "the Edwardian, Victorian, capitalist attitude."[50] While Grierson performed his influential work as a theorist and practitioner primarily in England, the history of reformist and working-class cinema in the United States goes back even further.

During this time, a collective, politically minded documentary film movement was mounting in the United States that was committed to documenting workers' strikes, foreclosures, and elections.[51] The Workers' Film and Photo League was the first body of activist filmmakers in the United States to connect around a shared commitment to documenting the economic and social crisis. The League was an international group that operated in major cities in the 1930s, producing a prolific body of workers' newsreels and films. Newsreels were short films produced on a regular basis to be shown in cinemas before the featured film events. They included image-based political news, capturing moments of significance in global culture, circulating postcard-like images, and offering distant and static portraits of daily life. While most newsreel operations were business or government projects, a thriving labor movement saw the potential of the form. The Workers' Film and

Photo League brought workers' consciousness to the public through documentary newsreels and organized collectives. In a 1977 interview published in *Jump Cut* by Russell Campbell, Leo Seltzer, who shot much of the New York Film and Photo League footage, explains:

> Ours was a total involvement in what was happening in the world on a very practical and realistic level. We filmed the everyday social scene, the economic struggle. And we put it together to represent a realistic, not dramatized point of view. Then we carried those heavyweight "portable" projectors and the films back to the union halls and the picket lines and showed them to an audience that was the living subject of the films.[52]

These on-screen reflections of the lives of workers, Seltzer maintained, provided a much-needed moral boost to the strike lines during the Great Depression. The representation functioned as a kind of affirmation, creating solidarity among those who were in struggle and providing energy for the workers' movement.

Filmmakers making nonportable film equipment movable was one of the first instances of documentary filmmakers using technology in unintended ways. In subsequent years, they continued to find alternative uses for technologies and completely redesigned camera equipment to better capture life as it unfolded before their eyes. This type of filmmaking required structural support and a flexible lifestyle. Seltzer continues: "For me the Film and Photo League activity was a way of life, often working all day and most of the night, sleeping on a desk or editing table wrapped in the projection screen, eating food that might have been contributed for relief purposes and wearing clothes that were donated."[53] The Film and Photo League was supported by the Workers International Relief, a Marxist organization that reinforced workers' struggles around the world, with a focus on cinema production. This was clearly groundbreaking work, but does documentary film have the potential, as Grierson suggests, to create instrumental social change?

In this interwar period, representation was the primary revolutionary action of social minded cultural texts like documentary film. Documentary films aimed to make visible the people and ideas situated at the margins of society. In these films, this mostly meant placing the lives of white working-class people on display for democratic ends. Filmmakers like Grierson assumed that multivocality through documentary would provide the missing ingredient to remedy a troubled and homogeneous democracy.[54] But, as social movements scholar Albert Melucci asks, are activist cultural strategies designed to constitute an audience, organize information, and create new meaning through cultural codes enough?[55] The following section analyzes the second wave of activist documentary film that grew out of the political and social strife of the late 1960s and continued into the 1970s.[56]

The Second Wave of Social Change Documentary

The second wave of social change documentary was a reaction against industrial documentary production closely tied to corporate sponsorship and interests: filmmakers of the early 1960s began embracing the role of observer. The films of this period—often called direct cinema—were ambiguous, documenting subjects that society was inclined to ignore and leaving conclusions up to viewers. Filmmakers liberated themselves from the tripod and began innovating with handheld camera work. In this form of production, life appears to unfold in front of the camera, long shots, and unsteady framing direct attention away from the production process. For filmmakers in North America, this style represented a commitment to observation at the cost of intervention and an attempt to transport viewers into unfamiliar places. Of course, these views of unfamiliar places were determined by those making these films. With few exceptions, this was a space of white, hetero-male culture and its amusements. The liberating potential of this observation-focused moment in documentary expression is the legitimacy it gave to groups at the margins of society, but it also exploded the rhetorical potential of documentary by foregrounding the ideas and speech of the film subjects. Unlike the earlier era of documentary film, in which the filmmaker—often the narrator—could manipulate footage to create their own arguments through voiceover, the methodological commitments of direct cinema demanded that subjects speak for themselves:

> In the new focus on speech—talking people—documentaries were moving into an area they had long neglected, and which appeared to have surprising, even revolutionary impact. Since the advent of sound—throughout the 1930s and 1940s—documentaries had seldom featured talking people, except in brief static scenes.[57]

Now film subjects, with the help of technology that recorded synchronized sound and image, took significant interpretive control out of the hands of the director. It was during this moment that the unfiltered vernacular voices of marginalized communities began to appear in documentary film representation. This evolution in form increased the rhetorical potential of social change documentary, allowing it to move from speaking for people to having people speak for themselves. The distance created between the "voice of God" narrator and the distant images of life was replaced with the voices of everyday people, speaking freely.

With this focus on observation, new ways of looking emerged. For example, in Robert Drew's *Primary* (1960), we see then-Senator John F. Kennedy chatting with constituents, speaking intimately with his wife, joking after the news camera were turned off, and collaborating with his handlers. In these moments, we observe the slippage between Kennedy the human and the political persona he projects.

This observational crafting of authenticity is one reason the documentary genre has historically functioned as a vehicle for public address. By foregrounding the voices and experiences of documentary subjects, filmmakers could do more than speak for communities: it could bring marginalized voices directly to the public as a means of bearing witness. *Town Bloody Hall* (1979) by D. A. Pennebaker and Chris Hegedus documents a 1971 public debate between feminist advocates and antagonist Norman Mailer on the shifting gender roles in society. A critical mass of women were speaking out about abortion, rape, and sex-based education, and this documentary provided an amplified platform. The amplification of "voice," in this case women's voices, is significant when we place this film in the context of the long-entrenched inequalities that still exist. Considered in this way, the concept of "voice" can be used as shorthand to describe the continuous human struggle for recognition in society, suggesting that "spaces for voice" are "spaces for power" and a petition to be acknowledged as "part of the landscape."[58] Giving expression to marginalized voices is a form of reflexive agency,[59] creating subjects of ourselves and linking us to others while addressing the universal human desire to make sense of our lives.

In the late 1960s, documentary film and social change found new life as direct cinema foregrounded vernacular voices and European *cinéma vérité* remained committed to intervening in the project of political dissent. The widespread political unrest of the moment and the development of low-cost video technology created fertile ground for a new generation of filmmakers. People living in the margins began making their own films, and activists created their own media. The late 1960s through the 1970s marked the flourishing second wave of social change documentary.

DOCUMENTARY AS A VEHICLE
TO CHALLENGE REPRESENTATION

For documentary to act as a vehicle to challenge representation, there had to be innovations in form and content that produced creative ways of including underdocumented experiences and stories. These unconventional articulations and representations prompted reevaluation and engagement in the world. This approach unified one of the most diverse movements in documentary industry. According to Deirdre Boyle in her book, *Subject to Change: Guerrilla Television Revisited*, the activist-video movement began with the development of lightweight, affordable, and portable video-recording equipment in the late 1960s and early 1970s. Although video equipment was developed in the late 1950s, it was cumbersome, stationary, complex, and expensive. The Sony Corporation did not launch its first major effort to market consumer-grade equipment until 1965. The first genuinely portable video equipment—the half-inch, reel-to-reel consumer video portapak—was released in 1968.[60] This gave baby boomers the resources to make their own brand of television. This "new brand of television," also called guerrilla television, was part of a larger alternative media tide that swept across the country during the late 1960s and 1970s. For a generation that grew up in the shadows of the civil rights and antiwar movements, television was "the window to the world."[61] Troubled by the political and social unrest of the 1960s, the guerrilla television movement—made up of autonomous groups with diverse and often contradictory organizing frameworks and interests—collectively imagined utopian programming to change the structure of information in America by creating a distinct parallel broadcast system providing oppositional content: "Optimism about television and its dynamic impact not just on communications but on contemporary consciousness was seized by the first generation raised on television, who found . . . a euphoric explanation of themselves and their changing times [in television]."[62] This section addresses the documentary impulses and interventions of this movement.

The political crisis of the late 1960s, provoked by the Vietnam War and ongoing resistance movements, in conjunction with technological innovations in video, precipitated new spaces and forms for the documentary impulse. The new medium of video recording provided challenges and opportunities for activists. For example, video is more accessible and less expensive than film, and it also allows an immediate playback function not available in film recording. Early activist-video collectives in the second wave capitalized on this playback function as a community-building mechanism, screening footage in popular spaces immediately after recording it. The portability of video also allowed activists to use the medium to screen footage in makeshift theaters and community spaces. The screen as an object transforms viewership. Where the screen resides, whether pinned to a community wall or traditionally framed among ornate design in a theater, influences the viewing experience. In practice, video provided portability and access to recording technology that had the potential to invigorate democratic practices. As documented in a video handbook produced by the Video Freex collective:

> We want to catch them in the action of their daily lives, record them on our magic tape. We want to introduce people to each other and we want to saturate them with information, information about human beings, "fellow Americans." Seize the time, capture the situation! History in the making, life recorded, but not just the life we read about in our mass media, or see on our network television stations.[63]

Video happened in real time, allowing communities to see themselves and the world differently but at the speed of broadcast television. Participatory organizing was influenced by anarchist-inflected practices, "establishing their own cells," adopting consensus decision making, rejecting hierarchy, occasionally promoting direct action, but more often, "attempting" to carve out a better world."[64]

DOCUMENTARY AS AN AXIS OF COLLABORATION

Documentary culture acted as an axis of collaboration, spurring autonomous organizing and early experiments, with documentary as a participatory commons. The term *axis of collaboration* refers to the ways groups used the documentary production process as a means to include diverse communities—locally and across geographical divides—around shared interests through participatory practice. New York City was one of the major hubs for experiments with activist documentary video in the late 1960s. Prominent video collectives included the Video Freex, the People's Video Theater, Global Village, and the Raindance Corporation.[65] The following section focuses on the function of activist documentary and political collaboration as practiced by three prominent collectives in the second wave of activist documentary: Video Freex, Top Value Television, and the Raindance Corporation. Although each of the video collectives worked autonomously and employed divergent strategies, they shared common goals and a similar mode of activism. Notably, each video collective group was bound by (1) an outright opposition to mainstream broadcast television, (2) a belief in the medium of television as a vehicle for critical analysis and information exchange, and (3) a commitment to universal access to video technology to allow underrepresented communities to create their own media. They were also insular and utopian, and they often were composed of privileged people who had the space, resources, education, and time to experiment with remaking culture through video. One of the first such media activist groups was a handful of citizens who called themselves Video Freex.

Figure 2.1 Some of the most important work of the Videofreex involved recording the growing political uprisings in the late 60s, including rare footage of a 1969 interview with Fred Hampton and the Black Panthers as well as Abbie Hoffman during the Chicago 8 trial.

The Video Freex collective began as a small group of video activists housed in an industrial section of downtown Manhattan. As one member remarked, "We were happy to blur our provenance and thus assume our rightful role among the elite if not the vanguard of the counter-culture and anti-war movements."[66] The group produced an array of video, including some of the more entertaining and accomplished work on the scene. Their Chicago travelogues provide an inside view into the workings of late 1960s radical activists and groups, including Abbie Hoffman, Jerry Rubin, the Yippies, and the Weathermen. These tapes also provide rare footage of the Black Panthers as they organized in Chicago, including the powerful oratory of Fred Hampton. The group sought to establish a countercultural lifestyle collective rooted in the production of activist documentary and video art. Beginning in the city but eventually moving to rural upstate New York to illegally broadcast their micro-power television station, they were committed to building community and providing democratic access to production resources: "[G]uerrilla television was configured not as a weapon, but as a cultural tool bringing people together."[67] By giving people access to tools that allowed them to document their lives and negotiate the world on their own terms, the movement created a vernacular space that countered the prevailing dominant ideology of broadcast television:

> [V]ideo could involve people by making them active participants in the "video environment" rather than passive viewers of network TV fare . . . video's potential [was] to offer people a variety of viewpoints rather than the official, objective one promoted by Walter Cronkite's "And That's the Way It Is."[68]

This kind of production happened around collectives and media centers, generating many fluid experiments in collaboration.

For example, in 1972, New York's Downtown Community Television Center (DCTV) was founded by Jon Alpert, who had worked as a taxi driver in a multi-ethnic area, and Keiko Tsuno. Together, Alpert and Tsuno produced a documentary about taxi unions and the issues of exploitation drivers faced. Seeing their lives mirrored on video, citizens became excited about the potential of television to provide an audience that would witness their concerns. As a result, Alpert and Tsuno launched free training sessions in video production in three languages. The work that emerged out of DCTV was produced in fifteen languages and broadcast by stations in various parts of the world.[69] DCTV continues to be a robust production company and community outreach program, providing production skills to underserved communities. When I talked to Tsuno, she explained how DCTV was able to survive the dire cuts in arts funding and the challenges of keeping a community media center functioning for over four decades:

> This is also one of the reasons we are still here. I think it . . . there are two things. Number one is we are not dependent on grant only. The people who are only

dependent on government grant, they just wiped out when, you know, big cutback happened. It was . . . once it happened in 1980s, and then again recently. But, also . . . well, this 1980, when our grant from government shrank from 90 percent to 15 percent, or . . . we knew that was very big, you know, turnaround time. And we started to rent our professional equipment and professional editing suite. That's how we survived. Then our lawyer and accountants start saying, "look, you are doing some commercial activities under name of, you know, non-profit." We said, "yes, it's a contradiction. But, that's the way people have to survive." So they said, "ok, make two organizations. And all profit goes to a non-profit. So this doesn't make money, but you have to, you know, file separately." So we did. And that one is still . . . it's . . . that one is ended by 1995. But, now we have also two organizations under the same DCTV name. One is DCTV Doc, which is basically who we're producing for, you know, HBO and other channels, networks. And, that is still big, large profit, 50 percent of our income to support this [nonprofit].

Sustaining community media collaborations took more than good intentions; it required crafty negotiation of income streams to fund social justice objectives that the market and government institutions did not reliably support. In addition to fundraising, these organizations also had to build the networks needed for community media broadcasts to reach the masses.

One of the most significant and historically unrecognized social change documentary filmmakers is George Stoney. With a career spanning more than sixty years, "Stoney, better than any other single figure, bridges the traditional Grierson world of documentary film production and the current digital democratization of the documentary."[70] He developed an understanding of documentary that "has work to do in the world,"[71] but he also invested in establishing activist media networks and infrastructure. Stoney's work began in the 1940s, when he used Pare Lorenz's documentary, *The River* (1939), as a discussion tool in meetings with southern rural communities that were organized by Roosevelt's Farm Settlement Administration. For Stoney, the postscreening discussions were just as important as the film, and perhaps even more important. In these discussions, biases were confronted, connections were made, and identifications were solidified. These sorts of critical engagements transform viewers into activists. Stoney's rich legacy profoundly affected how documentary filmmakers understand the possibilities of participation.

Stoney's films often existed in a strange vortex between educational, training, and social issue films, reflecting his commitments to bridging community problems with social institutions. One of Stoney's most revered documentary works, *All My Babies* (1953), addressed the culture of black midwifery in the South, focusing on procedures and processes of care. The documentary was used extensively as a training video for the medical community and helped contribute to lower maternal and infant mortality rates.[72] During the 1960s, when direct cinema filmmakers were embracing observation, Stoney stayed focused on the participatory possibilities of documentary intervention. He routinely invited his subjects to pick up the camera, give feedback on edits, and contribute to crafting the story. Stoney worked with institutions interested in using film for outreach, and he was not particularly skeptical of institutions or conscious of their tendency to control communities even as they served them. He worked with government institutional funding and never had problems with censorship or with making documentaries that went against his own principles. The result is an uncritical paternalism in some of his work that may explain why it was so well received by mainstream institutions.

When I interviewed George Stoney on a rainy summer day in 2009, a few years before his death, we talked about the care work of documentary, the telling of undocumented history, and the process of participation. In response to my question about how social change documentary functions in the world, he clearly and firmly answered: "It [documentary] confirms the conviction of the presenter. It causes the viewer to identify him or herself with the objective. And, it shows some methods of change, methods of bringing about change."[73] He believes the collective identification experienced through documentary is not just a matter of solidifying associations between like-minded people. According to Stoney, documentary also

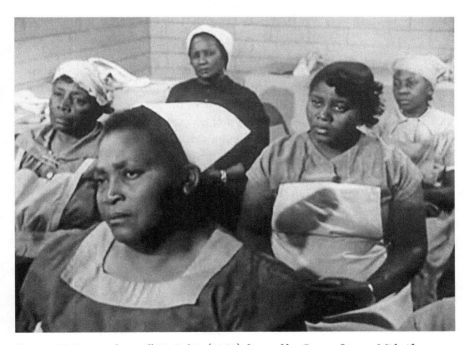

Figure 2.2 A scene from *All My Babies* (1953) directed by George Stoney. Midwifes are directed into formal education from the white, male medical establishment. Experienced midwifes sit and listen to doctors explain the medicalized procedures for birth.

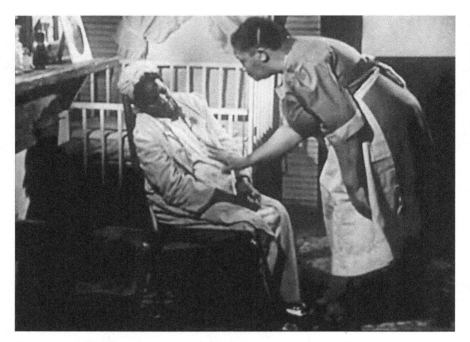

Figure 2.3 A midwife helps a woman through labor, a scene from *All My Babies* (1953) directed by George Stoney

informs us about how one should act in the world, generating a form of agency. His commitments to participation are more practical and less situated in an ethical framework. He explains, "I found when I involved the people who were gonna use the film in their production, they were not only much more useful, but the people had a commitment to use them. . . . I found that people responded much better when they did their own stuff. . . . I think that when people [are] involved in their own production, they are much easier about having the public see them."[74] Unlike a finished film, the process of collaboration during production is often invisible, though it has its own impact on the world.

In the early 1970s, while working as a professor at New York University, Stoney and others pioneered a project to realize the ultimate vision of every citizen having a voice and the access and resources to author their own media. This vision included building a network for broadcast distribution through local cable access channels to allow easy circulation of activist media. To achieve these goals, Stoney launched the Alternative Media Center in New York City and petitioned cable stations for community access resources across the country.

These early efforts worked to shift television content away from banal entertainment and negative images of youthful protest toward representations of countercultural values and a new television reality. As Boyle observed, "fueled by adolescent rebellion and utopian dreams, video promised an alternative to the slickly civilized, commercially corrupt, and aesthetically bankrupt world of [broadcast] television."[75] The aim of the portable-video movement "was 'guerrilla warfare' insofar as it enabled citizens to fight the 'perceptual imperialism of broadcast television' on a small scale in what was then an irregular war."[76] If this was the goal, how exactly did activist media collectives use documentary to create social change?

While George Stoney and DCTV worked to build open and accessible community media collaborations, groups such as Video Freex became mired in building alternative lifestyle communities around video production. The video production lifestyle, rather than the shared political principles, acted as the marker of the community. Activist-video collectives, an outgrowth of the commune movement, had an ecological vision that attempted to subvert "commercial media, state bureaucracy, and the nuclear family."[77] As one Video Freex member recounted:

> We called ourselves Video Freex. Officially, it was a corporation as well as our collective name. It had become a generic term as well, with the pejorative sense of freak undermined by the prevailing sub-culture, such that any enthusiast or aficionado, regardless of the subject—sex, drugs, rock 'n' roll, food, video—was non-judgmentally classified as a freak."[78]

Although many experimental projects evolved out of the Video Freex collective, their approach fostered experimentations with production and exhibition rather than significant social change. Still, this work picked up the autonomous, radical impulse that was fomented during the early moments of cinema. Still other activist-video collectives—in an attempt to directly combat the homogeneous news environment—were reformist in nature, confronting the mainstream media from the inside.

DOCUMENTARY AS A CONDUIT FOR INFORMATION EXCHANGE

In the late 1960s, the Newsreel movement was particularly active across the United States. Politically focused independent filmmakers within specific geographical locations, pooled resources to document life in urban spaces. These documentary representations in the form of motion picture newsreels captured the unseen people and circumstances that did not penetrate the thick veneer of broadcast television, with organizations developing in San Francisco, Los Angeles, Chicago, and Boston. New York Newsreel's focus was on cinema as a tool to engage spectators, an organizing mechanism of bringing new people to the movement and prompting action in real life.[79] The Newsreel movement and the larger guerrilla video movement shared a resistance to the aesthetics of production and what those choices symbolized. There was an outright rejection of the professional culture and the slick production of mainstream and broadcast media, which were deemed inauthentic, consumer-based, and empty of vision or political principle.

Newsreels produced by the movement were not just new representations of unseen content, but rather the production process was made transparent through experiments with montage and perspective. These production interventions had visceral impacts on communities, narrating stories that straddled the space between oral history and urban lore. Chris Robé documents two such incidents illustrating their impact. First, Newsreel's *Columbia Revolt* (1968) captures protests at Columbia University when students discovered links between the university and the institutional apparatus of the Vietnam war as well as the compounding issues of segregation on campus. The documentary represents the story of those occupying five university buildings for social change, the camera capturing the story from inside while the press waited outside. The documentary screened at the State University of New York (SUNY) at Buffalo and provided the energy that led 500 students to burn down the ROTC building. Second, at the University of California, Santa Cruz, embolded by the screening it "strengthened student resolve" to confront the Board of Regents the next day with their own set of demands. Within many of these organizations, there was a push and pull between artistry and activism, a focus on aesthetics that often traded off with authentic connections and relationships with working-class members of Newsreel and the communities they documented.[80] The way Newsreel and a nationwide collective documented the bubbling undercurrents of culture was unprecedented. The diversity in representation straddling class, race, and gender was striking, as these works became some of the most important historical documents in our visual history.

Documentary's function as a conduit for information exchange is bound up in the politics of representation, as well as the structures of alternative distribution and exhibition. Alternative media networks circumvent gatekeepers and create pathways in which information can flow with minimal top-down obstruction. In traditional media structures, some information is more accessible, documented, privileged, and accepted than other information. When documentary functions as a conduit of information exchange, it provides information that had been missing, submerged, or undocumented. This manifests in the form of unheard of perspectives, undocumented history, and alternative archiving and cultural production. Alternative networks make space for this underground information to be broadcast publicly and forcefully. At the other end of the guerrilla television spectrum, Top Value Television (TVTV) was an ad hoc group organized to cover the United States' 1972 national presidential conventions for a growing cable television market. Equipped with the newly available portable-video technology, activists flooded young Republican rallies, cocktail parties, antiwar demonstrations, and the convention floor.[81]

The TVTV group produced *Four More Years* (1972), a behind-the-scenes look at the 1972 National Republican Convention. Focused on capturing the counternarrative of the convention, *Four More Years* edits together loosely connected scenes from the events, showcasing undocumented moments and opinions, especially those that counter the slick veneer of broadcast television narratives. The documentary recorded news reporters complaining about their work circumstances, the production crew playing harmonica on the convention floor, and images from the production side of television culture, shown in close and intimate framing. As one member of the TVTV noted, the goal was to "cover the media covering those actions and cover the people planning for or reflecting on them. The [convention] actions themselves are of negligible importance to us."[82] In this context, activist video recorded events from a perspective that countered that of mainstream television. The videos challenged the objectivity of the news by focusing on events that traditionally fall outside the television screen. As one member of TVTV recounted, "Our tapes must represent the event—far less than traditional media trips—but the content of the event must be there. Our role is unique."[83] Unlike mainstream television reporting that focused on events, this approach to activist video attempted to capture the missing contexts of those events. Although TVTV was not overtly advocating a particular ideological stance, the texts produced a new aesthetic and a fresh position on the media. As prominent media activist DeeDee Halleck reminisced:

Spunky, restless, and iconoclastic, TVTV's tapes were a breath of fresh air in the seventies, in stark contrast not only to stodgy commercial fare but to the overtly earnest tapes from the New/Old Left with their interminable harangues from microphones at demonstrations. Although never willing to spell out a specific ideological stance, TVTV made the media their politics, and even their checklist for camera people has a stance of defiance against the standard broadcast mores."[84]

Underneath the innovative use of cameras and the ecological vision of media produced by collectives lay a current of white and middle-class privilege that impeded work with historically disenfranchised groups.[85] TVTV walked a line between counterculture and mainstream, embracing a narrow sense of agitation at combating mainstream broadcast production representations and practices.

While Top Value Television produced alternative media content, the Raindance Corporation functioned as the research and development arm of the video movement. Raindance operated as an experimental video collective and was most famous for coining the term *guerrilla television*. This name marked a new brand of television that emerged from the collision of activism, art, and the development of accessible video technology in the early 1970s. In his book, *Guerrilla Television* (1971), Michael Shamberg describes the activist collective as an "analogue to the

Rand Corporation—a think tank that would use videotape instead of print."[86] The collective's primary objective was to agitate against the slick world of mainstream television broadcasting.

Fighting the slick world of broadcast television, the collective was rhetorically more concerned with "appearing in public" as opposed to "acting in public." There are some notable exceptions, but the movement was more focused on projecting missing representations than using images to create social change, engaging in a kind of magical thinking about moving image discourse. Political contestation was addressed "not by directly assaulting the system—as in a political revolution—but by extending the unifying properties of electronic media to everyone."[87] Attempting to avoid the ideological warfare on broadcast television, early video activist Frank Gillette commented that he was not imposing his structure on people, but rather he was letting people "give their raps on tape."[88] The movement located the political moment of social change in providing access to technology resources, focusing on alternative expression and lifestyle community. Abandoning instrumental political goals, the new breed of video activist was connected through the aesthetic of the countercultural lifestyle. Film and media studies scholar Chris Robé argues that the retreat into a collective lifestyle—especially with more radical groups such as Video Freex and the Newsreel collectives—was an anarchist-inflected movement toward remaking culture. Regardless of the intention, these activist cultures abandoned direct political agitation, ultimately preventing their work from actualizing into effective media formations. This shift meant that any instrumental platform for social change documentary that had been established was lost or, at best, not prioritized in the 1970s. Marco Vassi, an active member of the early video scene, commented on the environment of a grassroots video collective: "We sit stoned and dig each other's worldview. We rap and eat and fuck and watch tape. And for us, it's about the same as it has always been: just living fully, openly, honest to what is."[89] Although the production process collaboratively engaged communities, the engagement was not necessarily instrumental.

The political moment was concerned primarily with disseminating multiple viewpoints and developing a counter political community rather than taking agitational actions that might better guarantee, as Nancy Fraser suggests, the cultural recognition and redistribution of economic resources that are the foundation of oppression and marginalization. The emphasis on community building resulted in not "much time thinking about strategies for changing even the policies that were of central interest to them: media policies."[90] The strategies of political agitation were misdirected. As Dee Dee Halleck concluded, "The video guerrillas were reluctant to undertake the exhausting and thankless work of infrastructure development, and there was little prospect of funding long-term progressive initiatives."[91] As a result, the movement failed to reach its objective of systematic social change, but it did succeed in displaying alternative media content:

As a part of the counter-culture, guerrilla television helped raise a critique of American Society that went beyond the bounds of the political Left, even if it missed essential leftist insights about power, economic exploitation, and class.[92]

The 1970s movement pioneers also successfully established the foundational infrastructure for activist production, training, and distribution. This impulse led to early experiments in collaboration and information exchange that helped build future pathways toward social change.

The activist-video movement was insular in orientation, not because of its commitment to a distinct parallel broadcast system,[93] but because of the drive toward producing politically polarizing videotexts that mostly addressed an insider community. A community that fetishized new media resided comfortably in the privilege of play, largely ignoring agitation and the power dynamics that undergirded this work. The movement experimented with different communities in a superficial way, for example, the People's Video Theater built a temporary grant coalition with the Young Lords, a movement within the struggle for Puerto Rican liberation. Upon receiving the grant, the People's Video Theater purchased four portapaks, giving one unit to the Young Lords and keeping the rest. Each group went its own way, not formally collaborating on any creative projects. In this exchange, the People's Video Theater replicates a "colonial relation of white benefactors bestowing goods upon the colonized receiver to ingratiate themselves into the tribe."[94] Remnants of this political tourism continue in documentary culture today. Reflecting on the objectives of the activist-video movement, Marco Vassi observed that activist filmmakers must realize "that all their complex equipment is just so much metal junk, toys and tools, which have no more worth than the hands and hearts of the people who work them."[95] At some point, countercultural interests must engage with dominant hegemonic interests that are conscious of replicating oppressive structures. Video activism needed to attract a massive viewership to engage in persuasive appeals that could push audiences past the stalemate between countercultural interests and dominant hegemonic discourse.[96] The presence of alternative viewpoints alone was not enough to translate facts into beliefs and then into common sense.

As the 1970s came to an end, a new assault on video culture was mounting. The 1980s brought drastic cuts to arts funding in general and documentary in particular. The Reagan era's hostility to the arts ushered in a new cultural regime in which documentary "did not imagine new social spaces, but rather affirm[ed] unique individuals."[97] The restructuring of the telecommunications sector, political targeting by conservatives, and congressional debates "turned documentary into a bloody political battlefield."[98] Patricia Zimmermann identifies this moment as a war over how public space and nationhood are defined. Documentary became a location for the expression of larger conflicts like the "war between the imagined white nation-state and the new formations of diaspora."[99] As U.S. culture adopted a more conservative stance in the 1980s, radical media found new platforms and escape routes. The last decade of the 20th century then ushered in more new technologies, a maturing neoliberal economic system, shifting political formations, and new democratic practices that further collapsed the line between politics and culture.

The Third Wave of Social Change Documentary

One thing becomes clear from the history of social change documentary: locating the political potential of the genre does not tell the whole story. Documentary filmmakers have used production and distribution to engage the process of social change, creating moments of fundamental political significance. The Workers Film and Photo League contributed to representations that created identification with the working-class struggle for survival deeply influenced by Soviet montage and Dziga Vertov, a Soviet documentary and newsreel director who deeply influenced theories of cinema and filmmaking. Video collectives in the 1970s located their activist production and distribution strategies in the choice to screen works in community centers and to teach communities how to make their own media. These shifting social and political contexts have dictated the strategies, texture, and civic potential of documentary over time. Therefore, different periods of social change documentary not only cluster around moments of political crisis, but also function according to the needs and limits of a given historical moment. For example, the Workers Film and Photo League of the 1930s was energized by the economic crisis of the time but was limited by the lack of portable technology available to record the personal and intimate struggles of the working poor. Much like the activist documentaries of other periods, a unique political and social context produced a particular kind of activist moment in the third wave.

The third wave of activist documentary fomented in the late 1980s, bursting onto the scene after the turn of the century and continuing to evolve today. Analyzing pivotal changes in the independent documentary in a post–1989 landscape, Patricia Zimmermann argues, "radical documentary practices graphing difference have been engaged in a civil war over the national imaginary."[100] This war began in the 1980s with the Reagan administration's draconian reductions of federal and state arts funding and the dismantling of the noncommercial media sector in the United States—reducing documentary to a more marginal practice. This historical moment also included accelerated media restructuring and mergers that demanded new production ecologies. These circumstances were accompanied by an intense cultural war on content. As national discussions about sexuality-explicit art raged on, documentary's historical reputation for repudiating "the fictions of the nation with the real, the document, the historical, the particular,"[101] meant the genre was at odds with conservative positions on cultural politics. By the end of the 1980s, these conditions realigned the production culture of documentary in the United States, pushing more documentary production to the nonprofit sector and eventually, into commercial institutions. As a result, "the entire project of documentary itself has been contested by realignments and new developments in new communications systems, the state and consumer culture."[102] Before 1989, independent media was framed as a common good for democratic ends: arts funding and public television were understood as spaces for voices denied access by capitalist interests. The third wave is a reaction to dozens of not-for-profit media centers closing their doors and the emergence of new documentary practices shaped by advances in new digital technologies and the internet. Understanding documentary as a robust commons is about returning to media production as a social good, a process to connect the underrepresented with a larger political and cultural horizon.

Varied contemporary documentary and social change strategies led to the third wave; they included an influx of labor documentaries that marked significant shifts in manager–worker relations, documentaries that recorded a living history of the growing AIDS crisis, and documentaries that questioned government and corporate globalization practices. In the late 1980s and early 1990s, there was a proliferation of union films that depicted a societal transition in worker–management relations. Films like Barbara Kopple's *American Dream* (1990) and Michael Moore's *Roger and Me* (1989) were portraits of American workers living through crisis. During this time, community access channels in the rising cable market continued to produce an interesting variety of activist programming that ranged from media literacy education programs such as "Herbert Schiller Reads the *New York Times*" to the expansion of parallel broadcast networks such as Paper Tiger TV.[103] Then, the explosion of the AIDS crisis in the late 1980s and early 1990s produced a new kind of activist video. Those afflicted by this disease, about which the U.S. government remained silent, made their voices heard through documentary production.

The AIDS activist-video movement documented demonstrations, the struggle for visibility, and the evolution of the disease from the perspective of those experiencing it. The videotexts functioned as a necessary and powerful counternarrative to the consistently negative depictions of AIDS in the mainstream media.[104] During this time, ACT UP, a prominent gay activist group, created a video collective called DIVA TV (Damned Interfering Video Activist Television). Gregg Bordowitz, a DIVA TV member, produced some of the most influential work in AIDS activist video, such as *Voices from the Front* (1991) and *Fast Trip, Long Drop* (1995). Using a combination of personal and autobiographical modes, activist street-tape recordings, and reused silent and found footage, Bordowitz captured the essence of living with HIV. He used montage to construct familiar relationships with unknowable experiences.

The videos provide stirring portraits of the political struggle surrounding the AIDS crisis in public and in intimate close-up as Bordowitz struggles with the effects of the disease on his own body. AIDS activist video, Paper Tiger TV, and DIVA TV all played an important role in developing the foundation for the third wave of activist documentary. While these works continued to sit at the margins of popular culture, a new form of social change documentary was about to explode into the mainstream.

Unlike the second wave of documentary, which characterized social change as a fight between surly commercial broadcasting and activist media, the new struggle for power is issue driven, underscored by the tensions of exploitation and marginalization that are amplified by a maturing neoliberalism in the United States. In fact, popular contemporary activist media is at home in the slick world of corporate broadcasting and commercial distribution, which is dependent on maintaining a loyal viewership through subscription, advertising, and sales. A familiar strategy of third-wave activist documentary is to place films in major distribution outlets, hoping to reach the maximum viewing audience without compromising critical political content. The most significant test case of this phenomenon was the wide release of *Fahrenheit 9/11*.

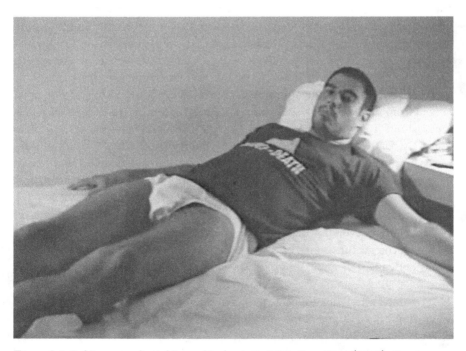

Figure 2.4 In his personal autobiographical epic *Fast Trip, Long Drop* (1993), Gregg Bordowitz stiches together a narrative about living with HIV through archives, personal performance and activist street tapes.

DOCUMENTARY AS A TOOL OF POLITICAL INTERVENTION

Documentary's move into mainstream commercial culture shifted strategies for engaging social change. Previously, documentary functioned as a mirror, an axis of collaboration, or an information exchange, but with the move to commercial culture, it began to intervene more frequently in larger political discussions, policymaking, the news agenda, and legal proceedings. The walls of the theater have long been porous for documentary, and this new kind of exposure, amplified by the comfortable circulation of documentary discourse in commercial and institutional networks, increases the genre's productive and destructive consequences in public culture. In the summer of 2004, the United States was embroiled in a questionable war against Iraq. In this heated political moment, provocateur and documentary filmmaker Michael Moore released his fourth feature film. It addressed the Iraq War, condemning the sitting Bush administration and the mainstream press. *Fahrenheit 9/11* is one of the most commercially successful documentaries, yet its significance resides elsewhere. While media makers frequently address social issues on a local level, it was rare at the time for a film of this magnitude and genre to attempt to mobilize a nation around a national political issue during an election year.[105] The most interesting and significant aspect of *Fahrenheit 9/11* is the film's evolution into something bigger than the documentary itself.[106] With *Fahrenheit 9/11*, Moore entered into an agitational relationship with the mainstream media while simultaneously existing within it.[107]

Fahrenheit 9/11 marked a new evolution in the third wave of activist documentary. The controversial film received significant attention from mainstream news media, allowing it to defy traditional activist documentary positioning. Instead of being situated at the margins of the counterculture, today activist documentaries like *Fahrenheit 9/11* take center stage in popular culture. The popular activist documentary is one aspect of the third wave that can either explode or bury the potential of social change. Does intense visibility make audience members numb to social injustice, or does it urge different populations to engage beyond the viewing moment? Many other activist documentaries followed *Fahrenheit 9/11*, comfortably existing in the stratosphere of popular, mainstream reception.

The political and social context of third-wave activist documentary is distinct from that of previous periods. As McChesney and other scholars have noted, media is becoming a more pervasive and persuasive aspect of contemporary life.[108] In this historical moment that is characterized by media saturation and participation, commercial political protest is around every corner: "Capitalism, at least as it is envisioned by the best-selling management handbooks, is no longer about enforcing order, but destroying it. 'Revolution', once the totemic catchphrase of the counter-culture, has become the totemic catch-phrase of boomer-as-capitalist."[109] Unlike other periods of history, perpetual revolution and rule-breaking are the orthodoxy of the day.[110] During the first and second wave of activist documentary, recordings were always outside the mainstream, while today's commercial media often adopt edgy counterhegemonic media for profit.[111]

The texture of contemporary social change documentary reflects the blurred boundaries between counterhegemonic ideas, political dissent, and commercial culture. Distribution outside the commercial media apparatus is no longer a clear marker of an activist documentary. Recent mass-marketed documentaries have targeted the media and corporate exploitation: filmmaker Morgan Spurlock attacks fast-food corporations in the blockbuster *Supersize Me* (2004), Michael Moore routinely targets corrupt corporations and inefficient political institutions in *Bowling for Columbine* (2002), *Fahrenheit 9/11* (2004), and *Capitalism: A Love Story* (2009). Moore released *Fahrenheit 11/9* (2018) in an attempt to revive his 2004 success bearing a similar name but in the Trump era. By most accounts, Moore continues to speak for social change, though his approach and style are wearing thin in a different political moment. Josh Fox exposes the practices of fracking in *Gasland* (2010), and Gabriela Cowperthwaite's *Blackfish* (2013) helps expose and dismantle the practices of Sea World, a multinational corporation. The benefits of commercial media lie in its power of mass distribution. In order to reach the maximum audience, activist media may benefit from tapping into the commercial media apparatus. The pressing question facing the rhetorical situation of third-wave social change documentary, however, is how activist messages exist in the mass media environment and resist cooption by commercial interests. One popular HBO documentary and its sequel managed to circumvent this dilemma by finding an audience in the mainstream media while extending political work that led to social change.

The HBO documentary films *Paradise Lost: The Child Murders at Robin Hood Hills* (1996) and its sequel *Paradise Lost Revisited* (2000) chronicle a murder trial in Arkansas in which three teenage boys were convicted of killing three younger boys. The first film documents the trial, while the second film reflects on the first film's impact on the trial. There arose a significant question as to whether the convicted were indeed guilty, and an instrumental social movement developed from the viewership of the first documentary.[112] The first film helped turn passive consumers of communication into deliberating agents. The audience collectively turned public communication into political communication in the counter-public sphere by sharing evidence in the case on a public website, gathering support internationally with a postcard petition, and forming an instrumental social movement organization called Free the West Memphis Three. In praxis, the impersonal, passive, and relaxing aspects of the consumption of mass media were overcome in this instance by participatory internet use. An analysis of these two films and their publics suggests that the internet has the potential to unite unlikely citizens. It does so by providing a way to overcome geographic distances between activists and facilitate connection through affective affinity and critical-rational exchange.[113]

This documentary event is especially intriguing because the directors had no activist intentions. As seasoned filmmakers, Joe Berlinger and Bruce Sinofsky were on assignment for HBO and were not motivated activists working from the margins. Yet, the culmination of their work is perhaps one of the most significant instances of documentary confronting the legal structure; it ultimately resulted in the release of three innocent men from prison, one of whom was released from death row.

The third wave of activist documentary is also distinct in that it coincides with the proliferation of mobile recording and online engagement. Much as developments in recording technology and television drastically changed the project of the activist documentary, the internet and mobile recording created a new paradigm for culture and social change. Audiences can now extend the documentary viewing experience by seeking more information online and connecting with others who share their concerns. In online forums, collaborations are created, shared interests are expressed, and connections are strengthened through participation. This means documentary production can use online engagement as a clearinghouse for information and connection.[114] With features like live chat, blogs, listservs, and grassroots archiving, the internet has the potential to make the documentary viewing experience interactive and consequently more conducive to the formation of participatory media cultures around collective identifications for facilitating social change. Picking up the work of collaboration in a new digital landscape, mobile recording and internet streaming made possible a new population of media makers.

DOCUMENTARY AS AN ORGANIZING AGENT

The collaborative impulse found new traction with the introduction of new technology and growing political unrest. New digital technology created a new playing field for organizing with the documentary impulse in order to gather diverse communities for agitational action. At the turn of the 21st century, there was a resurgence of street tapes and participatory media collectives. Perhaps the most significant grassroots site for global citizen journalism in the last several decades was the Independent Media Center (IMC). Although the IMC has been inconsistent in recent years, its video networks and experiments at the turn of the century were essential to media activism from 2000 to 2010[115] and after, ranging from Occupy Wall Street to Black Lives Matter. In the early days of the third wave, the IMC was touted as the "newest phenomenon to hit the political scene," and it subsequently became a "surprisingly effective news organization"[116] that included thousands of volunteer reporters in thirty-seven cities in the United States and forty-five locations around the world. It is an internet-based activist-video movement "born out of protest against corporate interests and governments' role in globalization. It is a movement that has joined diverse groups, from grassroots organizations to labor unions."[117] The IMC is the newest iteration of a larger activist-video movement committed to the marriage of low-format sound and video technology and activism that began in the early 1970s and was revitalized at the turn of the century.[118]

The IMC website reported over one million hits during the 1999 World Trade Organization (WTO) meeting and subsequent protest; people visited the website to view streaming videos of stories investigated by IMC volunteers and captured with donated video and audio equipment. The volunteers—many of them WTO protestors themselves—logged footage of protest events around the clock and conducted street interviews with everyone from black-dressed anarchists to the police. The stories emphasized the concerns of the protestors and functioned as a means of bearing witness to the numerous acts of police brutality that occurred in an effort to control the crowds.[119] These street tapes depict a celebration of life in the streets: puppets, performers, drum circles, elaborate costumes representing wildlife, and free-form dancing. Arresting moments of the video streaming out of the IMC during the protests included, among other types of video, repetitive violent sequences and montages of police dominance. The street tapes bear witness to police use of excessive violence and to the protestors' helplessness against a well-equipped military unit. The videos feature scenes of protestors forcefully pinned down, thrown around, and beaten by police; these events are captured in close and intimate proximity, where the camera translates the experience of such repression. Jill Friedberg, co-director of *This Is What Democracy Looks Like* and an activist who was part of the first meetings to organize the IMC in Seattle, describes the experience as frenetic and fast paced. In our conversation about Seattle in 1999, she explains: "It felt a little like getting shot out of cannon, and everybody in the Independent Media Center in Seattle felt that way. After the tear gas cleared and everyone went home, we all felt like we'd been launched out of a cannon, and in the process, I had to do a lot of thinking about, you know documentary and social change, and what we were making and what did we want to do with it." This kind of collective organizing and the images generated during protest form a specific kind of production culture. The fast circulation of images is emphasized, sometimes at the expense of taking time to consider the best ways to approach the process. The internet alters traditional political participation by overcoming the limitations of geographic distance and access to information; it can even multiply strategies of agitation.[120] The onset of mobile recording exponentially increased our exposure to images of real-time political struggle and vernacular history.

If we pay attention to the lessons of documentary history, we come away with several clarifying observations about social change that seem most salient: First, as scholars, we must study a wider documentary ecology. Interventions in the process of social change manifest in the production, distribution, circulation, and uptake of documentary as well as in the participatory culture(s) that emerge around them. This insight suggests that we might revisit how we study documentary and question our preferred methods and the limitations. The study of documentary and social change demands new methods of scholarship, connecting the knowledge of those who make documentaries with those who use documentary in political struggles and in conversation with those who study this work. Second, cultural and theoretical assessment of social change must take into account the widely varied scale and effects of these films. This could challenge iron-clad theorizing about this process, but it matches the nature of this political exchange. Finally, the theoretical and historical space for investigating documentary and social change should balance the project of productive political intervention with the craft of cinema, engaging in knowledge production that is inclusive of the entire media ecology.

The third wave of social change documentary reflects a movement toward systematic analysis of social injustice, illuminating a web of problems and uncovering possible solutions. One way to assess the effect of social change documentary is to consider how it contributes to a broader public dialogue about its content. We can also measure the success of documentary in terms of its capacity to elicit feelings and new perspectives in audience members through the process of storytelling. If social change is our concern, we must consider the rhetorical capacity of documentary to contribute to larger civic-sector conversations by calling together publics and sustaining participatory networks. The field of documentary studies must begin to directly investigate how the genre has become part of social life. In the 1930s, the documentary moving image stood in for critical rational debate and social change. In the early activist-video movement of the 1970s, attempts to foster critical rational debate took a backseat to community building and providing access to resources. It is not enough to visually and aesthetically parade a series of countercultural values and images in front of audiences. Effective documentary must leave a footprint in the sphere(s) of politics and in the hearts of its audience, opening up spaces for social change.

Documentary and Social Change

A common response emerged in my interviews with filmmakers, activists, and other media professionals: these media practitioners expressed a visceral desire to make clear that the documentary object alone does not have the capacity to create social change. In my conversation with George Stoney, he repeated: "the activist documentary is one that is useful in bringing about social change as a part of a movement and a part of an activity. It's not. . . . It doesn't stand on its own. When a film just stands on its own, it doesn't bring about social change. It has to be applied and absorbed by the audience." Documentary is part of a system of relationships and communities, built on networks that harness the kinetic energy of agency. Living, breathing bodies are needed to connect documentary to the process of social change. Despite advances in online communication in the last twenty years, on-the-ground accountability and agitation are most powerfully expressed in person, using new channels of communication as innovative tools and repurposing technology for specific needs. Retelling the history of documentary and political struggle with an emphasis on participatory media cultures yields a spectrum of possibilities for future exploration and intervention. This history uncovers the genre's patterns and strategies and yields abstract models for understanding media engagements as well as practical information for practitioners.

We currently find ourselves in the throes of documentary's third wave and in the middle of a digital revolution that reconfigures pathways of communication, diminishing barriers, and changing conditions of participation. These changes are beginning to reshape social relationships between activists and the state, communities, and law enforcement, and the documentary impulse and power. There is a new and growing media commons with evolving participatory investment in documenting everyday life, exchanging political ideas and urgencies with the documentary impulse. The smart phones carried in the back pockets of many people in the United States hold tremendous participatory potential. The ability to capture, remix, and circulate live content—faster than the news media—is now routine. Recording bits of our daily lives and recirculating these images for pleasure and business are now deeply stitched into our culture. The ubiquity of public cameras, mobile recording, and surveillance means that daily life, in all its complexity, is documented more frequently than ever before. Exploring the currency of these images can reveal how social change documentary circulation becomes a culture in itself and for itself, developing into a media commons. Collective organizing around the commons does not appear in a vacuum: it requires intention and labor. The commons is "an activity, not a result,"[121] defined by "the positive, material and innovative capacity to build."[122] In the midst of dire circumstances and political strife, people find innovative ways to build community, organize, and fight back by any means necessary.

In this chapter, we have explored how documentary can function as a political platform, mirror, vehicle of representation, axis of collaboration, conduit of information exchange, tool of political intervention, and organizing agent. While those strategies provide categories of documentary engagement with participatory media publics, they give us little in the way of assessing the political impact of this work. Given documentary's range of potential social change outcomes and functions, I propose the following framework as a starting point for exploring the political potential of documentary and social change:

> *Representing Social Change*: This category refers to activist documentary that petitions for various underrepresented stories to be included in public memory. It includes historical works documenting radical social movements, street-tape recordings of direct action, and other works focused on recording the process of political struggle as a form of historical documentation. A wide range of documentaries fall into this category, ranging from Sam Green and Bill Siegel's acclaimed *The Weather Underground* to Big Noise Film's *This Is What Democracy Looks Like*.

Speaking for Social Change: These works are focused on speaking for the
  marginalized, identifying problems, and making arguments for social
  change. These documentaries function as free-floating signifiers of political
  discourse and are only loosely connected to the process of social change.
  These works don't direct action to particular political struggles, nor do they
  point to any specific movement or propose coherent calls to action.

Collaborating for Social Change: These are production collaborations between
  filmmakers, activists, audiences, and institutional stakeholders that articulate
  new visions, document unheard voices, establish underrepresented views,
  and seek justice. This would include documentaries like Kirby Dick and
  Amy Ziering's *The Hunting Ground* but also questionable applications of
  collaboration such as Joshua Oppenheimer's *The Act of Killing*.

Engaging in Social Change: This form of documentary intervention holds space
  for activism, utilizing media work as a tool of organizing and agitation.
  Coupled with new media technology, these documentary works create
  and sustain participatory culture and activism, engaging with communities
  who agitate for the interests on the documentary screen. Popular films like
  Berlinger and Sinofsky's *Paradise Lost* and grassroots video focused on local
  political struggles are examples of this kind of intervention.

The modes of social change documentary in this framework have various
ramifications for collective identification and agency. In the following chapters,
I discuss how these categories map onto collective organizing and engagement,
producing an emerging documentary commons. As Stuart Hall suggests, the role
of theory is to provide better maps and tools for furthering political issues and
motivating various projects.[123] At its best, theory gives us maps that allow us to find
ways to struggle more effectively against forms of injustice. The territory mapped
here straddles the borders of theory and practice, moving between disciplines and
through politically charged terrain.

Conclusions

To sustain social change, documentary circulation requires social movements and
participatory media publics. In examining the lessons of historical documentary, we
see that media texts must play out in larger publics.[124] Michael Warner suggests that
publics form partially through the construction and circulation of text.[125] This may
help explain how documentary film and video achieve a civic function. Circulating
through networks, the documentary travels pathways of exposure as new meanings
and connections emerge, giving the discourse a central place in various political
struggles. However, circulation of documentary is only one part of the process of
social change, which also requires agitation opportunities in production, collective

organization, and instrumental action.[126] The documentary alone cannot maintain the complicated process of social change or sustain the embodied political struggle necessary for social transformation. Discussion of the role and function of the documentary is important heuristically for practitioners and scholars alike, especially those concerned with the social change potential of the genre. New objectives could draw documentary audiences into spaces of collective investment where they are inspired to act instrumentally to alleviate injustices foregrounded on the screen. Social change documentary must be less concerned with developing community to *appear* in public and more concerned with *acting* in public to create a space for agitation.

3

Documentary Goes Popular

The Rise of Digital Media Cultures

In the early years of the 21st century, the United States found itself in turmoil, mired in the September 11 tragedy and increasingly aware of an impending environmental crisis hastened by climate change and our insatiable thirst for fossil fuels. In moments of political and social crisis, music, film, television, and magazines often reflect the chaos of their context, demonstrating a dynamic relationship between popular culture and political life.[1] This was evident in the surge of popular activist documentaries released after the turn of the 21st century, including *Fahrenheit 9/11* (2004), *An Inconvenient Truth* (2006), and *Gasland* (2010). The popularity of these films left politicians, media pundits, and funding organizations wondering about the real effect of the documentary genre on the contemporary political landscape. While documentaries like *Blackfish* (2013) and *Paradise Lost* (1996) helped bring substantive change in legal judgments and the global marketplace, other documentaries proved to be nothing more than passive Netflix entertainment. The recent uptick in popular social justice documentary and the increasing popularity of video streaming demands more rigorous attention to how social change documentary is theorized and understood as it travels through networks of popular culture. More specifically, we must identify the circumstances that move the documentary experience beyond entertainment, generating the potential for participatory media cultures to develop.

Documentary has always attracted large audiences, despite its tendency to exist in the shadows of its flashier and more lucrative cousin, fiction film. Popular documentary is a relatively new phenomenon; throughout most of its history, production cultures were closely tied to peoples' history, undocumented stories, do-it-yourself production culture, participatory modes, and community screenings. Documentary media makers were generally suspicious of institutions and the government and placed themselves directly in opposition to corporate interests, especially those of the mainstream media. Documentary film history rested in countercultural spaces rather than in the realm of corporate media production and distribution. Until now.

Contemporary documentary culture is comfortably positioned in mainstream corporate media, circulating in popular and accessible distribution outlets, and enjoying mass audiences and years of circulation in syndication or through popular streaming. These films are distinguished from those made in most other periods of documentary history by their mass accessibility, the size of their audiences, and their circulation patterns. In addition to these differences, the political work of commercial, mass-distributed, popular documentary is different from that of grassroots production work. While mass media directs its content at a general audience, grassroots media is often focused on unwanted stories petitioning for inclusion in pubic memory, regardless of their appeal to mass commercial audiences. The recent exposure of documentary in popular culture coincides with an evolving digital culture that is reorganizing flows of political communication in public life.

The outlook for activist documentary production changed dramatically from the bleak post–1989 independent documentary landscape outlined by Patricia Zimmermann (2000), transforming with media technologies of the late 1990s. At the end of the 1980s, most documentary production work was funded through commercial institutions or the nonprofit sector because the conservative war on content and draconian reductions to federal and state arts funding had dismantled the non-commercial media sector. Just one decade later, however, technological innovation in developing online networks and strides in mobile recording upended this kind of media gatekeeping. Documentary production changed in two ways: First, we saw the rebirth of grassroots media production practice, which flowered with the ubiquity of compact and mobile cameras and the widespread use of the internet, opening new opportunities for participatory media cultures. Second, around this same time, reality TV was hitting its stride and feature-length political documentary began to occupy a visible place in commercial entertainment media. In the midst of these shifts in the status of nonfiction discourse, however, the mainstream media and its corporate interests continued to underestimate and ignore grassroots activist media.

The ways documentaries make contact with social and political structures as they circulate through popular culture remain little understood. We need to investigate how commercial culture changes documentary's intersection with political and social life, both directly, in the form of witnessing, and by creating a space for publics to organize, ready to pick up the political work on the screen. The effects of activist documentary intervention may multiply or change with popular visibility and widespread recognition, but these interventions may also have unintended consequences.

Popular culture can be understood as a site where "collective social understandings are created,"[2] terrain in which power is negotiated and attempts are made to persuade others to shift their worldview. These power struggles, which are often bound up in media representation, happen between powerful groups in society and the resistance of oppositional culture.[3] As many scholars have noted,

"Basically, the 'cultural war' is being fought, via institutions such as the media, over who has the right to define what is 'acceptable' or 'normal' behavior in US society."[4] There is widespread pessimism, however, about the potential for dissent or resistance in a popular culture directed by market logics. It is fair to ask whether the popularization of documentary has taken our dreams of diversity and social justice and sold them back to us for entertainment. Is popular documentary able to circumvent the profit engines and institutional interests that motivate popular culture? Before we dismiss popular culture as a location of protest and resistance, we should consider that the oppositional culture courted by popular activist documentary is sizable, comprising a constellation of diverse audiences capable of organizing into social formations.

Arts funding agencies and other media institutions have recognized the increasing influence of popular activist documentaries, and they are now conducting their own research to understand the dynamics of popular documentary and social change. In these studies, the category of social change actors is defined broadly to include corporations, media, and policymakers. Three recent studies in particular draw considerable attention to documentary's capacity to create change. The first study, which focuses on the film *End of the Line*, was spearheaded by the Channel 4 BRITDOC Foundation and funded by the Esmée Fairbairn Foundation. It offers recommendations for maximizing a film's stakeholders. A second study, focused on *An Inconvenient Truth*, also emerged from the Channel 4 BRITDOC Foundation—specifically, from the foundation's chief executive, Jess Search, who conducted the study as part of her MBA dissertation. Search's work sought to determine the documentary's social benefit through a valuation process previously adopted by government agencies and nonprofit organizations. The third study, focused on *Waiting for Superman*, was produced by the nonprofit Harmony Institute and funded in part by the Ford Foundation. It is the most qualitative of the three reports, focusing on the film's impact on viewers' perceptions of the U.S. education system. These three studies reflect a desire to know more about the influence of documentary in public life. They are part of a larger trend in the industry to measure impact as a model for engagement. Bill Nichols describes this misguided approach to understanding social change as "impact in a fishbowl, measurable and demonstrateable but safely contained at the same time. It is ameliorative rather than transformative, liberal more than radical."[5] It is the social currency of hits, likes, purchases, hashtags, and donations. In this funding environment, the government has mostly abandoned support for civic media, leaving commercial documentary to saturate the plentiful media pathways with social measures that encourage political tourism over substantive social change. Nichols concludes, "Social impact, measured empirically, is not the same as social justice, achieved broadly."[6] It could be argued that documentary—as a field of both practice and study—is undergoing a major transformation and that practitioners and scholars are in the process of trying to understand these shifts.

One industry-wide meeting led to crucial insights into the state of documentary, as the genre increasingly enjoys popular circulation. The Documentary Sustainability Summit was held on February 10, 2017, at the National Endowment for the Arts offices in Washington, DC. In collaboration with the International Documentary Association, the summit featured eighty filmmakers, producers, distributors, film festivals, film-festival representatives, funders, and other stakeholders. The meeting resulted in the publication of a report designed to explore the state of the professional field of documentary production. Findings from the report indicate that over 90 percent of participants were "optimistic" or "very optimistic" about new audiences discovering the documentary genre and about the potential of the genre's social impact. The summit revealed a professional urgency to understand the various networks and registers of documentary engagement because technology is shifting faster than our understanding of how documentary influences public life. Participants' concerns were largely focused on economic sustainability, including their ability to make a living from documentary production work. Although documentary is experiencing increasing mainstream success, the field of documentary production is almost impossible to pursue as a career without additional employment or other support. These conditions select who can afford to sustain documentary production as a career path. Organizations and independent producers operate with lean budgets and staff, all of which contributes to isolated professional networks. The report emphasized that the documentary community must "commission and execute a well-planned quantitative and qualitative research agenda [that] will be essential to play an active role in determining future economic structures" of the documentary production field. One step in this direction would be more rigorous scholarly investment in understanding documentary as a material force in public life by placing different elements of the documentary ecosystem in conversation with one another through participatory field research.

The studies and reports that issued from this meeting largely circulated in trade magazines and websites geared to practitioners and other industry professionals. Overall, the findings were optimistic about the potential for corporations and governments to act in top-down ways as useful engines of social change. They were mostly uncritical of the profit interests at stake in such sponsorship, ignoring the grassroots sentiments of widespread alienation from corporate-funding institutions. Perhaps we need a study of corporate funding of documentary film that approaches the phenomenon from a critical perspective that is informed by historical patterns of intervention by institutions and corporations. Such a study could question the perceived benevolence of these funding organizations and their true stakes in serving the interests of the most vulnerable among us. When looking at the history of documentary and social change, we see that governments, institutions, and market interests have not consistently operated in the interests of people or for the civic good. Checking institutional interests against the discourse of practitioners and other relevant communities could provide useful theoretical insights into documentary and social change in cultural life.

Cinema has a profound power to reconfigure our world, penetrate our thoughts, influence our conversations, and help us see through new eyes. A radical or activist politics can indeed exist within a commercialized and commodified media structure. Yet, the circulation of popular media discourse depends on preexisting frameworks of understanding that are likely to be tolerant of radical ideas but intolerant of radical action. This leads to circumstances in which radical discourse is subject to rearticulation in reformist terms. This reformism can be mitigated when popular documentary is able to slip through a porous wall within commercial culture, amplifying resistance and protest and triggering change as the documentary circulates, transforms, and connects with other community struggles. This chapter addresses the various modes of documentary and the patterns of circulation that shift participatory culture and political agency. These documentary modes—the filmmaker as advocate, participatory sleuthing culture, and coalition building with popular documentary—produce different participatory cultures with various ramifications for social change. Before addressing these popular documentary modes, we will look at how rhetorical theories of circulation capture the movement of discourse through time and space.

The Rhetoric of Popular Documentary Circulation

Optimism that popular political documentary will create social change is not widespread. Noted documentary theorist Bill Nichols argues that "the triumph of the political documentary will remain a great achievement well worth celebrating but not the political victory that will turn the tide of recent events from their catastrophic direction." Documentary does political work, but there is a blind spot about how and where this work happens, making it difficult to study the social change process. Documentary history is shot through with revolutionary optimism in which it is seen as a radical act and a vital organ of the people that has not been fully realized. It is difficult to reconcile the seemingly opposing notions of documentary opening up space for significant social change and simultaneously failing to dramatically mediate at the level of global, intersecting problems. There is an art to documentary production work, requiring creative teams to decide what tools best help audiences see anew. With any art, the shifts are not formulaic or routine; they require committed engagement and spontaneous flexibility. That means our theory must be flexible enough to explain how documentary moves "us in those mysterious, unfathomable ways great works do."[7] Contemporary rhetoric theories could inform how documentary discourse circulates as a material force in society.

Through Bill Nichols's foundational work, documentary studies have integrated the focus on rhetoric into the foundations of its investigation. Nichols rested the study of documentary on the canons of classical rhetoric, gravitating toward focusing on documentary as a form of political oration with a creator and an audience. This exchange becomes the basis for the beginnings of documentary studies as it circulates in the world. Carl Plantinga (2015), a cognitive film theorists, and Thomas Benson (2008), a rhetorical scholar in communication, previously focused on this cross-disciplinary engagement, bringing classical and formalist approaches of rhetorical theory to account for documentary's contributions to public life. Relying on theory derived from the oral traditions of ancient Greece and Enlightenment-era Europe, these interventions established the civic function of documentary. Rhetoric scholars in U.S. communication studies tend to situate documentary within a traditional political context, focusing on how documentary influences larger civic-sector discussions. For example, Thomas Benson and Brian Snee narrate the politics of documentary history as the story of great white male directors making films about great white political leaders. This inaccurately implies that the political potential of documentary emerged the first time the documentary camera was used by politicians.[8] This top-down story of political documentary tells the history of the camera used as government propaganda to sell war[9] and establishes the legacy of political campaign documentaries,[10] missing the use of the camera's grassroots history of being used as a tool for survival by those alienated from traditional political structures.

Theories from a broad range of subfields can contribute to creating a more nuanced understanding of political documentary. Today, contemporary rhetorical theories around agency and circulation have a great deal to offer documentary studies. These theories focus on how communication travels, transforms, and connects to other things that can illuminate documentary discourse's movement in time and space. Theories of participatory media culture also contribute to the understanding of circulation, shedding light on how people act in relation to the issues on the screen. Circulation theory helps us understand how documentary discourse flows, not just as an object but also as a force that accumulates and transforms. With a specific focus on the dynamic and distributive aspects of documentary in social life, circulation theory explains the way storytelling unsettles the historical and political ground we stand on.

The documentary impulse is becoming something we embrace as a condition of survival. This urgency requires us to investigate how contemporary rhetorical theory, together with its attention to rhetoric as an ongoing condition of human experience, can contribute to our understanding of documentary's circulation and evolution across the digital landscape. Documentary circulation is not linear: it begins before the screen, and it circulates long after the premiere, remixed into other media objects, appropriated for alternative uses, and reemerging at the whim of historical demand. Documentary circulation theory is a blind spot for cinema and media studies, a field often occupied with screen culture and a canon of films. It is essential that we now work to understand how "material artifacts do 'live' on beyond their initial moments of production and delivery. And during circulation, material artifacts generate traceable consequences in their wake, which contribute to their ongoing rhetoricity."[11] Attending to documentary's changing rhetoricity as it flows through networks defines one dimension of its social change potential.

The following chapter will address selected recent instances of popular documentary coalescing with participatory media culture, which happens in three ways: vitality, agency, and virality. As Laurie E. Gries outlines in her book, *Still Life with Rhetoric: A New Materialist Approach for Visual Rhetorics*, the elements of vitality, agency, and virality help explain the dynamics of human and nonhuman matter and the construction of collective life. As the rhetoric of documentary circulates and documentary objects travel through culture, we see some unexpected assemblages emerge as documentary connects various participatory cultures. These are instances of "vitality," a term that refers to how things, like documentary films, take on lives of their own and move in and out of "various assemblages and trigger diverse kinds of change." The next element, "agency," refers to "diverse entities intra-acting within and across assemblages." In this sense, agency is a process of understanding how participatory relationships move into action. Finally, the principal of "virality" is used to refer to "the tendency of things to spread quickly and widely," with a focus on contagion as a framework for understanding the distribution of rhetorical force.[12]

The rhetorical ecology[13] of popular activist documentary is unique. The fluidity and circulation of these works in mass media institutions is specific to this historical moment. Popular documentary distribution engages in continuous emergence, circulation, flow, and reemergence, moving audiences toward or away from action in the world. The genre exists in a visible register of media history, responding to controversy on a much larger scale than previous independent documentary films were able to do. Through this process of circulation and uptake, popular documentary makes contact with social structures, and its thingness becomes rhetorical "in divergent, unpredictable ways as they circulate, transform, and catalyze."[14] It is not just provocative content that animates documentary's connection and influence. We must also look at how these works materialize, create associations with movements and institutions, and work with other entities to change collective life. Action takes place in networks, "it is how something performs or is made to perform within a given network that determines how it's situated and therefore temporary meaning and significance."[15] Observing the interactions between meaning, materiality, and social practice in a particular historical context contributes to the long-term understanding and appraisal of documentary and social change.

In my own documentary-production experience, I found that some screenings and actions are intentional on the part of the filmmaker, whereas others are motivated by other people, institutions, and circumstances. Sometimes documentary objects are put in service in new and surprising ways, outside the filmmaker's intentions. Just as vernacular communities develop unintentional technology use to meet their own needs, documentary as a technology functions in the same way.

For example, one night I received a call from a friend telling me that *778 Bullets*, a short documentary I made about a Black Panther shootout in a rural Illinois town, was being projected on the wall of the police station in the small town where the shooting occurred. Local activists were using the documentary to underscore the historically problematic relationship between the community and the police. It was an impromptu and unannounced screening, powered by a generator and a group of frustrated community members. This is an example of the kind of agency possible at a local level; imagine the scale of impact when this kind of intention is harnessed as a result of a mass-broadcast documentary event. When previously immobilized viewers find like-minded others—locally or online—new communities emerge, creating possibilities for collective identity and agency to find life beyond the intentions of the filmmaker, situated in networks for future circulation. Next I highlight three approaches to popular documentary that produce patterns of participatory organizing: the filmmaker advocate, documentary sleuthing culture, and collaborative coalition building.

Radical Publicity and Activist Personas: The Filmmaker Advocate

The earliest and most visible forms of popular activist documentary were character-driven stories, often featuring the filmmaker as the protagonist. Examples include *Roger and Me* (1989), directed by journalist-turned-filmmaker Michael Moore. The film, which grossed over $7.7 million and was released in 265 theaters,[16] documents the devastating impact of General Motors CEO Roger Smith's decision to close several auto plants in Flint, Michigan. *Hoop Dreams* (1994), directed by Steve James, follows the story of two African American high school students from Chicago and their dreams to become professional basketball players. The documentary earned over $11.8 million worldwide and was released in 262 theaters.[17] Blockbuster wildlife films like *Winged Migration* (2003) and *March of the Penguins* (2005) helped pave the way for large-scale theatrical distribution of documentary. After *Roger and Me*, Michael Moore turned entertainment logic on its head, generating a career out of making commercially popular activist documentary. In the highly competitive and saturated media environment, the success of his film *Fahrenheit 9/11* was unprecedented. As one reporter remarked: "People don't like to pay money to see something about politics and they don't pay money to see documentaries, so the success of this movie is all the more remarkable because of that."[18]

Before Moore's *Roger and Me* (1989), *Bowling for Columbine* (2003), and *Fahrenheit 9/11* (2004), political documentary was considered the opposite of entertainment and commercial culture. Moore's early "aw shucks," everyman appeal was transformed as he became a darling of commercial culture over two decades of work. Moore's rise is even more groundbreaking when we consider that it happened before the widespread popularity of *The Daily Show, The Colbert Report,* and other popular political entertainment in mass culture. Moore's films led mainstream commercial industry to recognize the profit possibilities of mass-distributed controversial documentary. With this recognition, Moore shifted from his original proletariat persona into being the most visible, political, and highest-grossing documentary filmmaker of all time. His 2003 documentary, *Bowling for Columbine,* earned $58 million worldwide[19] and *Fahrenheit 9/11* earned over $222 million.[20]

What power do these popular political documentaries really have? It remains unclear whether a mass-marketed and massively popular documentary film could sway a national presidential election, at least so far. Held up as a watershed event in politainment, *Fahrenheit 9/11* was the test case to demonstrate whether a single media event—a highly visible documentary—could have a significant and decisive influence on a presidential election.[21] Released in late June 2004, approximately four months before the November election, *Fahrenheit 9/11* evoked immense public controversy and achieved the distinction of being the highest grossing documentary release to date.[22] As one reporter noted, the film became "a water cooler subject, where everybody wanted to talk about it on talk radio and around the country."[23] The act of buying a ticket or not became a new kind of political statement,[24] making *Fahrenheit 9/11* a landmark event in political filmmaking.[25] In the media frenzy surrounding the film, congressional representatives on both sides of the aisle, as well as the White House communications director, were asked to weigh in on the political debate initiated by the movie. In their essay on Michael Moore and *Fahrenheit 9/11,* Shawn J. Parry-Giles and Trevor Parry-Giles present a well-crafted reading of the film's historical context, situating the documentary within the longstanding "national reluctance to challenge presidential wartime policies."[26] With this attention to historical context, the documentary is identified as a "unique deliberative and campaign text."[27] The present work, like many in the field of rhetorical studies, ties documentary to traditional forms of political communication in the lineage of the oral tradition, establishing documentary's legitimacy as a form of mainstream public address.

In the months leading up to the election, news organizations speculated about the film's potential to rally apathetic voters and help Democratic presidential candidate John Kerry ascend to the White House.[28] The documentary presented a scathing attack on the Bush administration. Specifically, it condemned the mainstream media, the corporate war machine, and the laissez-faire government, accusing them of being uncritical of the administration's rally to war. In the end, *Fahrenheit 9/11* (2004) proved to be enormously popular but failed in its electoral aims. Moore was not shy about his intentions for the film: he publicly proclaimed that his hope was for the film to become the first big-audience, election-year film to unseat a sitting president.[29] In November 2004, President Bush was reelected by three million votes. Though *Fahrenheit 9/11* failed to intervene decisively in the results of a national election, it still broke ground for the genre. No other documentary in U.S. history had attempted to rally a nation around a particular political position months before a presidential election. It was ambitious to imagine that a single media event could prompt a nation to vote for one candidate over another. Though Bush was reelected, the activist potential of the film was present in its ability to circulate critical ideas, generate discussion, and foment public dissent.

Much of Michael Moore's work is unable to activate agency that translates into collective participatory actions or formations ready to pick up the political work featured in his films. Moore is skilled at producing a dedicated fan culture with his documentaries, but not organized political agents. In the case of *Fahrenheit 9/11*, Moore's radical political critique circulated as a call for reformist advocacy in the form of voting. In press interviews, Moore urged people to vote, the same action he urges at the end of *Fahrenheit 9/11*. This framing of the documentary and Moore's public articulations limit the possibilities for political action other than voting. The strategy Moore outlines fails to encourage broader public pressure on the political and economic system as a response to the documentary, pressure that could potentially address the structures at the roots of the problems on screen. Though his work fails to generate activist publics, it does contribute to the genre. The most unique aspect of Moore's work in general—and *Fahrenheit 9/11* in particular—is its vitality and virality. His documentaries generated significant media controversy, sometimes for content and other times for his agitational position on mainstream-media institutions.

Constructed with a significant amount of archival news footage, *Fahrenheit 9/11* creates a counterhistorical narrative out of familiar mainstream-news images. Instead of adopting more predictable, noninvasive, *direct cinema* production strategies, Moore utilized an unapologetic advocacy approach. In addition to letting individuals speak for themselves, Moore uses the ever-present voiceover narrative which was frequently used in the political documentaries of the 1930s. The technique projects Moore's critical, omniscient, and off-screen narrative presence onto the story. For example, while visually displaying footage of President Bush reading *The Pet Goat* to an elementary school class while the World Trade Center Towers are under attack, Moore speculates in a narrative voiceover:

> As Bush sat in that Florida classroom was he wondering if maybe he should have shown up to work more often? Should he have held at least one meeting since taking office to discuss the threat of terrorism with his head of counter-terrorism? Maybe Bush wondered why he had cut terrorism funding from the FBI. Or perhaps he just should have read the security briefing that was given to him on August 6th, 2001, which said Osama bin Laden was planning to attack America by hijacking airplanes.[30]

In his voiceover, Moore frames Bush's actions, attributing intention and thought to a "simple-minded" president stunned in a tragic moment. These narrative attributions were one of the film's tactics that the mainstream press criticized as heavy-handed and unfair.[31]

Most of Moore's satire relies on incongruity. His editorial decisions juxtapose visual images with popular musical scores. In an attempt to bring levity and humor to the early scenes in the film, Moore insinuates that President Bush was not paying attention to the security needs of the country in the months before the September 11 attacks. He uses visual images of Bush at play during the early months of his presidency, golfing, fishing, and playing with his dog. Moore scores these images with the upbeat song "Vacation" by The Go-Go's and says, "In his first eight months in office before September 11th . . . George W. Bush was on vacation, according to *The Washington Post* . . . 42 percent of the time. It was not surprising that Mr. Bush needed some time off. Being president is a lot of work." Moore's use of music layers a lighthearted tone over his critical words while the images function as evidence for his argument.

Sometimes Moore's pointed questions lead to unlikely and powerful responses from his interviewees. In one memorable scene, he asks Congressman John Conyers how Congress could pass the Patriot Act without reading it. Representative Conyers responds: "Sit down, my son. We don't read most of the bills. Do you really know what that would entail if we were to read every bill that we passed? Well, the good thing, it would slow down the legislative process." With sit-down access to government officials and the use of direct questions, Moore uses the documentary to unveil the institutional practices that led to this political moment of crisis. In his other films, Moore relied primarily on aggressive tactics such as finding and ambushing public officials and business executives in public. It would seem that Moore's emerging legitimacy as a filmmaker and visibility as an activist sometimes allowed him access to important officials who shared his interests. His desire to speak to a wider audience resulted in less aggressive tactics.

Moore appears to be most interested in speaking for social change, manifesting agency as a filmmaker-advocate, synthesizing information, and presenting audiences with a forced choice. He doesn't collaborate with particular political struggles, but he does collaborate with affected groups to confront those fleeing accountability. *Fahrenheit 9/11* is a case against the mainstream media's framing of the Bush's administration's previous four years. He primarily accomplishes this task by taking familiar images—news broadcasts—and decontextualizing them with critical analysis. In many of his press interviews, he makes this intention explicitly clear. In one interview, Katie Couric criticizes Moore for his lack of ideological balance, asking why he did not show Saddam Hussein as a horrible leader. Moore responds:

You guys did such a good job of—telling us how tyrannical and horrible he was. You already did that. What—the question should be posed to NBC and all other news agencies: Why didn't you show us that the people we are going to bomb in a few days are these people, human beings who are living normal lives, kids flying kites, people just trying to get by in their daily existence. . . . We killed civilians and we don't know how many thousands of civilians we killed . . . and nobody covered that. And so, for two hours, I am going to cover it. I'm going to—out of four years of all this propaganda, I'm going to give you two hours that says here's the other side of the story.[32]

Moore's articulation of the documentary and his press interviews position *Fahrenheit 9/11* as a debatable resolution for some of the more pressing political questions of our time. Moore sees himself as a conduit of information exchange, providing the missing information the public needs to make a sound political assessment. But in this world, he is the sole proprietor of facts and evidence and there is no uncertainty in his case. The film is a sounding board for critical opposition, presenting an alternate history that purposefully identifies points of contention with the political actions of the Bush administration and the mainstream media's framing of those events. He uses this information as a mechanism of polarization to make the audience choose one side or the other. The film constitutes a loosely connected and unorganized deliberative public that engages in debate about core systematic problems of sacred U.S. institutions such as the free market, the military, the process of governance, and the "free" press. These conversations took place across the media, on talk shows, in the news, outside the theater, between family members, at the water cooler, and within friend circles.

There was significant speculation in the press about whether *Fahrenheit 9/11* could bring about civic participation; this question argues that attention does not guarantee movement toward social change. Although there are a variety of opportunities for civic engagement, voting behavior was the focus in both the news coverage of the documentary and Moore's own commentary on the film. In an interview, Moore remarked, "If I do nothing else but just get people out to vote, regardless who they vote for, if they can get that 50 percent, or part of that 50 percent out that has chosen not to vote, to engage and come back in and—and care about what is going on, then I will feel like I've done something important."[33] Moore's self-proclaimed intentions are to produce civic participation in the form of voting, regardless of political commitments. His remarks characterize his intentions as altruistic and grounded in reformist liberalism. His intended audience, as characterized in the press, was the mainstream voter, emphasizing that the vote was the primary political power to be seized. Given the outcome of the 2004 presidential election, this position may be problematic.

The press's framing of civic participation also pivoted around voting behavior. While opinions varied widely about the potential of *Fahrenheit 9/11* to prompt civic participation, increased voting behavior was the primary, explicit goal of the documentary. As one reporter noted:

I think that people getting worked up on either side in the advocacy of his particular project or in dissent against his ideas will at least get mobilized and then perhaps the documentary, having mobilized that discourse, will mobilize people's passions even further to be able to organize people to get out and vote. So, in that sense, I think it will have a direct and indirect relationship on this debate and on the upcoming election, and that's a good thing, and I think Michael Moore has done an admirable job of stirring up some conversation that needs to be had.[34]

What is striking about this particular description of civic participation is the promotion of political action (voting) without engaging the question of prudent political decision making. The 2004 election did have an elevated voter turnout, but that did not translate into Moore's ideas being reflected in the voting booth. This suggests that it might be more effective to cultivate an activist audience, willing to take up and agitate for the issues foregrounded in the documentary, rather than focus on a mass audience and position voting as the apex of civic action. Unprecedented commercial success does not translate into the ability to produce the space for activism and social change.

I talked to D. A. Pennebaker just after Moore released *Capitalism: A Love Story* (2009). After explaining the connection between Marx, Engels, and Moore—all of whom began their work with real problems in the world—Pennebaker theorizes about Moore's documentary practice:

The only way people understand things, whether it's a black hole, gravity, or anything, is they see it . . . it's not enough to see a person in the gutter to say, "here's poor people." You have to see people who are working hard and have nothing. You have to understand the connections. And so, film is a way to do that. Film is the first way to do that . . . I guess my connection to documentary has been I want the movies to be like theater, to be like plays. I want . . . that's why dialog was so crucial, because you couldn't make films like Daybreak Express with Duke Ellington, even though I love the . . . what Duke did on that, that's great, but that's not the movie for me. That's a little escape, that's entertainment you do for somebody to get them through the next hour. But, a real piece of theater is something that you think about for a long time after, you know? . . . Michael is the extreme example for me of somebody doing that. We have . . . an entire country. It's prosperous beyond belief when it sets out to be, and yet, most of the people in it don't get a million dollar bonuses, you know, at the end . . . no matter what they do, no matter how hard they work. So, what's wrong . . . what kind of a place is this? Or is it a good idea? What's a good idea if this isn't, you know? Whatever it is, he's trying to examine the thing. And, that's a different kind of theater, and I don't know how to make those films, and I'm not up to do it, and I don't. . . . But, I think there . . . I feel kind of protected knowing that Michael's out there on the case. And, when he writes and says he's tired and he doesn't know how long he can keep doing it, I want to cheer him up. I want to tell him, "keep going! You're doing great!"[35]

Pennebaker makes several noteworthy points here. First, showing is a powerful and distinct tool of documentary, creating a map of understanding and a grid of intelligibility that explains why people make the decisions they do. Second, there is a very real difference between Pennebaker's direct cinema work and Moore's activist work; they share a connection as documentary theater, but the distinctions between them should be further explored with other practitioners. Finally, the work Moore is doing is understood as a form of political protection, difficult work that is not for everyone. He is skilled at taking facts and producing spectacle to create a targeted response.

Fahrenheit 9/11 spread globally through the national and international news media.[36] The response extended beyond the content of the documentary until the very question of what constitutes an "authentic" documentary was up for public discussion. Many of these discussions provoked effects that Moore did not intend. Several documentaries were produced in response to *Fahrenheit 9/11*, which actively referred to, targeted, and refuted the arguments Moore presented in *Fahrenheit 9/11*. For example, *Manufacturing Dissent: Uncovering Michael Moore* (2007) asserts that Moore used misleading tactics in the film. Featuring people interviewed by Moore who later had grievances about the use of their participation in the documentary, the filmmakers adopted Moore's confrontational style for their own ends. *Celsius 41.11* (2004) was another documentary response to *Fahrenheit 9/11*. While documentary filmmakers have often influenced each other, *Celsius 41.11* contends directly with the political articulations in *Fahrenheit 9/11*. Taking the form of an academic argument, the film addresses claims made in Moore's film and provides specific and detailed counterarguments. The documentary was produced for $1 million by Citizens United, a conservative nonprofit organization, and earned less than $100,000 at the box office.[37]

The nonprofit Citizens United had previously filed a complaint to the Federal Election Commission (FEC) charging that ads for *Fahrenheit 9/11* constituted political advertising and so should not be aired thirty days before a primary and sixty days before an election. The FEC dismissed this complaint as well as a second complaint in which Citizens United claimed *Fahrenheit 9/11* constituted illegal corporate spending as it set out to advocate for the defeat of an election candidate, which is illegal under the Taft-Hartley Act of 1947 and the Federal Election Campaign Act Amendments of 1974. The FEC did rule that screening *Celsius 41.11* would violate these provisions because Citizens United operated as a political entity, in contrast to Moore's commercial documentary venture and reputation as a filmmaker. These conditions inspired Citizens United to establish roots in commercial filmmaking before the 2008 election, with significant consequences. They produced several documentaries between 2005 and 2007, including the biggest little documentary you never heard of: *Hillary: The Movie*.

Before airing commercials for their new documentary during the 2008 election season, Citizens United filed a complaint with the U.S. district court challenging the constitutionality of electioneering communications. The complaint asked the court to lift the prohibition on corporate and union funding on the grounds of free speech and unconstitutionality, applying these conditions to the distribution of *Hillary: The Movie*. The statute they challenged was the same statute and ruling that allowed Michael Moore to advertise *Fahrenheit 9/11* during election season, but it denied Citizens United the right to run commercials for *Celsius 41.11*. The complaint made its way to the Supreme Court, and *Citizens United v. Federal Election Commission*, 558 U.S. 310 (2010) became a landmark constitutional, corporate, and finance law case, the effects of which still linger today. The Supreme Court ruled that the free speech clause of the First Amendment prevents the government from restricting independent expenditures for communications by nonprofits, for-profit corporations, labor unions, and other associations.

Conservative political operatives were exploiting the political possibilities of popular documentary practice as an unregulated form of political advertising. The court ruling about popular documentary advertising changed decades of election regulations and freed corporations and unions to spend money on "electioneering communications" directly advocating for the election or defeat of candidates. This led to the rise of super PACs (political action committees), which are political organizations that do not give money directly to candidates and can therefore receive unlimited contributions. President Obama and others criticized the ruling as giving special interests more power by eliminating checks on campaign financing and allowing foreign entities to gain influence through corporate subsidiaries. The ruling, which was incredibly unpopular, did not overturn the ban on political donations by foreign corporations. In a February 2010 *Washington Post* poll, 80 percent of those surveyed opposed the law[38] and sixteen states have since called for a constitutional amendment to reverse the Court's decision.

When considering the vitality, agency, and virality of *Fahrenheit 9/11*, it becomes clear that as a documentary's popularity, perceived influence, and political stage increase, so do the film's stakes and consequences, both intended and unintended. Would we be living with the legacy of the Citizens United decision without *Fahrenheit 9/11*? Maybe, but this legal dispute over popular political documentary advertising altered decades of general election regulations, radically affecting the processes of democracy in the United States. Every action has a reaction, and there is no guarantee the reaction will be desirable; unintended and unwanted assemblages are always a possibility. Moore's popularity and success have made him one of the leading leftist intellectuals in the United States, but, as noted in Chapter 2, the popularity of his documentary work is waning; a recent film, *Where to Invade Next*

Figure 3.1 Michael Moore is one of the most recognized documentary filmmakers of our time and celebrated with appearances on popular late night shows, seen here with Stephen Colbert.

Figure 3.2 In his latest documentary, *Fahrenheit 11/9* (2018) Michael Moore attempts to revive the election season fervor generated from *Fahrenheit 9/11* (2004) with only modest results.

(2016), was not distributed globally and grossed only 3.8 million.[39] His fan culture remains strong, however, and audiences continue to watch his documentary work, although he is now more significant as a political commentator and social organizer, appearing on the news, Twitter, Instagram, and other media outlets. In the end, although diverse assemblages were created around Moore's work, they failed to act in a way that could alleviate the dire circumstances of the lives of the vulnerable people who appear on Moore's documentary screen. Moore represents one well-known orientation of popular documentary, but there are other participatory media cultures at work more successfully moving people into action.

True Crime Documentary and Sleuthing Culture

The documentary film *Making a Murderer* (2015) was released in the midst of a popular true crime revival. Audiences at the time connected around Sarah Koenig's podcast *Serial* and HBO's *The Jinx*. This moment also marked the fiftieth anniversary of Truman Capote's iconic true crime book, *In Cold Blood*. In this new era of true crime, the relationship between documentary and participatory sleuthing has emerged as one of the most interesting phenomena in media and popular culture. Viewers are inspired to investigate the cases featured on the documentary screen, collectively and individually, often building connections between audience members. Surprisingly or not, participatory media cultures quickly form around specific true crime documentary. Addressing audiences as jurors or judges, these documentaries present evidence, and an unfinished or unjust investigation becomes the object of audience focus and collective participatory energy.

Making a Murderer (2015) documents the life of Steven Avery, a man from Manitowoc County, Wisconsin, who served eighteen years in prison for a wrongful conviction before being fully exonerated by DNA evidence in 2003. In 2007, he was then convicted for the murder of Teresa Halback. To ensure the circulation of the series, when Netflix released the first episode to its customers, it simultaneously released it on YouTube. The strategy worked: over nineteen million viewers watched the documentary within the first thirty-five days of release.[40] Hundreds of thousands of viewers signed petitions requesting that President Obama overturn Avery's conviction,[41] to which the White House responded: "The President cannot pardon a state criminal offense."

While true crime is not new, contemporary media consumption patterns that include binge watching and listening have changed how stories are made and consumed.[42] What is the effect of these interventions beyond the screen? Can binge-watching lead to systematic social change? Where do careful consideration and deliberation fit into this budding participatory media culture? Or do media cultures matter at all? A popular HBO documentary series provides an interesting example of a sleuthing outlier.

The Jinx (2015), directed by Andrew Jarecki, is an episodic documentary series that investigates the life of Robert Durst, the wealthy son of a New York real estate mogul. Durst, the heir to a tremendous fortune, is surrounded by decades of suspicion regarding the mysterious disappearance of his wife and the murder of his confidant, Susan Berman. Before *The Jinx*, Jarecki made a feature fiction film, *All The Good Things* (2010) starring Ryan Gosling and Kristen Dunst that was inspired by

Figure 3.3 During the first season of *Making a Murderer* (2015), defense lawyers for Steven Avery became national celebrities, going on lucrative speaking tours to talk about justice in America.

Figure 3.4 Chicago lawyer Kathleen Zellner takes on Steven Avery's case post-conviction, navigating the intense media frenzy in the second part of *Making a Murderer* (2018).

the life of Robert Durst. Robert Durst was a fan of that film and contacted Jarecki and offered to be interviewed. This initial taped conversation was the first of 20 hours of recording Jarecki collected over several years. Jarecki develops the documentary series around these taped conversations.

The Jinx is an interesting example of documentary sleuthing because the investigative work took place during the actual production process rather than from a participatory media culture after the initial screening, circumventing the collection

Figure 3.5 Chicago lawyer Kathleen Zellner takes on Steven Avery's case post-conviction, navigating the intense media frenzy in the second part of *Making a Murderer* (2018).

of participatory publics as a mechanism to address justice. The night before the final episode in the series was aired, the lead character, Robert Durst, was arrested for first-degree murder as a result of the new evidence presented in the documentary. Durst gave filmmakers unrestricted access to his personal files, which included an incriminating videotaped deposition. In the time it took for serial broadcast circulation, the audience had the satisfaction of Durst finally being held accountable for his crimes. In quick succession, these documentaries, Sarah Koenig's podcast *Serial*, and the Netflix documentary series *The Keepers* (2017)[43] solidified true crime documentary's critical success in contemporary popular culture. The most interesting case of long-term struggle and action, however, began in the 1990s with HBO's *Paradise Lost* documentaries (see Chapter 2), which stand out as critical examples of popular true crime documentary and social change.

As discussed in Chapter 2, the HBO documentary films *Paradise Lost: The Child Murders at Robin Hood Hills* (1996) and its sequel *Paradise Lost Revisited* (2000) chronicle a murder trial in Arkansas in which three teenage boys, Damien, Jason, and Jessie were convicted of killing three 8-year-old boys, Stevie, Michael, and Christopher. The first film documents the trial, while the second film reflects on the first film's impact on the trial. In the first film, the guilt of the convicted boys was far from certain. Eventually, a social formation, comprised of viewers of the first film, emerged to seek justice and truth in the sequel.

The strongest case for the guilt of the West Memphis Three is made in the first ten minutes of the first documentary. Playing into the framing of the local news reports, the documentary opens with the actual crime scene footage, the film's most gruesome and shocking images. The footage shows the decomposing bodies of three little boys found on the shore of a shallow creek. The subtitle reads: "Police Crime Scene Video, 6 May 1993." From the beginning, the audience bears witness to the space and place of the crime, including the mutilated bodies of the three boys. By opening with the crime scene footage—a camera moves slowly over the river-bank, a shaky handheld frame hunting for pertinent clues—the film immediately asks the audience to take in the visual details of the case. This preferred reading of the text, provided by the filmmakers' appropriation of crime scene footage, allows the audience a direct connection to the evidence. Through the viewfinder of the po-lice camera, the audience is placed in the subject position of investigator, taking in the images that are later disputed in the murder trial.

These documentaries characterize the accused, Damien, Jason, and Jessie, as outsiders in their devout Christian rural community. The film's opening moments develop audience identification with the families of the three murdered boys: Stevie, Michael, and Christopher. Raw moments of grief are recorded in intimate interviews with the victims' parents and edited together, culminating in a final interview with Stevie Branch's mother, Pam Hobbs. This interview marks a shift in the tone of the film. At this point, the filmmakers begin to trouble the case and those victimized by it. Instead of showing an intimate interview, the camera records a local news media crew interviewing Hobbs. We see a grieving mother experiencing a moment of ex-citement about being on television. When the camera goes live, she begins to talk about her loss, performing a complicated subject position that suggests a distinction between lived experience and media spectacle. The audience is left suspecting that an alternate story exists beneath the media caricatures and partial circumstances released to the press. From this point on, the film begins to bridge identification with the boys charged with the crime, exposing the Satan-worshiping mythos projected in the media and public discourse around the case.

As depicted in the second film, a group of viewers in Los Angeles began meeting on a regular basis to discuss the facts of the case after they watched *Paradise Lost* (1996). This group began to research the case, share information, and gather on a regular basis. The movie acted as a catalyst for social change by creating the environ-ment for a public concerned with injustices, while simultaneously creating rhetor-ical identification with alienation and the convicted boys, who were known as "The West Memphis Three." Before the film, counternarratives were silenced in official court hearings and by the mainstream media; without the film's intervention, these narratives might never have proliferated in a significant way. These two films acted as a catalyst, galvanizing participatory publics invested in seeing through the pro-cess of justice and change.

The *Paradise Lost* phenomenon marks the beginning of a much-theorized and new form of democratic practice facilitated by popular documentary distribu-tion, true crime sleuthing, and the internet. *Paradise Lost* highlights the potential of high-profile, popular, and mass-distributed documentary discourse to create a collective audience identification invested in instrumental political action. The

Figure 3.6 Early members of the Free the West Memphis Three group meet with reporter Mara Leveritt to explain how they became involved as activist in a scene from *Paradise Lost 2: Revelations* (2000).

Figure 3.7 Activist Kathy Bakken of the Free the West Memphis Three group explains the origins of the activist website that helped organize viewers online in a scene from *Paradise Lost 2: Revelations* (2000).

Figure 3.8 Members of the Free the West Memphis Three group that formed online meet with reporter Mara Leveritt in person about why they travel to Arkansas on vacation from work to support the convicted young men in a scene from *Paradise Lost 2: Revelations* (2000).

audiences that form around the films are addressed as juror–citizens by the framing of the documentaries. After the opening of the documentary, the story is structured around the evidence and procedural sequencing in the court case. Viewers are encouraged to collect and analyze evidence and render a verdict. As a consequence, audience members organized as participatory activist publics in defense of the West Memphis Three. The documentary disrupts dominant mainstream news frames, while building collective identification with an audience sympathetic to the injustices of social alienation and scapegoating. The film turned passive consumers of communication into deliberative sleuthing agents who shared the evidence they gathered on a public website and generated support internationally with a post-card petition. They formed a social movement organization called "Free the West Memphis Three." The manner in which documentary crafts social problems, how it characterizes people and actions, and draws connections between events and actions provides understanding for previously unknown stories. Documentary representations create openings for change and help produce roadmaps for imagining collective action.

Filmmaker George Stoney, a leading force in social change documentary, suggests that, "Given the historical background, a humanistic background to the political and social situation is extremely important in bringing about its change. When you present a problem and you present the possibility of change, if you present the characters and the human situations in which it can happen, then the people whom you want to engage begin to understand how they can bring about change." An analysis of these films and their publics suggests that the internet has the potential to create unlikely citizen alliances because it provides a means to overcome geographical distances between activists and facilitates critical-rational debate.[44] Viewers, activated by the documentary, are set in motion and into the world motivated by justice and with the resources to participate.

The long-term vitality of the participatory media culture around the *Paradise Lost* documentaries is astounding. The first film was released in 1996, in the early days of the internet, and multiple participatory cultures quickly formed around it on message boards. When these disparate media cultures joined forces to create a "Free the West Memphis Three" movement, the assemblages and connections around the documentaries gained visibility that produced needed resources to see through the process of justice. The West Memphis Three group gained cultural recognition for the case by agitating against the legal establishment in Arkansas through face-to-face public protest; they also raised awareness for the case in media outlets including *People* Magazine,[45] and two episodes of CNN's *Larry King Live*.[46] The documentary generated support from celebrities such as Eddie Vedder, the front man for Pearl Jam, Natalie Mains of the Dixie Chicks, and actor Johnny Depp. This celebrity attention brought valuable contributions and experts to the case, including DNA expert Barry Scheck. The website for the organization functioned as a gateway for information and action for the larger activist community, but the core early activists were on listservs, debating the evidence and circumstances of the case. As a result, the website collected a legal library of evidence, encouraging visitors to adjudicate the facts. The early participatory culture connected around deliberation over legal arguments. These community members educated themselves in legal rhetoric and crime scene investigation in order to understand the trove of information that was collected and to gain the support of valuable legal experts. Participation, in this instance, cultivated the necessary skills and tools for action, bridging the gulf between need and motivation.

This movement brought experts, celebrity visibility, core activists, and collective grassroots participation to the case, exerting tremendous material force in public culture that ultimately resulted in the release of the three young men from jail. The various connections between the social actors involved situated diverse support from multiple agitational fronts in mainstream media, providing resources for legal processes and local protests to produce powerful demonstrations of widespread support.

The documentary presented a debatable resolution, and the website provided the audience with evidence and grounds for discussion. The "how to help" section of the website highlighted an extensive writing campaign in which supporters were encouraged to write to the governor of Arkansas, the Appeals Court judges, and the media. All contact information for letter writing was provided, along with a

Figure 3.9 Instructions on the Free the West Memphis Three website in the late 90s where a grassroots collective archiving project about the case united a variety of diverse people across a geographical divide.

Figure 3.10 The splash page for the Free the West Memphis Three website in the late 90s where viewers could connect with others concerned about the case.

Figure 3.11 Members of the Free the West Memphis Three group sell t-shirts outside the courtroom during the appeals process to support the defense in a scene from *Paradise Lost 2: Revelations* (2000).

sample letter and pointers on how to write effective correspondence. The documentary compelled viewers to learn more, and the website functioned to collect and organize viewers into participatory actors. Over time, the participatory culture of those who organized around this case grew into interconnected movements fighting wrongful conviction and the death penalty, including assemblages with international social movements. The solidarity created by members of these movements grew into a powerful, collective force. Whether or not the filmmakers intended to create change, the *Paradise Lost* films become an example of documentary agency engaged in social change.

This documentary event challenges the notion that virality always means speed. As we see with *Paradise Lost*, contagion can move slowly but steadily toward collaboration and action, significantly affecting injustices on the screen. The *Paradise Lost* documentaries are significant because they present a clear example of how the circulation of popular documentary can create new social movement organizations rather than just tapping into existing organizations. The connections formed around the films were strong and long lasting, sustaining the organization for over a decade and eventually making powerful connections with the international movement opposing the death penalty. Intense intellectual investment in the details of the case, the debates that emerged on message boards, and participatory engagement over a sustained period of time produced significant investments in a community able to sustain the long and incremental process of social change. This counters concepts of viral speed as a primary sign of influence, indicating that documentary can inspire other, more incremental modes of connection. Long-term connections are at least as important to solidarity and social change as quickly spreading virality, or maybe they are even more important. Certain modes of media circulation might develop patterns based on routine cultural practices and historical context. Still, images might generate a particular pattern of circulation based on the ease of editing, remixing, and circulating and the low investment in attracting audiences. Although documentary discourse can't draw on still photography's remixing and circulating capacities, it can lead to more cultural production and participation. Documentary is associated with moving audiences and connecting social problems with decision makers. As we have reviewed, Michael Moore and documentary-sleuthing represent two dimensions of popular activist documentary, but other approaches have yielded less dramatic interventions by amplifying the work of existing social movements and facilitating coalition building, resulting in important structural change.

Amplifying Movements and Creating Coalitions

Many popular documentary productions collaborate with existing social movements and their outcomes vary in quality and longevity. Some filmmakers coordinate with social movements or engage in organizing tactics during distribution. As Mike Bonanno from The Yes Men, explains, ". . . the idea is that we contribute to campaigns that already have momentum that will continue to have momentum after we do our intervention." From Bonanno's perspective, social change is a vehicle driven by social movements. Temporary collaborations are developed between media makers and social movements as a means of amplification or as a way to increase the speed of a process already in motion. This intervention is part of a system. A filmmaker like Michael Moore engages in systematic critique, but he is driving his own vehicle and there is public reluctance about going along for the ride. The lines between filmmaker and activist often blur in these situations. When the filmmaker and the struggling community find productive collaborative roots, agreed upon interests, and bonds strengthened by collective identification, this coalitional ground can be fruitful for social justice objectives. One example is found in the documentary work of Kirby Dick and Amy Ziering.

Dick and Ziering did not set out to make multiple films about sexual assault. Their first film, *The Invisible War* (2012), tackles the complicated and widespread problem of sexual assault in the U.S. military. It features stories of veterans from multiple branches who survived rape culture in the armed forces. The storytelling is intimate and the framing of the interviews is quiet, set in safe places with closely framed shots of the painful testimony. Multiple women share some of the most diffi-cult moments of their lives, telling stories of being violated, ignored, and left behind by one of the most venerated institutions in our country.

The Invisible War begins by exploring the media representation of women en-tering into the military for the first time. Several decades of military advertising and propaganda are edited together with archival footage of capable women doing im-portant work for the institution. The documentary calls together the parts of the audience that intuitively understand these values. In this montage, the conditions women naively entering the military will experience are laid bare. Women are depicted gleefully marching in pencil skirts, taking the military oath in white gloves and matching floral print dress and fixing an airplane with beautifully flowing hair. This archival footage represents women enthusiastically molding their lives around this burgeoning open military culture, taking advantage of opportunities that were once unavailable.

Contemporary women representing each branch of the military begin to share their stories in unison. During sit-down interviews, there is a collective expression of appreciation for what armed forces institutions offered in terms of direction, disci-pline, and camaraderie. We meet intelligent and enthusiastic women, many of whom come from military families. These are mothers and daughters, clearly articulating their whole-hearted belief in the military as an institution of self-improvement. Home videos of these women, living their lives as important members of families and contributing to their communities, are edited together over these testimonies. The voices of these women are melded together, one picking up where the other leaves off, an editing choice that powerfully demonstrates the shared aspirations of military women.

Dick and Ziering don't begin where they want you to end; they summon par-ticular collective identifications, calling together an audience that is invested in military institutions. This approach to storytelling is built on the assumption that institutions are detached and self-preserving, but people who work within them have more complicated experiences. This is central to the appeal of Dick and Ziering's work: they begin their story with an openness that allows the most unlikely of audiences to step in and experience the stories before them. As is standard in most feature-length, theatrical documentaries, the initial attempts at collective identification with the audience are fairly consistent for the first ten minutes, until the complexities seep in. In this instance, the complexity arrives in the form of a petite, pretty blond woman named Kori, who is a member of the Coast Guard.

We see Kori in civilian life as an active mom and wife; her husband also belonged to the Coast Guard. Her sincerity and love for the institution are clear as she talks about repeated sexual violence and assault she suffered at the hands of her commanding officer. After her moving story, the cascade of women's stories in the opening institutional montage returns. The uplifting stories turn dark, testifying to the consistent, routine ways military culture preyed on women and protected assailants, including their own experience with sexual assault in the military. Trina, a middle-aged woman who served in the Navy, concludes by recounting her own assault: "If this happened to me, surely, I am not the only one." What follows is a powerful and diverse display of new women, of various ages, races, and ethnicities, sharing their assault experiences. Ten new women enter the story, presenting a powerful argument about the prevalence and severity of the problem.

The military organization is often lauded as a model of safety, security, and our national understanding of protection. The documentary skillfully weaves the individual story of each survivor into a common narrative with systematic implications. We see that the military is an institution with a history of empty promises to address the consistently high rates of sexual assault. The careful documentation of negligence and the widespread culture of harassment and assault in the film create a sense of urgency to act. The audience witnesses so many lives already damaged and so many still in harm's way.

I interviewed Kirby Dick while he was making *The Invisible War* and thinking through how to invite a mass audience into the topic of military sexual assault in a way that was productive and not divisive:

> It's unbelievable. I mean, I did a calculation, and if the figures are right, there's been 600,000 women who've been raped or sexually assaulted who are. . . . You know, over the life of the military there's tens of thousands a year. But the film will take an approach where . . . whether you're for the war or against it, whether you're even pro-military or anti-military, everybody can agree on the fact that these women are daughters, mothers, husbands, lovers. They should be supported and they should be protected. And so it's . . . We're really trying to avoid. . . . In fact, we're trying to actually reach an audience that normally is not reached. Most liberal documentaries, you know, mine. . . . Well, I don't think *Twist of Faith* (2005) is necessarily liberal, but certainly *Outrage* (2009) I would say is . . . you know, in some ways, preach to the converted, which is fine, and that does cause change, but I'm interested also in trying to reach across that divide.

Like Michael Moore, Kirby Dick is trying to reach a mass audience, but their strategies for generating collective identification differ. Moore levels a radical critique that is ambivalent about vernacular voices and pushes audience members toward polarization around voting as a primary civic action. Dick and Ziering locate the most vulnerable and invisible within the scope of the problem and build the story around these perspectives. These approaches have generated different results in terms of how spectators understand the problem at hand, and, as George Stoney suggests, how they understand their role in creating change. The way the story is crafted around the problem has implications for shared identification and agency.

The Invisible War includes a great deal of institutional participation, including interviews with eight members of Congress and nine former and current military personnel. In his 2014 memoir, *Worthy Fights*, Secretary of Defense Leon Panetta stated that watching *The Invisible War* was one of the main factors that influenced him to issue a directive ordering all sexual assault cases to be handled by senior officers,[47] ending the practice of commanders adjudicating the cases from within their own units.[48] Senator Kirsten Gillibrand points to *The Invisible War* as her inspiration to create the Military Justice Improvement Act. In her 2014 memoir, *Off the Sidelines: Raise Your Voice, Change the World*, Gillibrand writes, "Nothing in my life . . . prepared me for what I saw in that film . . . whatever it took, I had to help bring justice to these survivors, and I needed to work to prevent further crimes."[49] In 2013, President Barack Obama signed the National Defense Authorization Act, a law that included improvements to the military handling of sexual assault cases, eliminating enlistment waivers and forming special units in the military to investigate sexual assault. Dick and Ziering created networks and pathways for the documentary discourse to travel into military and policy circles. These pathways made sure the documentary discourse found its way to the most productive audiences. This could happen on its own but more frequently, these are intentional choices made by filmmakers to create pathways of communication to decision makers. Other times, these empathetic pathways are developed through storytelling. Judith Helfand,[50] a filmmaker, field builder, and activist, is known for her high-energy and personal documentaries about social injustice. She articulates a way to think about this process. Referring to George Stoney's influence on her production process, Helfand explains:

> [W]hat will happen to the community sitting in the room when the lights come up? Will they be more willing to work with each other and know each other and communicate with each other and think out loud? Or will they be more divided? . . . and you know the job of a movie is to sort of make it more complex when the lights come up. If your goal is "we are going to do documentary" well at least move the dial on the dialogue a little bit . . . let's make sure that your views and your attitudes when you walked in are different.

Certain storytelling modes generate affect, spectacle, narrative, and identification, activating the audience's imaginings about participatory intervention, a process also shaped by the historical conditions and technical capacities of the medium. Gries theorizes that circulation virality varies, based on design, production, and distribution. Vitality, how media objects take on a life of their own, moving in and out of assemblages for change, is also contingent on the specific media cultures. Documentary moving-image discourse does not circulate like still photography in meme culture.

Beyond its influence on policymakers, *The Invisible War* also did important cultural recognition work, addressing the systematic problem of sexual harassment and assault in the military, including exposing the climate at the Marine Barracks Washington.[51] Over 235,000 military service members viewed the documentary after Air Force Chief of Staff General Mark Welsh met with all the active wing commanders to screen the film and talk about the problem.[52] According to the *New York Times*, the film "has been credited with both persuading more women to come forward to report abuse and with forcing the military to deal more openly about the problem."[53] The documentary prompted the Armed Services Committee to hold a hearing on sexual assault in the military on January 23, 2013.[54] The problem took center stage again during a Senate Subcommittee hearing on March 13, 2013, in which lawmakers and military officials described the documentary's impact on military training programs dealing with sexual assault. Despite its cultural impact and wide recognition as a policy influencer, *The Invisible War* was not a commercial hit, earning just over $71,000 at the box office.[55]

Dick and Ziering started working on a second film while still screening *The Invisible War* on college campuses. After the screenings, young women would compare their own experiences with sexual assault and harassment on campus with the stories of the military on the screen. Ziering explains, "Every time we went on a campus, a student or more than one student would come up to us and say, 'actually, something you pointed out, going on in the military, happened to me here. There is a lot of analogies there that I experienced.'"[56] The filmmakers found themselves doing research for a documentary project on campus sexual violence in the midst of a growing student movement addressing this silent problem. Instead of beginning their film with institutions, the filmmakers started with activists and survivors. As Dick aptly observed, "[C]olleges and universities are no different than any other institution. Their first impulse is self-preservation and their reputation. Unless they are pressured to do the right thing, all institutions will do the easy thing which is cover it up."[57] Dick goes on to explain why working with institutions can be problematic. At other times in documentary history, institutions were sometimes seen as important collaborators, but Dick's skepticism is not unwarranted and his reasons must be acknowledged. The perspective is especially important as the larger documentary industry embraces the impact model of success, which welcomes institutions and commercial interests without critically analyzing motives that might facilitate a kind of political tourism. What would *The Invisible War* be like if Dick and Ziering had decided to work with the military before aligning themselves with those systematically harmed by the institutions? After a period of investigation, the duo moved forward with production on *The Hunting*

Ground (2015), tackling the issue of sexual violence on college campuses across the United States.

An important exchange happened between student movement leaders and the filmmakers during the production, postproduction, and distribution process of

Figure 3.12 In the *Hunting Ground* (2015) activist from around the country and at separate universities hold press conferences to expose the systematic problems that compound sexual assault on college campuses.

Figure 3.13 In the *Hunting Ground* (2015) activists from University of California, Berkeley hold a press conference to expose the problem of sexual assault on their specific campus.

the film. The directors did not operate in isolation from those struggling on the ground; instead, they collaborated with frontline activists and survivors. Dick reported that after spending time with student activists, new collective ideas would emerge. In a discussion of one montage for the documentary, Dick was looking for a catchphrase to represent the way educational institutions habitually respond to sexual assault. He explains, "I think it was either Annie or Andrea who was in the office at that time, and she said, 'They all say, "we take this very seriously." So, we started to look for that phrase and bam! It always came up. But I really like to work with subjects and include them into the creative exploration of the process."[58] The directors used conceptual, creative collaboration, as well as field production collaboration, putting the tools of authorship in the hands of people closely tied to the circumstances. George Stoney pioneered these kinds of commitments to community, religiously advocating for an engagement between the production process and the communities being recorded. This included activities such as screening footage and providing opportunities for community feedback, media workshops, and pursuit of collective production practices and archiving. Through these types of participatory activities, communities become co-authors who gain agency in the process of documentary production. Often, the community becomes an essential part of the production process. Kirby Dick explains how this happened during the production of *The Hunting Ground*: "[S]tudents are able to get [to] places with cameras that even we couldn't because we'd have to get permits. In some ways, the film was crowd sourced. Not only were we working with the hundreds of survivors, but we were interacting with dozens of student filmmakers."[59] Dick and Ziering employ practical and effective methods of collaborative documentary production in their films, making strategic decisions about the interests with which the documentary will align. Kirby Dick has developed this collaborative approach over several decades, beginning with his early documentary, *Chain Camera* (2001).

Within a year of *The Hunting Ground's* release, it was screened more than one thousand times on university and college campuses across the United States, creating a national conversation among students, parents, administrators, government, and media that resulted in an increased awareness of the problem of sexual assault and violence on campus.[60] Inspired by the onscreen accounts of activists featured in the documentary, Annie E. Clark and Andrea Pino, Senators Clare McCaskill and Gillibrand introduced the Campus Accountability and Safety Act, which requires colleges to designate advisors to serve as a confidential resource for victims and to standardize university processes for dealing with sexual violence.

Documentary discourse has tentacles that reach out into the culture and wrap around other objects and assemblages. This is seen in the circulation of underground tapes, use of documentary in diversity job training, viral video, or use of the documentary form to situate collective memory. Documentary is cut up, circulated in parts, and used as court evidence. We often come to it with the

Figure 3.14 At Columbia University, Emma Sulkowicz, a fourth year visual arts major carries a dorm mattress representing the painful burden rape victims carry, a scene from the *Hunting Ground* (2015).

Figure 3.15 College activists turn their apartment into a central command center for activism against sexual assault on college campuses, a scene from the *Hunting Ground* (2015).

intention of bearing witness to what is depicted onscreen. Gries's conception of circulation focuses on the transformation of the object, specifically the still photo. Moving-image discourse transforms as it circulates, often evoking participation with, for, and around documentary. Documentary discourse can be used in

Figure 3.16 College activists organize online, turning their living spaces into community organizing spaces, a scene from the *Hunting Ground* (2015).

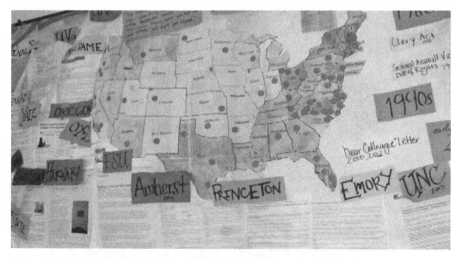

Figure 3.17 A map of complaints and sexual assault history on college campuses organized by activists, a scene from the *Hunting Ground* (2015).

ways that are embodied and agitating, seeping from one public space to another, visual representations transformed into different cultural objects. *The Hunting Ground* had only modest opening-weekend success, but real change began to happen when the film was screened on campuses. These screenings sparked confrontations across the United States between existing student movements and university administrators.[61]

Figure 3.18 College activists turn their dorm rooms into a central command center for activism against sexual assault on college campuses, a scene from the *Hunting Ground* (2015).

Figure 3.19 College women gather in a dorm room to express how these conditions of sexual expectations and unchecked party culture create dangerous circumstances for assault, a scene from the *Hunting Ground* (2015).

A year after the release of *The Hunting Ground, Variety,* Hollywood's trade periodical, interviewed Andrea Pino,[62] one of the student activists featured in the documentary. Dick and Ziering are not invisible in the interview, but they have retreated into the background while the issue of campus sexual assault lingers in popular culture. At the time

Figure 3.20 College activists turn their kitchen tables into a central command center for activism against sexual assault on college campuses, a scene from the *Hunting Ground* (2015).

Figure 3.21 After Emma Sulkowicz carries a dorm mattress to expose the lack of university accountability for sexual assault, mattresses become a symbol of emotional weight and the lack of justice, a scene from the *Hunting Ground* (2015).

of the interview, Lady Gaga and Diane Warren were nominated for an Academy Award for best original song, "Til It Happens to You," written for *The Hunting Ground*. Pino was onstage—with many other survivors featured in the documentary—for the Lady Gaga performance of the nominated song at the 2016 Academy Awards ceremony.

The song and the Academy Award ceremony performance were evidence of a powerful transformation of documentary discourse into another form and network of exposure with global scope. The song is "robust and orchestral,"[63] with lyrics that "command attention,"[64] providing "an extra jolt of poignancy"[65] in the film. At the 2016 Academy Award ceremony, one year before the shocking exposure of widespread sexual harassment and assault in Hollywood and elsewhere, Lady Gaga performed a powerful, stripped-down rendition of "Til It Happens to You." Dressed in all white and playing a white piano, she gave an emotionally piercing performance that slipped between pain, helplessness, anger, and strength. The track was backed by the gravitas of a string orchestra, which was juxtaposed against the force of the pounding piano keys. Lady Gaga performed on stage but played to the camera; she knows where her audience sits. During the last chorus, the screen behind the piano lifted, and the dark shadow of a group of people was silhouetted behind a cobalt-blue screen. As she sings the last chorus, young women and men from all backgrounds step forward in casual clothes, distinct from the audience watching in the theater, revealing themselves as survivors of sexual assault. Pino was one of those survivors. Some of them had messages written on their forearms: "not your fault" and "unbreakable." The performance forced audience members not only to feel but also to bear witness to the extent of the problem. Famous actors in the theater leaped to their feet in applause and tears; the song may have hit close to home. Kirby Dick explains: "We received emails from around the globe for weeks following the Oscars from survivors and advocates saying it was a watershed historic moment in the victim's rights movement."[66] This transference of documentary discourse into a different cultural expression creates new networks and strengthens connections to participation. Interestingly, both *The Invisible War* and *The Hunting Ground* were critical successes and accomplished in terms of intervening in social justice struggles, but they had only marginal commercial success.

Impact Partners financed Dick and Ziering's last films, *The Invisible War* (2012) and *The Hunting Ground* (2015). Since 2007, the company has been involved in financing over 80 films, including *The Cove* (2009), *How to Survive a Plague* (2012), and *Icarus* (2017). Impact Partners is a company focused on financing and advising strong cinematic stories that explore urgent social issues through documentary. We know little about the influence of these kinds of production companies, which are a mixture of philanthropic inspiration and business venture, except for their intention to affect the social and political landscape. The company takes on ten to twelve projects a year, advising some of the more popular activist documentaries of the moment. The cofounders, Dan Cogan and Geralyn Dreyfous, are particularly focused on promoting social change with film.

Unlike *The Invisible War*, *The Hunting Ground* became the subject of considerable backlash. The U.S. military embraced *The Invisible War*, using it to begin organizational changes. Universities, in contrast, launched counterattacks against

The Hunting Ground, including campaigns addressing the numbers and analysis in the documentary. National fraternity and sorority organizations stepped up lobbying efforts for legislation that would make it more difficult for colleges to punish sexual assault. Kirby Dick explains, "There has been some backlash from a few of the institutions that were criticized in *The Hunting Ground*. This is not surprising; they are reacting defensively by attacking the messenger and denying there is a problem rather than addressing the problem. This response is proof that we've touched a nerve, that we've uncovered something these institutions don't want exposed."[67] The work of Dick and Ziering demonstrates a powerful mode of production harnessed through popular culture. Notably, these films are less visible in a popular, commercial sense than other documentaries; they earned very little in comparison to most of the films discussed in this chapter. However, the production team and the documentaries have received a great deal of critical praise and circulation in major commercial streaming outlets, as well as award recognition and high-profile festival exposure. It is evident that popular exposure helps, but a film does not need box-office commercial success to be effective in facilitating social change. Juxtaposing Michael Moore's films with Dick and Ziering's work, we can reasonably conclude that popular commercial success might, in fact, complicate social justice objectives. Dick and Ziering are working on a third documentary about the cultures of sexual assault, this time they will take on the Hollywood establishment.[68]

Conclusion

Cinematic discourse turns the dial on how society sees itself. Trends in the mass media environment make it clear that one function of contemporary activist documentary is to "go popular." This strategy is not without its perils, but it does open up new avenues of public advocacy through the circulation of documentary discourse. An agency emerges from our engagement with the documentary screen. The way a problem is presented in the crafting of the documentary experience constitutes a form of action or inaction. The problem's presentation provides a grid of intelligibility that suggests how the viewer should act in relation to the world, encouraging a particular agency based on the documentary experience. When a documentary functions as an event film, the discourse circulates in public networks and becomes a gateway to a number of taboo and not-so-taboo political discussions.

There is also a form of agency that emerges from circulation. As documentary discourse travels through networks, it makes connections and uses and creates new pathways. Sometimes the circulation picks up where the documentary left off, extending the viewing experience. Other times, it may draw new audiences to the documentary participatory culture. These audiences are different from the one addressed by the documentary. In the case of *The Hunting Ground*, this happens as the documentary discourse transforms into a popular song that brings many more people to the struggle the documentary represents. This circulation process is often slow, with the cultural impact of the exchanges unfolding over time. In circulating *The Invisible War*, Dick and Ziering did not anticipate making another documentary about sexual assault. It was in the face-to-face interactions during college campus screenings of the first documentary that the directors realized the systematic and culturally rooted patterns that exist across institutions, including both the military and education. This propelled more cultural production; inspired by those campus interactions, the filmmakers created *The Hunting Ground*, providing a mirror for the educational facilities that hosted them.

The *Paradise Lost* documentaries produced circulation pathways unimaginable at the time, overcoming the limitations of rudimentary listservs and websites. Audiences collected materials in an online community archive, solidified their collective arrangement around miscarriages of justice, and organized on message boards with core activists directing actions on a website. The documentary prompted viewers to know more, and the internet provided easy access to information, creating a participatory media culture that lasted approximately 10 years. The connections between activists were strengthened and deepened by critically reconstructing the details of the case together as a collective engine of information exchange and knowledge production.

The circulating patterns of *Fahrenheit 9/11* are plentiful and difficult to track. Books, films, speeches, TV shows, and other terms of cultural production responded to the documentary. Collectively, these circulatory engagements created precious critical space in public culture for dissenting opinions against the Bush administration after the attack on the World Trade Center. The circulation of documentary discourse created a tremendous impact on public culture but lacked the ability to mobilize a participatory media public willing to pick up the political work on the screen in any organized manner. The scope of the documentary addresses everyone in general and no one specifically, framing the problem in a way that makes intervention seem overwhelming and impossible. Moore levels a radical critique of major U.S. institutions and then asks audiences to go out and vote, putting faith in the institutions he condemns.

The ideas of ecology and interconnectedness are not new. People in non-Western, integrated frameworks have long been aware of the relationship flows between things and people. This object-oriented ontology is another version of systematic thinking, which is now necessary to describe the rhetorical flows before us. Understanding life as a series of dynamic networks, independent and diverse but responsive to feedback, is useful in understanding documentary and social change. Human agency and thing-power are distinct, and the study of popular documentary indicates that humans and objects have comparable but distinct input into the systems of meaning construction and circulation through networks. As radical and/or activist ideas become more prevalent in popular culture and these ideas enter more homes, exist in more movie theaters, and take up more space on streaming services, we must be cautious not to conflate wider visibility, distribution, and box-office success with political acceptance, influence, or engagement. Instead, we must investigate the relationship between documentary circulation and the ability to collect audiences invested in political action and social change.

The popular turn complicates and magnifies the possibilities for the documentary commons. In many ways, the popular documentary tested the genre's capacity to collect diverse, not previously organized publics into collective formations. The *Paradise Lost* documentaries brought audiences together in a long-term social formation, initially through collective identification bound up in alienation but sustained for over a decade by an activist and archiving culture that created a commons of shared evidence, collective theories developed through debate, and community actions. All of this took place at a time before social media and extensive online networks existed.

Documentary has achieved a level of prominence in public culture—a wider global documentary commons—that is difficult to assess. Michael Moore produced documentaries that shifted the national conversation and made international news. His films plug into social change at the level of mass consciousness, adding to activist discourse without being directly tied to participatory media cultures and appearing as documentary speaking for social change. The documentaries identified problems and provided arguments for change, but they were not connected to social formations willing to pick up the political process. *Fahrenheit 9/11* is a case of unintentional political formations having a profound impact on our culture. The case of this film, Citizens United, and the engagement of popular documentary testing election communication regulations should be a cautionary tale of unintended political formations and assemblages of popular engagement. We may live with the legal legacy of these struggles for decades, changing the playing field for fair elections in the United States for generations to come.

The goal of theory is to move forward by developing wider horizons of understanding with the specificity of concrete detail. Documentary studies are positioned to provide helpful theories and maps for real-world problems, rendering a complex world more understandable through research and field study. We need to expand our perception of what kind of social change is possible with documentary discourse in the contemporary media environment. This endeavor includes taking stock of all the ways popular documentary circulation is changing the game and influencing congressional, legal, and executive discussions and policymaking. Popular political documentary discourse circulates, and its potential assemblages and effects comprise a substantial new political playing field. Media makers, politicians, activists, lawyers, philanthropists, and industry institutions already understand the importance of this emerging documentary commons as a significant domain of political struggle. It is time for scholars to connect cumulative knowledge production, history, and dedicated research to these discussions.

4

Laboring under Documentary

*Collective Identification and the Collapse of
the American Working Class*

Examining documentary history reveals a consistent and robust record of labor struggles in the United States. From the beginning of cinema until now, labor agitation has inspired documentary, and documentary has supported and amplified labor movements. The history of this symbiosis is long and sordid, but one thing has remained consistent: those who document labor struggle often find themselves in the crossfire of intense and violent conflict. In 1972, Barbara Kopple began filming the "Miners for Democracy" movement in Harlan County, Kentucky. Filmmakers and production crews routinely place their bodies on the line to record labor documentary footage, and Kopple's film was no exception. In a tense moment during the miners' strike, "gun thugs" violently attacked the workers. Semiautomatic weapon fire was directed at the picket line and Kopple found herself in the middle of a violent attack:

> They pushed me up against the rocks, and I just started swinging to keep them off of me. They took each one of us individually and did that to us. The cameraman, Hart Perry, was yelling, "The camera's broken, the camera's broken," and that's all they really wanted to do was to make sure that we weren't functioning.[1]

The striking workers were held at gunpoint and attacked with pipes and other weapons. The dark, grainy footage and erratic camera movements do not provide a clear picture, but the screams captured are haunting and inescapable; you don't need to see clearly to sense the danger. This moment is featured in Kopple's Academy Award–winning documentary *Harlan County, USA* (1976), demonstrating the volatility and precariousness of producing labor documentary.

Over the last century, collectives and filmmakers—who often thought of themselves as labor activists first—experimented with the possibilities of documentary as a form of protest, agitation, and resistance. While the category of labor documentary might evoke images of miners striking or labor newsreel footage from the 1930s, the scope and diversity of representation in U.S. labor documentary is far-reaching. From the radical interventions of films exploring how women and people of color existed at the center of the larger labor struggle to the documentation of migrant workers' campaigns in the 1950s, there have been ongoing efforts to articulate a resonant radical history.

Collectively, these documentaries capture violent clashes over workers' rights and decades of police brutality, establishing early experiments with participatory media culture. Workers organized around the cultural production of media that represented labor struggles when mainstream media did not. Despite labor documentary's long history, we still know little about how documentary practices construct collective-identity formation and how this correlates with participatory agency, political action, and social change. To address this, I survey notable labor documentaries in the United States, focusing on the varied collisions between collective-identity formation, agency, and political action. The contexts in which labor documentary emerges are linked to an already organized global labor movement. This means that collective organizing around labor documentary is more deeply rooted in social movement history than the organizing that forms around other threads of social change documentary.

Positing documentary as a potential conduit of social change, while insisting, "filmmakers themselves cannot make revolutions but can only provide 'working tools' for those who can," Thomas Waugh addresses documentary as an instrument. The way it is used defines its political potential. How does documentary discourse enter the collective imaginary in a way that motivates revolutionary actions? Waugh identifies best practices for utilizing documentary as a means to change. Notably, establishing connections with viewer-activists and social movements is essential; organized people have always been crucial to social change documentary. Waugh's work is significant for its commitment to understanding the "gaps between political intention and achievement. It is only by exploring how committed artists of the past have come to grips with—or failed to come to grips with—their historical context that we can learn how to act within our own."[2] Waugh wrote this as the field of documentary studies was coming into its own, exploring methodologies and building on the work of early historians like Eric Barnouw, Jay Leyda, and Lewis Jacobs. Despite Waugh's call to orient documentary studies around the social change capacity of the genre, the field has been slow to address how filmmakers have failed or succeeded in bringing intention and action together. To fill this void in the scholarship, this chapter asks, "How does labor documentary influence documentary work culture as both a production process and a system of representation?"

This chapter extends Waugh's thoughts about the connections between audiences and social movements by exploring collective identification and its relationship to viewer agency. How has labor documentary navigated this terrain over the last 100 years? I argue that documentaries have encouraged identification with a laboring subject that is confrontational toward capitalism and forced to contend with the collapse of the American working class under the strains of neoliberalism. This history documents untold stories and features underrepresented people who have confronted patterns of exploitation and abuse, working in opposition to capitalist interests and the internal reproduction of marginalization within the labor movement. A radical media tradition emerges from this history, elevating voices of resistance that thwart compliance with racist, classist, sexist, and homophobic cultures of domination. Labor documentary helps the audience recognize itself as an object, a capitalist commodity. This process of recognition reveals the basic motor of capitalism as exploitation. The documentary impulse lays bare the expectation of free labor that follows from exploitation. This knowledge produces an opening for conversation, education and an opportunity to resist the capitalist structures that seek to contain us.

What is particularly astounding about the body of labor documentary is that much of it was made in the tides of an intense anticommunist backlash. Blacklisted filmmakers, underground cultural producers, industry sympathizers, and longstanding political networks shaped this history. The ways anticommunist retaliations transformed Hollywood are well known, but the same sentiments also ravaged documentary production culture. The apparatus of control, shifting between local law enforcement, the Federal Bureau of Investigation, the judicial branch, and the executive office is a consistent presence in the history of documentary.

Through explorations of labor documentary, this chapter first addresses collective-identity formation and agency; then rethinking documentary beginnings, histories of labor struggle, radical solidarity, documentation of workers' lives; and finally, feminist labor documentary intervention. Understanding the successes and failures of labor documentary is essential to harnessing the potential of the form. From the initial impulses to record and distribute images of the labor struggle, media producers have been wrestling with the potency of documentary in public culture.

Collective-Identity Formation and Agency

Understanding the process of collective-identity formation is critical to how groups organize around documentary to create participatory media publics. Collective identity is "an individual's cognitive, moral, and emotional connection with a broader community, category, practice, or institution. It is a perceived shared status, which may be imagined rather than experienced directly, and it is distinct from personal identity, although it may form part of a personal identity."[3] Documentary media practice initiates collective identification by positioning the audience through images, story, editing, framing, argument, discovery, and the many other choices that create a grid of intelligibility for the onscreen experience. Audiences collectively identify through stories, expressions of voice, and performances, while also absorbing the curated point of view made possible by the camera and through the screen. Functioning on a variety of registers, collective-identity formation can be forged through reason, dialogue, self-reflection, consciousness-raising, and affective exchanges.

Depending on which scholar you ask, collective identity in social movement formation has been understood too narrowly or too broadly,[4] or has been neglected altogether, especially in relation to online activism, where digital culture has played a central role in the process of collective-identity construction.[5] Although all scholars seem to agree that the formation of collective identity is an essential aspect of the social change process, we still know little about how this happens with documentary. Jasper and Polletta address sociology's approach to collective identity, mostly in an effort to fill in the gaps left by structuralist, state-centered, and rational-choice models.[6] I suggest there are arenas of political agency to be explored, gaps left by the focus on the cinema screen—participatory media cultures and the collective commons that emerge from these engagements. Gerbaudo and Trere argue that a shift toward digital culture demands that we reinvest in collective identity as a possible nodal around which social change spins—a concept that could inform how groups mobilize to meet the needs of social justice communities.[7] Karma R. Chavez views this collective-identity formation process as coalition building—the temporary coming together of a group of people with shared interests who grow together toward goal-oriented action. Chavez argues that differential belonging—a desire to create relations across difference—can lead to possibilities for tactical subjectivity. She writes: Social actors "resist in ways that are not bound by fixed identities . . . that allow for further connections between individuals and groups that are very different."[8] Studying participatory media cultures allows us to focus on the organizational and strategic consequences of collective-identity formation as coalition building as well as the micro-interactional factors that help collective formations shift into political action.

Collective-identity construction is a rhetorical process. Documentary facilitates this discourse by delivering an experience that unites the audience around common ideas, allowing them to share a substance of humanness: audience members become consubstantial in their shared values.[9] This perspective understands documentary as more than a tool or channel and instead embraces the interactive, fluid, and symbolic nature of the participatory media cultures that grow around documentary. Although collective identity can be crafted intentionally, it can also occur independent of strategic efforts.[10] As Kaja Silverman asserts, "Political cinema cannot be understood apart from identification, since it is the privileged mechanism whereby the spectator can be not only integrated into a new social collectivity, but also induced to occupy a subject-position which is antithetical to his or her [original] psychic formation."[11] I am primarily interested here in collective-identity formation and documentary that produces sustained investment and collective action rather than mere engagement. As we trace this process in a world before and after the emergence of digital culture, understanding of collective action must not collapse into "connective action" in which engagement becomes flexible and individualized.[12]

The understanding of collective-identity formation in this book is specific to communities where members have access to most or all rights of citizenship, including legal assembly and free speech. Under these conditions, people are most free to "engage in the creative reformulations of who they are"[13] and politicize their belonging.[14] Rhetorically, crafting collective identification means creating frameworks for sharing interests and fostering a shared status or relationship. Rather than assume that shared social interests already exist and that social movement actors are aware and ready to act, this book posits collective identity as being fluid, with the potential to shift and reprioritize interests, calibrating the urgency to act. What triggers this urgency, motivating audiences to respond to specific images on the documentary screen with collective action? In exploring this question, Dana Cloud identifies several rhetorical strategies that help explain how "divergent experiential knowledge (episteme)" transforms into "common sense (doxa)" that motivates actions for social change.[15] These strategies include (1) emotion as the experience of making sense of feelings, (2) embodiment that involves bodies as sites of physical agency in the world, (3) narrative storytelling as a way of making meaning in the world, and (4) spectacle as a striking ritualistic visual display. These strategies mediate the process of transforming experience into common sense, creating urgency to act in the world. The following sections focus on dynamics of collective-identity formation that use these and other rhetorical strategies to prompt communities to embrace instrumental agency.

Rethinking Documentary Beginnings

Archives of labor documentary hold some of the most complete and diverse visual narratives of working life in the United States. Most of this visual history was constructed by and for workers in conjunction with the longstanding labor movement. The history of labor documentary and social change in the United States precedes John Grierson's towering presence in film history and theory. In his foundational book on documentary history, Eric Barnouw positions Grierson as the essential documentary theorist and filmmaker, responsible for uncovering the form's civic capacity. As a filmmaker, Grierson came from a relatively privileged background and developed a well-established affinity with working-class culture,[16] which produced significant interventions into representations of British working life. His desire to shift the focus of documentary toward social change was important, and his use of the film platform for these goals was foundational for documentary history. His films are well preserved, the scholarship about him is robust, and his thinking stands as a pillar of the origin story of documentary studies. Many critics found Grierson's work void of politics and uncritical of social hierarchies,[17] and, though Grierson's civic focus was important, the tradition of films galvanizing audiences to undertake political work in response to what is shown onscreen goes all the way back to silent-film production in the United States. This early documentary history is less well known, however, because it is found outside the traditional white, Western orientation of documentary history.

Early silent-era newsreel documentaries produced new representations of black life. Often called "actualities," these newsreels brought "attention to the progress and pride of ordinary citizens" in documentaries such as *Youth Pride and Achievement of Colored People of Atlanta, Georgia* in which "communities celebrated themselves and told their own stories."[18] Some of these early films were commercially released, and others were shown at community screenings in lodge halls, neighborhood churches, and civic halls. There were also showmen who traveled a circuit with projection equipment, putting on eclectic picture shows in which documentaries about black life were often featured. With the emergence of race theaters and race films at the turn of the 20th century, black documentary found space in a parallel community, a phenomenon that traditional documentary history has not fully embraced. Uncovering the history of black documentary practice, which was producing moving images decades before Grierson, has implications for how we understand documentary, collective identification, and social change today.

BLACK DOCUMENTARY IN THE SILENT ERA

The phenomenon of people recording their own lives with the moving-image camera—as a survival mechanism—has historical roots in U.S. black production culture. Black citizens emancipating themselves from the legacy of slavery found a particular urgency to use documentary as a means of social change and a radical tool to combat oppression. In 1910, census data indicates that black people made up 11 percent of the total population but accounted for 1 percent of professional registered photographers.[19] The percentage of black professional photographers just forty-five years after the end of slavery indicates that there was an intense desire for photographic documentation of black life at the beginnings of cinema, reflecting the ways necessity often gives birth to new and unconventional uses of photographic and moving-image recording.

Black photographers, grounded in their communities and beginning to encounter emerging motion picture technology, recorded a changing black culture framed by the rhetorics of improvement and advancement. Showmen would advertise the presence of a motion picture camera in town, inviting communities to be part of the public record, with the promise of a subsequent screening of the footage. Pearl Bowser explains that early black documentaries were race movies, promoting and documenting economic and political movements and organizations, such as Booker T. Washington's National Negro Business League (NNBL) and Marcus Garvey's United Negro Improvement Association (UNIA). Washington commissioned the first black documentary, and Garvey's UNIA established its own film company to publicize the activities of the movement. Photographer James Van Der Zee and others produced portraits of Garvey and elite guards in uniform and recorded the August 20, 1920, rally that brought 50,000 Garveyites to Harlem's West Boulevard.[20] The UNIA film company captured a range of social movement activities on film. As Bowser concludes, "most if not all of these early films are lost to us," but can be studied through newspapers in news, ads, and information buried in other stories.[21]

Black documentary in the silent era experimented with shifting representations of laboring black subjects and ways to manage power relationships with these images. Creating representations of life after emancipation, black documentary was ahead of its time. It functioned as more than a mirror, a project Grierson later championed as a goal for filmmakers. Booker T. Washington was practicing documentary as a vehicle to challenge representation. He commissioned specific but unconventional representations to prompt reevaluation of the dignified black working man, using powerful visual narratives and striking representations. His film, *A Day at Tuskegee* (1909), was one of the first and most influential short documentaries of the silent era. The film depicted the vocational training of young black men and women at the Tuskegee Institute. Newspaper accounts describe the documentary as forty-three scenes of industrial education shot inside the institute, creating black identification with working-class culture while managing white culture's anxieties and fears of an emancipated slave class.[22] This documentary screened around the country at UNIA events and attracted the attention of influential politicians. It debuted to an audience of 2000 people in New York City's Carnegie Hall on January 24, 1910.[23] Washington commissioned the film to promote his vision for industrial education and the integration of black people into white culture. By seeking to transform black agency into job training and away from activism, Washington was able to leverage resources and support from powerful white businessmen, politicians, and former President Theodore Roosevelt, enabling him to pursue his long-term goal of an economically self-reliant and independent black workforce at the Tuskegee Institute. For Washington, documentary images were a way to expose larger audiences to new representations of black working people through traveling film screenings and incipient fundraising possibilities. These were documentary works created as a means of survival and with a desire to engage with a more equitable world. Booker T. Washington was not the only pioneer of early documentary.

After the release of D. W. Griffith's racially charged *The Birth of a Nation* (1915), nationally renowned leader Dr. George E. Cannon established the Frederick Douglass Film Company out of his home. The film company produced four feature films depicting black people as distinguished, professional, and successful citizens. One of the films, a documentary, *Heroic Negro Soldiers of World War* (1919), features black soldiers as they trained for war. At the time, lynching was highly visible and racial tensions ran high; these films of military "heroism and sacrifice in battle, shown not only in theaters, but also in community churches and lodge halls, helped to strengthen African American resolve to fight against the prejudice, hatred and the oppression they faced at home."[24] The representations of black life shown onscreen created collective-identity formations around American nationalism and patriotism. The calls to serve in the military provided dignity and credibility for black people, who were under tremendous threat in the United States but had the opportunity to show themselves resilient and patriotic enough to take on external threats to the country.

In 1909, a time when print communication dominated cultural discourse, the use of film for social change represented a risky and innovative strategy. Washington recognized cinema as a powerful educational tool and effective fundraising tactic, as well as a way to build coalitions with different constituencies. He used documentary to challenge commonsense thinking around race and labor, producing unconventional representations to prompt reevaluation and different engagement in the world. Washington and Cannon were documentary innovators who hailed from the elite business class of the black community, a position that affected their creative understanding of what documentary could be. They walked a line between speaking for and speaking with the black community. Despite the economic class of the filmmakers, these films were still not regarded as valuable to the larger U.S. culture. Preservation and documentation of early black documentary film culture, especially race films, is sparse for many reasons: distribution outlets were not well documented, screenings were held in small commercial venues with limited advertising budgets, and as films eventually lost their value as educational materials, they disappeared from public and institutional archives. Nonetheless, the existing artifacts show that these films provided critical representations of black subjectivity at a time of dramatic change and functioned as a petition for black agency in a white-supremacist culture. Many early black documentaries worked to include black life in the larger public imaginary and political landscape. This was significant, as labor documentary more broadly remained ambivalent toward issues of race for decades to come.

NEWSREEL AS AGITATION

The discovery of the Workers' Film and Photo League and Frontier Films by scholars in the 1970s came as an exciting revelation that provided evidence of a dynamic and radical activist documentary tradition in the United States.[25] The Workers' Film and Photo League was an offshoot of existing political movements. In the early 1930s, Communist International, specifically the United States Chapter of the Workers International Relief (WIR), organized revolutionary drama groups, dance troupes, orchestras, bands, and choirs, and produced newsreels.[26] Their interests were similar to those of black documentary filmmakers two decades earlier, who sought to reach a mass audience and provide representation that was not easily available elsewhere. They shifted from feature films to newsreels because newsreels could be produced and screened quickly, creating a more immediate impact. The Great Depression prompted a focus on strike lines and other demonstrations, but there was also a growing agitational impulse. As film critic Samuel Brody wrote in *The Daily Worker*: "[T]he capitalist class knows that there are certain things that it cannot afford to have shown. It is afraid of some pictures. . . . Films are being used against the workers like police clubs . . . we will equip our own cameramen to make our own films."[27] The impulse to control documentary images out of fear of the political volatility these images could trigger continues throughout this history.

In the United States in the 1930s, documentary screenings held for workers in their own communities became a potent organizing tool. These documentary efforts were made by and for workers committed to agitation. The filmmakers understood the power of circulation, harnessing these events for strategic intervention and organizing. The screenings demonstrated how quickly a single group could transform from a film audience into a dangerous threat to the status quo. In 1934, Lester Balog, a founding member of the New York Workers Film and Photo League, was jailed while working with San Francisco's Film and Photo League for showing *Road to Life* (1931) and *Cottonpicker's Strike* (1933) to agricultural workers in California. He recounts the following:

> So while I was projecting, about four troopers came in, big son-of-a-guns, you know? I am not tall, but they were about 6 1/2 feet, and they stood around me—I didn't know what to do, I finished the film. I understand Pat meanwhile sneaked out, and when it was over they practically picked me up and took me to jail . . . they charged me with running a business without a license . . . they kept me 13 days in the police station, and then I got 45 days.[28]

Balog, like many before and after him, found himself targeted by law enforcement who acted to protect corporate interests.

Balog and the larger Workers Film and Photo League experimented with documentary as a tool of political intervention; he put his body on the line to serve the struggles of the larger labor movement, powerfully encouraging workers to agitate for better working conditions. These documentary interventions held political space and legitimacy for the working class. Other documentary films acted to protect workers who found themselves in sudden and violent clashes.

On Memorial Day 1937, Republic Steel workers were on strike. A larger action was in progress across the steel industry, but the Republic Steel factory in Chicago stayed open. The strike escalated when Chicago police brutally attacked the crowd of protestors and ten workers were murdered. As the political struggle became more violent, so did the production culture of labor documentary. Footage produced by Paramount Pictures and distributed as part of their newsreel series recorded the attack. The documentation of the event depicts an aggressive police line descending upon a running crowd; smoke obscures the frame, but a clear view of police beating the crowd with batons remains. The spectacle was striking, producing awe at the brute display of the police working in unison to attack striking workers. The circulation of these images cultivated an exchange of public views about the workers who began the strike and their vulnerability to police brutality. The newsreel was so damning that it was illegally banned by the Chicago Police Department on the grounds of potentially causing unrest. In this first wave of labor documentary, we see representation intercede to curtail violence and establish support for workers. This was especially trenchant for Republic Steel workers, whose previous strikes lacked public support. The documentary impulse, in the form of the newsreel, aided labor organizing by giving workers images of themselves and their interests magnified onscreen and projected across the United States and around the world. We begin to see documentary engaging social change in a very specific way, challenging the authority of police and curtailing violence. As far back as 1937, there is slippage between community media, as represented by the Workers Film and Photo League and commercial media: Paramount Pictures documented the Republic Steel workers strike for their commercial newsreel series. Documenting news events for political ends was one of many fronts of agitation in the ongoing labor struggle.

Histories of Labor Struggle

From the late 1940s into the 1960s, there were few instances of labor documentary. McCarthyism sent social action film underground; filmmakers who engaged labor documentary were at risk because they were suspected of communism. In the 1960s, early newsreels and amateur recordings of labor struggles began a second life as source material for historical documentation. Filmmakers constructed large-scale labor histories with dramatic scripts, oral testimonies, and archival footage. The films built grand narratives of historical labor struggles and featured unlikely workplace agitators. Documentaries were particularly adept at interrogating and conceptualizing history because they "fill in gaps, correct errors, and expose distortions in order to provide counter-narratives."[29] Primarily relying on an epic narrative framework, these films created identification with working people across industries, suggesting a broad identification with "the worker." This included depictions of sacrifice and loss made triumphant through solidarity. These documentaries often targeted union-sympathizing audiences, but frequently the human struggle of emancipation from exploitation became the fodder for powerful storytelling that translated to a mass audience.

Released to celebrate the fiftieth anniversary of the Amalgamated Clothing Workers of America, the earliest of these large historical narratives, *The Inheritance* (1964), represented clothing workers' union successes over five decades. Like many other historical labor films, this film takes a reflective tone rather than attempting to keep time with current events. It builds public investment in workers' historical legacy through documentary discourse, representing historical events as a way to solidify inclusion in public memory. *The Inheritance* is an optimistic story of workers' struggles in the 1930s as seen from the perspective of immigrants pursuing mobility in an abundant American culture. The script reads like a radio drama paired with powerful images of an industrial culture with a penchant for child labor and worker exploitation. As the documentary progresses, so does the precariousness of the conditions faced by the workers onscreen. The narrative is held together by celebratory images of solidarity and the good-life juxtaposed against montages of police violence toward protestors. This sweeping documentary represents a harmonious labor movement in conflict with a capitalist system but without internal struggle. Conspicuous omissions include any mention of the labor movement's racist positions and the exclusion of women. Representing social change requires negotiating the impulse to present a cohesive and unified history at the expense of accurately representing nuance, contradiction, and complexity within a movement.

These documentaries establish labor's public significance and serve as public pedagogy in the worker's struggle, circumventing commercial media gatekeepers. *The Uprising of '34* (1995) directed by George Stoney, Judith Helfand, and Susanne Rostocks, documents the suppressed story of the General Textile strike, in which 500,000 southern mill workers walked off their jobs in the 1930s. This historical narrative holds space for the epic tale of this strike, while attending to its inherent contradictions and exclusions. For example, the specific strike ends in defeat, but the failure is framed as a success because it builds community solidarity. The labor campaign was traumatic and unsuccessful; one union leader underscores the importance of documenting these actions:

> When we would hear what was happening in other places, like the big city, New York, Chicago, San Francisco. . . . The people were aware of this new freedom and protection and they were taking advantage of it. And then we

began to feel like we could be a part of a great movement. That we wouldn't be an individual group down here. That was a wonderful feeling.[30]

A potent collective identification is forged through the subject position of "the worker." The audience is allowed to contemplate their own relationship to production and their position as an object of capitalist exploitation.

In the late 1970s into the 1980s, labor documentary moved toward constructing history as recorded by workers themselves, rather than the interests of government or news corporations. This impulse continued through the turn of the 21st century, as workers' rights continued to erode and older labor industries disappeared. *Brothers on the Line* (2012) follows the journey of three brothers, all United Auto Workers, who led a social justice movement that transformed the landscape of union organizing through their struggles for workers' rights. A later film, *Mine Wars* (2016), depicts the culture of mining in West Virginia, raising profound questions about freedom and democracy among working people.

While filmmakers and activists were using archival footage to construct labor history, documentation of workplace struggles —in a manner reminiscent of newsreel footage—never ceased. Many labor documentaries focus on the conditions and concerns of one specific labor struggle and the people who make extraordinary decisions and take on monumental risks in support of that struggle. These documentaries create collective identification with workers and against capitalist values as represented by bosses and corporations, creating a portrait of an American working class crushed under capitalism.

SOUTHWEST DOCUMENTARY JUSTICE

The films of Harvey Richards comprise some of the most significant—and least documented—contributions to labor history. There are no better extrainstitutional, long-term examples of documenting political struggle to sustain the historical record. Richards's career as a photographer spanned roughly twenty active years, from 1958–1978. During this time, he amassed one of the most influential archives of documentary history footage in the United States. In the 1960s and into the 1970s, he produced twenty-two documentaries featuring various social and political movements. His films have been licensed for use in over seventy documentaries, TV productions, books, magazines, and exhibits.[31] Richards began using a camera in his mid-forties to capture labor and civil rights struggles across the southern United States. After a 1957 subpoena to testify at the congressional hearing for the Committee on Un-American Activities, Richards, who had been a union organizer in Philadelphia and Boston, decided to grab his camera and "take a vacation" to avoid testifying. He traveled throughout the Deep South and to Latin America but ended up working in the shipyards in San Francisco as a machinist. He augmented his still photography equipment with a motion picture camera, first creating a hand-wound

Bolex 16 millimeter camera and then using an Arriflex battery-powered camera with synchronous-sound capabilities. He was frequently present at protests with his camera mounted on a tripod and propped on the back of his car; his was an intervention of mobile cinema before equipment allowed an easy transition into such a mode of production.

Richards found himself on the front lines of social justice struggles in the late 1950s and into the 1960s, before these movements became newsworthy. He was often one of the first with a camera on the picket line, and then, as a struggle gained more media attention, he would move on to the next project. He worked closely with communities, especially the farmworkers' movement and unions, capturing working conditions. He edited his films independently but worked with activists to use documentary in political struggle. His most extensive body of work focused on agricultural labor; in introducing the farmworker to white audiences to compel support for the Braceros, he exposed the inhumane working conditions that existed on U.S. soil.

One of Richards's early films, *Perch of the Devil* (1960), was about the 1959 copper mine strike in Butte, Montana. The documentary focuses on the Workers Local Union No. 1 in Butte, which faced many violent struggles over the years. To support the miners' strike against Anaconda Copper, the film documents the dangerous working conditions that produced silicosis and fatal lung disease. Audiences identify with abused and policed workers whose survival is compromised by the greed of mine owners. The FBI trailed Richards during the film's production, concerned that his lack of participation in the UnAmerican Activities Committee Hearings and focus on the labor struggle had created a certain "energy" around his film activity. Richards persisted nonetheless, creating solidarity and organizing with documentary when most radical filmmakers went underground, fearing exposure and accusations. Richards later produced the most significant documentation of migrant worker struggles in the West (which are addressed later in this chapter). Whereas Richards captured the labor struggle in the Southwest, fifteen years later a significant labor documentary culture was building in the Midwest.

DOCUMENTARY AGITATION IN THE MIDWEST

In the 1970s, the Kartemquin Film Collective in Chicago produced notable labor documentary that should receive more attention than it has. While most media collectives in New York and San Francisco were abandoning worker agitation as a mode of political struggle in favor of countercultural lifestyle communities and experimental expression, Chicago was producing labor-influenced documentary that experimented with political engagement. *Where's I.W. Abel?* (1975) was created with rank-and-file steel workers to help oppose the no-strike agreement between the company president and the ten major steel companies. *U.E. Wells* (1975) documents an organized drive by the United Electrical Workers at the Wells Foundry in Chicago, where the company used race to drive a wedge between workers. *HSA Strike-75* (1975) is the story of interns and residents at Chicago's only public hospital striking for better patient care. *Taylor Chain I* (1980) follows a seven-week strike at a small chain factory in Indiana, and *Taylor Chain II* (1983) represents labor and management working together to save the plant from anti-union legislation and the impacts of globalization. *The Last Pullman Car* (1983) tells the story of workers fighting the closure of a Chicago railcar plant. These documentaries feature a multiethnic workforce, testimony committed to rank-and-file interests, and unparalleled experimentation with workplace agitation and documentary intervention, picking up some of the agitational impulses of early workers' films in the thirties. The Kartemquin Film Collective also experimented with collaboration. *Where's I.W. Abel?* was made in collaboration with the steel workers' caucus, aligning the film with their struggle. Gordon Quinn, one of the early founders of Kartemquin, explained how their approach to social change documentary shifted with this experience. In the beginning, he explains, "we sort of thought that if you held a mirror up to society and just showed it what it was like, that would be enough to create social change. Well, we learned very quickly that that was not enough . . . you had to go much deeper and you had to not only have an analysis, but you also had to have a kind of way of putting the film into venues and getting it used in ways that were gonna lead to social change."[32] Quinn recognized the need for an analysis of power that goes beyond the "screen-as-mirror" function of documentary. He advocated for public exhibitions that reached change makers. Several other films followed his model of collaboration and intervention.

Judy Hoffman was an early video producer of labor documentary for the Kartemquin Film Collective. Her film *What's Happening at Local 70* (1975) is a notable example of activist experimentation with the camera and workers' struggles and was screened in workers' spaces unedited immediately after shooting. This workflow helped make the union campaigns successful. *What's Happening at Local 70* (1975) covered a local labor strike in a Chicago unemployment compensation office, which led to a walkout. Hoffman documented the events using video, which allowed for immediate playback. Communities were able to see themselves and their world projected on the screen on the same scale and speed as broadcast television. This innovation changed documentary's function, expanding possibilities for collaboration with labor struggle. The camera became part of the street protest, interacting and engaging with political struggle rather than representing it from a distance. The result was the emergence of an anti-slick street aesthetic marked by shaky handheld camera images, out-of-focus segments, beheaded protesting bodies, fast and out-of-focus pans, in-camera editing, and various technical imperfections. The video displayed unconventional-yet-refreshing visual framing in the form of unstable close-up shots, center framing, long sustained shots, and frequent reframing during interviews. The visual characteristics made activist video distinct from mass-produced broadcast images, creating credibility through markers of visual authenticity to develop a vernacular cinematic discourse.

Grassroots documentary screenings in the 1970s were playful, experimenting with unconventional spaces for public exhibition. Video allowed for an immediacy prohibited by the formal constraints of celluloid film. Early activist-video collectives capitalized on this as a community-building mechanism—recording footage and then screening it immediately in makeshift theaters and community spaces. For example, in *What's Happening at Local 70*, interviews were shot, edited in camera, and screened for nine weeks at local bars and restaurants. The screenings were accompanied by discussions of the labor struggle. Union officials attempted to suppress a viewing of the tape at a Chicago-wide union meeting, but the rank-and-file demanded a screening and the tape was shown. After the screening, the entire membership voted to support Local 70 and hold a one-day solidarity strike and rally. The workers of Local 70 were rehired, but dispersed to other local offices. Video had a real-time effect, allowing communities to see themselves and the world differently. Their own images took on the same gravity as broadcast television.

Hoffman uses the documentary as a tool of innovative political intervention, harnessing the capacity of video to capitalize on productive intervention with the strike campaign. Like many of her peers, Hoffman learned video production in the field, and the imperfections of this process produce a kind of authenticity; the anti-slick representation creates a from-the-streets aesthetic that resonates with

Figure 4.1 On the strike line, Judy Hoffman interviews striking city workers and the people supporting the strike in *What's Happening at Local 70?* (1975)

Figure 4.2 In *What's Happening at Local 70?* (1975) families come to the strike line to help support the workers.

Figure 4.3 On the strike line, Judy Hoffman interviews striking city workers in *What's Happening at Local 70?* (1975)

Figure 4.4 Judy Hoffman features women as workers and documents the invisible support work to aid the continuation of the strike in *What's Happening at Local 70?* (1975)

Figure 4.5 Judy Hoffman captures a strike by a union of interns and residents at Chicago's only public hospital, a struggle for better patient care in *HSA Strike '75*.

real people. Hoffman interviews strikers but also supporters of the campaign, including the women working to feed the protestors, thus shining a light on the invisible labor behind the strike line. Her films challenge conventional aesthetics by offering a vernacular cinematic discourse that creates a visual authenticity. At that historical moment, many people felt that film production was the domain of men but that video was an open and exploratory culture. In video's emerging potential, Hoffman and other women found their own ground to experiment with social change documentary.

Kartemquin films, such as *HSA Strike 1975* and *What's Happening at Local 70*, disseminate a distinct vernacular cinematic language connected to the communities seeking social justice, which should be understood in contrast to simple representation of the interests of marginalized and exploited communities. This vernacular cinematic discourse creates an experience of authenticity that allows viewers to feel like they are watching life unfold before their (camera) eyes. It is a difference between engaging in social change as opposed to speaking for social change, which involves aesthetic and conceptual distance. The markers and cues of this vernacular cinematic language emerge from the social conditions of their production and include visual forms such as unconventional framing and a significant focus on public speech as a means of bearing witness. This language reflects a labor movement characterized by negotiation and struggle. Shared interests and contestation become the basis for collective experience, creating an environment of labor narratives that come together to construct a public authenticity.

The 1970s were a vibrant time for labor documentary and one of the era's most popular and well-studied labor documentaries, Barbara Kopple's *Harlan County, USA*, provides a documentary account of a 1974 Kentucky miners' strike. Kopple captures the backbreaking work of the miners and the inevitable destitution that lies ahead of them, carefully recording both the mundane and dangerous parts of the strike, which included several shootings. Responding to her experience working and living with miners as they struggled to sustain a strike, Kopple reflects, "It made me learn that you can't do anything by yourself. In order to achieve something or in order to win some kind of victory, you all have to be united under the same ideas or the same cause."[33] As we see with Kopple, filmmakers' understandings of collective identity and audience are important to the co-creation of meaning around the documentary event. In a later film, *American Dream* (1990), Kopple further pursues this notion of collectivity as she returns to the strike line to document the dramatic and heartbreaking events surrounding the union battle at the Hormel meatpacking plant in Austin, Minnesota.

THE BIRTH OF NEOLIBERALISM: LABOR UNDER DURESS

As the 1980s began, stories of dangerous work environments and violence enacted on workers' bodies persisted. In *Song of the Canary* (1979), male workers confront chemical plant owners about working conditions that have left them sterile. The birth defects that resulted from toxic working conditions are documented in *Worker to Worker* (1980). *Pregnant but Equal* (1982) follows a group of factory workers fighting to pass the 1978 Pregnancy Discrimination Act. In the 1970s and 1980s, forty-plus years after the first major U.S. workers' strikes hoped to make work spaces safe, there remained a great deal of conflict around worker safety and reflection about who had been left out of the gains of the early labor struggles.

Signed, Sealed and Delivered: Labor Struggle in the Post Office (1980), directed by Tami Gold, Dan Gordon, and Erik Lewis, addresses the dangers of mechanization to speed up worker productivity. The film represents government workers who are not allowed to strike. It focuses on a wildcat strike held to address mandatory over-time, forced speed-ups, and hazardous working conditions. The strikes of the 1930s addressed unregulated worker exploitation by corporations, while this representa-tion of worker struggle depicts unethical government workplace practices and the desperate acts of workers fighting for safety and fair working conditions. This docu-mentary is aligned with the interests of rank-and-file workers, fired postal workers, and the union campaign to maintain a focus on workers' interests. It documents the erosion of workers' protections in a moment requiring increased vigilance and regular documentation of the labor struggle. The government was cast in a new role, that of the unrelenting and exploitative boss.

Fast Food Women (1991), directed by Anne Lewis, explores the lives of working poor women employed by the fast-food industry in eastern Kentucky. It begins with a series of sit-down interviews with fast-food managers; the men talk openly about efforts to exploit the emotional loyalty of the female workers and the pressure they put on the women to increase their speed and maintain consistency in output. It is a story of a growing contingent labor force that holds positions for which little skill is required. Workers become replaceable, and this dispensability spreads across industries, from college professors to technical professionals. *Fast Food Women* becomes a gateway for policy changes to address labor instability. Director Anne Lewis explains:

> And it came out and I think it was somewhat helpful to expose things way before *Nickeled and Dimed* and all of this kind of stuff came out about the working poor. Well, remember when Hilary Clinton was pushing for health-care? So I got a call from the White House and they wanted to bring some of the women (one of the staffers had seen *Fast Food Women*) and they wanted to bring some of the women in it up to Washington to testify before Congress about their health insurance, or lack of health insurance. And what was re-ally cool was that they, in the same room in front of Congress, this Congress subcommittee, they were also going to have the CEO of, you know, Pizza Hut, which is PepsiCo and the CEO of some of these other companies. So they brought these two women up from my film, who'd been in my film, from

Kentucky. First time either one of them had been on an airplane. They put them up on a hotel, and then they took them over to Congress to testify. And I saw it on C-Span. It was covered by C-Span. It was phenomenal. It was absolutely wonderful. I mean the women just were terrific, and they absolutely confronted the CEO.[34]

The subjects in the documentary had a public platform for sharing their experiences. Traveling to Washington, D.C., gave them the chance to participate in shaping the policies that affected them, and they were also able to confront the CEOs responsible for their exploitation. Real bodies that walk off the screen and into the congressional hearing room. In this unprecedented form of intervention for this time, the documentary becomes part of policymaking and other forms of decision making by providing footage for evidence and documentary subjects who can be asked to testify. Documentary production has tentacles that reach far beyond the film object itself. Many connections and networks coalesce around the process of production, making filmmakers a resource and their research as data in the political struggle as well as the legislative process and legal battles. Although these stories are compelling and effective in engaging policy, historical labor documentary is often ambivalent or dismissive toward internal race and gender struggles.

SOLIDARITY SOMETIMES

The reproduction of exclusion and bigotry within the labor movement is not a new story. How these articulations find ground in documentary expression is scattered and varied. Documentary representation of the black and latinx workers who built the United States in the steel, automotive, and agriculture industries is scarce. Documentary representation tends to romanticize and sanctify worker struggle at the expense of telling uncomfortable truths about inequality. This myopia is the starting point for *Struggle in Steel* (1996) by Ray Henderson and Tony Buba. The film documents the stories of African American steel workers who are confined to doing the most backbreaking, dangerous, and low-paid work. One worker explains:

> About 10 percent of the country's steel workers were black but we never seem to show up in the official history of steel. You would think we never worked in the mill. A documentary aired on a local TV station about steel workers who lost their jobs and not one black person was in it. For them to say we have played no significant role as steel workers angered me. It hurt my heart because black people helped build this country.[35]

The documentary details the specific experiences of black workers as a response to the lack of black representation in widespread narratives of labor history. Labor history tends to underplay nuances and internal tensions in favor of telling a universal (if incomplete) story of workers' solidarity. An exception, *I Am Somebody* (1970), which received funding from the Carnegie Corporation of New York, depicts a successful 1969 strike by black women hospital workers. This representation of black workers' struggle is unique because it elevates the voices of working-class black women. *At the River I Stand* (1993) represents the dramatic climax of the civil rights movements with documentation of the Memphis sanitation workers strike in the spring of 1968. This history is a powerful illustration of the deep connection between economic and civil rights. *Miles of Smiles* (1982) tells the story of Pullman porters who organized America's first black trade union because white unions would not support their struggle. *A. Philip Randolph: For Jobs and Freedom* (1996) positions the civil rights leader as the preeminent black labor leader of the century. Randolph, who was responsible for organizing the Pullman porters, was known for his commitment to socialist ideas and persistence in organizing workers. A radical impulse to address structures of capitalism as a way of rethinking exploitation emerged from these efforts to document workers' struggles and construct a more inclusive workers' history.

Like addressing race in union organizing, documentaries focused on issues of sexual orientation and/or gender discrimination in the workspace are rarely found. When they appear, they are a necessary correctives to the dominant romanticized labor narrative. Ellen Spiro's *DiAnna's Hair Ego* (1989) follows a hair salon owner in the South who uses her workplace to disseminate information about HIV and AIDS in the face of the cultural silence around the disease. *Live Nude Girls Unite* (2007) documents the labor struggle of peep show dancers at one of San Francisco's longest running adult entertainment establishment, The Lusty Lady. These and other films attempt to address the intersection of gender, class, sexuality, and identity-based organizing, representing the struggles and bigotry that require workers (and the audience) to rethink their own alliances. As union organizer and filmmaker Amber Hollibaugh suggests, "Good organizing needs to speak to the complexity of private life. If you can't do that . . . ultimately you haven't created a space that makes it possible for people to talk about what effects them as they try to survive economically."[36] Documentaries create an opening for excluded stories to gain recognition and empathy in the larger workplace discourse. One of the most controversial and visible of this cause is *Out at Work*, a film that circulated in two versions.

Out at Work (1997) and (1999) by Kelly Anderson and Tami Gold documents what it means to be LGBT and unprotected in the workplace. At the time, over thirty states had no protections against discrimination based on sexual orientation and/or gender identity. Fighting for nondiscrimination laws, *Out at Work* documents workers struggling for workplace safety, job security, and benefits in a political climate that was still outwardly aggressive and violent toward any visible recognition of LBGT personhood, specifically within the union context. Cutting across the service, automotive, and financial industry, the documentary stiches together a common storyline shared by those facing discrimination based on sexual orientation and/or gender identity.

The outreach campaign, the controversy that emerged from the documentary's circulation, and the nerve it hit in the larger labor movement created a contestable space for agitation. *Out at Work* was an official selection at the Sundance Film Festival, reviewed in the *New York Times*, and broadcast on HBO's America Undercover series, but its circulation did not come without resistance. Before it aired on HBO, PBS considered it for their Point of View Series but ultimately refused to air it because a modest portion of the budget came from union organizations. Devastated, Gold and Anderson argued that these calculations were made without considering the total cost of the documentary, excluding free labor and in-kind services. Another controversy arose around a fundraising screening for the documentary held at a hotel with an active labor dispute; HBO stepped in and suggested it would take its fundraising screening elsewhere, shaping labor relations for the workers at that hotel. *Out at Work* traveled in the world, making contact with the global labor movement and its struggles. KipuKai Kuali'I of the AFL-CIO reports: "*Out At Work* is the single most important organizing tool we have had for our educational work within workplaces and labor unions." While discriminatory policies continue, films like *Out at Work* expose those uncomfortable discriminations we often avoid in cultures of worker's struggle.

Radical Solidarity

While labor documentary clearly and directly opposes capitalism, it often ignores marginalization within the labor movement. This is evident in limited representation of marginalized groups and the omission of internal conflicts from the dominant labor documentary narrative. A radical impulse in labor documentary history seeks to expose romanticized elements of labor struggle and the nuances that trouble solidarity, including suppressing underrepresented viewpoints and sustaining discriminatory cultures. This radical impulse directs the camera at root systems and problems, moving toward complete political and social reform.

Like many women in the early 1970s independent film scene, Julia Reichert imagined film as a tool to help the women's movement grow. Unlike mainstream media makers, Reichert was interested in producing documentaries about real people and screening them where people lived and worked, in places like colleges, high schools, YMCAs, and churches. As Alexandra Juhasz explains in her book *Women of Vision*, Reichert, a socialist feminist, and her filmmaking partner James Klein, approached documentary as political organizing that uses film as a tool. Reichert explains, "We did not see ourselves as artists or even primarily filmmakers. I saw myself as an activist who had skills to make film."[37] This distinction is important; labor documentary filmmakers manage multiple identities, often prioritizing the role of activist worker. Other identifications—as artist or filmmaker—could obscure the primary goal of political agitation. Reichert and Klein were interested in viewer insights, participation, and political organizing through film.

Reichart and Klein's *Union Maids* (1979) was shot in Chicago over three days and featured women who were movement leaders and labor organizers in the 1930s. The documentary creates an intersectional space, connecting the insights of the women's movement and labor struggle. It frames workplace struggle as consisting of brave people, principled actions, and unlikely leaders who emerge from everyday work conditions. Labor struggle is depicted as what average people do to survive the unrelenting forces of capitalism. The featured women provide the missing stories of radical organizing in the early labor movement, stories omitted from the epic, romanticized narrative. This challenge to traditional representation prompts a rethinking of labor history. Katie, one of the film's protagonists, describes the desperation workers felt as the economy began its downturn in 1930. After her company announced layoffs, Katie recounts how she felt and what she said to herself:

> My gosh, Katie. You have some responsibilities after all, you're a radical. You can't let this thing go by and keep your mouth shut and be a coward. So I lift my hand and said, "I protest." And everyone was shocked. I wrote an article to the *Daily Worker*, cut out the article and hung on the walls at work.[38]

When Katie returned to her department after hanging up her article, the women had turned off the machines and refused to work. Katie was fired along with the other women. Katie's identification with the larger radical-labor movement placed her action and subsequent firing as a success by disrupting the company work conditions for the greater good. She had earned her place as a radical leader. She was part of creating workplace "counter-rationality,"[39] an expression of worker subjectivity that demands human dignity. In the process of struggle, new identifications can form, and workers have opportunities to reconsider previous commitments with collective interests in mind. The audience identifies with this process of realignment and has a chance consider their own position. These representations of collective power and individual agency to combat powerful capitalist interests contribute to the substance of *Union Maids*. Recording history that is in danger of being lost to time by pointing the camera at undocumented stories elevates the narrative. Documentary becomes an act of preserving the memory of unrepresented existences and offering these silenced voices powerful recognition in the patchwork of history.

As the documentary unfolds, there is space for complexity and contradiction. Sylvia, one of the protagonists in the film, recounts a little-known laundry workers' sit-down strike, "not in the history books." She suggests that it might have been the very first sit-down strike. The missing premise of Sylvia's statement is clear: some history is not counted, especially history made by black people. Sylvia talks about growing up with a father who was a Garveyite, a follower of a form of Black

Nationalism founded on the thinking of Marcus Garvey. She describes the pride of black culture and the undocumented narratives of black people articulating resistance to white supremacy during the Progressive Era in the United States. In their filmmaking, Reichert and Klein are particularly skilled at constructing a broad narrative that takes into account contradictions in history, such as the longstanding racism that pervaded the labor movement.

Both *Union Maids* (1976) and the documentary I will address next, *With Babies and Banners* (1979), create representations of womanhood that are strong, resilient, outspoken, and physically capable of fighting police. These films counter privileged representations of womanhood. When asked about the women's movement, one participant explains, "When you come from an area or economic base where you have choices, you know, you can't relate to people who have to work for a living in factories or in homes or offices."[40] There are hints of a socialist tradition in these projects and whispers of a radical history. Normative priorities for women are rejected in favor of a working-class subjectivity that is active and militant.

With Babies and Banners (1979), directed by Lorraine Gray, focuses on a 1937 United Auto Workers sit-down strike that won union recognition and increased wages, leading to better working conditions. The documentary exposes the ruthlessness of capitalist exploitation in the United States. Labor struggle is represented as an act of self-defense in the face of deadly working conditions, starving families, and workplace sexual assault. The women onscreen question authority and find meaning in union participation, becoming active agents and pioneers in the history of struggle.

The documentary reveals the specific ways women suffered in the workplace. Young women, who flooded into factories to seek work to support their families, were subject to sexual harassment, dangerous working conditions, and sexual blackmail. Women's presence in labor organizing contributed to the struggle but also changed the union culture. One participant recounted:

> When we first started coming up to the union hall, you must remember, that the union had been the domain of men. All of the craft unions, women never went up to the union meetings. They weren't wanted and when we first started coming up there, men were suspicious. Some would say, "They are on the make." No. So I didn't wear any make up. I let my hair go straight to let them know. I had to tell a number of men off. When I began playing a little more aggressive role, then they thought perhaps, there is a deeper reason why we were up there and they called us "the queers" at that time.[41]

In response to labor representations that were predominantly heteronormative and white, these films document labor history from the bottom up, revealing the shortcomings of union culture and society in general. This challenge to traditional labor documentary representation suggests that audiences adopt antiracist, feminist, and queer labor identifications. Audiences see women who fought back; they carry concealed weapons, and they act in self-defense if necessary, projecting an image of embodied agency that challenges traditional union culture and gender roles:

> One thing, I think, came of the women being active, it gave men a different outlook on the ordinary housewife. Before, it had always been a housewife or a mother, that is the only image they had, but after the union was organized, it gave men a deeper respect for the working woman.[42]

With Babies and Banners (1979) tells a story of political struggle that confronts difference by forging solidarity. When done well, the representation of collective-identity formation around solidarity transforms the people involved, helping groups become more inclusive. The historical function of this documentary works in representing social change for public memory includes a largely unexpected labor protagonist, working women of which many are young and unmarried. The documentation of submerged labor history creates recognition and helps integrate the inclusion of marginalized stories into a larger public account of political struggle.

A thematically consistent collection of labor documentaries addresses solidarity organizing and the radical-labor tradition. Radical media makers are in a specific rhetorical situation as their discourse is fundamentally more active, appealing to resistance rather than petition or asking the powerful to change. Radical documentary calls on audiences to actively thwart compliance with injustice and to assert agency. There are hints of the radical labor tradition in *Union Maids* and *With Babies and Banners*, but the following documentaries represent an intentional recovery of suppressed labor histories woven with elements of socialism, anarchism, and communism.

In 1979, Deborah Shaffer released *The Wobblies*, a long-form history of the Industrial Workers of the World, a militant and historically marginalized organization formed to attack corporate greed. The IWW stood for "work, good wages, and respect" and fought for its members "to be people and not nobody." The documentary re-creates the material struggles of the 1930s with archival materials, moving images of industry, and still images of notable capitalists, edited together with recordings of their own public statements about exploitation. The narrative challenges conventional representations of labor from the perspective of those marginalized by the movement. This challenge expands the scope of potential political intervention. Mainstream labor viewed the radical IWW with suspicion. AFL President Samuel Gompers said the Wobblies were a "radical fungus on the labor movement, those who could not fit into a normal, rational movement."[43] Rearticulating workers' history through the story of the IWW provides a portrait of a labor struggle comprised of fully committed frontline fighters who purposefully walked into unorganized factories with the intention of confronting capitalist exploitation. The film places the IWW on the forefront of organizing immigrants and shows women in essential leadership roles. Given their propensity for street fights, the Wobblies suffered from intense police brutality and harassment that led to prison for some and the death penalty for others. *An Injury to One* (2002) represents a shift in the history of labor documentary in that it draws on experimental media strategies to explore the turn-of-the-century murder of union organizer Frank Little in Butte, Montana. *Joe Hill* (2015) is the story of charismatic union and labor organizer Joe Hill, whose controversial execution by the state of Utah in 1915 ignited protests across the country. Eventually, the Red Scare and police persecution fragmented radical organizing and pushed it into underground and countercultural spaces. This legacy is picked up in *Anarchism in America* (1983).

Anarchism in America (1983), directed by Steven Fischler and Joel Sucher, provides a time capsule of American cultural misconceptions about anarchism and the reverberation of anarchist ideas in popular culture. The documentary takes a broad look at anarchism as a concept; labor is part of the story but it is not at the center of the narrative. More time is dedicated understanding countercultural spaces occupied by diverse efforts to combat exploitation through the creation of new self-determined microsystems. The narrative attempts to make sense of disinformation and representations of anarchism that pivot around violence, disorder, and aggression. It dips in and out of the historical mode to explore how Americans negotiated this political inflection in the early 1980s. The camera maneuvers through a confrontation with police and a cocktail party at the First International Symposium on Anarchism in Portland, Oregon, and also embarks on a road trip to explore fragments of anarchism around the country. This story of alternatives to capitalism is a marginalized narrative in U.S. culture, and documentary filmmakers are among the few historians taking up these missing parts of history. After reflecting on the stories in *Union Maids*, Reichert and Klein embarked on their own effort to document an epic history in *Seeing Red* (1983). The documentary looks at the activities of members of the American Communist Party. Funded by the National Endowment for the Humanities and predigital crowd funding, the film was nominated for an Academy Award for best documentary feature. Like early labor films, these radical documentaries tend to use cultural production as a political act, attempting to shift labor's white male heteronormative identifications with new articulations of labor's more diverse protagonist, embodying an intersectional solidarity.

Radical film shifts the horizon line of possibility for change and action. Manifestations of radical labor struggle continue in underground spaces, on social media, and in autonomous community centers across the country. In the conclusion of his book, *Breaking the Spell: A History of Anarchist Filmmakers, Videotape Guerrillas, and Digital Ninjas*, Chris Robé laments the tendency of radical media culture to revisit familiar self-involved modes, glossing over the needs of the underrepresented voices of the radical community. He challenges radical media culture to reassess how participatory cultures negotiate privilege and inclusion. Our best way forward, according to Robé, is to become actively literate in the history of radical media traditions like Third Cinema,[44] the newsreel movement, the video guerrillas, and the impulses of radical documentary traditions. The knowledge enables contemporary activists to tap into the rich imagery, lessons, and possibilities of the past: "We don't have to watch history painfully repeat itself as farce . . . critically observe the wreckage of the past that keeps blowing us inexorably into the future."[45] These historical loops of repeating painful patterns suggest that different interventions are needed. Theories and concepts help order history, but critically informed production practice, an orientation of learning, thinking, and doing might move us out of these painful historical reveries.

COMMUNITY MEDIA INTERVENTIONS

The void of worker-created newsreels representing the interests of the rank-and-file resonated acutely throughout the 1970s and 1980s. Drastic cuts in public media funding required community leaders to intervene. The Labor Video Project began as a community access labor show in 1983 and grew into an international labor media production hub. One summer morning at a café in the Mission District in San Francisco, I met Steve Zelzer, the founder of the Labor Video Project. Reflecting on his thirty years of making grassroots labor documentary, he concluded: "[T]his world among working class people has to be recorded. Because otherwise it's lost. People go through struggles, and unless it's recorded, it's gone, it's just memories. And so the actual work of recording the struggles of the working class is vital to show the history of their struggle."[46] The nonfiction image fixes people in history, like a stamp of authentication or a photographic trail of existence. As a researcher, I have traveled this unpaved road of history where the only records are found in newspapers, official recordings, and forgotten archives in the closets of people who lived through this history. Leaflets, papers, and photographs are common, but when you find moving images, it is like discovering a pot of gold. Moving images freeze time in specific ways, capturing with it the sensory texture of the space recorded. Sometimes this includes a cacophony of sounds, providing remnants of the way people moved in the world, spoke for themselves, and held themselves in front of a crowd. Other times film captures the brave things people did when no one was looking. The history of labor documentary in the United States is the story of media makers leaving pieces of our collective soul behind in the form of documentary, so that it is not forgotten. The undeniable sensory experience of this history is there for us to experience, again and again, on the screen.

Labor Beat is a community news and television program born in Chicago in 1986 to bring labor news to people across the country. By the 1980s, the cultural labor support work present in 1930s in the form of theater troupes, newsreels, and other creative projects had disappeared. Recounting the lack of media infrastructure around labor struggles and the inspiration for *Labor Beat*, Larry Duncan explains, ". . . from the official labor movement, no publication in print or electronic that presents its view to the public" existed.[47] This prompted rank-and-file workers to pick up the camera again to defend themselves from the conservative media onslaught propping up neoliberal interests. This Chicago-based media organization was created to tell the stories of the working class. Still active today, it produces the longest running cable-television labor series in the United States.

I met Larry Duncan at a quiet labor hall on a week night, just outside of downtown Chicago. Larry was a founding member and backbone of Labor Beat, a cable access show that grew into a media archive for documenting rank-and-file union struggles throughout the United States and around the world. As Duncan states, "There's a lot of anti-union propaganda that's spread out through this big media ocean that the public is exposed to." From his perspective, big labor institutions have "made no efforts, really, to counter it."[48] This situation has a long but recent history. Duncan remembers that in the "'60s and '70s and '80s and '90s as a lot of the union internationals, in many ways, became more ossified, became more oriented toward accommodating the corporations, the membership had evolved and become more and more aware that they needed an independent voice in all of this."[49] Duncan stepped into this void and created Labor Beat, which became the longest running cable access labor series in the country. At the same time, Steve Zelzer was on the West Coast, working independently to address the need for cultural production around labor struggle.

From Duncan and Zelzer's perspective, in the last fifty years labor institutions have been too scared of losing control of central messaging or ambivalent about developing community media focused on labor struggle. The labor movement has no dedicated media apparatus to circulate the perspectives of the workers in public culture. Duncan recalls a moment in the mid-1970s when these media needs were required: "AFL-CIO called . . . contacted me and wanted to know if I'd go to Kansas City to record this [teacher's strike], cause they didn't know anybody else who was doing this kind of thing."[50] In the absence of support from big labor, Duncan and Zelzer took advantage of the opening cable access market to produce labor documentary, a project that was not always welcomed, as Zelzer explains:

> I think here in the United States we've made a concerted effort to get the AFL-CIO, the unions to have a similar priority to the development of labor media. One of the problems with [union] bureaucracy . . . is they're afraid of it. Because if it goes among regular people, if regular people start to make their own media, then it's not going to be a centralized top down control. And they're not necessarily interested in a lot of stories going out about what's

going on. They want to control the information. But this new technology means that the ability to control it is limited.[51]

The democratization of media and the inclusion of multiple voices through production can challenge the rigid institutional patterns that hamper collective engagement. Documentary is an effecting intervention with the capacity to confront the micro and macro conditions of power within the labor struggle. As these radical filmmakers fought the normalization of capitalism, others were addressing the contradictions of the migrant working class.

Documenting Lives across Borders

The capitalist drive to maximize profits increases the demand for cheap labor—a demand that crosses borders, evades laws, and seeks out vulnerable communities for exploitation. The story of labor documentary in the United States is inextricably tied to the U.S./Mexico border, a central gateway for bodies seeking survival under duress. Under neoliberal capitalism, labor has the freedom to migrate that people do not. This section outlines efforts to document labor struggle in the context of capital moving across borders to extract valuable resources from vulnerable communities. Most of this visual history is documented by people outside of migrant communities working in various collaborations with the people who struggle directly under these conditions. New representations seek to inspire political intervention, and early representations find a second life in contextualizing the historical narratives of these times.

Harvey Richards's archival interventions and robust documentation of migrant worker struggles made a unique contribution to documentary history. He documented some of the first images of migrant workers putting down their tools and walking off the job in the late 1950s. He recorded industrialization and mass production taking over farming practices as companies began to use giant machines to replace workers. He provided some of the only midcentury representations of striking farmworkers standing on roads in front of fields, holding protest signs. With the fires of the McCarthy era still smoldering, when most cultural producers went underground, Richards openly and prolifically recorded workers' struggle. His framing of images tended to be wide, creating moving portraits that speak to his initial practice as an amateur photographer. His style is reserved, occupied with work practices rather than the specific stories of workers' lives. In his films, though the narrative advances with a paternalistic voiceover, the content aligns with the interests of workers. Richards often names unions, such as United Packinghouse Workers of America (AFL-CIO), as producers of his documentaries, but it is unclear what sort of working relationships he had with the unions.

Documentary studies include little to no documentation of Richards's work. There are a few books about his photography,[52] a few articles from labor studies journals regarding his documentary work,[53] and little additional information about his production practice.[54] What we do know is that Richards had a significant career organizing unions, and his commitment to solidarity carried over into his documentary production practice, influencing his decisions about where to point his camera. He spent a lot of time traveling up and down the agricultural corridor of California, a route that produced three documentaries, including some of the first images of migrant farm culture in the 1950s.

In *Factory Farms* (1959), Richards introduces the conditions of migrant farmworkers to a middle-class white audience and the larger labor struggle. After photographing working conditions in California's Central Valley from 1958 to 1959, he made this documentary to provide portraits of family farming devastated by profit-hungry capitalists. The film provides representation for the migrant worker, a figure largely invisible in the growth economy of the United States. The voiceover begins with an attempt to position audiences in this unfamiliar world: "This is a story of California's greatest industry and its forgotten man. He doesn't work in oil or steel or construction. Nor aircraft or ship building or long shoring. He works in

Figure 4.6 Harvey Richards records the struggles of migrant farm families with arresting images of children in *Uno Veintecinco: the Lettuce Strike of 1962.*

Figure 4.7 Harvey Richards documents the early farm worker struggles in the early 60s in *Uno Veintecinco: the Lettuce Strike of 1962.*

Figure 4.8 Harvey Richards captures some of the first images of migrant farm workers striking in front of the fields during the early 60s in *Uno Veintecinco: the Lettuce Strike of 1962.*

Figure 4.9 Women were a significant part of the migrant farm workers, whole families worked in the fields during the early 60s in *Uno Veintecinco: the Lettuce Strike of 1962*.

agriculture, a 3 billion dollar industry." The documentary represents the agricultural laborer who is missing from the wider labor narrative focused on factories, mills, and mines. The conditions for the agricultural workers are dire; their bodies are used up by corporations that leave families in never-ending cycles of poverty.

In his subsequent documentaries, *The Harvesters* (1960) and *This Land Is Rich* (1966), Richards documents the impoverished and deteriorating conditions in which farmworkers labor and live. Viewers see children without shoes and people living on dirt floors with no running water or electricity. Richards creates a relationship between his production practice and union organizing through positioning of the audience, image montages, and voiceover. As other industries were reaping the benefits of the labor struggles in the 1930s, Depression-era poverty conditions persisted in the agricultural industry. This was one reason why Edward R. Murrow's *Harvest of Shame* (1960) was so galvanizing. Richards's and Murrow's works offer images that confront white middle-class culture with the underbelly of the working poor and the labor conditions behind the food consumed in American households. In the 1970s, filmmakers began documenting the growing agitation in the agricultural sector and beyond.

As part of the Deep Dish TV organization, Glen Pearcy directed *Fighting for Our Lives* (1975), a two-part series focused on the history of the United Farm Workers.

Unlike Richards's work, which can be abstract and focused on work practices, Pearcy's documentary begins with a scene of police brutality and an antagonistic confrontation between bosses and union workers. It is an immersive experience; the camera is in the middle of the confrontation and is later pushed off the farm field by company security. This documentary encourages identification with the power of collective agitation through solidarity and strikes and includes powerful representations of the march from Delano. In 1966 Cesar Chavez led a 300-mile march from Delano to Sacramento, the state's capital. A coalition of Latino and Pilipino workers embarked on this march in protest of poor pay and working conditions. The audience sees workers as active agents of self-determination in the face of police resistance. Farmworkers speak for themselves, in contrast to the heavy-handed narration of Richards's earlier documentaries.

At the turn of the century, we begin to see the wide expanse of capitalist exploitation represented in documentaries and a flood of activity around migrant labor documentary. These works extend the struggle beyond the agricultural fields. *Senorita Extraviada* (2002) addresses the missing and murdered women around the factory towns on the U.S./Mexico border. *Maquilapolis* (2006), by Sergio De La Torre and Vicky Funan, depicts working conditions in one of Tijuana's *maquiladoras*—factories run by multinational companies that come to Mexico seeking cheap labor. These films document exploitation as it moves out of the fields, finding other vulnerable markets for exploitation. Undocumented and migrant workers, desperate for a better life and suffering under the global market that allows for the free movement of products but not people, find themselves trapped between worlds.

Los Trabajadores (2003), directed by Heather Courtney, captures the construction and real estate industry boom that created demand for a flexible class of workers leading to a controversial day labor program in Austin, Texas. Hart Perry's intriguing *Valley of Tears* (2003) tells the story of agricultural workers' struggles in Raymondville, Texas, as filmed over twenty-four years, beginning in 1979. While films like these echo the themes in Richards's work, they tend to take a more agitational stance. *Valley of Tears* captures workers standing up to the white bosses who exploit the migrant community. *Maid in America* (2005), by Anayansi Prado, addresses the rise in demand for domestic labor, tracing the lives of three of the 100,000 domestic workers living in Los Angeles. *Made in L.A.* (2007) follows three powerful Latina garment workers as they fight exploitative working conditions while global corporations fight culpability. The documentary addresses issues of immigration, factory flight, and organized demand for economic justice. Anne Lewis takes on the global shifts affecting migrant working communities living in the mountain towns of east Tennessee in *Morristown* (2007). In 2008, another labor struggle involving mostly Latino immigrant workers at a window factory in Chicago made the headlines. Andrew Friend directed *Workers Republic* (2010) to document the people whose lives and livelihoods were radically transformed by the 2008 economic downturn. As millions of workers lost their jobs, these workers in Chicago fought back and occupied their factory. The situation was a throwback to the kinds of labor stories documented in the 1930s, but this time the camera was inside the factory. *The Harvest* (2010) portrays the current horrors of child labor in the agricultural industry in the United States. Between the time of the early farmworker struggles documented by Richards and the present, working conditions have become increasingly dire, especially for undocumented children under the age of twelve who are subject to heat exposure, pesticides, and dangerous working conditions. Throughout the extensive body of documentary work centered on migrant communities, immigrant workers, and capitalist exploitation, patterns of globalization and neoliberalism are clear. We see this association again each time the workers make gains and exploitation moves or shifts into a different form.

The most iconic documentaries of the farmworker struggles are those focused on the best-known leader of the farmworker movement, Cesar Chavez. *Fight in the Fields* (1997) tells the story of the successful drive to organize farmworkers in the United States, canonizing Cesar Chavez as the center of this narrative and documenting his life from his adolescence as a migrant farmworker to his early years as a community organizer. It also documents Chavez's political alliance with Robert Kennedy. After this film came *Cesar's Last Fast* (2014), directed by Ray Perez and Lorena Parlee, which told the story of Chavez's thirty-six-day water-only hunger strike in 1988. Chavez embarked on this hunger strike to draw attention to the poisoning of migrant workers.

While Chavez is widely known in the popular imagination, the stories of the Filipino community, which has always been a sizable segment of the farmworker struggle, are rarely told. *Delano Manongs* (2014) begins to address this lack, telling the story of labor organizer Larry Itliong, who instigated the Delano Grape Strike of 1965 and helped create the United Farm Workers. He organized 1500 Filipinos to strike, forming a collaboration with Chicano workers that would continue for years. Intersections of identity formation, such as the role of groups like the Filipino agricultural workers in the largely Chicano farmworkers movement, remain part of labor history that requires further exploration. The case of Harvey Richards' documentation of early farmworker struggles and other political movements illustrates the circulatory patterns of this unique footage.

The power of Richards's work is felt when it is transformed into historical documentary source material. His films are particularly intriguing in their secondary life as historical source material, recontextualized in a variety of cultural objects, artifacts, and other movies. Richards's films have been licensed for use in over seventy documentaries, TV productions, books, magazines, feature films, and exhibits.[55] His footage is used as historical source material in documentaries such as *Berkeley in the Sixties, Eyes on the Prize, Fight in the Fields: Cesar Chavez and the Farmer Struggle*, and *Chicano! History of the Mexican American Civil Rights Movement*. It also appears in feature fiction films such as *Fear and Loathing in Las Vegas* and *Panthers*. In this case, the transformation of documentary footage into historical source material means that Richard's representations live on as iconic images of historical record.

The Great Recession of 2008 and the resulting shifts in labor exploitation produced a new wave of documentaries. The legacy of antiglobalization organizing and the emergence of the Occupy Wall Street movement demonstrate shifts in how groups organize against capitalism. As lines of exploitation expand, a new representation of the exploited worker takes center stage.

Labor and Public Work

Public workers' struggles are an untold story of the labor movement. Most labor documentary focuses on tensions between workers and corporate capitalism. As foreshadowed in Tami Gold's *Signed, Sealed and Delivered* (1980), however, public workers are consistently exploited by state entities, complicating the traditional agitation between workers and for-profit companies. In 2010, waves of Republicans were elected to political office as the Democrats were blamed for the failing economy. In Wisconsin, Republican Scott Walker won the gubernatorial race by a narrow margin. Once in office, he attempted to fix the state's financial problems by cutting wages and benefits for public workers. The "boss" in this case is the state government, a situation that significantly redraws the lines of the labor struggle. The unprecedented regression of workers' rights and benefits in Wisconsin ignited waves of demonstrations and protests. This time, the hostile working conditions were not found in fields, assembly plants, or factories, but in the offices and classrooms of state employees, representing the imploding middle class and all its fragility.

We Are Wisconsin (2011), directed by Amie Williams, follows the twenty-six days that Wisconsin citizens occupied the state capital in response to Walker's cuts. This representation of labor struggle shows new activists, former anti-union sympathizers, and young students rising together to address the governor's attack on public employees. The documentary represents middle-class white people who are surprised to find themselves on the protest line. A new alliance emerges as police officers, who are employees of the state, join the protest by bringing food into the state rotunda, where students are occupying the capital, carrying signs that say, "Cops for Labor" and "Deputies for Democracy." This appearance of the police in a labor protest was unprecedented; from the 1926 riot footage until this moment, law enforcement was exclusively represented as antagonistic to labor and engaged in protecting business interests.

As Goes Jainsville (2012) is a portrait of a small town in Wisconsin recovering from the decline of the auto industry. Opportunities had evaporated in a place where families used to make a working-class living. The documentary covers the attack on collective bargaining in 2011 through the lens of the people struggling with the collapse of the middle class and a widening gap between rich and poor. In the opening scenes of *Wisconsin Rising* (2014), directed by Sam Mayfield, we see state lawmakers strip collective bargaining rights from citizens. The state rotunda is packed with activists chanting, "Occupy! Occupy! Occupy!" The film portrays Wisconsin as the canary in the coal mine for America's working class, focusing on workers' rights issues with the backdrop of the state's labor history.

Figure 4.10 In *Wisconsin Rising* (2014) solidarity is forged across many different communities of workers.

Figure 4.11 Feeling the impacts of unregulated election funding, an activist in *Wisconsin Rising* (2014) carries a sign against the Citizens United ruling.

Figure 4.12 Police march inside state capital in support of the state worker protest in *Wisconsin Rising* (2014).

Figure 4.13 Early in the protest, police did not remove anyone from the capital sit-in, those conditions changes when the state settles a contract with police unions but not the rest of the workers in *Wisconsin Rising* (2014).

Figure 4.14 Police use cameras to record activities in the occupied capital in *Wisconsin Rising* (2014).

Figure 4.15 Damon Terrell talks about his experience protesting at the capital in *Wisconsin Rising* (2014)

In this crisis in public work, there is a return to documentary as mirror. The representations in these films force a difficult look at a familiar struggle. Audiences are confronted with the vulnerability of working life that affects a broad spectrum of professionals. Political lines shift beneath the lives of middle-class Americans faster than representations can reflect these shifts, and the narratives overflow with sadness, anger, and regret. The safety net of the New Deal is quickly evaporating, and contemporary labor documentaries forge collective identification with a widening class of working poor. The focus is on unrecognized and exploited workers, from state employees to contingent professionals.

In 2011, Occupy Wall Street emerged in opposition to global economic inequality to protest the influence of corporations on government. This ushered in a series of documentaries capturing radical opposition to corporate greed and the creation of oppositional space. *The Hand That Feeds* (2015) represents the cultural patterns of struggle, consensus decision making, and alternative need networks influenced by the Occupy Movement that gave shape to the workplace struggles of undocumented immigrant workers. The film shows one group of workers' fight for human rights and dignity in the service industry of New York City. As labor culture shifted, so did the production culture around making labor documentaries. The last section of this chapter considers the production culture of labor documentary from the perspective of those shaped by this history.

Production Culture and Documentary Labor

"Do we really talk about women and labor anymore? As part of a workforce? Or class-consciousness? I mean, those issues have been swept under, I think, in favor of the personal story."
> —Judy Hoffman, documentary media maker and activist

As I was completing field interviews for this project, I found my way to the office of independent media producer Barbra Abrash, who served as the associate director for the Center for Media, Culture, and History at New York University. Abrash was one of the early independent filmmakers on the scene. I naïvely asked, "Can you talk a little bit more about what it was like to be a woman entering into a field that was male-dominated?" She replied, amused: "Oh, independent film was never male-dominated. Not when I came in to it. There were a lot of rowdy women."[56]

While popular memory encourages us to consider women in the United States during the 1970s as Betty Friedan-reading housewives, there is another dimension of women's history that is rarely explored by scholars. Women in that era assumed leadership roles because of the radical subjectivities they produced in the workplace. A focus on these activist requires considering a representation of womanhood that threatens the social order. These radical subjectivities—those of women committed to root causes and changing deeply ingrained systems—are among the missing stories of documentary history. The labor documentaries of the 1970s and 1980s produced by women provide an abundant opportunity to understand this production culture through the representations it produced. These women are also navigating unequal labor conditions and production processes in an active space of public agency that was unprecedented at the time.

The guerrilla media movement was a loosely connected network of activist and video artists across the United States who produced media that challenged the aesthetic form and content of mainstream institutions in the late 1960s and throughout the 1970s. The work of award-winning documentary filmmaker and labor activist Tami Gold, who was affiliated with what was then known as New York Newsreel, and the work of labor activist Judy Hoffman of the Kartemquin Film Collective in Chicago, represented an expressive political resistance and instrumental agency negotiated with the documentary camera. Media history is often silent about the women who significantly contributed to this culture.

Tami Gold has been producing social justice films in New York City for over thirty-five years. In the early 1970s, she began developing her skills at New York Newsreel and DCTV, and working with the revered George Stoney. Gold intentionally produced work outside mainstream documentary practice, creating collaborations with the communities she documented. Around the same time, Judy Hoffman was becoming an early producer of alternative video at the Kartemquin Film Collective in Chicago. Hoffman, who worked closely with Jean Rouch for several years, was interested in process filmmaking for social change.[57] She sought to capitalize on video's unique potential as a medium for political struggle. Both women began working in alternative media at the time of the transition from 16-millimeter film to early video portapaks. Both worked as antiracist and radical labor activists in their communities, maintaining pedagogical commitments to community media training through DCTV in New York City for Gold, and Videopolis in Chicago for Hoffman. What is unique about both of these filmmakers is how intimately they are connected to the working-class communities they document and how profoundly that connection affects their productions.

The next section, which focuses on Gold and Hoffman's experiences as alternative media producers, addresses these filmmakers' innovative approaches to inscribing activist elements into the production process. We see how their strategies for resisting a production culture were situated deeply in lifestyle politics and male leadership. Together, Gold and Hoffman produced a body of video work that functions as a critical interruption to mainstream media and its systems of labor.

GUERRILLA TELEVISION: "NO ONE OWNS THIS SHIT"

Gold and Hoffman encourage a critical reading of guerrilla production culture, free from the idealized utopian notions of alternative media. Both filmmakers describe alternative media as a place where working-class people could have a voice, working comfortably within constraints. As Hoffman remembers: "Video was a way for women to work. It was a new, you know, technology, and women who had been kept out of film because it's so nepotistic and you had to be male . . . white male born into it, video seemed to be a choice that women could, you know, could do."[58]

However, "there was a kind of a false democracy that we didn't, you know, want to address. I think we're in kind of a denial about it. But there was no doubt that the men had the power for the most part."[59] Here Hoffman is referring to her experience as part of Chicago's Kartemquin Film Collective, one of the participatory media groups that emerged in the 1960s to provide broader and more democratic access to resources and media production training. Tami Gold recounts a similar experience working with New York (now Third World) Newsreel: "So, in Newsreel, I was pretty voiceless, to be honest. I was young, I didn't come from a school, I, you know, felt insecure. So, being with the educated folks that were the filmmakers and things like that, I really deferred totally." Gold continues, "And just because we're alternative cinema makers doesn't mean that we have the recipe for how to treat each other better. I don't think so."[60] On the West Coast, filmmaker Lourdes Portillo echoes this experience with production culture: "[T]hat was the only way a Chicana could get into film. I don't think that the possibilities of entering the industry, the film industry, were there for us at all. But I saw them in documentary. People were open, were willing to take you on." While independent media culture provided unique spaces for alternative expressions of agency, articulating this agency in documentary culture was still challenging. Gold concludes: "I think that I found the space within that world to carve out my voice, but [I also found that my voice] was not one that could find, you know, very easy homes."[61] Existing on the fringes of the mainstream, women in independent media created direct relationships between lived experience, the camera, and political engagement, producing a kind of radical media discourse magnified by the documentary camera. As Judy Hoffman explained, "So I think it, you know . . . you wanna . . . like Eisenstein, put a . . . throw a firecracker . . . have firecrackers in the seats of people in the audience."[62] Hoffman understands radical documentary as a jolt that can prompt realignment with action in the world.

The political upheaval of the years of early video combined with the emergence of video technology helped create new visual forms of vernacular moving images. Street recording made it possible for citizen-produced content to come out of everyday life. Recordings of the streets, meetings, and private conversations provided a window into events and spaces that older, more cumbersome and expensive, equipment rarely recorded. These new recordings captured places that were the domain of the working class, where the camera could meet citizens in public spaces of vernacular dissent. When recording a labor strike in Chicago, Hoffman remembers a discussion about distribution: " 'Well, let's show it in Grant Park'. So, we got a generator and a couple of TVs and stands and put them up and played the tape for all the, you know, the general strikers to watch, but also to embarrass the people in the offices and other people would come by, and there were no rules at that point, you know?"[63] Radical discourse carries its own conditions, functions, and orientation to power, especially when leveled by women; this is not your mother's public dissent.

Both women made a concerted effort to resist the dominant means of media production and traditional filmmaking conventions. Gold reflects on her time working in independent media production: "On the other hand, I've been very clear. I could not make it in a mainstream sector, section of life. I couldn't, because I would resist too much. I wouldn't be able to make all the compromises."[64] Hoffman says she is, ". . . not just counter-culture in a kind of hippy way, but to have counter-media, you know . . . at least for me, I was not looking for inclusion, you know? I wanted to be on the edge in that, you know, and on the border."[65] Incredible political work with documentary happens in the community, on the margins, in the streets, and with pop-up political sites of our choosing.

BODIES THAT MATTER

Documentary history occasionally acknowledges its own exclusionary undercurrents and the absence of women in the field, but it is still difficult to address the issue of the bodies of working women making contact with the patriarchal structure of culture. In my research, I discovered that the results of this contact include everything from equipment constraints to the repercussions of assault and violence.

Workplace systems that marginalize women require women to make adjustments and confront unexpected obstacles. Gold recounts being on one field shoot while breastfeeding her first child. She strapped the portapak camera onto her chest because it was easier to carry: "It was not a long time after giving birth. And, I had to press play and record all the time so that we could record on the tape. And, having been in this state of nursing, my breasts were pretty large and they kept turning the machine off."[66] Gold is referring to the power button on early portapaks, located near the area where the pack was strapped on the chest:

> **A:** [*laughter*] That was one time where physical . . . the physicality of the chunkiness of the equipment felt like a drag.
> **A:** I kept saying, "Oh, something's wrong with the deck! It keeps going off."
> **Q:** And you're, like, "Oh, those are my boobs." [*laughter*]
> **A:** Yeah, I said, "These are my boobs. Just lactating. . . ."[67]

While Gold's experience was quite lighthearted, that is often not the case for women when their bodies come up against male-oriented and designed production equipment.

Every day women encounter a culture that encourages violence toward their bodies. In the study of production culture, we rarely understand how women navigate the intersections of this violent culture and the demands of production. Recounting how long it took to edit an important activist film about striking medical professionals, Hoffman recounts:

A personal thing happened during that time. I was raped. And that really sent me for a loop, you know? They did catch the guy. And . . . so, I was in the criminal justice quagmire for years dealing with it. And I think it really screwed me up and affected my, you know, my ability to, you know, really, like, work on the tape. So . . . but it did finally get finished, in a different form than, you know, I would have maybe initially anticipated. But it got cut.[68]

Women's bodies collide with the urgency and importance of their activist media work. The stakes of activist media demand rapid production and circulation because real life unfolds as the camera stops recording. Representations of struggle can only function as intervention within a limited window of time and in conjunction with organized movement. Often, the life of media makers comes up against the arena of political struggle, causing conflict in time, ethics and resources. Gold and Hoffman articulate the ways working-class identification can affect the production process and their experiments with the camera as a mode of engagement.

CRAFTING COALITIONS

Filmmaker Barbara Kopple, director of *Harlan County, USA*, reflects on issues similar to those faced by Gold and Hoffman as she discusses negotiating working-class identification in the film production process. Kopple first became politically engaged when she was in college and joined the antiwar movement. In her early career, she worked with the Maysles on the documentary *Salesman*. She describes her commitment to community as she struggled to finance *Harlan County, USA*, "I went to a few producers who'd say, 'Why is a little girl like you doing a film like this?'" Kopple's challenges in making *Harlan County* were determined by the gender and class barriers to her filmmaking rather than the difficulty of the subject matter. Her commitment to collective identification extended beyond the production of the documentary. The needs of the community in Harlan Country were more immediate than the needs of the production process. Kopple reflects:

> It was also feeling that I was engaged in a struggle, and that even if I didn't have any film in the camera, it was important for me to be there because having a camera there kept down violence. Also, the people there really needed to know that there were other people that cared about them and supported them. It was a part of my life. I was there, and I lived there for a long time, and I lived with them, and I wanted to stay.[69]

She moved to Kentucky, lived in the community, and, by her own account, that experience changed her. In the distribution contract, she asked for the following conditions: ". . . that the film will not be recut; that the film will be able to be used by workers for free or the cost of the mailing or whatever they can afford; that it can be used for political benefits—things like that."[70] The workers' struggle came first. Many of the ethical problems surrounding the practice of documentary and social change arise when these priorities are inverted.

Radical women making media declare their public agency while critiquing power relationships through the documentary camera. These media makers are not circulating petitions or asking for grievances to be acknowledged by the power structure. Instead, they consistently defy the powerful in the interests of the working class, limiting the authority of others. These are not the conditions in which the privileged, institutionalized, and sanctioned directors of documentary history operated. Radical documentary discourse systematically rejects the normative in the name of a better tomorrow and urges an awakening of consciousness. Protest or dissent is more widely studied in documentary discourse when it is directed against institutions and the structural authority to seek power, justice, and solidarity. Radical documentary discourse takes the form of rebellion, challenging systems and power structures with an act of refusal to enter the system as a means of seeking freedom. Tami Gold, Judy Hoffman, Julia Reichert, Lourdes Portillo and Barbra Kopple's early work represents a small part of a whole community of radical activist women who carved out spaces for themselves in the counterculture beginning in the early 1970s and who continue to engage in social change activism with their documentary cameras. With the exception of Kopple, their films are rarely hailed as part of the canon of documentary film history; but the political engagement and impact of their work is worthy of more documentation and study.

Conclusion

Labor documentary in the United States produced rare progressive representations of people from diverse cross sections of society. Most histories of documentary's civic potential begins with British filmmaker John Grierson. While I do not deny the importance of his civic interventions, when we focus on social change documentary more broadly, the historical markers shift, and we must begin by focusing on black film production in the United States during the silent era, a largely ignored and only ambivalently integrated history. Historians must critically consider decolonizing our familiar canons of documentary. We need to interrogate what is missing, making documentary history more inclusive and reflective of all people.

Women have played a dominant role in labor documentary, providing some of the most progressive images of workers and struggling communities before these representations were accessible and considered significant to mass audiences. Women directors, sometimes working in dangerous and hostile environments, foregrounded the stories of marginalized people as a way to contribute to public memory. Some of the most progressive representations of women in documentary history come from these labor narratives that unapologetically articulated working-class perspectives and interests as a means of survival.

A more complete picture of labor documentary history requires us to expand our understanding of collective identification. I have argued that collective identification is often understood as a rhetorical device located on the screen, but collective identification happens throughout the documentary production process. Collective identification can take place long before a film is screened. It is a function of how the director understands the relationship between him or herself and the community being recorded; it is in the way vernacular communities are integrated into the creative process; and it is endemic to the circulation of documentary discourse and its connection to movements of people organizing for change. The articulation of collective identification in the documentary process is a rich source for exploration.

Collective identification and agency are central to understanding political mobilization. Documentary is remarkably effective at facilitating collective formations, especially when audience members have contact postviewing. The quality and investment of audience dialogue is important. It can range from hashtag discussions to in-person political organizing meetings. For labor documentary—in a world before online communities—face-to-face organizing provided the space for discussion, speaking out, and solidifying collectively shared interests, with the intention of engaging in struggles beyond the screen. Organizing is the foundation of documentary history, particularly labor documentary history, so the focus on collective identification and social change reflects the ways agency expands and contracts under specific historical conditions. It is why so many media makers in this chapter understand documentary as a powerful organizing tool. Documentary can create a public commons grounded in working-class subjectivity that can revive working-class identification and instill urgency in viewers to act in the world.

The gap between intention and achievement is wide in labor documentary, as it is in most areas of social change documentary. Agency generated through collective identification remains even when a specific labor campaigns fails, however, and this is essential for the long-term achievement of political ends. Emotion, embodiment, narrative, and spectacle may trigger the urgency to act, but sustained relationships of solidarity are built on broader, more systematic critiques of power. The effects of capitalist exploitation compound themselves in people's lives in ways that can be located, defined, and identified in terms of working-class interests.[71] Although worker experiences are individual, clear patterns of exploitation emerge in worker relationships to capitalist modes of production. These shared experiences, when articulated through documentary, create a powerful mode of consciousness that addresses root causes and engenders solidarity.[72] Workers have a great deal to gain from parsing counterarguments to neoliberal capitalism. This articulation is essential to gaining support for campaigns, creating widespread cohesion, and galvanizing people to choose a side in the struggle. Documentary production creates a space not only for collective-identity formation but also agency. By telling stories—especially those narrated by vernacular and undocumented voices—workers are transformed into subjects in self-authored narratives that offer an active and reflective agency that has repercussions beyond the immediate struggle.

5

Subjugated Histories and Affective Resistance

Abortion Documentaries as Botched Political Subjectivity

> *[T]here is no pain worse than a story that needs to be told*
> *and has been kept suppressed.*
> —Jennifer Baumgardner, feminist writer and
> producer of *I Had an Abortion*

Since the 1970s, documentary media have engaged the shifting cultural climate around women's reproductive health in the United States in complex ways. Many documentary efforts have sought to mediate, intervene, and shift the confounding tensions around women's reproductive health issues, including access to abortion. In the last fifty years, abortion documentary has adopted various modes of production, from conversation films to grand historical narratives. Abortion documentary gives voice to the "unspeakable problem" in *It Happens to Us* (1972), spans multiple perspectives in *What If You Had No Choice?* (1982), employs powerful storytelling in *Leona's Sister Gerri* (1995), and explores the extensive historical narrative in *From Danger to Dignity* (1995). These documentaries are not always easy to watch, even for an audience politically aligned with the politics of reproductive justice. The films detail sustained traumatic violence on the bodies of women, a repressed history, and well-documented political aggression by religious conservatives that continues unabated. The persistent violence of abortion rhetoric produces a representation of abortion that pivots on emotion. The affective responses this tactic elicits in the bodies of audience members has yet to be explored. Film theory's focus on revolutionary aesthetics means we know too little about "the politicized body of [the] spectator."[1]

Some scholarly works have considered the representation of abortion on television and in motion pictures[2] but have paid little attention to how the documentary genre crafts public space for this controversial issue. In one of the few research articles on women's reproductive health films, Shilyh Warren observes, "Nonfiction

Figure 5.1 *It Happens to Us* (1973) by Amalie Rothschild represent women discussing the conditions of abortion.

Figure 5.2 The condition of abortion come with fractured feelings in a culture of shame in *It Happens to Us* (1973)

Figure 5.3 Women directly address the camera with their point of view in *It Happens to Us* (1973).

Figure 5.4 The issue of abortion reverberates across a women's lifespan in *It Happens to Us* (1973)

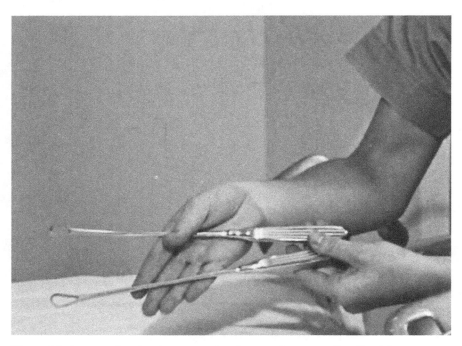

Figure 5.5 In many abortion documentaries, the narratives attempt to dispel the secrecy around the procedure by showing instruments in *It Happens to Us* (1973).

representations of abortion are rarely singled out for attention by the mainstream press, and these generally come into the public eye through sensational reporting."[3] This sensational reporting often frames abortion in terms preferred by social conservatives, as a source of shame and the result of unruly sexual behavior.

In addition to traditional documentaries about abortion, a growing archive of grassroots videos constitutes an emerging, loosely structured participatory media culture. Young women are using their mobile recording capabilities—mostly webcams and cell phones—to document the process of having an abortion, in real time and in retrospect. These representations are personal and vulnerable affective exchanges. Streaming on YouTube and circulating among interested viewers, these media works are not positioned as products for paid entertainment. Instead, they act as expressions of what is usually shrouded in private and unavailable for public view. These documentaries about abortion are a form of video confessional, creating intimacy through self-disclosure and exploring the emotional experience of abortion as a form of political action.[4]

This chapter considers how documentary practices engage affects, feelings, and emotions as strategies of activism and resistance. Affect, often understood as the opposite of reason and deliberation, is not well understood as a component of documentary activism, protest, and resistance.[5] Emotion, the narrativizing of affect, is accepted as a part of political struggle. We know little about how affective registers shape and guide public discourse; this gap in scholarship has contributed to political silence, narrow frameworks of understanding, and deliberative stalemates. The present chapter explores how the affective registers around abortion shape the public rhetoric, impacting agency, collective identification, and documentary circulation.

Many abortion documentaries belong to a category of production that is often ignored by historians and film scholars: the smaller than micro-budget documentary. These media exist primarily thanks to the will of their creators, with little to no institutional support. Evolving with a strong Do-It-Yourself impulse, these works are not motivated by the prospect of economic return. Instead, these political interventions are inspired by the possibility of imbuing audiences with the urgency to act in the world. Existing on the fringes of the market, these films are financed by their creators and sometimes circulate for free; by removing cost barriers to access, they intensify the documentary's impact. These smaller-than-micro-budget films often exceed the concept of entertainment. This media can take many forms: the social and political utility of the documentary is significant, but the cinematic experience can range from dull to uncomfortable and may be unwatchable. We might not want to see what the director asks us to witness; the message may go against the collective wisdom of the day; or the documentary may give space and dignity to people or issues that are not recognized in public culture. These forms of feminist documentary intervention often utilize a talking-head political aesthetic and other realist strategies that have been relegated to the dustbin of cinema history.

Alex Juhasz has documented the steady erasure of conventional political documentary—talking head, cinéma vérité, or realist approaches—from legitimate film history. In the 1980s and 1990s, these kinds of working-class documentary approaches were characterized as "not sophisticated, or even legitimate, formal strategies."[6] Responding to scholars like E. Ann Kaplan and Eileen McGarry, who are skeptical of realism's ability to challenge political consciousness, Juhasz points out that working feminist media makers have steadily relied on realism, despite scholars' preoccupation with psychoanalytic feminist analysis.

In the last fifty years, documentaries about abortion have served a variety of utilitarian and community needs. In the last ten years, these works have become more mainstream, circulating in popular commercial outlets like HBO and Showtime and successfully screening on the festival circuit. In spite of this critical success, they still experience a modest commercial return. The documentary efforts of the past decade signal an important shift from the tight focus on confession to a larger structural critique of the unavoidable circumstances women encounter without access to safe and affordable reproductive health care. This chapter traverses this terrain, tracing abortion documentary from Do It Yourself confessions to representations of a street war that continues to rage in the United States.

The history of feminist abortion documentary is full of contradictions. Feminism is a contestable space where conflicts around ideology, inclusiveness, tactics, strategies, and positionality work themselves out through cultural expressions, objects, and rituals. In 2005, third wave feminists seeking public language for their experiences with abortion began to produce documentary media. The tension that contextualizes these films is generational, demonstrating the rhetorical and affective chasm between second and third wave feminist. Director Penny Lane explains the source of this tension as "anger on the part of some older women who didn't understand why the younger women didn't care" about abortion.[7] At the same time, another tension is coming to the surface of the U.S. feminist discourse, a fissure around social mobility. Scholarship has examined how modes of education, professionalism, and social mobility influence feminist movements. We see this borne out in feminist documentary film, where production processes and creative choices reveal ideological positions. These insights provide a critical window into how specific feminist expressions navigate issues such as mobility and inclusion within larger feminist rhetoric and its strategic alliance with neoliberalism.

This chapter focuses on a moment —in 2005 and beyond— when third wave feminist filmmakers, who were mostly white, professional, and activist in orientation, attempted to engage abortion politics through a confessional mode. In 2005, feminists Gillian Aldrich and Jennifer Baumgardner directed *I Had an Abortion*. Aldrich and Baumgardner are professionals and activists: Aldrich works in activist filmmaking, producing for Michael Moore, and Baumgardner is a noted feminist author, writing such notable third wave feminist volumes as *Manifesta: Young Women, Feminisms and the Future* and *Grassroots: A Field Guide for Feminist Activism*. Baumgardner is known for her contributions to the public articulation of third wave feminism, exploring the disconnection between generations of women and the new politics that merge in this shift. *I Had an Abortion* (2005) had visibility in professional activist circles, including coverage by institutional and commercial feminist establishments. In contrast, filmmaker Penny Lane created a similar, but more independent, documentary, *The Abortion Diaries* (2005). This film presents a do-it-yourself aesthetic, including kitchen table discussions about how abortion affected the lives of educated, working-class, and poor women as they resist the tendency to make the act of abortion a secret. Both documentaries circulated in feminist and educational communities, and both highlight the tensions that exist in neoliberal inflections of feminism between mobility feminism and intersectional feminism, tensions that reverberate today.

Mobility feminism operates within the logics of neoliberalism. The focus is on the (re)creation of a feminist heritage tale, establishing women's equal representation across sectors of society, even when those mobility paths exist in oppressive organizations, and establishing freedom through the discourses of representation in professional careers. Intersectional feminism includes those interested in apprehending social reality for people through an integrated approach, invested in "social, cultural, economic and political dynamics as being multiple and determined simultaneously and interactively through various significant axes of social organizing."[8] Intersectional politics are an amplified response to the mobility priorities of popular feminism, which routinely aligns itself with neoliberal political interests at the expense of the most vulnerable within a community. Intersectional feminism amplifies voices and perspectives drowned out in dominant culture, providing space for narratives that are often eclipsed by the hegemony of mobility feminism. From this perspective, women do not have a single unified universal message. This impulse produces an alternative documentary vernacular that is messy, multivocal, contradictory, and process oriented. The recognition of all peoples' interests is made central to political action.

The post–2010 shift in documentary storytelling around abortion is notable for its intersectional impulses. With a few exceptions, white, middle-class women are the ones producing this documentary discourse, but there is a greater reflexivity about class and race, an awareness of the social and political structures that funnel women into choiceless circumstances. Yet, the tone and aesthetic of this documentary discourse is almost uniformly constructed for commercial broadcast. The films offer the distance of direct cinema paired with intimate, confessional interviews with women, and they address the political and heath care ecosystems that circulate around abortion. The earlier DIY impulse continues on YouTube and other streaming media, where young women share their own experiences in a youth culture still hungry for answers.

After five decades of documentary articulations of gendered subjectivity and reproductive health, certain cinematic strategies have become ingrained in the genre. The telling of experience and history through abortion documentary has constructed "a collective, visible, political subject who demands a universalized set of legal and social rights over her reproductive capacities, desires and possibilities."[9] Shilyh Warren argues that these documentaries are so preoccupied with telling women's stories that they fail to represent the actual abortion procedure. The lack of representation and the cultural silence surrounding abortion have produced a collective anxiety. From Warren's perspective, the "feminist audiovisual campaign in support of abortion has failed to fully exploit the possibilities of showing." She concludes that, "despite decades of productive telling, reproductive rights advocates are arguably losing the culture war over abortion."[10] I agree with Warren's conclusion. After five decades of feminist film on women's reproductive health, there is little evidence that documentary discourse has significantly contributed to resolving this ongoing political impasse. In fact, support for access to reproductive health has considerably retreated over the past several decades.

Despite failing to engage the political process directly, the participatory cultures of political engagement that emerged around media work focused on abortion should be explored. Warren makes a strong argument for showing the medical procedure itself, but I contend that this documentary work has an affective dimension that complicates its political force in the world. In her book *Moving Politics*, Deborah Gould articulates the force of emotion in the struggle for social change as *emotional habitus*, which is defined as socially constituted ways of feeling and emoting that can foreclose or open political horizons. The unruly quality of affect can disrupt emotional habitus, and these moments provide possibilities for social change.[11] Film scholar Jane Gaines identifies this process as political mimesis, a relationship between the bodies on the screen and the audience that produces a visceral impetus to "go beyond the abstractly intellectual to produce a body swelling."[12] Although emotional habitus are shared, they are also shaped by social conditions.

Marginalized groups have emotional habitus "influenced by a reigning emotional habitus in a society, but their contours derive as well from specific experiences of oppression."[13] The collective affective responses of marginalized communities, which are not widely understood in the dominant culture, result from social and structural oppression in the larger cultural habitus. The emotional habitus that surrounds abortion documentary is shaped by the affective regime that holds together a longstanding conservative heritage myth. The myth is a preservationist narrative that seeks to solidify the authority of the already powerful. According to Celeste Condit, this conservative heritage tale posits that "throughout the Western tradition, abortion has been written and spoken against by important institutional and moral authorities."[14] This potent myth contextualizes most of the public discussion about abortion in the United States.

Documentaries focused on abortion create affective encounters that move through the object of the documentary, orienting and (re)orienting localized and individual perceptions of hegemonic social relations. The films make use of the activist media practice of consciousness-raising, making the private experience of abortion public through confession. Known in feminist communities as "speaking out," documentary amplifies this confessional mode. Individual confessions become broadly compelling through their connections to a constellation of similar stories. This strategy emerges from an affective regime that precedes the production of these documentaries and contains the possibilities for identification and potential political agency. This tension between marginalized communities and the wider habitus must remain present in discussions around emotion and political intervention. This chapter traces the condition of affect in the history of abortion and the documentary impulse. Next, I explore the limitations of emotion as a form of political intervention with focus on two documentaries, *I Had an Abortion* and *Abortion Diaries*. Finally, I consider the bodily horror and nightmare heritage tale that continues to reverberate throughout U.S. cultural politics and its representation in documentary discourse.

Histories of Affect

American cultures rest on an assumption that political ideologies play out on the bodies of women, creating an affective environment that rests on a history of bodily subjugation. Tracking abortion advocacy rhetoric over decades in the United States, Celeste Condit identifies several shifts.[15] In the 1950s, we saw the emergence of widespread public rhetoric centering on powerful descriptions of illegal abortion. Doctors reported concern but only addressed professional issues, avoiding the larger social problems that suffused the discussion with unease and strong emotional responses.[16] Doctors and lawyers pushed professional boundaries while responding to the increased demand for abortion. In 1959, the American Law Institute sought to broaden permissions for abortion to include "committee-approved cases of rape, incest, fetal deformity and threats to the pregnant woman's health."[17] The voices of American women were largely absent from the discussion. In the 1960s, the "abortion problem" went from a professional issue to a public discussion. Magazines and newspapers began publishing vibrant descriptions of women's lives, tales of bodily trauma, and great loss. The women in these stories were sympathetic, and grisly descriptions of illegal abortion methods were dramatized in detail, framing illegal abortion as a racket—a seedy underworld of horrific abuse.[18]

Tension between new and old beliefs arose; people clutched at an ideal of motherhood defined by complete self-sacrifice, while also acknowledging the social conditions that motivated women to terminate pregnancies. In order to find public support, "abortion narratives had to use images of motherhood to argue for a choice against specific instances of motherhood."[19] If abortion was a "good" act, it had to be undertaken by "good" women. The larger public vocabulary began to accommodate stories about abortion, arguing that it was justified under certain conditions and for a certain kind of woman: a neoliberal subject who took full responsibility for balancing work and family. This led to enough public support to usher in a set of laws and commitments to abortion access, especially as public rhetoric incorporated the concerns of working women and their important role as wage earners.[20]

In response to these changes, a new and wildly persuasive anti-abortion narrative emerged. It wielded a powerful "heritage myth" to unify diverse groups that opposed abortion. The tale was simple and potent: This myth positioned the history of Christian morality and American culture on the side of eradicating abortion. Abortion was framed as an affective binary choice between murder and a life of love, motherhood, and sacrifice.[21] The rhetoric of reproductive choice attempted to challenge these terms by asserting women's agency and autonomy, but through the lens of the conservative heritage myth, this autonomy is equivalent to narcissism and selfishness.

In the 1970s and 1980s, the rhetoric around abortion centered on life, equality, and choice. These terms become "ideographs"—words open to interpretation that can be used as though they had clear meaning by people with competing ideological positions in the process of political struggle.[22] Over the next several decades, the ideological divides around abortion remained, and the conservative heritage myth grew more persuasive. Throughout the 1980s and 1990s, the conservative heritage tale became an accepted framework for public understanding about abortion, complete with an intense affective regime, complicating the reproductive justice struggle for years to come. This potent affective regime became a roadblock for any documentary attempting to navigate this public deliberative space. The flows of information are so powerful and the affective regime surrounding this issue is so pervasive that most people avoid trying to persuade others. This silence and resistance to public discussion, however, has not always been the case.

ABORTION DOCUMENTARY AND EMOTION

> *And if you [go through] all the history books on documentary, you won't find . . . you won't find that history.*
> —Debra Zimmerman, Executive Director of Women Make Movies

In 1982, Aimee Frank and Abigail Norman wrote *The Guide to Films on Reproductive Rights* and distributed it out of the New York City office of the Media Network, an organization that provided activists and educators with information on films and how to use them. Following a new wave of conservative electoral victories, activists and others were bracing for aggressive attacks on abortion access. Activists addressed these political conditions by producing films and creating screening cultures around reproductive rights documentaries. Frank and Norman began researching how reproductive rights films were being used and found that "the same half dozen films" were being screened again and again as tools of political organizing. In response, they gathered all the reproductive rights films circulating at the time, called together fifty panelists from diverse backgrounds, and screened over 100 films, videotapes, and slideshows. The project had a clear focus: "Our goal was to create a valuable resource for organizers, and we hoped that the Guide would encourage more of them to use media."[23] *The Guide* brought visibility to alternative film culture and included guidelines for stimulating productive discussion about the political issues at hand. For over five decades, feminists have initiated experiments in developing participatory media cultures and activist practices with the documentary impulse.

As these cultural battles are fought on the bodies of women, the documentary telling of this history—which often details how the violence of illegal abortion is exacted on the bodies of women—makes for difficult listening and watching. Women were experimenting with the documentary form, resulting in "further modification of the cinéma vérité legacy, unmaking not merely the camera but also the filmmaker, a reversing of the prior exploitation of the subject to create an empowerment of the subject."[24] Early abortion documentaries focused on the entire field of women's reproductive health, addressing the lack of information women were given about their bodies, reproductive capacity, and birth control. Amalie Rothschild's *It Happens to Us* (1972) is one of the first documentaries to give voice to women's experiences with abortion. The film, which offered stories from both before and after legalization, was presented in collaboration with New Day Films. Margaret

Lazarus's *Taking Our Bodies Back: The Women's Health Movement* (1974) is a powerful film that offered women information about their own bodies that had been withheld by the male-dominated health care industry. The documentary represents an active movement of women rethinking their own embodied subjectivity. This film covers a participatory self-exam, an educator's cervix display, and the birthing process at a women's clinic. One of the last scenes features a middle-aged woman walking into the health clinic seeking an abortion.

It was a documentary about reproductive health justice, *Healthcaring: From Our End of the Speculum* (1976), that prompted Women Make Movies to become a formal media distributor. Women Make Movies was founded in 1972 with the specific mission of training women to become media makers. It was the unprecedented success of distributing *Healthcaring* that encouraged the organization to eventually become the most important distributor of feminist film. Directed by Denise Bostrom and Jane Warren, *Healthcaring* focuses on the abuse women have suffered at the hands of male doctors and the lack of comprehensive health care for women. This intervention is revelatory in that "women [were] experts, people experts, not doctors necessarily, but women who have actually experienced problems with health care."[25] Debra Zimmerman, director of Women Make Movies, reflected on the organization's impromptu beginnings as distributor of this documentary:

> [The] film [was] called *Healthcaring: From Our End of the Speculum*, which was kind of like *Our Bodies, Ourselves* on film. And it was a really important film in terms of women's health care, but nobody would distribute it because they said there wasn't a market for it . . . but the organization felt it had to distribute it, and it did, and it was very, very successful. It won a Blue Ribbon at . . . a very important educational film festival, the American Film Festival. And, because of that success, other women came to us and said, "would you distribute my film." So, we started acquiring other . . . other films, and that's how we became a distributor.[26]

Alternative distribution networks were needed to circumvent market logics based on mass appeal that devalued unrecognized voices. This has always been the case for the underrepresented: the network of information flow are cut off prior to circulation. The pathway to authorship have always been more plentiful than the privileges of circulation.

The documentary archive of abortion films produced during the 1980s is sparse because many of these films were lost or never properly archived. Those listed in *The Guild to Reproductive Rights Films* are often impossible to locate and screen. *Our Lives on the Line* (1980) features a group of black women discussing abortion, problems with access, and the pervasive racism experienced in counseling and health care delivery. In *What If You Had No Choice* (1982), one black woman and three white women explain their reasons for having had illegal abortions ten years earlier. They talk about the trauma they experienced and how economic conditions influenced their decisions. *A Mother Is a Mother* (1982) features seven black teen-aged mothers discussing their lives, their hopes and dreams for their children and themselves, and the obstacles they face in reaching their goals. These films are rarely, if ever, mentioned in institutional documentation and scholarship about the history of abortion. The voices of the women of color who appeared in the films have been erased by the lack of perceived value of these works and the preservation politics that follow, especially in comparison to the treatment of films such as *It Happens to Us* (1972) and *Taking Our Bodies Back: The Women's Health Movement* (1974), which can be easily accessed today.

By the mid-1980s, psychoanalysis had become the preferred mode of feminist analysis among film scholars.[27] This turn away from materialist film analysis and the subjugation of traditional political struggle as a focus of research had consequences for documentary theory and practice. At a time when praxis was desperately needed in feminist political struggle, the divide between theory and practice was driven deeper. Working-class women, amateurs, and those who do not typically have access to tools of media authorship used "unsophisticated" realist media-making strategies, eliciting harsh criticism from scholars. B. Ruby Rich recalls a time in the 1980s, when the elitist forces among feminist film scholars and those at *Screen Magazine* were so intense that a simple suggestion of media having political utility would be met with accusations of vulgar Marxism.[28]

The 1990s saw a flood of documentaries focused on the history of abortion access before *Roe vs. Wade*. The political climate produced an urgency to document the history of violence against women's bodies as a way to understand the present moment. Director Dorothy Fadiman contributed to this history with her documentary trilogy, which began with the Academy Award-nominated *When Abortion Was Illegal* (1992). This film documents the firsthand experiences of women living in a time when seeking abortion care was punishable by law. After thirty years of silence and informed by her own illegal abortion experience, Fadiman was galvanized in the early 1990s by the legal vulnerability of *Roe vs. Wade*. She explains, "So, I decided to make a documentary based on what I had lived through and survived, and what had happened to so many other women."[29] Her trilogy continued with *From Danger to Dignity: The Fight for Safe Abortion* (1995) and *Motherhood by Choice, Not Chance* (1994). During this time, established documentary filmmaker Albert Maysles directed *Abortion: Desperate Choices* (1992), which was later broadcast on HBO. Sundance Film Festival selected and screened *Jane: An Abortion Referral Service* (1996), a film documenting a little-known chapter in women's history: "Jane" was a Chicago-based women's health group that performed nearly 12,000 safe illegal abortions between 1969 and 1973, with no formal medical training.

The telling of abortion history through documentary cannot be separated from the embodied emotional response it creates in life, on the screen, and in the audience. *Leona's Sister Gerri* (1995), a film by Jane Gillooly, seeks to untangle the identity of a woman whose death on a bloody hotel room floor was photographed by police, leaked to the media, and used by the pro-choice movement in public advocacy for accessible abortion. *When Abortion Was Illegal* (1995) graphically depicts the horror of illegal abortion in the lives of poor and underresourced families. Penny Lane, director of *The Abortion Diaries* (2005), describes the disconnect she felt from early abortion activist rhetoric as a younger woman who never lived with the trauma of illegal abortion: "The language that was being used, even for things like bumper stickers or t-shirts or whatever, just didn't feel like it was for me."[30] This question of affect and how things "feel" in the process of social change is ripe for exploration. Emotions are an important dimension of political resistance and protest; affect can open the process of social change to new identifications just as easily as it can close off those opportunities. Gaines advances emotion and political engagement as "involuntary," understanding this process as a runaway train of expression. I suggest that emotions and their expressions build cumulatively, mediated through communication in a process of capture, release, and narrativization.

The distinction between affect and emotion is particularly important in considering strategies of activism, resistance, and disturbance. If affect represents the physiological response that comes before emotion, we must examine how it is captured, released, and narrativized into emotion for strategic and political interests. Erin Rand states that, for the purposes of political action, affect is "strategically interpreted into the language of emotion" and "harnessed in the service of political action."[31] Bryan McCann argues that political action requires affect to be captured so that it can it be expressed.[32] The categorical wall between affect and emotions is porous and imprecise. Sara Ahmed describes "the messiness of the experiential, the unfolding of bodies into worlds, and the drama of contingency."[33] In Ahmed's work, emotion is closely tied to social and cultural movements as an action that moves through objects, grounded in historical context, to solidify relations between people. Ahmed is less concerned with affect and more concerned with the social cement of emotions. While Gaines considers emotions as a motor for movement, Ahmed recognizes the relational capacity of emotion.

Affective responses have histories; while located in the moment of response, they are also informed by the way emotions are socialized, defined, and embalmed in history. The study of trauma has emerged in affect theory "in order to welcome bodies haunted by memories of times lost and places left."[34] Often, affective expression is a response to a history that is partial, not representative, and invested in white, heteronormative, patriarchal culture. In affect theory, investigations of bodily responses are about "endings that are not over."[35] Many times, they are "a collective experience that generates collective response."[36]

Despite harsh criticism leveled by film theorists, the activist strategies embedded in the realist codes of feminist documentary representations accomplish important political work, tethering "previously unarticulated knowledge" to history. As oppressed people and those who record their circumstances know instinctively, these "bad" and "unsophisticated" stories provide a rare space for vernacular contributions to public record. These films, bemoaned by critics for their lack of cinematic artistry, offer representation to people who are rarely allowed to see or present themselves on screen.[37] It is from this location that the documentary confession grounds its power in authenticity.

Rage Against the Silence: Confessionals as Affective Disruption

Experimental, avant-garde, and feminist documentary movements paved the way for autobiographical impulses to create new cinema spaces for political consciousness-raising. According to Julia Lesage, feminist documentaries created important political interventions by providing alternative representations of women and politicizing the domestic spaces that cinema historically ignored. Many of these works were motivated by consciousness-raising impulses to "establish a structure for social and psychological change and are filmed specifically to combat patriarchy."[38] Built into feminist film culture is an impulse to respond to long-standing problems of inequity and the traumas that flow from such conditions. Consciousness-raising with documentary involves "an act of previously unarticulated knowledge."[39] When an audience identifies with what is onscreen, documentary discourse performs political analysis. Identification with images of the oppressed makes shared empathic work of the "personal problems" onscreen. Documentary storytelling becomes a way to see our own oppression as political and connected into a larger network of experiences with collective expression. The cultural conditions around abortion, then and now, continue to demand address.

Before 1960, abortion was a whisper word that was not spoken about in public except in limited clinical terms. There was an accompanying silence around women's abortion experiences, which still haunts the broader dialogue. *The Abortion Diaries* (2005) and *I Had an Abortion* (2005) address this silence in different ways. *The Abortion Diaries* recognizes the structures that cause silence, celebrating the expression of complex individual stories, privileging the emotionally chaotic context of a women's decision with care and concern. As Penny Lane, the director of *The Abortion Diaries* explains, there is "a generational gap in language . . . people in my generation didn't . . . [we] had no access to these stories in a sense."[40] Her documentary is a dialogue between women, exposing the messy way life unfolds around abortion. Lane interviews women in their homes and backyards, often with comfortable surroundings. Common themes and contradictory emotions speak more loudly than any single unified story. Lane's film creates the feeling that people are letting you into their most intimate experiences. She is not speaking for the marginalized, identifying problems, and making arguments. She is using documentary as a collaborative tool, bringing unrecognized voices to the discussion and weaving together an emotionally unruly narrative.

Figure 5.6 Director Penny Lane comforts someone she is interviewing in *Abortion Diaries* (2005).

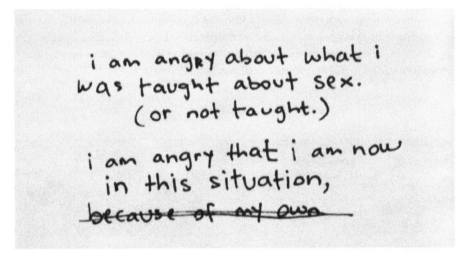

Figure 5.7 A sample of the hand drawn title cards in *Abortion Diaries* (2005).

The Abortion Diaries (2005) explores the emotional dimensions of abortion through chapters, delineated by handwritten title cards, generated from excerpts of Lane's personal journal as she went through her own abortion. On the screen, the animation title cards show sketches of images and words, phrases that express Lane's inner turmoil. She places the viewer in her confusion, writing on the screen: "I don't know who to talk to. I don't know who to trust" and "I feel . . . I don't feel guilty. I feel guilty for not feeling guilty."[41] In this narrative, unwanted pregnancy is the affliction and abortion is the relief, an idea expressed in hushed tones in safe domestic spaces.

The narrative of *The Abortion Diaries* (2005) explores the coexistence of competing and contradictory affective responses. Living room storytelling helps unbind the complexities of abortion to create space for dichotomous emotions to take root. In one static shot, Gwen, a middle-aged woman, explains, "I have no regrets for my abortion, my sorrow is that it's unlikely that I am ever going to have a child and I feel sad. I just feel sad about that." The lo-fi handheld camera moves slightly over the close framing of her face. Knickknacks, mementos, and family pictures sit on a table behind her. Gwen's voice turns quiet; the last few words start to crack as tears well in her eyes. She continues, "I am proud of myself, that I didn't fall prey to my religion and my society's opinion that just because I am a woman, I have [a] requirement to have a baby. I am proud that I didn't fall prey to that but I wish my life would have been different in some ways, that I had been supported to have a child. I never felt supported enough . . . my only sense of sadness comes from that."[42] Gwen expresses relief over having an abortion, yet sadness at not having a child. Both emotions are genuine, yet difficult to reconcile. Emotional expression fosters space for contradiction to take root. Emotion creates disruptions for new articulations of our most unspeakable stories, exposing the problems of a whisper culture. Lane does not attempt to resolve the perceived inconsistencies. Instead, she uses the tension inherent in these complex stories to invite audiences into a messy, process-oriented world of intersectional production practice.

Figure 5.8 Gwen expresses the emotional complexities of living with the abortion across her lifetime in *Abortion Diaries* (2005).

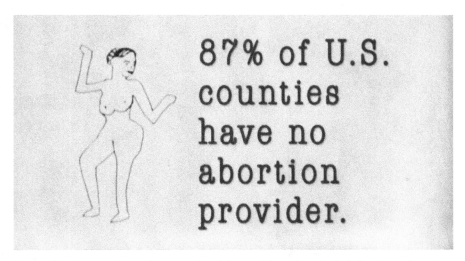

Figure 5.9 Director Penny Lane uses hand drawn title cards to include her journal entries describing her own experience in *Abortion Diaries* (2005).

Figure 5.10 Director Penny Lane listens to the stories of women who talk about the their own abortion in *Abortion Diaries* (2005).

The primary political act in the Aldrich and Baumgardner film, *I Had an Abortion* (2005), takes the form of women speaking out collectively.[43] The women on the screen stand in for all women. Their identical shirts and staged interviews with the same backdrop assert similarity in the face of difference. At the opening of *I Had*

Figure 5.11 Joh explains the circumstances around her abortion decision in in *Abortion Diaries* (2005).

an Abortion, we hear the high-pitched notes of "Hello Birmingham," one of eight Ani DiFranco songs featured in the documentary, as we see slow-motion images of an anti-abortion protest. This song, a haunting lyrical response to the murder of a doctor and the bombing of an abortion clinic, plays over images of clergy and modestly dressed women carrying protest signs on which the question: "Is this a choice or a child?" is written over an image of a fetus. This scene quickly fades into an interview with a spunky young woman, sitting before a camera wearing a shirt that reads, "This is what a feminist looks like." In an upbeat tone and with confidence she announces, "You never hear anyone saying, 'I had an abortion'. You never hear anyone saying, you know, being open about it." That statement fades into a series of portraits of different women standing in the center of the frame, wearing the same black t-shirt with white letters that state, "I had an abortion." At the end of the documentary, a similar montage occurs in which we see diverse women filmed with the same close camera framing and repeating the same phrase, "I had an abortion." These are strong, powerful images of women choosing to stand in front of the camera and publicly declare abortion as part of their own stories, in essence bookending the film.

Specific conditions and varying circumstances are erased by the universalizing aesthetic focus on coming out publicly to create a feminist heritage tale, a counterhistory of mothers who have been making these decisions for centuries. A collective power drives this message: women are not alone, and many have traveled this road before. Yet, this advocacy scours away the diverse socioeconomic backgrounds that bring women into the abortion experience, revealing the deep ideological divides at the center of the abortion struggle. Very diverse experiences of

Figure 5.12 A college student talks about the conditions of shame around abortion and the codes of silence that shut down information in *I Had an Abortion* (2005).

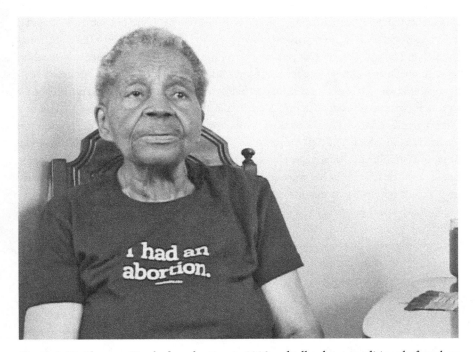

Figure 5.13 Florence Rice had an abortion in 1938 and talks about conditions before they were legal in *I Had an Abortion* (2005).

abortion are made equivalent, generalizing a narrow experience, held by a privileged few, as normative and representative of all others. In this way, mobility feminism guides the film's trajectory. Although a racial diversity exists among interviewees, their radicalized experiences are not discussed in any depth. Furthermore, the relative middle-class status of interviewees remains unacknowledged. This documentary could be a dispatch from professional feminism, branded and marketed to the masses. Many of the women featured are recognizable public figures with deep ties to privileged East Coast artistic and activist enclaves. The privileging of this universalized message embodied by those holding significant socioeconomic status masks the contradictions that sit at the center of the abortion struggle.

The privileged perspective of *I Had an Abortion* manifests itself in the series of interviews with Gloria Steinem, who speaks out about the abortion experience. "Speaking out" is a tradition of the feminist movement, particularly among white, middle-class circles. Steinem articulates her abortion choice as a form of self-preservation: "I could not see any way I could possibly give birth to someone else and also give birth to myself."[44] Steinem's assumptions assume a critical perspective on political power and motherhood, which is not widely circulated in a public culture that largely subscribes to the conservative heritage tale assumption that motherhood is a sacrosanct position and women should sacrifice everything for it. In such a framework, there is no space to talk about motherhood, femininity, and womanhood itself as cultural constructs or about the labor, time, energy and other resources that go into maintaining them. It is the great problem of rhetoric and social change: in order to be persuasive to a wider public, we must tap into the traditional values and language that give potency to a moment while simultaneously leveling critiques that can change the terms of our collective understanding. Steinem's realization that she had to choose between her own self-actualization and motherhood is not accessible to a broader culture mired in the assumptions of the conservative heritage tale. It fails to speak to women occupying underprivileged socioeconomic conditions in which self-determination is extremely fraught and difficult terrain to imagine. Steinem's critical perspective on political power and motherhood does not make rhetorical sense in the prevailing emotional regime, which simplifies the issue as a choice between murder and selfless care.

Women speaking out about their own reproductive agency fails to confront how the heritage myth frames the terms of the debate. Speaking out and confessional modes of expression about abortion function as a form of consciousness-raising and solidification among those who already share interests in favor of women's reproductive health. Within the conservative heritage framework, feminist confessional intervention seems self-indulgent and narcissistic. In *The Cultural Contradictions of Capitalism*, Daniel Bell claims that authenticity of the self takes precedence over social cohesion in a consumer-based society where "a composite of atomistic individuals . . . pursue only their own gratification."[45] This impulse toward confession and authentic expression is understood divergently within the same historical

Figure 5.14 Former anti-choice activist Robin Ringleka-Koltke talks about casting out the shame through speaking out about abortion in *I Had an Abortion* (2005).

Figure 5.15 Feminist intellectual and political activist Gloria Steinem talks about the condition around her own abortion decision in *I Had an Abortion* (2005).

context. It can be read as a manifestation of the need to break the silence and find new language or as an example of self-indulgent individuality. The heritage debate's resistance to confessional feminist rhetoric taps into the conservative interpretation of feminism as nothing more than the manifestation of a prevalent culture of narcissism.

Unfortunately, Baumgardner's *I Had an Abortion* gave further ammunition to conservatives, who saw it as evidence of self-promotion. The heavy commodification in the film's promotion even gave liberals pause. Baumgardner constructed a multimedia campaign that included the documentary, speaking engagements, and t-shirts that had the words, "I had an abortion," printed across the chest. Some commentators described the t-shirts as one of the most controversial feminist campaigns in recent decades.[46] Conservatives speculated in local newspapers across the country that the documentary was a marketing stunt for the controversial t-shirt, which conservative opinion columnists described as "callous," "insensitive," and "promoting abortion."[47] Baumgardner partnered with Planned Parenthood to sell the t-shirts as a fundraiser, in the belief that the organization helped normalize abortion, taking it out of the whisper culture and providing a tool to begin productive conversations. The sensational press surrounding the t-shirts, however, became louder than the aims of the documentary. Feminists debated whether the shirts expressed solidarity or acted as a glib and superficial way to address the experience of abortion. Does a t-shirt mark the beginning of a discussion that builds solidarity or the end of one? More broadly, we should ask how any commodity, whether documentary or t-shirt, can intervene to promote social change.

REDIRECTING SHAME

Articulating sadness, releasing guilt and shame, and finding the relief of acceptance form a familiar emotional arc for many of the stories in each of these documentaries. In the *Abortion Diaries* (2005), forgiveness provides a path to valuing the self. As women fight through the ramifications of silence and seek stories outside the murder versus self-sacrifice narrative, one woman reflects: "It seems to me . . . that the ability to decide if and when to be a mother is about self-determination."[48] This is a declaration of recognition that motherhood is a life-shifting factor and a determining force in a woman's life. Taking control over reproduction is a form of agency that shapes many parts of the self-determination project, including economic security. Many women recount the possibilities that would have been lost because of resource scarcity and unintended pregnancy: "I wouldn't have gone to school. I wouldn't have known myself."[49] The conservative heritage myth does not acknowledge issues of time, emotion, and labor in the practice of motherhood. Children require labor—physical and emotional—that leaves women with fewer resources to dedicate to themselves, friends, work, or their communities. The highest cost of the labor of motherhood is the inability to engage in self-discovery and the determination of one's own future. Forgiveness is shown as a release of shame and guilt, an opportunity to seek out different values.

Questions of process are at the center of *The Abortion Diaries*. Lane interviewed people she could physically visit using public transportation; there were no famous artists or activists, just a cross section of people who answered a request from their friend network or responded to an unsolicited email invitation. The patchwork process of collecting interviews allowed for the emergence of a complex map of emotions. Women report contrary emotions in the same expression: "I want to be a mom but I am not ready to be a mom. Not now, not because of a mistake."[50] Regarding the clinic experience, another woman explains, "I felt like I was alone in the world, and then when it was over, I felt relieved. I felt very relieved when I left the clinic."[51] These expressions run contrary to the prescriptions of the conservative heritage myth. In *The Abortion Diaries,* Lane creates an open space to allow complex and repressed emotions to emerge. The film acknowledges feelings and responses that the heritage myth robs of legitimacy in broader discourse.

I Had an Abortion takes a broader scope, both historically and conceptually. The emotions in this documentary are not complicated or contradictory. Shame around abortion causes pain; relief comes from access to abortion and speaking out. No regret, confusion, or ambivalence is structured into the narrative. Marion Banzhuf, a veteran in the AIDS activist movement, talks about the New York City abortion mills and recalls her own emotions about this procedure. "I was thrilled, I was so happy . . .I was so relieved . . . skipped down the street singing . . .sense of overwhelming relief," she reports.[52] The film seems to argue that freedom and happiness is universally waiting on the other side of the abortion procedure. Confession or speaking out becomes a critical aspect of this process of accessing relief and casting out shame. Robin Ringleka-Koltke had an abortion in 1992. She is a former antichoice activist and speaks extensively on the shame and guilt that comes from conservative heritage tale rhetoric. She explains, "When you talk about the issue, it casts out the shame."[53] To speak one's own truth in public is a cornerstone practice of U.S. feminism; women publicly declaring their experience with abortion contributes to the ongoing project of normalizing the medical procedure. Speaking out also builds solidarity with others who share reproductive justice and women's health interests, helping to develop a collective political community through shared experience. *I Had an Abortion* attempts to persuade an unfixed political spectator with the absence of diverse emotional experiences or contradiction. Paradoxically, the emotional contradiction in *The Abortion Diaries* invites vulnerability, an unfixed space for an unfixed spectator, opening up the ways audiences can emotionally identify with the story. When the film makes space for any expression to exist, no matter how untidy, it welcomes the audience into a confidential discussion contained by whisper culture.

Capturing shame and releasing it into anger helps drive women beyond the ide-ological limits of the conservative heritage myth, which positions women as sexual gatekeepers. This frees women of sole responsibility for reproductive outcomes. The ubiquity of the heritage myth makes guilt the most common emotion for women who get pregnant out of wedlock; unwanted pregnancy is a personal failure of moral character for women rather than the result of natural, healthy sexual de-sire. By expressing and releasing guilt, a process of redefinition occurs. Sara Ahmed observes that "feminism also involves a reading of the response of anger: it moves from anger into an interpretation of that which one is against, whereby associations or connections are made between the object of anger and broader patterns or structures."[54] Anger opens up the cognitive space for alternative interpretations of responsibilities crafted in response to newly visible forces that direct women into strict roles as sexual gatekeepers. The move from shame to anger allows the broader historical, cultural, and political context to inform the abortion decision. The move into anger helps women reject heritage tale guilt in favor of a more humane and compassionate grid of understanding.

This particular progression of emotions, articulated from the perspective of women, is still not part of the widespread public understanding of abortion. The conservative heritage myth framing of abortion as a choice between murder or a life of love and sacrifice forecloses the possibility of lived realities, such as a desire for self-actualization or resources too limited to support a child. Discourses of silence make it difficult to describe an experience for which there is no public vocabulary. Future arguments are more difficult to make because the reasoning and rich de-scription around the experience of abortion are not in public circulation. This guilt–shame–relief arc articulates an invisible experience while detailing the contexts in which women choose abortion. This arc allows us to see self-preservation, safety, and resource scarcity as legitimate reasons for making decisions. When we look at the contexts of abortion decisions, a familiar theme emerges: the choice to have an abortion is really no choice at all.

SMALLER THAN A MICRO-BUDGET

Both 2005 films, *I Had an Abortion* and *The Abortion Diaries*, were designed as tools of political intervention, and both were made very quickly, in response to political efforts to erode access to reproductive health care. Since 1979, legislative efforts to defund Planned Parenthood and restrict access to affordable reproductive health for women have escalated. In 2001, George W. Bush reinstated the Reagan-era policy of prohibiting foreign aid to health care programs offering abortion. In 2003, Missouri and Texas took aggressive measures to defund Planned Parenthood. Abortion clinics continue to be under violent assault. Doctors, clinic escorts, patients, receptionists, and security guards are in the crossfire of an increasingly violent anti-abortion movement, which is now armed and backed by the violent heritage myth. In classrooms, churches, rural communities, and other spaces, the culture war on reproductive choice has only intensified. Crisis pregnancy centers outnumber Planned Parenthood clinics in rural communities and anti-choice organizations have a notable presence on college campuses.

The Abortion Diaries (2005) and *I Had an Abortion* (2005) represent a spectrum of documentaries produced for less than a micro-budget. The films lacked significant institutional support and emerged from communities that were historically silenced by the shame of conservative heritage myth thinking. The films were produced almost against the odds in an attempt to keep time with the movement of the larger public discussions. Aldrich, Baumgardner, and Lane crowd-funded their films in a pre-social media age. Political projects outside the commercial and entertainment milieu have always used communal financing, volunteer labor, and in-kind donations. Filmmakers have found that sometimes, if the project can be done inexpensively, the conditions of communal financing are preferable to institutional support because of the bureaucratic and legal oversight that comes with institutional arrangements. *I Had an Abortion* was largely supported by Baumgardner's personal and professional networks; her friends, family, and colleagues gathered resources and contacted people in their networks for support.[55] Similarly, Lane financed her own project with several hundred dollars and copious amounts of free labor. As a working graduate student with limited finances, she also obtained modest grants from the Puffin Foundation and New York State Council on the Arts.

Yet, tapping personal networks for financing is not sustainable for most media makers. If one is not already connected to well-resourced communities, it is difficult to return to personal networks for future funding. Additionally, a certain amount of socioeconomic privilege is required before a media maker can even consider her project worthy of fundraising in the first place. The personal funding model is best suited to those, like Aldrich, Baumgardner, and Lane, who already belong to professional activist networks and feminist organizations. In addition to production funding, their networks and associations also paved the way for the films to screen on an activist circuit. Lane went on several self-organized regional tours on the East Coast and throughout the South. Her appearances ranged from large university auditoriums filled with hundreds of students to sparsely attended screenings in community centers. She eventually worked with Planned Parenthood, which used the documentary for fundraising opportunities and information sessions with women seeking abortion. The partnership created an easy connection to the women Lane hoped to reach. Her documentary functions as an organizing agent and a tool of political intervention because of her commitment to community screenings and the collaboration she developed with Planned Parenthood.

Aldrich and Baumgardner activated their established activist networks to do screenings across the country, often featuring documentary participants in postscreening discussions. Their distribution incorporated a marketing campaign that included a press rollout plan, media outlets, t-shirts, screenings with feminist organizations, and other tie-ins. Most people do not have the resources to effectively crowd source the funding to produce a documentary, stage a sustained promotional campaign, and conduct outreach into impacted communities. Even for those who can capitalize upon such resources, it is unclear what kind of political work emerges out of these engagements. The escalation of political conflict around abortion and the absence of consistent legal precedent or policy continue to increase cultural anxiety.

The story of social change is not linear; it moves back and forth and in a circle. Documentary does not need a starring role in this story to be of value. It could move the dial on social change indirectly or in unmeasurable ways. Barbra Abrash, media theorist and practitioner, reminds us that there are many avenues that lead into social change:

> I think life happens in a lot of different ways, right? I mean, sometimes a social movement can be sparked by some public event. It doesn't have to be sparked by a documentary film. So I think documentary film lives in a media environment, and it's one of many kinds of ways of communicating ideas and triggering social response.[56]

Documentary's ability to trigger social response depends on political circumstances and the public credibility of documentary discourse as a form of meaning production.

In the 1970s and 1980s, the landmarks of abortion agitation were bound up in legal precedent. *Roe vs. Wade* and other legal cases brought contradictory outcomes. *Bellotti vs. Baird* (1981) allowed minors to petition the court for permission to seek an abortion, and *Webster vs. Reproductive Health Services* (1989), a law in Washington State, declares life begins at conception. These dichotomous legal precedents added to tensions around abortion. Violent clinic bombings and practices of intimidation outside health care facilities proliferated throughout the 1980s and 1990s. As pro-choice President Clinton took office in 1993, the extreme pro-life movement began to assassinate abortion care providers. Dr. David Gunn was shot outside a clinic in Pensacola, Florida. The perpetrator was Michael Griffin, an abortion protestor later sentenced to life in prison for his actions. This would not be the last murder or violent act; the murder of Dr. Gunn marked the beginning of an escalation and an enactment of a horrific heritage myth nightmare that shaped the formative impulses of abortion documentary representation. The documentaries discussed in this chapter gained little traction, and reproductive health care access was quickly eroding, precipitating shifts in documentary storytelling. Strategically addressing the systematic violence and denial of care, this shift in abortion representation challenges the murder versus self-sacrifice model put forward by the persuasive undercurrents of the conservative heritage narrative.

Bodily Horror and the Nightmare Heritage Tale

An anti-abortion activist murdered Dr. George Tiller, age sixty-seven, in the sanctuary of his church. At the time of his murder, he was one of four doctors in the United States who provided late-term abortion services. Tiller had been a target of anti-abortion activists for two decades; in 1985, his medical clinic was bombed, and in 1993, he was shot in both arms. In the documentary *After Tiller* (2013), directors Martha Shane and Lana Wilson embark on a dark tale of labor, risk, and human need. The story outlines the most recent fatal attacks perpetrated by anti-abortion extremists—those who organize violence, kidnapping, assault, murder, arson, and bombings directed against abortion care workers and patients. *After Tiller* tells the stories of four late-term abortion doctors dealing with escalating threats, harassment, and the recent murder of their colleague. The observational representation of the doctors humanizes the medical care work by focusing on "the calling" of the occupation in the face of bodily harm and harassment. This narrative breaks down the moral high ground claimed by anti-abortion protestors as protectors of life.

This documentary exposed the calculated acts of violence committed by armed people motivated by the conservative heritage myth, who engage in violent action toward abortion care workers, seeing themselves as serving God and protecting the country. A survey published in 2017 by the Feminist Majority Foundation found that 34 percent of abortion providers reported "severe violence or threats of violence."[57] This is an increase of 19 percent in reported violence since 2014. This harassment comes with evaporating rights and increasing restrictions on access to abortion. As explained by Dawn Porter, the director of *Trapped* (2016), "There is a so-called 'abortion desert' from Florida to New Mexico where women have little to no access to abortion services."[58] For most of the past five decades, there has been little media representation of violence and harassment toward abortion providers outside of the nightly news. As a result of the rise in violence after the turn of the century, abortion documentary moved away from the confessional mode toward a new representation of the issue. While these documentaries never completely abandoned confessional elements, new strategies evolved as media makers struggled with how to address the growing and increasingly violent anti-abortion movement.

After Tiller (2013) and *Soldiers in the Army of God* (2000) were two of the first mainstream documentary representations of the armed heritage myth. These films offer a portrait of those who pray in huddled masses outside of clinics and moments later engage in aggression, intimidation, harassment, and murder. *After Tiller* frames these oppositional cultures—pro-choice and anti-abortion—by juxtaposing scenes that expose the gap of understanding between what happens inside the clinic and the tone, emotion, or action of those outside the building. In one scene, a concerned prayer group huddles on the sidewalk and talks about the evil inside the clinic. The next scene immediately cuts to a mundane clinic break room—pastries on the table, a lunch bag opened and unfinished, community table condiments; the doctor sits and reads the newspaper, moralizing about the new cannabis laws in Colorado. The anti-abortion demonstrators' dehumanization of clinic workers is placed alongside a mundane scene of workplace boredom and supportive care.

Soldiers in the Army of God (2000) documents the connection between the anti-abortion harassment outside a clinic in Pensacola, Florida, and the eventual murder of Dr. John Britton. The documentary uncomfortably provides unobstructed camera time—without boundaries or consequence—to the members of an anti-abortion group that organizes violent political actions. Directed by Marc Levin and Daphne Pinkerson, the film depicts a small but deadly movement of people willing to use violence to intimidate and kill abortion providers. Convicted of murdering Dr. Britton, Paul Jennings Hill explains in detail what it was like to get up in the morning and shoot an abortion doctor. At one point he says, "It was very difficult. I am smiling now about it but I wasn't smiling then. It was a very grim task."[59] The film occupies the perspective of the anti-abortion assailant, and the documentary structure places viewers in this perspective for long stretches of time without much critical interruption. This pairing of the seemingly neutral observational mode and starkly controversial issues can be problematic. At what point do unobstructed camera time and extended identification with a violent offender turn from criticism into endorsement? This documentary pulls at the limitations of the observational mode to wade through controversy, especially when the camera focuses on an unreliable and predatory narrator.

These new representations tap into fear of unbridled government constraints on the bodies of women. These documentaries are a signal from the most vulnerable families among us that our basic liberties and self-actualization capacities are at risk. The story of increasing government constraints on reproductive health care also includes a monster in the form of violent actors who subscribe to an aggressive, unrelenting nightmare heritage myth and who are armed and causing bodily horror.

After Tiller (2013) directs the camera toward late-term abortion, offering access to conversations between members of families of pregnant women whose fetuses show significant and fatal abnormalities. It places viewers in the subject position of sitting with the terrible choice between the future suffering of a child and an abortion. This is a significant attempt to rearticulate abortion as a public health issue; it parallels the early rhetoric of the 1950s, when doctors spoke out against the dangers of illegal and self-induced abortion. Significant screen time is dedicated to humanizing doctors and abortion care workers, the process itself, and those who find themselves in need of these services. Scenes of an actual abortion procedure accompany these humanizing details. Nurses talk in detail about the labor and delivery of late-term abortion, and the audience is in the room during parts of the medical procedure. In *After Tiller* (2013), we see that the small fringe group shown engaging in anti-abortion violence in *Soldiers in the Army of God* (2000) has become a nationally networked movement. In *12th and Delaware* (2010), organized groups systematically harass patients and workers outside clinic grounds and organize violence against care providers. The aggressive force of the early 2000s has become mature, institutionalized, and forceful.

Heidi Ewing and Rachel Grady's *12th and Delaware* (2010) offers a microcosm of the larger street fight around abortion. The filmmakers document two opposite street corners in Fort Prince, Florida. On one side of the street is a women's health clinic that offers abortion services. On the other side is a crisis pregnancy center, run by local religious groups. The crisis pregnancy center represents the conservative attack on women's health clinics across the country. The documentary captures the coercive ways crisis pregnancy clinics use emotional appeals to direct pregnant women away from abortion services using fear and promises of financial help and emotional support. During one counseling session, a young woman clearly states her desire to have an abortion because of her lack of resources; she had no job, insurance, or place to live. In response, the intake specialist at the crisis pregnancy clinic places tiny plastic fetus dolls in the hands of the young woman. The pregnant woman's demeanor changes, and she begins to feel the fetus dolls at different growth stages. The intake specialist leaves the room to commiserate with the ultrasound specialist. With urgency in her voice, resembling the emotional intensity of a salesperson closing in on a deal, the intake specialist provides the ultrasound tech with patient information: "She had an abortion in December. She might do it again. She's guessing, it puts her at seven weeks but maybe we can get a heartbeat?" The documentary reveals the motives and ideological underpinnings of the crisis pregnancy center, uncovering an emotional war to keep women pregnant without regard for their health, resources, or quality of life.

The film also captures the persistent street occupation of the grounds around the women's health clinic by anti-abortion activists who yell at women as they enter, "God made you pregnant, it's not a mistake." A man shouts into the window of a clinic exam room: "Think about yourself, 95 percent of women will tell you they regret their abortion. You are not going to be any different. This just makes everything worse." The representation of the anti-abortion movement—a heritage myth army—establishes the context for the street fights, manipulative crisis pregnancy centers, and assassinations. More recently, there have been further aggressive government policy assaults on women's reproductive health, also informed by a mature heritage myth movement. While fear is not an uncommon emotion within the context of abortion documentary, a shift in representation positions fear as a consequence of structural oppression, law, and policy outside the immediate control of those who need it the most. Restrictive government policy driven by the ubiquitous heritage myth movement appears as a menacing force.

Dawn Porter's documentary, *Trapped* (2016), focuses on politics, power, and dwindling abortion access following the passage of TRAP (Targeted Regulation of Abortion Providers) laws, which reproductive rights advocates believe are designed to restrict access to abortion. Concentrating on the abortion desert from Texas to Florida, Porter maps problems with access and the increasingly conservative policies that are chipping away at access to reproductive rights. The film profiles the doctors and staff who fight on the frontlines, balancing serving the needs of women with fighting a growing conservative legislative assault. The film points out the tragic irony of the fact that the new restrictive policies create a backlog of patients who must wait longer for access to an extremely time-sensitive procedure. The audience sees how and why TRAP laws create conditions that lead to more late-term abortions. By focusing on southern clinics, Porter's documentary makes it clear that TRAP laws disproportionally harm those who are most underresourced: poor women and people of color. The politicians who advance the TRAP legislation are part of an effort to construct punitive frameworks for women seeking care. These politicians also eliminate access to preventative birth control and reproductive health education, demonstrating a lack of concern about limiting unwanted pregnancy even as they work to restrict abortion.

One of the most appalling tactics revealed in *Trapped* (2016) is the strategic appropriation of race politics by anti-abortion protestors. Images of an African American doctor arriving at his clinic—with security escorts and wooden road partitions to block sidewalks—are edited with an emphasis on routine and exact procedure. The doctor's voice is now heard as he ponders his own safety: "People have been killed doing this work and I don't wear a vest because a vest doesn't provide me with any greater sense of safety. If I spend time processing what can happen to me, I will lose the courage to do what I know is the right thing to do." As the doctor's car pulls into the driveway of the clinic, we begin to hear the Lord's Prayer recited by the clinic escort team. Anti-abortion families with multiple children line the streets holding signs; people are camped out across the street with binoculars, and protestors are yelling at the women entering the clinic. As the doctor exits the car to enter the clinic, a white protestor screams, "What sickens me is that you are a black man and that you're having black women go in there and destroy black lives. All black lives matter. All black lives matter. All lives matter." This slippage between "all black lives matter" and "all lives matter" is telling. The obvious political tension around these terms is lost on the clinic protestor, who clings to a giant sign that reads "Black Lives Matter."

Tracy Droz Tragos's *Abortion: Stories Women Tell* (2016) tells a similar story, tracking the conservative movement in Missouri that is attempting to make the state abortion-free in a few years. The documentary marks 2001 as a significant moment in the struggle over abortion services because it was the first year since *Roe vs. Wade* that over half of U.S. states had significantly restricted access to abortion. The documentary represents women with limited means who need to work to support their existing families. The phones in the clinic ring constantly, and the staff takes time with each emotional caller. Outside, an anti-abortion protestor with a bullhorn shouts into the building. The documentary moves toward a return to the confessional mode. One woman featured in the documentary summarizes her experience toward the end of the documentary: "Telling our stories is so important because we keep those things locked up inside of ourselves and they kill us." The silence addressed by Lane, Baumgardner, and Aldrich in 2005 continues to haunt women seeking reproductive health care. Despite this shift in representation, the need to speak out never stops.

Abortion: Stories Women Tell (2016) is a portrait of American women stretched to their emotional and economic limits and often unable to command the resources necessary to get access to abortion. The forced waiting periods and growing abortion deserts means women must travel many hours and hundreds of miles to receive care, requiring multiple days off work, a driver to transport the patient, and money for the hotel stays, which the multiday mandatory clinic visits require. Many of these laws intentionally make the abortion process more difficult, no matter the cost to the lives of women and their families.

This documentary expands the social geography of the abortion struggle. We see millennial women pick up the conservative heritage myth campaign for a new generation on college campuses and new rhetorical tactics employed on clinic grounds. One tall and loud anti-abortion protestor shouted at a male supporter escorting a woman into the clinic: "Abortion does not stop making you a dad. It makes you a dad of a dead baby. Sir, you are guilty. You are accountable before God and your conscience knows it. And you feel guilty, you feel conscience driven. Sir. Sir. Be a man. Be a man and don't kill your baby." This well-orchestrated anti-abortion movement is now more mainstream, thriving in church gyms full of parishioners cheering, "All in Christ." Unlike the mostly male movement represented in *Soldiers in the Army of God*, this documentary details a mainstream and woman-led anti-abortion movement. Leaders, scarred by decisions to have an abortion in the past and fighting for a more just world, see "saving" women now as a way to find emotional absolution for themselves.

Trapped (2016), *12th and Delaware* (2010), and *Abortion: Stories Women Tell* (2016) create dynamic portraits of the policy assault on abortion access and the escalating street war on clinic grounds. This wave of abortion documentary is distinct in the way it directly confronts the heritage myth and the hypocrisy of the anti-abortion protestors. Post–2005 documentaries return the focus on confession, and there is a productive shift to tracking patterns of aggression and escalating efforts to deny women access to abortion. Realist strategies are never abandoned; analyses of political systems supplement, rather than replace, confession. This shift in documentary representation has the potential to challenge the shape and pervasiveness of the conservative heritage myth. Unlike the earlier generations of abortion documentaries, these films no longer exist on the fringes of countercultural expression and alternative cinema. Recent documentaries have been broadcast by visible popular media outlets, including HBO, PBS, and Sundance. HBO, in particular, has been a significant supporter of securing abortion documentary funding and circulating these works in high-profile broadcast outlets. These films reach millions of viewers through television broadcasts and streaming services, providing a popular representation of abortion that normalizes the procedure in public understanding in unprecedented ways. In an audience reception study that involved a screening of *After Tiller* (2013), researchers found that many people did not have prior information about late-term abortion and that the lack of knowledge contributed to a lack of sympathy. The study concluded that a lack of representation of the issue and widespread public silences and information gaps combined to create a space around the film that influenced audience views. As long-time media producer and activist Karen Ranucci suggests, "Educating someone is a first step in opening them up to the need for social change. So that's an essential element. And, independent media does a lot, has a lot to offer in that department. I think the biggest thing is, how do you take an educated public to become an activated public." The political subjectivity around abortion documentary often fails to build the scaffolding for political and moral grounding, and the emotional habitus makes these interventions challenging. We are still missing compelling pro-choice rhetoric that plugs into universal values that resonate across diverse publics.

It is still too early to tell if these newer representations of abortion struggle will have a significant impact on political outcomes for women. Will documentary representation help women gain autonomy over their own bodies and reproductive health care decisions? The desire to affect this social condition with documentary is fervent and critical in these hostile historical conditions. We desperately need to repair the botched political subjectivity around reproductive justice documentary.

Conclusions

More than four decades after *Roe vs. Wade*, we have moved very little toward a consensus about abortion as a legal reality, a medical decision, an ancient practice, and an experience that cuts across race, class, religion, and education. Reproduction is a job; it takes time, money, emotional energy, support systems, and so much more. If women cannot control their reproductive capacity, they do not have full autonomy to choose how to invest resources in themselves and their communities. Although gender roles are changing in the United States, women still lack the resources to establish themselves in public life. More women are in the workforce, but most do not occupy top positions of power. Women's reproductive options are also more restricted than they have been in decades. More than ever before, we need effective media work to intervene in this political struggle.

This chapter assesses how middle-class feminists utilized the documentary genre to recover women's history and reclaim public space for reproductive justice. We paid particular attention to a change that began in 2005, when feminists were combating silence with confession. A person's speaking out about an often-shamed experience is powerful to witness, no matter what the subject. Modest but important participatory cultures of political engagement have emerged from smaller than micro-budget documentaries about abortion rights. There is potency to animating political issues through the fusion of documentary, consciousness-raising, and affect. The educational and consciousness-raising efforts of documentary discourse are necessary political moments of participatory media activism that need further articulations.

Still, the unique and significant representations found in these documentaries are limited by the emotional habitus of the conservative heritage myth about abortion that prevails in U.S. culture. Attempts at feminist expression around abortion in the confessional mode is too easily absorbed into the emotional habitus of the conservative heritage tale. The heritage myth twists women's personal stories to support the narrative of the selfish, callous, and insensitive woman who seeks abortion. Attempts to redirect documentary work at the assumptions of the heritage myth, its rendering of domestic labor as invisible, the unrealistic conditions of the family, and the unequal burdens upon women might help unsettle the emotional habitus around this myth. It is also possible that representations of the increasingly violent anti-choice movement, which kills abortion doctors, intimidates women on walkways, and bombs clinics, might help disrupt the integrity and moral high ground of the heritage myth, redirecting the frame of violence to those who are the persistent aggressors.

Future scholarship could focus on how collective identification and agency is animated by the fusion of documentary, consciousness-raising, and affect—especially as documentary media makers attempt to tackle topics that feel unspeakable, even among politically like-minded people. Since mobile recording equipment has taken hold with the ubiquity of smart phones and the birth of social media at the turn of the century, the confessional impulse in documentary has taken a radical vernacular turn. No one can escape the confessions of the mobile recording age. More research is needed to explore how confessional modes established by online participatory media cultures might effectively challenge wider discourses that deny women's complex emotions, desires, and needs for self-actualization.

6

Street Tapes

The People's History of Unjustified Police Force

> *For many of us, you know, whose families lived through this, who are*
> *extensions of this kind of oppression, we don't need to see pictures to*
> *understand what's going on. It's really to kind of speak to the masses who*
> *have been ignoring this for the majority of their life. But I also think there's*
> *trouble just showing, you know, black bodies as dead bodies, too. Too much*
> *of anything becomes unhealthy, unuseful.*
> —Cory Greene, formerly incarcerated activist and cofounder of How
> Our Lives Link Altogether, an organization by and for the formally
> incarcerated, quoted from the documentary, *13th*

Representations of police brutality pepper the reels of documentary history. In these films, groups swarm the streets, police batons fly in the air, Molotov cocktails are tossed, bodies slam into asphalt, rocks and bottles rain down from rooftops, and National Guard tanks drive through city streets. We witness police dogs attacking protestors, shattered glass from broken windows, fire hoses shooting water at bystanders, and unarmed people being trampled to the ground. Documentary discourse centered around political struggle reveals a consistent pattern of unjustified police force. We see the state using armed police to exert control over its citizens in a cycle of aggression that transcends geography, specific political struggles, and historical context. Documentary often finds its way into vernacular cultures[1] to represent those without a secure place on the political stage. It is therefore no surprise that the camera picks up citizens' cries of distress in response to this violence.

Structural power relationships in crisis—like those between citizens and an armed police force—set the stage for documentary to enter the existing public conversation about police brutality and excessive force. Documentary becomes a part of the scene by documenting physical conflicts, reporting on their significance, and providing stories about what these exchanges signify for those who confront state control. Access to vernacular authenticity comes from the previously untold nature of these stories; documentary practices rearticulate the spaces in our community where historical amnesia has ossified the narrative around police into a static story of protect and serve.

Police are caught in a bind between state control and pressure from their communities. Police brutality and unjustified force are tactics of state control embodied by law enforcement and directed toward specific bodies and communities when those communities assert agency. Representations of physical hand-to-hand combat between police and citizens appear frequently in civil rights documentaries, stories about black urban rebellions, labor documentaries, and recordings of political actions around various social movements. The consistent theme of state violence against black bodies warrants further documentation: "Black boys and men present a particular kind of physical threat in the white American imagination, a threat that needs to be contained."[2] This narrative is a shadowy part of the foundation of the United States and documentary discourse around unjustified police force attempts to confront those who want to ignore that reality.

Filmmakers and activists who document police violence face a choice between two undesirable courses of action. On one hand, representation must continue as a form of protection and resistance to problematic patterns of state control. On the other hand, this form of media production depicts black bodies as brutalized subjects rather than active subjects with agency. As Cory Greene pointed out in the chapter-opening quote, these images are not created for the communities in crisis, which are already aware of what is at stake. These recordings are directed to the "the masses who have been ignoring this for the majority of their life."[3] The inherent double bind in representing police brutality has hit a critical point as the tools of digital image recording and news broadcasting are carried in the back pockets of most people with smart phones. I am mindful of Kent Ono and John Sloop's call for scholars to privilege communication rooted in vernacular expressions of the cultural margins. These vernacular expressions open spaces for new concepts of communities and their contingencies to emerge. This use of documentary strengthens the public platform for challenges to the status quo, especially in the lives of marginalized peoples. As Calafell and Delgado argue, "vernacular discourse is also always in process, pursuing the aims of creating a community and interrogating the ongoing and also never finished expressions of power and asymmetrical relations between the dominant and the dominated."[4] We must address the function of documentary media as vernacular communication in the context of armed violence in the United States. Visual media provides an opening because "it constructs new cultural forms reflecting a fluid community that constantly and continuously forms and redefines itself."[5] The recent saturation of everyday life with screen media and digital culture has led to dramatic shifts in public communication, challenging our sense of what it means to be a citizen in the 21st century.

Digital technologies have expanded the public capacity to author and circulate information in unforeseen ways. This has a tremendous impact on communities in crisis as they struggle for recognition of their own interests in the face of state control. The digital activist communication shift began in the early 1990s with the Zapatistas in southern Mexico, who broadcast communiqués of their grassroots revolution to a global community through a new technology called the internet. Then, in 1999, global activists armed with cameras and audio equipment hit the streets of Seattle to report on the mass demonstration against the World Trade Organization (WTO). While the mainstream media focused on fringe actions and broken business windows, the activists countered official police stories with their own media dispatches. Activist street tapes documented a narrative that mainstream media missed, telling the stories that brought a broad range of protestors to the streets. The tapes captured and distributed images of a militarized, weapon-wielding police in aggressive engagement with peaceful demonstrators. A decade later, activists recorded the bloodied body of Michael Brown lying dead in the streets of Ferguson, Missouri. This time, dozens of mobile phones captured the scene, and the videos immediately circulated online, causing a media firestorm. The cell phone recordings became evidence of biased police investigating and unprovoked police attack, leaving traditional news outlets with little original content. Shifts in online engagement and mobile recording patterns allow people outside of business, state, and mainstream media sectors to create a visible digital presence that circumvents traditional media content.

This has led to new and reinvented forms of communication that sometimes involve unconventional uses of technology, such as live-streaming broadcasts, memes, podcasts, hashtags, blogs, mobile photography, and interactive discussion boards. No technology is single use, and we must consider the specific practices and distribution networks that create vibrant new pathways for communication. Countercultural communities develop media practices that help them "sustain their group ethics and identities."[6] As Jessa Lingel suggests in her book, *Digital Counter-Cultures and the Struggle for Community*, "Looking at counter-cultures' appropriation provides a way of identifying (and critiquing) mainstream narratives and their underlying structures of power."[7] The standardization of the internet at the turn of the century brought people together in new ways, paving the future for social media and newly formed social networks. Twitter, Facebook, Tumblr, Reddit, and many other networking platforms allow for a peer-to-peer parallel broadcast network that has the potential to challenge traditional hegemonic structures and institutions. Visibility through digital production, online self-publishing, and circulation through social networks are more than ways of gathering an audience; these forms of communication consistently disrupt, create, penetrate, challenge, focus, and reframe important public conversations.

This chapter focuses on documentary representations of police brutality, examining how the intersection of race and the incidental witnessing of unjustified police force has grown into global documentary practice. It is important to note that documentary representation of police brutality did not begin with digital culture. Its roots extend far back into documentary history, including early labor and civil rights documentary, vocational training videos, recovered undocumented histories of urban uprisings, and accidental recordings of police brutality. This predigital history foregrounds and overlaps with the prolific contemporary digital culture that has emerged around conflicts with police. Street-tape cultures that first manifested around Rodney King now extend to the deaths of Michael Brown, Eric Gardner, Tamir Rice, and Sandra Bland, as well as live streaming and the Black Lives Matter movement. Citizens are discovering new ways to generate influence that are similar in form to oral and textual traditions but different in capacity and function. Although some of this digital rhetoric provides a powerful affront to systematic oppression and exploitation, the technology alone is incapable of sustaining long-term struggle or providing proper protections for those recording injustices on the streets. Nonetheless, documentary production practice plays an important role in confronting cultures of white supremacy, especially in organizations tasked with "protecting" our communities with a barrel of a gun.

These little-documented stories of unjustified police force are removed—often purposefully and forcibly—from the historical landscape. Stories that are deliberately silenced may be stilled and some may die, but many live on. The very energy of disappearance builds tension toward the remembrance and revelation of what has been forgotten. As Avery Gordon suggests, the past always haunts the present. We are "tied to historical and social effects"[8] that haunt us and demand recognition. Our history is a "seething presence, acting on and often meddling with taken-for-granted realities, the ghost is just the sign, or the empirical evidence if you like, that tells you a haunting is taken place."[9] Ghosts speak through and with the documentary screen, revealing what is submerged, placing it on the political landscape for consideration.

Vivian Sobchack, Bill Nichols, and Linda Williams have considered the witnessing of real danger and death through the documentary camera. Nichols developed a taxonomy, addressing this process of witnessing as a form of gaze, including (1) the accidental gaze, which occurs at the moment of violence or death captured unintentionally; (2) the helpless gaze, which encourages a passivity or lack of engagement; (3) the endangered gaze, which happens when the camera person is at risk and captures the perilous conditions of production; (4) the interventional gaze, which appears when the camera becomes a physical embodiment of the human operating it; (5) the humane gaze, which emphasizes the human agency behind the camera marked by compassionate recording of an unavoidable death; and (6) the clinical or professional gaze, which is a mode of personal detachment and movement away from empathy.[10] These categories provide insight into the practices of looking with little critical apparatus to assess when these strategies can be exploitative. This chapter addresses these approaches as an attempt to position audience for social change.

Every new technological development brings new hope for efficiency, equal representation, and equal access to technology. Our individual worlds have been transformed by emerging technology, but does technology have the same power to transform our collective movements for social change? Can technology make social change more efficient, robust, immediate, and accessible? This book examines how concerned citizens engage in documentary resistance and activism in a bourgeoning digital world; we witness media makers exploring the opportunities for social justice that emerge in this new terrain. This chapter specifically addresses how documentary representations of police brutality changed with the shift from analog to digital culture. This story begins with street-tape culture and the vernacular cinematic discourse that emerged in the process of recording undocumented history. I then analyze police training videos as part of the larger representation of unjustified police force. The remainder of the chapter offers a conceptual map of representations, including urban rebellion documentary, Rodney King and the aftermath, patterns of unjustified force, and live streaming as mobile cinema.

Street Tapes and Vernacular Cinematic Discourse

"Street videos" or "street tapes" appeared in the late 1960s and continued into the 1970s as cable access channels provided access to equipment and community media training. Televisual culture in the late 1960s notably offered a public site where agitational vernacular publics could challenge hegemonic practices of media production and content. New media makers borrowed or appropriated media authorship for their own arguments while also creating a vernacular cinematic discourse. This approach amounted to an aesthetic refusal of the slick visual logics of mainstream media production. The style evolved from the first inexpensive, lightweight, and portable handheld cameras (1/2-inch reel-to-reel portapaks), used to generate vernacular images of public life.

Street tapes are characterized by amateur production quality and spontaneous interviews with people from all walks of life, carried out in streets, workplaces, and the community. The result is in an anti-slick street aesthetic marked by shaky hand-held camera images, beheaded protesting bodies, fast and out-of-focus pans, in-camera editing, and various technical imperfections. Many of these impromptu visual markers functioned to distinguish activist video from mass-produced broadcast images, establishing credibility with markers of visual authenticity. This aesthetic emerged from the awkwardness of early portable video technology and new users picking up equipment in unpredictable, sometimes volatile, environments.

This moment was defined by the new accessibility and portability of production equipment, which allowed more diversity to emerge in who could take control of the tools of authorship and presence on the screen. Early street-tape culture sought to build grassroots community institutions and democratize access to production resources. Giving people access to tools that allowed them to document their lives and negotiate the world on their own terms opened a vernacular space with the potential to counter the prevailing dominant ideology of broadcast television. For example, the League of Revolutionary Black Workers in Detroit used film to "challenge the institutional racism of business, unions, and the police, as well as wider government policies."[11] The League was a Marxist-Leninist umbrella organization comprised of revolutionary unions across trades whose struggles extended beyond the shop floor. In the late 1960s, with help from former Newsreel media producers, they created Finally Got the News. The documentary was a representation of black working conditions at midcentury, "where contemporary labor, in spite of being paid, becomes an extension of slavery's regime and ideology."[12] As is the case in many political organizations, there were intense internal struggles between the white filmmakers and black workers, as well as widespread sexism that helped create a cavern between production practice and the solidarity commitments of the struggle.[13]

The aesthetic was a part of a political statement that validated the argument the street tapes presented: "The low quality, grainy, and shaky footage was usually black and white and unedited, which offered a new type of straight-from-the-scene authenticity that challenged the presumed objectivity of broadcast television."[14] While broadcast television was sanitized, narrated, overproduced, slick, and run by elites, street-tape cultures could define themselves against the mainstream in form and content. The spontaneous, untrained, shaky footage is edited in a way that does not draw attention to the creative decisions that make street tapes partial and selective. This aesthetic allows the action on screen to have the appearance of raw footage, giving audience members the feeling that they can piece together their own story about the events on the screen. As Horsfield and Hilderbrand argue, "Media activists saw handheld video equipment as a tool to document a new type of direct-from-the-scene reportage that was not manipulated, biased, or reshaped in any way to distort reality."[15] Although street tapes carry the author's imprint in the form of decisions made about framing, stopping, and starting the camera, and placing shots next to each other, the production aesthetics and the dissemination of content not readily found in the mainstream media foster a sense of authenticity. The form—unsteady and unpredictable—meant audiences could look at onscreen images as raw data in an uncertain world.

Karen Ranucci reminds us that in the early practices of community media, "the process of making video itself was often as important as the finished product, or more important in many cases." Ranucci worked at DCTV in her early career, collaborating with the New York public schools to teach media to underresourced students. The focus on media pedagogy built liberating pathways of literacy. Ranucci continues:

It was inspiring to me as a teacher, but it was really inspiring to these kids because for the first time, they were beginning to feel, like . . . in control of their own lives, having the tool to really analyze things, to be able to express themselves where . . . you know, because of their lack of writing skills, they always felt deficient and couldn't express themselves. Now with video, they could really express themselves. So, it was really energizing and revolutionary in many ways in terms of transforming people's lives from being victims who felt isolated and alone. . . . In other revolutionary situations where people would pick up a gun to fight, a camera is even more powerful sometimes in terms of its effect on others, and trying to prove a point and change a situation.[16]

While academics might focus on systems of documentary moving-image representation and circulation, Ranucci identifies the importance of identity construction in the process of making media. This creation process can transform the self with new possibilities for expression, agency, and especially community.

"Bicycling" was one of the earliest types of participatory media networks in video culture. This term referred to the funneling of video projects and media practices through person-to-person networks and across geographical divides. This is the digital network of another time, when the challenges of analog technology did not stop people from connecting with media. I received an education in "bicycling" one afternoon in lower Manhattan when I met Skip Blumberg to talk about early video activism. Recalling his early work with the Videofreex, he explained:

Videofreex was really practical and production oriented. We made videos and we edited them and we would mail them out and, you know, it was called bicycling. And we would just send our tapes, sometimes even original tapes, to people that we knew and when something important happened, we would cover demonstrations. We were aligned with the alternate culture a lot, so we would cover different events and subjects with the alternate culture.[17]

The tapes circulated as an exchange of information as well as an alternative representation. Recording the political counterculture expanded cinema's capacity for entertainment; media making became a kind of cinemocracy.

I was curious about the term "bicycling." How did it emerge, and how did the practice offer such rich and complex ways to address media's need for networks to move the circulation of vernacular images and ideas? Blumberg continued: "Well, it's called bicycling, but there were no bicycles actually. We just mailed tapes to people. Well, again, the earliest days, it was about being in touch with groups of people, with these other production groups and collectives that could play back. So, we would send it to places that could play back." As a manner of circulation, couriers or ambassadors would literally transport the documentary impulse to different places across the United States. Dorothy Thigpen, executive director of New York Newsreel (now Third World Newsreel), explains that the movement began in the 1970s and spread across the United States. Documentaries and their makers traveled through informal countercultural and political networks. Newsreel people and media "bicycled around different states, because there were a lot of things going on in all the different states in the U.S. related to all of these social issues. So, that's how it started." Collectively, the Newsreel movements and the video activists produced some of the most captivating and important cultural history of our time.

The 1980s brought Ronald Reagan and deep cuts in funding for the arts, perhaps partially as a response to this newly powerful vernacular cinematic impulse. A new legion of video activists, organized around combating nuclear proliferation, took to the streets to record underreported protests and demonstrations. In the late 1980s and early 1990s, a proliferation of street tapes documented a societal transition in worker–management relations, a burgeoning critique of media conglomerations, and an impending health crisis.[18] In this exploratory environment, more militant activist collectives began to form.

The explosion of the AIDS crisis during these years produced a new kind of participatory video culture and activist intervention. The AIDS activist-video movement documented demonstrations, the struggle for visibility, and the evolution of the disease from the perspective of those experiencing it. The videotexts functioned as a necessary and powerful counternarrative to the absent or flatly negative depictions of AIDS in the mainstream media.[19]

The evolution of mobile technology in the late 1990s coincided with a massive political uprising against globalization and an increased reliance on online information streams to find up-to-date, underground, asynchronous information. This was a significant moment for street-tape culture, as technology became more compact, mobile, and inexpensive, the internet became standardized, and political conflict was plentiful. The WTO street tapes, which emerged before the advent of social media, reveal a participatory media culture transitioning away from analog production and distribution models toward early experimentation with digital formats and the internet. These varied predigital efforts to address the troubled relationship between police and community deserve further study.

Documentary Pedagogy and Police Training

The bulk of this chapter explores how communities have used documentary representation to resist police brutality. Before we can explore this multifaceted articulation, however, it is important to address the use of documentary as a pedagogical tool in the troubled relationship between law enforcement and community. Films created for police training harness the educational capacities and demonstrate the role-modeling possibilities of documentary discourse.

In 1964, social justice filmmaker George Stoney made a series of five films on police work culture that included representations of officers working to serve communities rather than just bring down criminals. These films were used in group discussions that allowed law enforcement officers to share their immediate experiences with one another and the health care professionals in their communities. Made in cooperation with the New Orleans Police Department, *Booked for Safekeeping* (1960) instructs police officers on how to respond to people with mental illness. Written materials supplemented the films during these discussions. *The Cry for Help* (1962) teaches police officers how to interact with people suffering from suicidal ideation. In an effort to help police understand that alcohol can disguise or mask serious physical and mental illness, Stoney directed *The Mask* (1963). Addressing the conditions of police work culture, *Under Pressure* (1964) discusses personal and emotional problems related to law enforcement work. *The Man in the Middle* (1966) demonstrates how police officers can work more sensitively with the communities they serve. These films were produced through the Louisiana Association for Mental Health and in collaboration with its executive director, Dr. Lloyd Rowland. The International Association of Chiefs of Police co-sponsored the series with support from the National Institute for Mental Health. The last film in the series was made with the New York Police Department.

George Stoney was friendly and cooperative with state institutions during his documentary career, seeing organizations like the New Orleans and New York Police Departments as collaborators. He consulted with mental health organizations on how to help represent the process of care. Collaborations with these kinds of institutions can be problematic for activists, however, as organizations sometimes act to protect entrenched institutional cultures in the face of confrontation and change. Could Stoney's representations of idealized New Orleans Police Department (NOPD) procedures have glossed over corruption within the department police culture?

For example, in 1964, a decade after the Metropolitan Crime Commission exposed rampant misconduct in the NOPD, Joseph Fichter conducted a study that found that the department still needed to take steps to improve professionalism when handling arrests and other interactions with citizens. Sections of the report detail continued racist and abusive language, informal bribery, sexual harassment, and physical abuse of arrestees.[20] This was happening at the same time Stoney was making his documentary series, which featured reflective, understanding, and compassionate police officers.

The documentaries are instructional in tone and clearly speak to police officers; the humane gaze of Stoney's production practice creates identification with an altruistic beat officer. There are attempts at reflective moments and productive modeling of professional practices for interacting with a variety of community members. In *The Cry for Help* (1962), the main narrator, who is also a police officer, recounts a situation when he made a bad decision answering a call to a non-English-speaking Latino family. A white bystander remarks, "They always hollering for nothin." Police responding to the call find an unarmed and possibly emotionally unstable man who lunges at the officers. The officer makes the mistake of approaching the situation in a way that creates a more dangerous encounter. The documentary shows proper procedures and explains why a gun would be useless in this situation. The police officers demonstrate grabbing pillow cushions to subdue the attacker. The documentary goes on to explain common patterns and temperaments experienced on such calls. At the time, ambulances did not transport mentally ill patients to care, and police officers had to handle this duty. Back at the jail, the arresting officer checks in on the man he arrested, taking the blame for the wounds he received. The documentary voiceover declares: "Whether they understand what these people are like or they know what to expect and act accordingly, the police can do the job safely and effectively until a better solution can be found." The documentary ends with a question: "What is the situation in your community?" These films address an audience of officers and community members, using documentary as a pedagogical tool. In the following decades, pedagogical police training videos continue but strike a very different tone. Stoney's idealism and compassion is gone, and the works represent officers under assault. The films become defensive, focusing on how to control citizens at all costs.

Police Officer Stress (2001) deals with the everyday trauma involved in police work and features police clinician Dr. Angela Wingo. The documentary represents officers as benevolent helpers in the fight against an uncontrollable criminal force. Unlike Stoney's documentaries, which provide instruction on nonviolent approaches and professional behavior, this documentary depicts a police force with

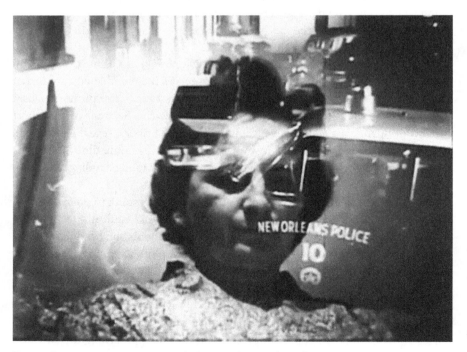

Figure 6.1 In George Stoney's *Booked for Safekeeping* (1960) a women struggles with calling the police on her abusive husband.

Figure 6.2 The police arrive to assist a Spanish speaking family in George Stoney's *Booked for Safekeeping* (1960). The police ask the English speaking bystander for information, the man describes the family to police: "they always hollerin."

Figure 6.3 Police subdue a mentally ill person with a family living room chair in George Stoney's *Booked for Safekeeping* (1960).

Figure 6.4 Police subdue a mentally ill person with living room cushions in George Stoney's *Booked for Safekeeping* (1960).

Figure 6.5 A police officer displays empathy and listening skills when talking with an emotionally distraught wife about her husband in George Stoney's *Booked for Safekeeping* (1960).

combat fatigue in an unending war against the criminal element. There is a similar educational framework, but the focus is exclusively on officer stress and not the ways officers' behavior affects others. There is a sharp turn toward the clinical or professional gaze in these representations and a growing dispassion toward community that is chilling. *Fresno, CA-Multi-Ethnic Community Policing* (1999) focuses on a community-policing program in a multiethnic environment. It highlights the Fresno and St. Louis Police Departments, which have taken a community approach to policing. A St. Louis police officer explains his relationship to multiethnic communities: "Their mistrust is already built in, maybe for years and years. As they become more Americanized and they're here longer, they realize that we are actually here to serve them." Although this documentary focuses on the relationship between the St. Louis Police Department and the Bosnian community as an example of successful community policing, it is silent about the department's fraught relationship with the city's African American community, a situation that would explode in nearby Ferguson, Missouri, less than two decades later.

Use of Force: The Death of Eric Garner (2015) documents veteran trainer Eric Austermann's perspective on Garner's death at the hands of police. Cameras and video are becoming ubiquitous in law enforcement, and this documentary asks what police can learn from this documentation. The trainer featured in this documentary, a sixteen-year veteran of the St. Louis County Police Department, provides training in tactics of arrest. During the 2014 uprising in Ferguson around Michael Brown's death, he served on the frontlines and in supporting roles, "defending" administrative offices. He explains the procedure followed in the arrest that killed Garner without addressing questions of ethics and prudent professional behavior. Unlike Stoney's documentaries, this training film does not foster generosity or empathy for the arrested; the assailant is to be contained and controlled.

Documentary representations that focus on compliance citizens and the concerted efforts to sidestep empathy illustrates how the dispassionate professional gaze extends the apparatus of state control within the framework of cultural production. Garner is described as "emotionally barricaded," and the narrator recounts the police "giving Mr. Garner a long time to vent" but he "refused to comply." The documentary narrator, the St. Louis-based trainer, shows the footage of a lifeless Garner on the ground as medics report he is still breathing. The narrator goes on to list health afflictions that contributed to Garner's death without addressing the fact that Garner was upright and breathing before police intervention. The narrator concludes: "We have to put this on Mr. Garner. Mr. Garner dictates what happens in this situation. That happens with every use of force, every resisting arrest with any police officer in the United States. The subject in custody dictates what happens next." The documentary then declares, "NYPD sources confirm that Eric Garner was a player in an organized crime cigarette smuggling syndicate." There is no evidence, documentation, or explanation for this statement. The medical examiner concluded that Garner died of compressions of the neck and chest and prone positioning during physical restraint by police. Eric Garner's wife, six children, and three grandchildren survive him. The person who recorded Garner's death at the hands of police, Ramsey Orta, is serving a four-year sentence for unrelated gun and drug possession charges, arrests that transpired after recording Garner's death on his cell phone and drawing scrutiny from police.

In the evolution of these training videos, we see a steady move away from identification with community toward an increasingly narrow focus on police authority, coded in the gaze of professional discourse. The identification with police authority does not include consideration of multiple viewpoints or alternative frameworks of policing. The exception is *Fresno, CA-Multi-ethnic Community Policing* (1999), which addresses difference and community, providing a small space for the problems associated with this collision. In the end, however, this documentary examines idealized policing programs while failing to confront the existing problems between police and community.

Urban Rebellion Documentary

In the 1960s, a flood of urban uprisings drew the attention of white Americans across the United States. Neighborhoods burned to the ground, and commercial sectors were looted and destroyed. Riots, uprisings, and rebellions act as collective expressions of a community pushed to its edge; in these situations, we see mounting frustration over a lack of opportunity, consistent police brutality, and a lack of political representation that festers and explodes. Media makers have recorded these moments, documenting their significance to our understanding of difference, community, and structural inequality. These documentaries often simultaneously represent tremendous acts of unjustified force and police misconduct.

Some observers understood the urban uprisings as the result of structural inequity, and others saw them simply as criminal behavior. In an attempt to manage these outbursts, state control clamped down on communities in crisis, sometimes exacerbating the initial destruction of property with violent, physical containment of citizens. Early labor documentaries provided our first encounters with documentary representations of police brutality. The urban uprisings of the 1960s were one expression of black agency that ignited fear and aggression in law enforcement, the apparatus of state control. Documentaries about urban uprisings provide our first representations of a racialized citizens' war in the streets, where "armed conflict erodes the social and cultural fabric of unarmed communities."[21]

July '64: Unrest in Rochester New York (2006) documents police brutality and the citizen uprising in Rochester that began on Friday, July 24, 1964. The events that followed changed the city of Rochester and reverberated throughout the state and the nation. The film addresses the underlying causes of rebellions that swept through black communities during the 1960s, providing an alarming wake-up call for America in the form of visible community struggle. There is a distant, hopeless gaze to the early representations of urban rebellion, a contemplative sadness of justice deferred.

Revolution '67 (2007) documents the explosive urban rebellion in Newark, New Jersey, in July 1967. The film reveals stories about the longstanding racial, economic, and political tensions that have perpetuated inner-city poverty and unrest in Newark and around the country. Tom Hayden, one of the founders of Students for a Democratic Society, was active in the community at the time. In an interview for the documentary, he describes the context: "There was a good deal of bigoted stereotyping of young black people. It was as if they were already a mob, even when they were peaceful and apathetic, they were a mob in the making. So, when they actually became a mob, I could imagine, from the police standpoint, only crushing force could stop them." The documentary shows the perspective of city officials, community leaders, and law enforcement officers who address, among other things, unjustified force employed by the city and state police as well as the National Guard during the uprisings in the summer of 1967. The film exposes the armed apparatus of the state, with structures of racism and classism solidly in place, using excessive force against the poor black community. Examples on screen include the state's use of automatic weapon fire on its citizens and official reports documenting that the police fired 13,000 rounds, while the alleged perpetrators of the unrest fired fewer than 100 rounds. Twenty-four of the twenty-six people dead were African Americans, killed by law enforcement.

Let the Fire Burn (2013) captures the longtime feud and eventual stand-off between the political organization MOVE and the city of Philadelphia, which culminated in a day-long battle in which police used tear gas, fire hoses, and over 10,000 rounds of ammunition to forcibly remove the organization from its residence. The authorities ordered military-grade explosives dropped on MOVE from a helicopter. The quickly escalating conflict and the extreme response by authorities resulted in the tragic deaths of eleven people, including five children, and the destruction of sixty-one surrounding homes. It was later discovered that authorities left the fire to burn and destroy the surrounding neighborhood. The documentary uses only archival news coverage and interviews, giving the audience a feeling of being present as events unfold in real time. There is an interventionist gaze, a sense of embodying the perspective of the reporters, first responders, moving in and out of the line of fire. It is the creation of space shared with historical actors as a mode of being transformed back into time. This choice and the decision to use realist narrative strategies, never breaking the frame for a contemporary interview, allow the audience to remain in the time the events occurred. The story transports us to Philadelphia in the late 1970s–mid-1980s, and we stay there. The film depicts life under a chronic police assault that creates a culture of terror. Military tanks, a bomb dropped from a helicopter, and encroaching police show a community under constant attack. The action happens in a time and place that doesn't exist now but that has consequences that still matter to us tremendously. These films establish an intimate relationship between survivors of racism and viewers, forging collective identification with those in the margins.

Documentary representations of police brutality and race fall mainly into one of three categories. First, urban rebellion documentaries present complicated community relations and the experiences of watching an uprising in the United States during the 1960s. Second, a collection of documentaries, produced mostly in the last two decades, focus on excessive force and the killing of community members by police officers in the line of duty. This is a submerged history that is not readily or easily available. These films create a visual map of casualties, connecting events, people, and action in ways that mainstream institutions refuse to make transparent. Third, we are currently experiencing an emergent vernacular cinematic discourse composed of live-streaming responses to the political struggles around practices of police misconduct. These documentary representations of police brutality pivot around historical moments of video witness that galvanize discussions around law and order in the Unites States. The most iconic of these moving images is George Holliday's camcorder footage of the beating of Rodney King by officers from the Los Angeles Police Department in 1991.

Figure 6.6 The unplanned recording of the Rodney Kind beating is perhaps the most influential street tape of our time.

Witnessing Brutality: Rodney King and the Aftermath

The United States has a history of community media culture. Groups have long "pinned a sheet to the wall" and projected films in community spaces. Early African American cinema "created by Black artists that portrayed the Black community in a positive light was not accepted into normal distribution chains,"[22] and so it was shown in these ad hoc spaces, confronting the white supremacist logics of commercial and mainstream culture. One of the best-known instances of video documentation of accidental witnessing was the footage of the beating of Rodney King by members of the Los Angeles Police Department. The 1990s marked a significant moment for African American bodies on videotape as "the site on which national trauma—sexual harassment, date rape, drug abuse, AIDS, racial and economic urban conflict—has been dramatized."[23]

In these moments, "black bodies and their attendant dramas are publically consumed by the larger populace."[24] The eighty-one-second videotape of four white police officers beating Rodney King provided viewers with evidence that exacerbated a great public division of opinion around racial inequity. It is an accidental witnessing at the moment of attack that evokes a sense of horror at its length and hopelessness to stop the violent act. The videotape as witness supported opposing narratives and viewers imported their own beliefs onto the screen,[25] bringing a polysemic moment of cultural confusion and chaos. Most importantly, the Rodney King video emphasized "the power of the local, organized video teams."[26] One example of this power is Cop Watch, which began in the 1990s as a way of organizing community members to observe and document problematic police practices.

Several documentaries took note of the cultural importance of the Rodney King beating. *Let It Fall: Los Angeles 1982–1992* (2017), directed by John Ridley, documents the decade leading up to the 1992 Los Angeles Riots. *The Lost Tapes: LA Riots* (2017), created by the Smithsonian Channel, offers a reconstruction of events from news footage, without narration. The use of an internal LAPD video in the documentary captures Los Angeles police chief, Daryl Gates, joking about the "good lighting" in the Rodney King Video. *Uprising: Hip Hop and the LA Riots* (2012), directed by Mark Ford, was narrated by Snoop Dog and broadcast on VH1. It addressed the subject of how hip hop predicted the LA riots and mended the community in the aftermath. *LA Burning*, directed by Erik Parker (A&E), focuses on memories of the three-day event; it includes new interviews, news reports, and found footage from street videographers who covered the riots on the ground. *LA 92* (2017), directed by Dan Lindsay and T. J. Martin, uses the B-roll news footage in the seconds before the feeds go live to explore the volatility on the ground in the most active neighborhoods. The film also uses a great deal of aerial footage, building distance between the audience and the reasons why people flooded the streets. The documentary is bookended with the Watts Riot, building the sense of systematic problems lurking below the surface. There is a passivity built into these representations, a gaze upon a caricature of the actual event. The King video and the documentary impulses it inspired generated broad discussion and revealed a great cultural divide that continues to fester.

Most of these documentaries are investing in the project of representing social change in an effort to secure a narrative foothold in public history. The tone is retrospective; the documentary camera is a vehicle to shake complicated understandings into clearer focus. The narratives attempt to make sense of urban uprisings from the outside, committed to the framework of civil society and its promises for equity. Recently, many of the commercial documentary projects focused on the issues surrounding the Rodney King trial brought back paternalistic voiceover narration, which excluded the perspectives of the community members most affected by the uprisings. These interventions are a challenge to news and mainstream media representation but are not well connected to the movements of people around these issues that continue to pull communities apart.

Resistance and opposition are foundational to street-tape culture. Like most radical media, street tapes oppose the professional practices of media production and seek to transform them. The opposition reflects the failure of mainstream news to represent and report on the interests of a significant portion of the global community.[27] Most activist video collectives that produce street tapes are characterized by "their attempts to free themselves from the power of government, the state and other dominant institutions and practices."[28] Many of the documentaries above benefited from the abundance of prosumer video recording equipment in the hands of average people who can grab a compact camera and press "record" at a moment's notice. It is this accessibility that transforms police abuse into something that can be documented and evidenced by those in close proximity.

The digital rhetoric[29] that emerged at the turn of the century came not only from the digitization of our world, but also from the ways these processes affected rituals of communication. Digitization changed how we communicate and with whom, shifting private/public distinctions and altering structures of control over the means of representation and witnessing.[30] This phenomenon manifested itself in emerging forms of communication such as street tapes, memes, podcasts, hashtags, blogs, mobile photography, and discussion boards enabled by an evolving digital culture.

Patterns of Unjustified Force: No Justice, No Peace

The history of purposeful observation of police misconduct goes back to the Black Panther Party's practice of following abusive police officers in California to protect the most vulnerable in the community. In the 1980s, public access television was an important outlet for video witnessing of police brutality, as well as providing access to video equipment and editing spaces.[31] Organizations like Cop Watch later emerged to counter unprofessional and unconstitutional police behavior in a variety of contexts. Documentary representations of police brutality opened communication spaces for interventions around points of community tension and their possible resolution. The framing of these documentary representations is critical to the community outcomes that follow. We see that storytelling can begin to repair "torn social fabrics, reconstruct eroded social bonds, re-appropriate public spaces, and strengthen strategies of nonviolent conflict resolution."[32] Where does this documentary work fit in the process of social change?

Every Mother's Son (2004), directed by Tami Gold and Kelly Anderson, addresses policing in communities of color from the perspective of three mothers whose sons were killed by officers. The film documents the confusion and outrage brought on by unjustified police force. Mayor Giuliani's tough-on-crime agenda meant police practices such as "stop and frisk" and "slam and jam" proliferated and intensified. These trends led to situations in which plain clothes officers stopped people on the streets, often without probable cause, to find guns and drugs. Community members describe these raids as treasure hunts. Police targeted young men of color, and sometimes these interactions went so badly that otherwise innocent people died. The documentary shows police officers manipulating family members by asking for information about the victim's history before allowing them access to the victim. These efforts to gather information, such as whether the victim had a history of mental illness or criminal activity, were intended to obscure accusations of police misconduct.

The documentary captures communities expressing exhaustion after decades of police misconduct and demanding immediate structural change, such as civilian review of police in light of decades of abuse. This film articulates the nuances of losing a family member at the hands of law enforcement, a shared experience that connects those who are fighting for change. As one mother reflects: "I think there is a certain feeling we all share because our sons didn't die because of an illness. They didn't die because they were hit by a car. There was no accident. Our children were killed by the police. And that is a far different thing than losing your son any other way." This point of collective identification is complicated and emotionally porous. Avery Gordon (2011) writes of the disorientation that comes as "ghosts" haunt people and social institutions. As Gordon (2008) suggests, "Being haunted draws us affectively, sometimes against our will and always a bit magically, into the structure of feeling of a reality we come to experience, not as cold knowledge, but as a transformative recognition."[33] Even if we don't share this experience at first hand, documentary storytelling offers us a way to develop empathy for struggles of that position.

Every Mother's Son includes a range of protest activity organized by Parents Against Police Brutality, including a sit-in at the Bronx District Attorney's Office. The story is told from the perspective of parents doing what all parents would do to seek justice for their child. The communities onscreen—largely immigrant and poor—live in a context where parents cannot sleep until their children come home at night, young people of color are suspect on sight, police act with impunity and with the protection of criminal justice institutions. Clemencia Rodriguez argues that, when operating in a world where citizens are unarmed and under siege by armed forces, "the role of citizens' media is to go beyond the journalistic coverage and focus on community needs and daily realties of people in their communities."[34] These documentaries depict collective action to meet the everyday needs of the community. They project images of an energetic, relentless struggle characterized by a collective force of strength. *Every Mother's Son* is powerful because it captures a turn in community consciousness in the form of representing the widespread loss of trust in government and policy institutions in communities of color. The patterns of unjustified force identified in *Every Mother's Son* (2004) persist, pushing increasingly desperate communities to the edge. In this film and others, the documentary representation of an unjustified police force is multifaceted and includes reports from the streets, mediating conflicts, recording undocumented history, and representing the most recent urban uprising.

REPORTS FROM THE STREETS

Before 2014 mainstream media outlets seldom address the unjustified use of force by police. For much of the historical scope of this chapter, pubic dialogue about police misconduct was taboo, controversial, and characterized as anti-police. Documenting police brutality was a defiant form of resistance. The documentary work we now turn to navigates different emotional terrain. Representations of police brutality were transformed with the development of cell phone recording; a decade into the 21st century, the mobile camera in everyone's pocket provided an unexpected plot twist. Political movements around unjustified police force that have been agitating for decades can now record police acting with impunity in their communities. Though compact video cameras had been around for a while, smart phone technology allowed community members to record and circulate an event with simply a slight movement of the fingertip.

Easy access to mobile recording created a new generation of street-tape activist. In the collision around poverty, policing, and representation, this new generation understands image production as a tool of political intervention. This includes up-close and intimate reports of daily life; the camera is the physical embodiment of intervention into a shared historical space. These media makers are attempting to challenge dominant representations of the "scary black perpetrator." These street recordings provide protection and simultaneously challenge the conventions of representation. These video clips are dispatches from the community, shifting the axis of collaboration from balanced perspectives to a focus representing unheard voices.

Through the stories of Oscar Grant, Lovelle Mixon, and journalist JR Valrey, *Operation Small Axe* (2010), directed by Adimu Madyun, represents life "under police terrorism" in Oakland, California. Fear of police brutality and misconduct has percolated in the community for decades, resulting in uprisings that are a form of self-defense for communities pushed to their edge. This documentary represents militarized and racist police forces occupying Oakland's communities of color. JR Valrey narrates the story through his community, his networks, his radio show, and the public spaces of protest, speaking directly and candidly to the camera, sometimes in rhythmic cadence. We begin to see the ways mobile camera phones act as witness to longstanding institutional abuses of power. In the opening scenes of this documentary, we have the cell phone recording of Oscar Grant's detainment at the Fruitvale station metro stop and his killing by police. It is the accidental witnessing of death on camera, a representation that is distant and produces jerky framing with the imprint of anxiety physically marked on the recording, a consequence of the shaking hands of the camera person. The result is the undeniable but arresting documentation of death at the hands of police.

Community members report that, after the shooting, police attempted to take away the cell phones from nearby witnesses instead of helping Grant receive medical attention, but there were too many cameras to suppress. The documentary incorporates cell phone recordings of intense moments of street protest and routine surveillance by police. Scenes illustrating the historical power relationship between citizens and police are edited together, connecting back with earlier attempts to control the actions of the Black Panthers. The film reveals the pattern of this excessive force and ways communities address safety concerns under these conditions. Especially "[i]n a culture of terror, unarmed civilians live with the knowledge that at any moment their sense of normalcy could shatter." Such experiences with armed police are shared by communities in San Francisco and across the country, but they are also familiar to communities in Afghanistan, Iraq, and Palestine. This larger critique of police force is underscored by closely framed street interviews in which people testify to their own experiences with unjustified police force. In these interviews, we see how "citizens' media can help resignify the memory of violent attack" with historically informed representation, "recodifing the meanings that violence leaves behind."[35] The mobile recordings create a powerful evidentiary frame, shifting credibility from police to the victims of assault and murder.

Copwatch: These Streets Are Watching (2010) was produced by the Cop Watch organization, which is devoted to the idea that community members have the right to see what police are doing: "Showing concern for what police do in our communities is a small but real deterrent against police misconduct." Cop Watch began to use cameras as a mirror to document police conduct long before the development of mobile camera recording, embodying the interventionist gaze in practice and representation. Organized to document misconduct, highly mobile recording technology further amplifies the effectiveness of community witnessing with the camera, multiplying the images documented and the organization's ability to be a consistent presence in the field. The documentary reminds audiences that the police are community servants and employees of the government, and that as citizens, the people have a constitutional right to observe and review police conduct. The documentary impulse can mirror and record police conduct to prevent abuse. Cop Watch began as a neighborhood watch organization, working with vulnerable communities that needed protection from police. As one witness recounts, communities in the same city were being treated unequally by police and no one was watching. The nonviolent group legally observes police conduct and records interactions in case the need for accountability arises.

Copwatch begins with a montage of police officers encountering Cop Watch videographers in the field. Police greet the videographers with a familiar refrain, acknowledging that they know why the video camera is present and expressing appreciation for the organization. The film later uses montage techniques to highlight the cavernous gap between legal, professional conduct and actual police behavior in the field. New negotiations are happening on the streets as intentional legal observers appear with mobile cameras to document exchanges between police and community. These montages of misconduct are important because they provide a counternarrative to the unquestioned cultural credibility of police, who often operate with impunity.

No Justice No Peace: California's Battle Against Police Brutality and Racist Violence (2013) is a documentary produced by Liberation News that focuses on the struggles against police brutality and racist violence precipitated by Southern California's epidemic of police shootings. The documentary begins with a montage of recordings of incidents of police brutality for which the offending officers did not face jail time. The sequences highlight the pattern of brutality in a horrific montage of assault, one beating after another. One accidental witnessing of police violence after another is profound and disturbing, and later finding out that these incidents did not include justice for the victimized is horrific. The larger story centers on the organizing efforts of more than thirty families of police brutality victims after the killing of Manuel Diaz by an officer in Anaheim, California. The families document patterns of victims being shot in the back and executed at close range. There are repeated testimonies about false police incident reports issued to cover up crimes committed by police officers. Community members begin to call this situation as an "epidemic," recognizing that while only certain cases are highlighted in the press, these incidents happen regularly in communities, cities, and towns across the nation. The documentary features people responding to the cascade of police violence and lack of accountability. We see massive protests when George Zimmerman is found not guilty of killing Trayvon Martin. An emerging portrait of the structure of violence emerges, along with a growing vernacular mass consciousness that things must change.

MEDIATING CONFLICT

One branch of documentary about excessive force uses the perspectives of unlikely victims' rights advocates, such as former law enforcement officers, to ask viewers to mediate between the intentions of abusive state institutions and victimized citizens. Audiences must negotiate between two opposing sides as a way to promote understanding and leading audience members toward points of stasis as a way to solve the root problem. This strategy challenges core American values such as liberty for all and the presumption of innocence. This documentary work begins to suggest a quickly compounding narrative that challenges the authority of police in society.

Where Is Hope—The Art of Murder (2015) was directed by Emmitt H. Thrower, a retired New York City cop-turned-filmmaker. The documentary tells the stories of disabled citizens murdered by police and the activist communities trying to end this targeted brutality. An estimated 50 percent or more of the victims of police brutality are disabled, though disability status is not acknowledged or recorded on police reports. Like many others, this documentary lists the names and circumstances of those killed at the hands of police to underscore the gravity and volume of the problem. The viewer witnesses congressional hearings that include documentation of police lying to the press and the press protecting the police.

When Justice Isn't Just (2015), directed by David Massey, explores why so many unarmed black people have been killed by law enforcement personnel. The documentary creates a portrait of inequality in the criminal justice system across the United States. The filmmakers talk to legal experts, law enforcement officials, activists, and victims' family members about how to prevent this violence, putting multiple viewpoints in tension with one another. This draws the audience's attention to the points of conflict that keep longstanding abuses in place without consequences.

Peace Officer (2015) depicts the increased militarization of the American police from the perspective of William "Dub" Lawrence, a former sheriff who established and trained Utah's first SWAT team. Thirty years later, that same SWAT unit killed Lawrence's son-in-law in a controversial stand-off. He uses his investigative skills to uncover new details about an officer-involved shooting in his own community. The documentary depicts the increasing use of paramilitary tactics and the effects of the 1033 program, a U.S. military program that gives militarized equipment to American police departments with the stipulation that they must use the equipment within one year. We witness police escalating situations with citizens and creating increasingly hostile engagements with firepower inherited from the military. Here, the institutional alliances one would come to expect, through which law enforcement would support and protect themselves, begin to fracture. The story follows a main character who developed programs for police and trained within police institutions but who later becomes a victim of the police and transforms into an outspoken victims' advocate.

Policing the Police (2016) is a Frontline documentary told from the perspective of a *New Yorker* magazine journalist, Jelani Cobb, who typically reports on the police from the outside. In this film, Cobb goes inside, shadowing police officers and talking to administrators. Cobb examines allegations of police abuses made against the Newark Police Department, which leads to exchanges between Cobb and law enforcement that result in difficult conversations about race. When the conversation turns to black and Latino officers policing their own communities, an officer asks if a black or Latino police officer can be a racist in the process of policing their own community. Cobb responds: "What makes it racism is not who did it but that it happens to the same community." The police officers represented in this documentary feel under siege by cell phone cameras and a hostile community, while simultaneously operating without transparency or proper documentation. The film depicts a powerful collision between the rights of citizens and the realities of the everyday police work culture. These points of stasis are important and create representational maps for moving forward through conflict.

UNDOCUMENTED HISTORIES

The silence imposed on public critique of law enforcement has left a long trail of undocumented stories of brutality and violence. The representations that do exist and circulate with regularity frame this issue as an urban problem for embattled families. Documentary media makers attempt to push at the geographical containment of this narrative, moving beyond the city and focusing on the victims of unjustified force who escaped with their lives. Developing a more complete record of these untold stories requires collaboration between filmmakers and communities. It is likely that the deeper the emotions cut through these truths, the more resistance there is to the retelling.

Arresting Power: Resisting Police Violence in Oregon (2015) documents conflict between Portland police and community members over the past fifty years. The film features vernacular voices from the community, victims of police misconduct, and the family members of those killed by police. This documentary holds viewers in the space of violence with meditative footage taken at the sites of attacks, using a complex audio track that features narration and recorded law enforcement communications about the incidents. While other documentaries bombard the viewer with montages of violence, this documentary quietly reveals the haunting space of violence, the absence of bodies and blood, and the tension that follows an unjustified police attack. The film roots the historical context of the problematic relationship between police and the community in the origins of U.S. law enforcement institutions, which initially functioned as slave patrols. The connection between systematic abuse by contemporary police and the history of slavery is usually obscured. The film also creates historical ties between the Black Panther Party and community members monitoring police behavior, including conflicts in Portland. Fifty years after the peak of the Black Panther Party, communities continue to need this kind of collective observation of police more than ever.

Stop-Challenging NYPD's "Stop and Frisk" Policies (2015) focuses on the controversial police tactic that has long inspired front-page news. Ten years earlier, *Every Mother's Son* (2004) examined stop and frisk, depicting communities of color already pushed to their edge by targeting and violence. Within the public imaginary, the ghosts of police impunity continue to haunt communities that live under the threat of armed violence. In the years between the two films, the tactic of stop and frisk inspired activism, stirred passions, created divisions, and became a catalyst for change. The central mechanism for creating structural change was *Floyd et al. v. the City of New York*, a class action lawsuit filed by the Center for Constitutional Rights in 2008. *Stop-Challenging NYPD's "Stop and Frisk" Policies* (2015) follows David Ourlicht, one of the four named plaintiffs in the case. The lawsuit alleged racial bias in the stop and frisk tactics carried out by the New York City Police Department. The landmark ruling declared that the NYPD's application of stop and frisk was unconstitutional. The documentary places "stop and frisk" in the context of a long history of civil rights struggles and raises a key question: "Must we trade safety for civil rights?" The film holds Mayor Giuliani's proactive policing techniques and Mayor Bloomberg's workplace efficiency efforts responsible for an increase in overly aggressive and militarized police stops in communities of color. The director and

Figure 6.7 A solidarity protest in Portland for the uprisings after the shooting of Michael Brown in Ferguson, MO featured in *Arresting Power: Resisting Police Violence in Portland, Oregon* (2015) co-directed by Jodi Darby, Julie Perini, and Erin Yanke.

Figure 6.8 Kids march in the Kendra James Memorial Rally in May 2003, featured in *Arresting Power: Resisting Police Violence in Portland, Oregon* (2015) co-directed by Jodi Darby, Julie Perini, and Erin Yanke.

Figure 6.9 *Arresting Power: Resisting Police Violence in Portland, Oregon* (2015) withholds images of the brutalized Black body but recreates the scene of attack with experimental soundscapes and moving portraits of where brutality took place.

narrator articulates his own position as a white man of privilege and recounts his blindness toward these issues, exhibiting a vulnerability rarely articulated in the narrative constructions of these representations.

REPRESENTATIONS OF URBAN UPRISING AND POPULAR CULTURE

From the urban uprisings in the 1960s to the tragedy of Rodney King and the mounting documentary evidence of unarmed people dying in police encounters, documentary media makers continue to explore unchallenged patterns of systematic violence. These representations feature citizens attacked by police in public spaces, in protective custody, and in the privacy of their own homes. We see people assaulted and sometimes murdered in front of the camera. Unjustified police force, the circumstances around police killings, and the participatory culture that emerges to document these events constitute a kind of haunting, "animated state in which a repressed or unresolved social violence is making itself known."[36] Ghosts tell us that suppressed actions and memories do not remain hidden. Consistent and reoccurring representations of police violence appear as one of many ghosts that haunt the public imaginary, reminding us of unresolved social violence foreshadowing a future of inevitable horrors. The structures of systematic violence produce conditions of resistance. The body swelling introduced by Jane Gaines, the representation of the body in struggle on the screen can produce an audience to pick up the political work to challenge unjustified police force in waking life outside the screen. In this context, the relationship shifts between the bodies on the screen and those in front of it. At some point, systematic violence toward specific populations triggers self-defense mechanisms and documentary representation functions to demand recognition, redistribution, and protection. The works discussed in this section narrativize urban uprisings in the framework of self-defense, perhaps representing the last battle of worn-down and desperate communities. These works present undocumented histories of white vigilante gangs, neighborhood zones policed by law enforcement and divided by race, and divisions compounded by poverty and the lack of opportunity.

Archival footage and street reporting are important aspects of these narratives. These documentaries are significantly composed of crowd-sourced mobile recordings and other social media content, including live-streaming broadcasts. The repackaged representations slide between public memory projects and tools of activist intervention to disrupt the larger media culture. The narratives are crafted to reshape the street-tape materials, imprinted with an interventionist gaze, into official historical accounts with a small touch of professional discourses of detachment, in an attempt to garner credibility in the commercial market. The documentaries are unquestionably commercial and circulate in highly visible outlets, with less attention given to screening culture intervention or mobilizing publics around these representations.

Burn Motherfucker, Burn! (2017) was broadcast on Showtime and documents the massive uprising that took place in Los Angeles on April 29, 1992, when four police officers were acquitted in the beating of Rodney King. Los Angeles has seen racial tensions, injustice, and a troubled relationship between the LAPD and the African American community for decades. Told through first-hand accounts of police brutality from local residents, artists, and community organizers, the film draws a line of connection between the 1965 Watts rebellion, the rise of LA street gangs, and the 1992 uprising after the acquittal of the officers accused of beating King. Intimate archival footage shows Malcolm X speaking out against police brutality in Los Angeles after a police attack at a Muslim mosque in 1962. The documentary produces a counterhistorical record of the relationship between the Los Angeles Police Department and the black communities they policed, using community accounts of police patrolling neighborhood boundaries to contain black communities and white vigilante gangs that came into the communities to prey on the vulnerable. "Spook hunters" were a group of white men out of Compton who wore leather jackets with an image on the back of a black person being lynched. The community reports that street gangs first formed as a way to protect themselves from white vigilante groups that jumped people on the streets with impunity. The systematic and continuous containment of black bodies interweaves with archival footage of continuous waves of abuse, blood, curfews, martial law, and lack of opportunity that builds until there is an uprising. The film also documents the cultural renaissance of self-determination that emerges out of this intense systematic oppression.

Broadcast on HBO, *Baltimore Rising* (2017) documents violence and a critical crisis of community trust in the wake of Freddie Gray's death in police custody during the spring of 2015. Baltimore was a city on edge as its underserved and overpoliced citizens waited to hear the fate of the six police officers involved in the incident. Activists, police officers, community leaders, and gang affiliates struggled to hold Baltimore together as homicide rates skyrocketed and police tactics were questioned. The documentary captures rare moments between community members and police in which people tell stories of police abuse and create new connections through community football games. The documentary places viewers in a network of people who care deeply about the city but are burdened by the complexity of its problems. It profiles a grassroots research and policy group comprised of young people focused on making their communities safer. There are abundant representations of community and individual agency alongside intense emotional responses to the pending decision. A seventeen-year-old boy speaks to the camera, explaining that he smokes because he is always so anxious that he's going to die of a stray bullet or at the hand of a "killer cop." A young woman chants, with a sense of desperation in her voice: "Tell me what democracy looks like." The crowd chants back, "This is what democracy looks like." The chant continues as tears run

Figure 6.10 The origins of gang cultural in south central Los Angels is explored in *Burn Motherfucker, Burn!* (2017) directed by Sasha Jenkins. This noose image was the symbol for a white vigilante gang who created violence in the Black communities with the help of police, creating the need for the development of street gangs to protect the community.

Figure 6.11 Burn Motherfucker, Burn! (2017) documents a Los Angeles rally protesting police brutality in 1962.

down her face. People take to the streets to prevent the armed conflict in these communities from imposing total isolation. The film documents efforts to combat fear with representations of fearlessness. The street scenes communicate togetherness and the joy of collectivity. Representations of these lived moments can counter feelings of powerlessness.[37]

As part of PBS and the POV series, *Whose Streets* (2017) documents the uprising in Ferguson, Missouri, that followed the police shooting of Michael Brown and the controversial choice to leave his body in the street for hours. The circumstances surrounding Brown's death aggravated longstanding tensions between residents and the St. Louis Police Department, which came to a boiling point when law enforcement officers arrived at the protests with M-16 guns and military-grade tanks. Artists, musicians, teachers, and parents joined the marchers as the National Guard descended on Ferguson. The onscreen tensions between police and community in this documentary show an evolution from the tensions seen in previous documentaries; the police in Ferguson are outfitted with militarized equipment and come with a history of predatory bureaucratic practices. These practices include issuing so many tickets for minor infractions that large percentages of the citizenry are indebted to the city, unable to pay, and forced into mandatory jail sentences that further destabilize the already underserved population. The ubiquitous digital culture permeates the storytelling of this conflict; tweets and social media posts stitch together the fragments of a community under duress. The black community of Ferguson finds itself at the center of an urban war zone, where the National Guard tear gasses the mainstream press and clears the area by turning their equipment off. The only people left documenting the scene are the community members trapped by police barricades.

Historically, documentary images of black power and political agency have been muted. Kristen Hoerl argues that documentaries about black political struggle consign "activism to a tragic and traumatic past" and "implicitly discourage audience members who question the justice of mainstream economic and political institutions."[38] The documentary media responding to police brutality reveal a longstanding and complex public conflict. Conflict is represented as constantly unfolding in the present as a means of rectifying the past. The agents of change are active and collectively swarming for justice in a manner that questions mainstream institutions. Most of the documentaries in this chapter are not widely circulated. There are a few exceptions, including the most recent ones, which have found commercial distribution on HBO, Showtime, and Netflix. This is also how the networks of circulation materialize, street tapes become transported into a position of critical visibility with their recirculation in popular commercial documentary. The vernacular cinematic discourse presented in the next section, however, represents a discursive shift. The new vernacular cinema of street-tape culture is actively encouraging audiences to invest in the process of struggle. It is unapologetic, unprecedented, and now circulating in popular outlets and online.

Figure 6.12 Burn Motherfucker, Burn! (2017) features rare 1962 footage of Malcolm X speaking out against police brutality in Los Angeles.

Figure 6.13 Massive uprisings spring up in St. Louis and across the country to demand law enforcements accountability in *Whose Streets* (2017) directed by Sabaah Folayan.

Figure 6.14 Local Canfield apartment residents watch the escalation of police presence around them in *Whose Streets* (2017) directed by Sabaah Folayan.

Figure 6.15 A spontaneous memorial to Michael Brown is erected where his body laid in the street for hours after his death, featured in *Whose Streets* (2017) directed by Sabaah Folayan.

Figure 6.16 A local activist shares her experience of the uprisings after the death of Michael Brown in *Whose Streets* (2017) directed by Sabaah Folayan.

Figure 6.17 In the neighborhood of the shooting, some homes include a sign in support of Black Lives Matter, featured in *Whose Streets* (2017).

Figure 6.18 Rapper Def Poe takes to the street to organize constructive agitation in *Whose Streets* (2017) directed by Sabaah Folayan.

Figure 6.19 As police descend into the neighborhood of Ferguson, MO a women approaches police with her hands up in *Whose Streets* (2017).

Figure 6.20 One protestor is contained by six police officers after a road blockage on a major St. Louis highway in *Whose Streets* (2017) directed by Sabaah Folayan.

Figure 6.21 A protestor stands on top of a cement barricade after activist successfully shut down a major highway through St. Louis in *Whose Streets* (2017) directed by Sabaah Folayan.

Figure 6.22 Police in Ferguson and surrounding areas are equipped with military grade weapons and show a powerful display of force after the shooting of Michael Brown in *Whose Streets* (2017) directed by Sabaah Folayan.

Figure 6.23 In *Whose Streets* (2017) military grade vehicles were rode into town, presenting a show of force and control.

Streaming as Mobile Cinema: Black Lives Matter Brings You to the Streets

Occupy Wall Street ushered in a new wave of citizen journalism as people used live streaming as a form of activism. The movement harnessed the ever-changing relationship between "mobile video tools, online platforms, on-the-go reporting and mainstream media within the context of rapidly shifting protest movements."[39] However, the Black Lives Matter movement is where we have seen these tools used in innovative ways to hold political and social systems to account. Rodriguez defines citizens' media as production practices that turn individuals into citizens: "crafting their own languages, codes, signs, and symbols, empowering them to name the world in their own terms."[40] This provides the opportunity to restructure individual and collective identities into "empowered subjectivities."[41] This emerging video practice has profound implications for the police use of excessive force that propelled the Black Lives Matter movement into popular consciousness.

Live streaming depends on accessible mobile recording units—smart phones or personal devices—providing the ability to press a button and broadcast lived experiences as they happen. At its core, it is an interventional gaze, with the camera becoming an embodiment of the person operating it. But these live-streaming experiences slip between the endangered gaze of precarity as activists face tactics of physical control and the accidental gaze of witness to violence. This also involves capturing the unpredictable magic of cinema, in this case a performative uprising and unrelenting embrace of collective public agency, the undeniable visceral response of being part of fighting back through the embodiment of the underdog. The ubiquity of small, compact recording equipment and new habits of use creates a visual experience that resembles traditional cinema. I use the term *mobile cinema* to refer to the live-streaming process as well as the story that unfolds within and outside the camera frame, complete with tension, arc, and conclusion. The story unfolds in real time, impromptu cinematic arrangements that are communally shared and rapidly circulated. Mobile cinema enables documentary media to generate spaces for activist communication and interaction as interventions are happening. Media makers are showing up to document conflict while also occupying public spaces with the process of production.

On July 17, 2014, Eric Garner, a forty-three-year-old African American man, was confronted by plainclothes police officers for selling "loosies," single cigarettes without tax stamps, which is an act in violation of New York State law. Bystander and friend of Garner, Ramsey Orta, recorded the incident on his cell phone. Garner had a history with police; he had filed a complaint in 2007 after police officers conducted a cavity search on him in full view on the street. When officers approached Garner on July 17, 2014, he explained to them, "Every time you see me, you want to mess with me. It stops today." New York police officer Daniel Pantaleo approached Garner and put him in a chokehold from behind, pulling him to the ground and smashing his face into the concrete. Garner repeated his last words, "I can't breathe," eleven times while being held down by police. These words were repeated by activists in protest chants on the day the grand jury decided not to indict Pantaleo. You could hear these chants echoing through the streets of New York; handheld camera recordings functioned as a surrogate for thousands sitting in their homes across the country, transmitting visceral response.

An accidental witnessing inspired a large-scale activist intervention in the context of an already mobilized Black Lives Matter movement. In a two-week period in 2014, grand jury decisions dismissed charges against the police officers who killed Michael Brown in St. Louis and Eric Garner in Staten Island, after which protests erupted across the country. On December 3, "die-ins" were staged in New York City and San Francisco, broadcast via live stream. In New York, protests lasted for three days, and broadcasts documented protestors enveloping the city, walking in the streets and against the flow of cars, prohibiting travel. Large swarms of people emerged from side streets and metro stops, joining the protests. Activists walked the main thoroughfares of New York City shouting, "Hands up, don't shoot." Cars stopped in the street due to spontaneous pedestrian traffic, and slowly the vehicles began to follow along with the chants, beeping their horns to the rhythm, sometimes participating with the call and response in the streets. A cameraperson called this action a wildcat march, listing all the areas of the city from which protestors descended and where they were headed. When police blocked the path of the protestors, the swarms found escape routes and alternative pathways as the crowds separated and grew bigger.[42]

While documentary narratives about black power typically look back at radical movements of the past that were energized by assassinated leaders, the present livestream broadcasts show a contemporary representation of radical action that is raw, powerful, leaderless, and growing. These transmissions allow viewers to experience police cutting off the movement of people in the streets and the subsequent spontaneous new directions of resistance that grow and change to circumvent police control. Vernacular cinematic discourse in the form of live streaming is about how performance engages all the senses. These broadcasts allow the unfolding experience to help viewers feel the communication emerging at the intersection of experience and expression. These broadcast transmissions are not just an expression of what is; they also show us what we are and what we could be. Black Lives Matter solidarity protests emerged in Chicago, Washington, D.C., Baltimore, Minneapolis, and Atlanta. On December 5, thousands gathered on the Boston Commons, blocking traffic, including traffic on I-90. At least fifty protests in support of Garner occurred globally. One year later, the documentation of excessive force is escalating and emerging on live-streaming broadcast.

Vernacular cinematic discourse is the language of the unheard. It steps in when representative government does not serve the interests of the people. Its messages,

videos, and networks find a place on the cultural horizon as a form of political inclusion. In the 1970s, the United States saw an explosion of vernacular cinematic
discourse as technology became lightweight and inexpensive and government investment in community development proliferated, funding programs that facilitated
greater access to the tools of community media production. This expression now
finds roots in everyday digital life, with unique and unintended uses of technology.
Vernacular cinematic discourse does not act alone; its power comes from the movement of people around it, through which it often develops a vitality of its own, circulating as a force in culture.

Perhaps the most profound example of the power of live-streaming video of excessive force occurred in the case of the shooting of Philando Castile in Minnesota.
When the Facebook live stream of the event begins, Diamond Reynolds appears
on the screen and states in a clear but distressed tone: "We got pulled over for a
busted tail light . . . they killed my boyfriend."[43] The camera shakes and pans over the
bloody and critically shot Philando Castile. As Castile moans from the pain of his
injuries, Reynolds calmly explains the details of their circumstances for the world to
witness. After being pulled over, Castile informed the officer that he was carrying a
firearm. *The Star Tribune* breaks down the police dashcam exchange:

> Before Castile completed the sentence, Yanez interrupted and calmly replied,
> "OK," and placed his right hand on the holster of his own holstered weapon.
> Yanez said, "Okay, don't reach for it, then . . . don't pull it out." Castile
> responded, "I'm not pulling it out," and Reynolds also said, "He's not pulling
> it out." Yanez repeated, raising his voice, "Don't pull it out!" as he quickly
> pulled his own gun with his right hand and reached inside the driver's window
> with his left hand. Reynolds screamed, "No!" Yanez removed his left arm from
> the car and fired seven shots in the direction of Castile in rapid succession.
> Reynolds yelled, "You just killed my boyfriend!" Castile moaned and said,
> "I wasn't reaching for it." Reynolds loudly said, "He wasn't reaching for it."
> Before she completed her sentence, Yanez again screamed, "Don't pull it out!"
> Reynolds responded, "He wasn't." Yanez yelled, "Don't move! Fuck![44]

Reynolds's live stream begins immediately after Castile is shot, as she is talking with
Officer Yanez about what just occurred. She says, "You shot four bullets into him,
sir. He was just getting his license and registration, sir." The officer, in a heightened
state of panic, explains, "I told him not to reach for it! I told him to get his hand
open!" Yanez orders Reynolds, whose daughter is in the backseat of the car and
whose dying boyfriend is in the front seat, to get on her knees. The recording
captures the sound of locking handcuffs. Reynolds's phone falls to the ground but
continues to record. Yanez repeatedly screams, "fuck," which can be heard in the
background. According to Reynolds, police did not check Castile's pulse or call for
medical care; instead, one police officer comforted the shooting officer.[45] Within

twenty-four hours of Castile's death, the live stream was viewed over 2.5 million times.[46] "Bicycling" distribution networks have transformed in digital culture. Digital distribution networks streamline accessibility and visibility in real time.

What happened in the 103 seconds of the Philando Castile traffic stop and its aftermath is widely disputed, but it was recorded on police dashcam and live streamed by Reynolds inside the car. Within hours of the shooting, angry but peaceful protestors gathered in support of Castile, and the public demonstrations continued for a week. After a week of peaceful protests, violence erupted on July 9 and 10; one hundred and two people were arrested, and twenty-one police officers were injured. A number of activists started an encampment outside the Minnesota governor's office. On July 19, twenty-one members of the St. Paul and Minneapolis teachers' federations were arrested while protesting Castile's death after they blocked a street in Minneapolis and refused orders to disperse. On June 16, 2017, Officer Yanez was acquitted of all charges, which included manslaughter and reckless discharge of a firearm. With the emergence of these new technologies of media activism, we are still far from achieving justice, but, as Rodriguez suggests, "[m]edia technologies play key roles, strengthening people's actions of cultural resistance against armed violence."[47] Selective representation of police brutality, especially in a post–Michael Brown world, poses an ideological challenge to systems of power by exposing the contradictions of national identity and the experience of vernacular cultures.

When video cameras and audio recorders allow us to tell alternative histories, agency multiplies. Underrepresented voices gain visibility, circulation, and capacity to develop a public voice; media production allows people to find action and expression. But ultimately, people choosing to press "record" or "broadcast," speaking their situated truth with and through the camera, is a critical first step. This is especially true when it's a truth denied by the broader public imaginary. Speaking such truth becomes more difficult in a historical moment when the intruding patterns of violence continue without consequence. These are dire circumstances being recorded on video, yet justice for these actions is slow or absent. In the face of this impunity for the perpetrators, it is difficult to imagine why these recordings matter, but these documentary interventions are the small bits left behind in the dust bin of history for others to pick up. Future viewers can look back on these moving images to draw patterns and decipher the cultures of control, so that we can better resist them. Upon first encountering these moving images, people can be galvanized into doing political work in the immediate moment. Sometimes it is in this space of public circulation that these recordings have tremendous impact. There is a second life for these images when historians and activists begin imagining another world. The ghosts of police impunity are not erased; their movement in the world is captured and frozen in time; they become relics and, later, a story. So we press "record" knowing that it will not always lead to justice because the structures of control are sometimes too powerful. However, that does not stop our work. There are surveillance concerns to understand and guard against, but we route ourselves around such attempts. We press "record" and act in the world in the face of injustice because there is no other option.

What makes live streaming unique as a documentary form is its capacity for real-time broadcasting of images from cameras embedded in the moment of lived expression. At times, live streaming is better able to report how actions unfold than the mainstream news media. It is a means of direct reporting from the scene that can become source material for news broadcasts, documentary films, and historical archives. Bassem Masri's coverage of the Michael Brown protests[48] was widely used by news stations. Content from both Bassem Masri and Bradley J. Rayford's live streams[49] were used in *Whose Streets?* (2017). Even when these recordings do not find immediate audiences, their value grows over time. These recordings become image time capsules that scholars, artists, and filmmakers use to piece together history or imagine another world. And when these recorded stories culminate in collective expression, it results in some of the most profound rhetoric we have for understanding the strains and joys we share.

Mainstream journalism's interest in framing protestors as criminals exists in ideological tension with the work of activists live streaming for police accountability. It will be interesting to observe how this tension plays out as more mainstream media adopt social media feeds as the preferred b-roll of news broadcasts, especially when activists are the only ones left in the street recording the struggle between unarmed protestors and a militarized police force.

COLLECTIVE ARCHIVING AGAINST UNJUSTIFIED POLICE FORCE

Something needs to be in place to "help people use the information in a more concrete way," Cornelius Moore explains on a sunny afternoon at his San Francisco office, housed at the headquarters of California Newsreel. Moore, the co-director of California Newsreel, continues, "the door will be opened, but it will not be the end. They'll go maybe to find out other information, other movies, books hopefully where they'll find out more." The one thing missing from the representations of unjustified police force is documentation of cultural exhibitions or community organizing around these representations. Instead representations function as a form of polarization received at home over social media networks. It is not difficult to imagine why, especially as we consider Cory Greene's proposition in the quotation at the beginning of this chapter. We need these images as a society, but these images are not for black people. Most black people are intimately aware of the dangers they traverse every day, especially when they encounter law enforcement and security entities. Documenting brutalization can bring awareness, but too many of these images—the number that would keep pace with realist representation of such oppression—is "unhealthy, unuseful." These images of brutality are for those who do not believe these conditions exist and those who don't have to think about such dangers while walking through life. Who is going to build community around that work? We are beginning to see the growth of this community work in art exhibition and local organizing. Is it even fair to ask people of color to pick up the heavy lifting of this organizing? Communities don't traditionally gather around these documentary images in the same way people experiencing struggles documented in other media cultures organize around images on screen. The spaces of engagement around the issues of police brutality and the circulation and curation of these recordings find more traction in community archiving.

The archive is a construction that not only orders information but also becomes an "apparatus through which we map the everyday."[50] In a time of deep divides, "archives can give us direct access to the world of others."[51] The archive can be designed as an apparatus we want to be produced by strategically gathering information to capture the changing attitudes and culture that yield more inclusive outcomes. In other words, using the collecting process creates a framework to map absences, privilege and challenges to mainstream representations. Scholars, activists, archivists, and community members with social justice aims collect documents that provide a counterhistory to official reports of police violence.

The modern archival craze started in 19th-century Victorian England when cultural heritage workers collected and archived the materials that serviced the Empire. The new cultural heritage workers of the digital age exist formally in institutions but also informally in the streets, recording, archiving, and circulating images and sound with smart phones. The ephemeral character of digital rhetoric requires researchers to collect materials in real time, archiving history as it is happening. Efforts underway include the Peoples Archive of Police Violence in Cleveland, a community-based archive that collects, preserves, and provides access to stories of police violence. Documenting Ferguson is a collaboration between St. Louis University and organizations that preserve and make accessible media captured and created following the killing of Michael Brown. Similarly, the Preserve the Baltimore Uprising Collection is a collaboration between the Maryland Historical Society, Baltimore-area university faculty members, museums, and community organizations that was set up to preserve the oral histories of those connected to the death of Freddie Gray. With the introduction of mechanization and digitization in the archival process, "there is a growing popularity and importance of community-generated live digital archives."[52] Digital culture brings with it abundance, but in the absence of a concerted effort to collect and preserve vernacular history, it can quickly slip from the official record.

Conclusion

Scholars must address the lived experience of violence in all its complexity and ambiguity. These representations are a necessary form of protection and simultaneously problematic representations. As Rodriguez suggests, media production practices solidify communities together against armed violence. This cultural reach is made exponential with the capacities of live streaming. This kind of cultural production as political intervention is making and unmaking the larger political discourse around unjustified police force in a manner that occasionally produces accountability for those who have been murdered or those who are at the other end of a violent attack.

Violence, especially at the hands of state and corporate interests, is the equivalent of the denial of being. It is the opposite of recognition. It is naive to expect that local community media and isolated video activists operating without budgets can stop structural racism and toxic institutional cultures, with established patterns of violence directed at particular communities. Documentary resistance is the effort of ordinary people to engage in public communication to challenge dominant social formations and institutional logics. This site of knowledge production has the potential to help us speak to one another across divisions to create frameworks for collaborative organizing, but much work is needed for these goals to materialize. Digital communication is the literacy of the emerging generation, and it grows more ingrained in our world with every new technological innovation. This new way of being in the world requires media makers and users to develop rhetorical media strategies, a critical approach, and proficiency as producers of content—a production culture that harnesses history and theory as a means to guide intervention.

7

Conclusion

The Documentary Commons and Conditions of Resistance

As a media maker and production educator who frequently works with mobile recording, I am acutely aware of the rapid shifts that are occurring in public media literacy, particularly involving nonfiction moving images. This new literacy is transforming multiple sectors of society, ranging from educational paradigms to the articulation of mainstream political discourse. In 2017, when Senator Elizabeth Warren was ejected from the confirmation hearing for Jeff Sessions, who later became Attorney General Jeff Sessions, she stepped outside the chamber and pressed "broadcast." Warren read the letter she had planned to include in her testimony on the chamber floor, live streaming to a public audience interested in the materials censored at the hearing. The court of public opinion does not have the same gate-keeping procedures as the United States congressional chamber, but this possibility is now made accessible with mobile recording capabilities. With the exploding reach and power of audio and video, documentary modes of communication are multiplying. In this developing commons, the documentary impulse as a way of life and articulation of political information and democratic exchange constitute new patterns of public communication. This shift has been percolating for the last century, but now, in a time where cameras are at our fingertips and broadcasts go live through unpredictable networks, the documentary impulse is realizing its potential, reflecting experiences back to audiences, deepening social roots and connections, as well as centering conflicts for resolution.

This book stretches the definition of documentary to embrace connections to a larger social impulse that extends beyond broadcasting, theater, and the internet. As we have suggested, the documentary impulse is a popular habit of expression that people use to negotiate power. Stuart Hall insists that the purpose of theory is to provide better maps and tools for furthering political issues and motivating various projects.[1] The chapters in this book sketch a map of how portions of the world work, so we can struggle more effectively against forms of injustice. This process includes theorizing about a material understanding of collective identification that expands the possibilities for political agency in an attempt to understand how participatory media cultures collect around documentary in the process of social change. I have offered frameworks for understanding the micro-interactions of negotiating documentary and social change, the construction of collective identification and political agency that has various ramifications for political life. This includes multiple frameworks categorizing types of documentary interventions and the various modes of production that address the gap between political intention and outcome.

Documentary resistance is not the result of a magical, visceral cinematic response or hopes that revolutionary impulses will somehow leap from the frame; actually, it comes from a collaboration of events, recordings, historical circumstances, creative interventions, and collective action that moves the dial on social change. It requires intention, time, and labor; documentary does not routinely swim off into the great vast beyond of viral unpredictability and create change. Although documentary has this capacity, we need to account for such interactions without expecting all social change media to manifest in this way. More often, social change documentary is prodded, crafted, and launched into the world in a manner that takes consistent nursing by human caretakers who have investments in its connection with movements of people. The territory in question straddles the borders of theory and practice, moving between disciplines and through politically charged terrain.

The work of participatory media cultures and the emerging documentary commons concentrates on the collective reprioritizing of democratic values, radical impulses, and grassroots collective decision making in documentary studies. The emerging documentary commons puts weight on our collective capacity to express ourselves and listen in a variety of forms and contexts. Documentary facilitates the act of witnessing, collective identification, and political agency, but it is also a way to negotiate conflict. The genre allows us to craft and foreground the moment of stasis in an issue, the location where two opposing points clash. These negotiations often happen in vernacular spaces that are not part of the government or commercial sector, locations where we are invited to "work it out": theaters, community spaces, online, and our living rooms. In the United States where we are deeply divided by our collective inability to hear each other or speak across difference, understanding the possibilities of an emerging documentary commons is even more urgent.

PARTICIPATORY TRAJECTORIES

The field data and other interviews incorporated into this book paint a dynamic picture of the last fifty years of documentary production culture. We have reviewed the story of documentary's participatory heyday in the 1970s and early 1980s, when mostly urban people from all walks of life began picking up the tools of media authorship. These opportunities expanded as public development funds were funneled into access, training, and establishment of community media organizations. In the broader culture, participatory and community media were seen as necessary for democracy and the public good. Many women, people of color, LGBT communities, radicals, and other working-class creatives found a professional space in media production. Things shifted dramatically in the mid-1980s with cuts to arts initiatives and funding. Waves of conservative thinking curtailed the connection between media production and community development priorities. Even so, working-class cinema continued, and AIDS media activism flourished as these communities couldn't afford to lose this historical moment for intervention. Media makers now work in an environment that is fundamentally hostile to diversity and articulations of change.

These circumstances fostered the development of new media pathways and commercial experiments with vernacular cinema. The professional opportunity to develop long-term media production careers has thinned as a contingent media professional class has emerged. So nonfiction images have achieved higher status and have become more ingrained in our daily living and social negotiating, transforming multiple sectors of society. However, there are few pedagogical commitments to these literacies in K–12 education, and finding a financially stable career path doing this work is often untenable. The internet and mobile recording reshuffled the game of access as new amateur media makers entered an environment of networked media circulation that circumvents traditional media gatekeeping. We've seen a brave new world of broadcast news stations emerge in the back pockets of those with cell phones and the networked capacity to circulate images, often widely and with great impact. Documentary moved to the top of the box office at the turn of the century but the documentary profession is waning. Few media makers are paid professionally, and many work for free or for poverty wages; most documentary media makers hustle at multiple contingent jobs to pay their bills.

At the turn of the century, documentary production emerged as a necessary literacy skill for political engagement, and online environments became saturated with documentary content. With the tools of authorship more universally available and mobile, we now find ourselves in the third wave of heightened social justice engagement with the documentary camera. Although moving images, both professional and vernacular, saturate our culture, career paths for independent filmmakers are narrow and unsustainable. The role of the documentary filmmaker is significant because the genre's capacity to intervene in the process of social change is realized without focused effort. It is given shape by technology, historical conditions, and our intentions. If we value democracy, inclusion, and social change, we must prioritize documentary production as something more than an activity motivated by aesthetic acumen and market interests.

As patterns of media communication, organization, and production shift with the rise of digital culture, academic discussion of participatory media cultures must begin in earnest. As Henry Jenkins acknowledges, participatory media cultures do not begin and end with digital culture. This book provides a broader field for studying the ways participatory cultures intersect with technological innovation, but many of the practices of organizing, solidifying as a group, and taking action are not new.

AGENCY

The idea of agency—the capacity to act in the world—becomes more complex when considered in the context of media makers and the documentary object. Once set in motion, the documentary object can take on a life on its own, being caught up in intentional and unintentional assemblages. For example, in spring 2017, one of my documentary shorts was viewed over 1200 times in three days, for reasons that are not entirely clear to me. I did nothing to initiate this kind of circulation, and it is contrary to usual viewing patterns. Released four years earlier, the documentary normally generates a modest number of views each week without any effort on my end. I can only partially trace how the documentary circulated and moved though networks during this brief period. The important part here is that I did not control or initiate this spike; it was enabled by digital culture. This experience challenges my thinking about agency, its human-centered capacities, and the role the documentary object plays in the circulation of political discourse. Was this just another example of documentary rhetoric on demand, accessible yet disconnected from the motor of author-initiated agency? It seems like an example of how documentary takes on its own life in digital culture, circulating with an urgency driven by the demands of history and pop-up audiences.

This is not to say that the agency of a documentary object is comparable to that of human intervention. Once set in motion, documentary has the potential to travel pathways of automation and be utilized in unintentional assemblages, mostly in ways facilitated by human action. Documentary moving images exist across our media culture, on streaming websites, and on broadcast outlets, but historical conditions are required to make these works relevant at a given moment. Context drives circulation of the documentary object, not the haphazard circuitry of networks. The documentary as an object is tentative. As a digitized object, a collection of coded zeros and ones that transform into a narrative, documentary is not a stable object. The digital components of documentary can be edited and remixed for historical narratives in museums, on TV, and in policy hearings. The object-ness of documentary can be transformed, but the discourse seeps out of the object, leaving the shell of its digital code behind to transform into something else. From documentary discourse into a song, legal evidence, historical record or memory.

As a documentary media maker focused on social justice and intimate with the process of distribution and circulation, I am forced to concede two conflicting ideas about agency and documentary. Documentary has tentacles that reach far beyond the viewing experience and outside of its intended audiences. I agree that this reach is only partially controlled by human intention. But I also understand that media makers typically engage in tremendous efforts to get their work viewed, often producing subtle and sporadic engagement. In other words, the existence of a media object is not enough; it needs to be set in motion by human history. The kinetic energy of agency is essential. Some forces of motion are bigger than others, and some networks of documentary circulation are more robust or have pathways directly tied into communities of decision makers. It is this kinetic energy of documentary produced through agency that needs further exploration. Media work usually needs to be pushed, branded, and marketed. Then, you hope, something will catch fire, taken up and circulated with a force that is uncontrolled by its initial release into the world. This kind of contagious circulation, however, is the exception, not the rule.

COLLECTIVE IDENTIFICATION

Collective identification might begin when you realize you are not alone. Or it might start when you realize you are no longer willing to see something continue. It gathers force with the recognition that something is wrong. You discover others feel as you do, and they also recognize the need to act. These are the moments when viewing becomes resistance. Documentary, as a form, is persuasive in its capacity to reorganize the priorities of an audience, often with a sense of urgency. It facilitates connections between unlikely strangers in the process. Collective identification is the force that inches this relational process along.

The collective nature of this process provides affirmation and energy toward movement: "While the internet can be a splendid mobilizing tool as well as an information archive, the truly vital recourse's are collective energy."[2] Collective identitification orders information, creates movement through urgency, and can provide the audience with varying degrees of agency but they are not automatically political. As many filmmakers echo in this book, the context of the story gives the audience information about how to act, and circumstances provide connections with others. The consciousness of sharing collective identification with others creates the space for social formations to arise.

SOCIAL CHANGE

There is a kind of magical thinking about the ability of documentary to engage the process of social change. This hunch, articulated by filmmakers and scholars who see a function and role for documentary in the process of social change, is critical to our democratic practices. The global documentary commons has capacities for change that need to be less haphazard and more strategic in positioning the documentary impulse to contribute to resolving our ongoing political conflicts. This book project, I hope, begins to address the missing concepts and frameworks for understanding documentary as an artistic and political process.

Social change is not a progressive march toward some utopian horizon. It is not a linear line of progression toward civilization. Social change doesn't stop at the moment of revolution and hang up its hat. Rather, it is ongoing, regressive, mean-dering, slow, and responsible for significant social and political shifts, and some-times, ventures off into the wrong direction. This is why talking about documentary in the framework of impact is so narrow and consumer based. Impact for whom? Whose interest does the documentary discourse serve?

Documentary resistance is the refusal to accept the authority of others and to adopt strategies of agitation and protest through media interventions that thwart compliance with the social order. This is the step past the recognition of injustice, and it is the purposeful invention of media that intentionally or not is made to pre-vent injustice in status quo power relationships. Most documentary that engages in the process of social change includes movements of people sustaining a par-ticipatory media culture that enacts the process of social transformation through successes, challenges, and attempts at control. Participatory collaborations are es-sential throughout this process, from production to the circulation and screening cultures.

One key feature of documentary is the recognition of voice, featuring vernacular cultures speaking for themselves and situating the missing perspectives in society by crafting empathetic narratives that penetrate exclusionary grids of understanding. Sometimes through surgical precision, documentary storytelling has the capacity to provide witness that forces central processing with incompatible beliefs in the minds of audience members.

This particular capacity of documentary—to recognize and create empathy for vernacular voices—is essential to the social change process, as scholars such as Fraser and Couldry address, creating agency and connections with others. The doc-umentary impulse plays a central role in social change, harnessing individuals and groups as moral, political, and social agents capable of contributing to the political process and participating in "how life together is organized."[3] Documentary has the capacity to convey vernacular voices that have been left out of the larger cultural imaginary, representing marginalized people as possessing dignity and humanity. Documentary's strength is its unparalleled ability to deliver insights into unrecog-nized corners of our world, especially the dark corners we don't want to recognize as a collective body.

Documentary and social change happens in "dimensions" and to "degrees." A di-mension is a plane of struggle on which documentary makes contact with power. This occurs along cultural, policy, legal, structural, and institutional dimensions. Documentary often slides between dimensions, mediating conflict and power. In 1909, Booker T. Washington negotiated white fear of the emancipated slave class by representing skilled working life in his Tuskegee documentary. This happened using the cultural dimension of representation, but Washington also set forth a vision for the structure of the black business class. The documentary became part of the cultural apparatus for Washington's pitch to white philanthropic financiers to invest in black education. Kirby Dick and Amy Ziering's critically successful

Invisible War was released commercially but had marginal box-office success. The documentary is powerful because of its ability to penetrate military institutions, making allies with policymakers and generating a force to help turn the dial on the legal process.

In the context of documentary and social change, I use "degree" to describe the intensity or swiftness with which change happens. Sometimes the degree is measured by the time it takes change to occur. For example, it took a trilogy of documentaries and nearly twenty years before the West Memphis Three were released from jail. In contrast, Robert Durst, who eluded authorities for decades, was arrested for murder by the end of the last episode of *The Jinx*. Often, degree can signify how transformative the change is for those who are most closely involved. I advocate articulating documentary's ability to bring social transformation that attends closely to the needs of the most vulnerable and underserved in the context of the issue that is at the core of the film.

This book identified four modes of social change documentary, but this is not an exhaustive list of social change modes. The category "Representing Social Change" refers to activist documentary depicting social change. This includes historical works focused on radical social movements, street tapes recording direct action, and other works that record the process of social change. The category "Speaking for Social Change" includes works that try to speak for the marginalized, to identify problems, and to make arguments for social change. In these instances, the documentary functions as a free-floating signifier of political discourse and is only loosely connected to the process of social change. Films in the category "Collaborating for Social Change" focus on the relationships formed between the creative team and community to build strategies of co-authorship. "Engaging in Social Change" is an evolving category of the activist documentary moment, utilizing media work as a tool of organizing and agitation. Coupled with new media technology and a burgeoning participatory media culture, these works create and sustain the political space for participatory culture and activism.

"Speaking for Social Change" can cause problems that trigger significant consequences. When we attempt to speak *for* an underrepresented group in a film, we deny them precious space and time to speak for themselves. I want to recall A. O. Scott's comments about the overabundance of filmmakers who make social justice films that do little to change the world and more to satisfy the moral convictions of the maker. I want to hold this position in tension with the longstanding practice of filmmakers walking into communities to record injustice and leaving with images that only benefit the maker's professional goals. Sometimes, media makers are encouraged to claim they are creating social change as a necessary condition for funding applications. Others might recognize how social change objectives fit neatly into the trauma narratives of the contemporary documentary market. Disconnecting documentary production from historically grounded political struggle creates problems that need more direct attention.

Films in the "Engaging in Social Change" and "Representing Social Change" categories have the strongest connections to the emergence of participatory media cultures. The production process with these films requires engagement with people in struggle, grounding political articulation in lived experience. The most promising documentary engagement emerges from filmmakers who involve those connected to struggle in the creative and distribution process in a substantive way. Documentary finds its place in the world by creating community partnerships and collective visions.

We need more serious consideration of documentary practice as a mechanism to facilitate the micro-interactions of democracy, the negotiation of difference and representation of the silenced that encourage political participation. This focus on the potential of documentary must involve funding media literacy and production practice in K–12 education and restoring public-sector funding for the community and public media.

Critical Production Practice

Theory is useful when it structures our thinking and explains phenomena of consequence in the world. This chapter has outlined some of the key findings of this project. I want to address the larger context of documentary, social change, and pedagogy as a way to move forward. Media literacy and documentary production are increasingly essential components of education and political participation, and they demand more attention. The civic infrastructure for media production is crumbling just as the potential of these forms is more powerful than ever. Integrating media literacy and production into secondary and collegiate education is one powerful way to address this issue. The idea of critical media practice—as a system of learning, research, thinking, and doing—requires exploration. Scholars and media artists must build collaborations to address social problems. Joining production practice with critical studies creates a pathway for cultural studies to intersect with media studies around the collective goal of using media to confront powerful institutional structures.

AGENCY AND CRITICAL PRODUCTION PRACTICE

In this project, reflecting my interest in agency in processes of democratic practice and participation, I have explored concrete connections between documentary and social change. Rhetoric scholar Ronald Greene argues that these connections create an "anxiety over agency that pushes rhetorical critics and theorists into becoming moral entrepreneurs scolding, correcting, and encouraging the body politic to improve the quality and quantity of political participation."[4] Rather than scolding or correcting, this project offers analyses in the service of generating effective political action in the linage of Stuart Hall. Taking a page from the impulse of cultural policy studies,[5] the investigation of agency and documentary is a site for understanding production culture as generating knowledge for action.[6] This produces a "series of rationales for particular types of conduct"[7] that have implications for social change. Toby Miller explains this intervention in terms of cultural policy studies.

Cultural policy studies investigate the formation of collective subjectivity that "nurtures belonging; animating institutions practices and cultural industries" that are "submerged beneath more pragmatic discourse" of policy.[8] The field explores cultural citizenship, "the maintenance and development of cultural lineage via education, custom, language, religion, and the acknowledgement of difference in and by the mainstream."[9] It is a way of combining theory and practice that can be used by policymaking bureaucracies, a critical practice of thinking and acting in the world. Justin Lewis and Toby Miller have identified this activity, which is happening in educational institutions and cultural industries. The call is for theorists to find their way into shaping policy. It's a call to engagement bound by work within cultural institutions with a reformist agenda. In Stuart Cunningham's terms, this effort to combine theory and practice involves taking up "political vocation, displacing "revolutionary rhetoric" with "reformist vocation."[10] I would suggest that critical production practice can transform a reformist agenda into a practice of strategic resistance and radical intervention within the documentary commons.

Cultural policy studies bring into sharper focus Stuart Hall's call for scholars to let research begin with some "real problem out there in the dirty world."[11] I suggest that scholars and media makers begin research with social problems, both together and on their own, to investigate the root causes ripe for public engagement through a critical media production practice. In other words, researchers and media makers can find connections between their intellectual and creative interests and specific, local, pressing problems in the world. Choosing topics for investigation in a whimsical manner should be paired with occasional interventions directed at the social good. This approach fills a gap in the cultural studies agenda by offering "a program for change in addition to distanced critique."[12]

Lewis and Miller readily acknowledge that the history of academic participation in institutional policymaking is "not especially encouraging"[13] and that the conditions of U.S. cultural institutions are not ideal for this kind of intervention. Producing culture in the arts and humanities to support national character has never been properly subsidized in the United States. Commercial interests and market forces currently dictate cultural industries in the United States, with a healthy peppering of vernacular media discourse seeping onto the public stage. Creating culture, both within and outside the mainstream, is often an act of survival and sheer will. This history of cultural production in the United States is the story of people and communities creating art and engaging in creativity as a site of meaning construction in order to imagine a better world.[14] The documentary impulse sits at the center of this project.

The documentary impulse, in particular, has a long history of creating a collective subjectivity beyond the screen, crafting subjectivity with the tools of address, and producing different participatory media outcomes. Documentary production and circulation exist both within and outside traditional cultural institutions, the government, and the market. There is an open-media ecology where those lacking access, skills, privilege, and possibilities can intervene in production culture inside and outside institutions. The collision of the growing networked and digital environment with massive political unrest around every corner and the social shifts toward documenting as a way life have created conditions for a new moment. We can harness the rich practices we are already engaging with to create systems of thinking, learning, and doing that have profound movement in the world.

Despite the lack of subsidized media institutions in the United States, in comparison to places such as Australia or Canada, the cultural industry is massive, porous, and available for intervention. The assumptions of Cultural Policy Studies are noteworthy, especially their emphasis on practice, putting theory into action, and the acknowledgment that theorists have something to contribute to cultural life beyond academic institutions and pedagogical practices in the commodity classroom.

I would like to advocate a position influenced by Hall and the impulses of cultural policy studies but recalibrated for engagement within the context of the United States. I would like to suggest organizing around a *critical media production practice*, a system of thinking, learning, theorizing, and acting in the world for social change. This is the process of understanding media analysis and theory as a system to inform production practice and political intervention. This system of thinking and doing can intersect across educational enclaves, community needs, and our political organizing. More importantly, media production culture can and should have a profound influence on academic theory. *Critical media production practice* also includes integrating the experiences of production culture back into theorizing, a cohesive process of knowledge production that is connected and engaged with community needs.

DOCUMENTARY AND THE ARCHIVE

The tools of documentary authorship are expanding with the proliferation of mobile production, which makes it easy to record massive amounts of raw footage from our daily lives. The accumulation of digital material poses a challenge to archival practices. With so much recording, from surveillance to mobile production, it is often difficult to distinguish what should be preserved and in what format. In other historical moments, cultural heritage workers collected and archived materials that served the British Empire. Today, the activist cultural heritage workers of the digital age exist formally in institutions but also informally in the streets, recording, archiving, and circulating documentary footage with smart phones.

Working in oral history and community document collection means wrestling with the documentary archive, negotiating both its bounty and its absences. Nowhere is this more evident than in the abundance of public vernacular rhetoric available through social media and how quickly it disappears, rendering it absent. Collecting and archiving digital communication have transformed the archive from a highly controlled apparatus into an open and participatory idea. The current moment requires real-time archivists and curators, acquiring artifacts while history is happening, scraping public discourse from social media and other platforms in real time, before fast-paced social media feeds bury the public dialogue.

Critical media production practice can also intervene in the political process by examining the transformational and political power of the archive and exploring its capacity to prompt societal change. The archive not only orders information but also becomes an "apparatus through which we map the everyday."[15] In a world that is so greatly divided, "archives can give us direct access to the world of others."[16] The archive can be designed to capture the changing attitudes and culture that sow more inclusive outcomes.

Part of the power of the archive comes from the agency it generates by producing institutionalized facts. At the center of this research is a desire to preserve community dialogues and emotional expressions of dissent in their powerful authentic vernacular. In this context, collecting digital fragments is an essential tool for social justice as the "apparatus of the archive is the network of strategies we use to map everything in both space and time precisely so that we may find what is as yet unlived in our own lives."[17]

Limitations of Data, Methods, and Results

This study has several limitations. A more robust picture of social change documentary could emerge by expanding the fieldwork to include interviews with activists and community members involved in the social justice issues addressed on the documentary screen. Activists are best able to assess changes in political cultures. Their voices could help determine how documentary intervenes in the process of social change. This study focuses primarily on practitioners, filmmakers, critics and curators, funders, and activists. As mentioned throughout this book, however, the roles of filmmaker and activist are often blurred. When these subjectivities come together, interesting assessments of documentary's effects rise to the surface.

It is important to situate documentary within historically contextualized political struggle to understand how a documentary commons emerges. Throughout this book, we have explored how these interventions often structure larger civic-sector conversations and collective action toward social change. This project captures some core foundations of this kind of struggle, but much more work is needed, especially as documentary engagement is escalating. The broad approach of this book also limits the degree to which individual films are addressed, allowing close reading of critical scenes rather than a more comprehensive analysis.

Every chapter of this book harbors a constellation of political discourses that I was unable to explore in depth due to the breadth of this project. I sought to map documentary history around particular political struggles to mark absences and create signposts on the well-traveled territory for future research. Many future projects can be cultivated in the crevices of the previous chapters. The two most significant areas of significant documentary engagement not covered in the book are the environmental justice movement and the documentary impulses surrounding the movements of Indigenous people. There are scores of documentaries, live streams, and street tapes involving these political struggles that require attention, including Josh Fox's *Gasland* series; Judith Helfand's political interventions; the work of the Yes Men; the impact of films like *Blackfish*, Laura Dunn's portraits of environmental disasters; the live streaming around indigenous land struggles; and documentation of immigrant rights, including the struggles concerning the Deferred Action for Childhood Arrivals (DACA) program.

In 2018, the recording of public speeches, personal advocacy, and collective political actions of youth after the school shooting at Marjory Stoneman Douglas High School in Florida galvanized the country around the issue of gun control in the United States. This movement would likely not be viewed with the same intimacy and rawness without the live streaming of high school kids who poured out of their schools in protest following the shooting of their classmates. Streams captured teenagers gathering into the streets and ultimating going on to the Washington, D.C., Mall and into city centers, delivering impassioned speeches. After a gunman fatally shot seventeen of her peers, Emma Gonzalez gave a riveting eleven-minute speech that turned the country's attention and cameras to the budding student movement. The videos of her speech and the speeches of her peers circulated for weeks on social media, reshaping the gun control debate. The documentary impulse sits at the center of contemporary political struggles, and it is time that scholars place it at the center of their work.

The focus on agency, collective identification, and social change might begin the discussion about documentary resistance, but there are several other theoretical entry points to explore. I am still curious about the role of witnessing as an active mode of looking with political dimensions that affect social change. The very nature of documentary has a kind of normalizing function because the "performances" are less obviously performed, the filmmakers' interventions are often obscured, and the reading practice is directed toward learning and exploring. The documentary can cause viewers to confuse the camera eye with the human eye; this means the documentary screen can often do the work of witnessing. The very notion of people acting in their world while being recorded gives us a sense that we can somehow understand the human condition with the camera eye. More importantly, documentary assures us that we are not alone, we do not struggle in isolation, our experiences mirror those of others, and we can act together for change. Although there is a fine line between fiction and nonfiction film, this idea of bearing witness—the translation of experience that creates connections with others and to the world—is a distinct characteristic of documentary.

Participatory media cultures form and persist for many reasons. We must further explore the conditions that build productive cohesion and lead audiences to organize and act together over the long term. It is easy for participatory cultures to come together but more difficult for them to act in the world. How does documentary create investment in social formations that build coalitions with existing social movements and other publics? This book starts to explore the possibilities; more intentional focus on coalition building within the context of documentary and social change could help clarify these possibilities.

Documentary Prospects

As social and political inequality grows, so does our ability to see it.[18] We need more informed conversations, research, data, and insights to understand how documentary can become a counter-valiant force in a media ecology composed of institutions that place market goals before democratic interests.

The history of documentary and social change in the United States cannot be completely addressed in one book, but I hope these chapters pique your curiosity and provide insights that will illuminate this area of scholarship. This research is connected to the creative practice and has the potential to inform production cultures and on-the-ground social actors. Savvy scholars will take greater efforts to include the experiences of practitioners in their research to better understand documentary production culture as it relates to engagement with the social and political world.

Documentary history is woefully caught in an auteur framework for understanding its own origins, finding its historical significance and credibility in the stories of great men, colonial explorers who pioneered documentary's recognized heritage. We can do better, and we must do more to resuscitate the ghosts of documentary history, those who resisted with the documentary impulse as a means of survival. They are the unrecognized pioneers of this history, the ones who have been covered over with the sediment of silent injustice. Documentary bits have been lying there for us to discover our more complete history; will you join me in making this documentary historical record more inclusive and complete?

With the exploding reach and power of audio and video, documentary modes of communication are multiplying. Finding its will in the capacity to reflect an experience back at its audience, documentary deepens our social roots more often than retracting them. What was once an outsider media practice is now finding new audiences with the distinct allure that moving images bring, creating undeniable connections with others. Documentary is particularly adept at engaging private insight, challenging it, and turning it into public knowledge in a way that is common sense, translating knowledge into cinematic storytelling. As digital culture creates new pathways for networks of information to flow, the social connections generated from documentary constitute an emerging public commons. In this way, documentary becomes a public performance where ideas are exchanged, tested, and reevaluated, inviting audience engagement to help solve social problems. In the deeply divided United States with its now fractured democracy, understanding how communities negotiate power and difference is of the utmost significance. Investment in these documentary practices could bring attention to the cultivation of intellectual life in the margins—where documentary media practices function as a form of survival.

Notes

Chapter 1

1. Hands, "@ Is for Activism," 4–5.
2. Aguayo, "Paradise Lost," 2013.
3. Scott, "Documentaries (in Name Only)," 2010.
4. Barney, Sterne, Tembeck, Ross, and Coleman, *Participatory Condition*, vii–viii.
5. Manjoo, "Post-Text Future," 2018.
6. Hands, "@ Is for Activism," 7.
7. Kahana, *Intelligence Work*, 9.
8. Gaines, "Political Mimesis," 92.
9. Benson and Anderson, *Reality Fictions*, 37–106.
10. Boyle.
11. Halleck.
12. Conan, "Political Documentaries," 2004.
13. Scott, "Documentaries (in Name Only)," 2010.
14. LaMarre and Landreville, "When Is Fiction as Good as Fact," 2009.
15. Schiller, "Framing the Revolution," 2009; Whiteman, "Documentary Film as Policy Analysis," 2009.
16. Whiteman, "Out of the Theaters."
17. Barnouw, *Documentary: A History*, 1993; Kahana, *Intelligence Work*, 2008; Waugh, *Show Us Life*, 1984; Waugh, Baker, and Winton., *Challenges for Change*, 2010.
18. Nisbet and Aufderheide, "Documentary Film," 2009.
19. See Waugh et al., *Challenge for Change*.
20. Anderson, *Imagined Communities* 6.
21. Geiger, "American Documentary Film," 3.
22. Zimmermann, "States of Emergency," 12.
23. Kahana, *Intelligence Work*, 2.
24. Geiger, *American Documentary Film*, 5.
25. For example, documentary has the potential to create a variety of viewing positions for the audience. The screen may display images of social injustice, but how do those stories and representations position the movement and agency of the audience? A closer investigation of collective identification could include understanding how audience subject positions, such as spectator, deliberative, consumer, and/or viewer–citizen, may have varying ramifications for the process of social change.
26. For clarity, I am not referring to the commons in a feudal sense as bound up in connections to property ownership. Nor am I directly referring to the commons as an international, global, or planetary term, although it does not exclude such things. For the purposes of this project,

the commons is not bound by property but connected through media objects, participatory connection and events.

27. Hands, "@ Is for Activism," 171.
28. Hardt and Negri, *Commonwealth*, 121.
29. Hardt and Negri, 165-167
30. McLagan, "Imagining Impact," 306.
31. Kay, "Filmanthropy."
32. McLagan, "Imagining Impact," 309.
33. Gordon, *Ghostly Matters*, 4.
34. Pezzullo, *Toxic Tourism*, 3.
35. Fraser, *Justice Interruptus*, 1996.
36. Bowers, Ochs, and Jenson, *Rhetoric of Agitation*, 19–46.
37. Nichols, *Representing Reality*, 77.
38. Lewis Interview.
39. Daressa, "Is Social Change Media a Delusion?" 2000.
40. Tuck and Yang, "R-Words," 223.
41. Downing, "Social Movement Theories," 42.
42. Lewis and Smoodin, *Looking Past the Screen*, 2.
43. Caldwell, *Production Culture*, 5.
44. Giannachi, *Archive Everything*, 8.
45. Gubrium and Harper, *Participatory Methods*, 13.
46. McKinnon, Asen, Chavez, and Howard., "Text + Field," 3.
47. Ono and Sloop, "Critique of Vernacular Discourse," 19.
48. Many works have used interviews to inform documentary history, including Russell Campbell's *Cinema Strikes Back*; Alexandra Juhasz's *AIDS TV: Identity, Community and Alternative Video*; and Chris Robé's *Breaking the Spell*.
49. Chanan, *Politics of Documentary*, 19.
50. Foust, Pason, and Rogness, *What Democracy Looks Like*, 17.
51. For a broad and through framework for understanding social change, see *Communicating Social Change* by Mohan Dutta.
52. DeLuca, *Image Politics*, 36.
53. Cloud, "Fighting Words," 511–512.
54. Tuck and Yang, "R-Words Refusing Research," 224–225.
55. Ibid., 227.
56. hooks, "Marginality as a Site of Resistance," 343.
57. Tuck and Yang, "Refusing Research," 227.
58. Spivak, "Can the Subaltern Speak," 27.
59. Alcoff, "Problem of Speaking for Others," 23.
60. Foust et al., *What Democracy Looks Like*, 17.
61. Chávez and Griffin, *Standing in the Intersection*, 16.
62. Chávez, *Queer Migration Politics*, 27.
63. Waugh, *Show Us Life*, xiii.
64. Hill, *Cancer's Rhetoricity*, 294.
65. Ibid., 288–289.
66. Dutta, *Communicating Social Change*, 10.
67. Gaines, "Political Mimesis," 90–91.
68. Campbell, *Contemporary Rhetoric*, I.
69. Lundberg and Gunn, " 'Ouija Board'," 94; Greene, "Rhetoric and Capitalism," 189.
70. Gamble and Hanan, *Figures of Entanglement*, 265.
71. Bennett, *Vibrant Matter*, 3.
72. Ibid., 251.
73. Miller, "What Can Automation Tell Us," 1.

74. Ibid., 142–145.

75. Ibid., 147.

76. Juhasz, *AIDS TV*.

77. Ibid., 20.

78. Polletta and Jasper, "Collective Identity," 285.

79. Juhasz, *AIDS TV,* 18.

80. Burke, *Rhetoric of Motives,* 19–31.

81. Downing, *Radical Media,* 2001; Hands, *@ Is for Activism,* 2011; Kellner, *Media Culture,* 1995; Langlois and Dubois, *Autonomous Media,* 2005; Rodriguez, *Fissures in the Mediascape,* 2001.

82. Foust et al., "What Democracy Looks Like," 8.

83. Sandoval, *Methodology of the Oppressed,* 58–64.

84. Chávez, "Queer Migration," 47.

85. Ahmed, *Politics of Emotion,* 2014.

86. Edwards, *Circulatory Encounters,* 2017.

87. Holling, *Centralizing Marginality,* 533.

88. Nichols, *Introduction to Critical Cinema,* 2011.

Chapter 2

1. Barnouw, *Documentary: A History of the Non-Fiction Film,* 87.

2. Ibid., 111–112.

3. Ibid., 263.

4. Boyle, *Subject to Change,* 26–33.

5. Nisbet and Aufderheide, "Documentary Film: Towards a Research Agenda," 450–456.

6. Anderson, *Imagined Communities,* 6.

7. Diani, "Social Movement Networks," 391.

8. Downing, *Radical Media,* 2001; Hands, *@ Is for Activism,* 2011; Kellner, *Media Culture,* 1995; Langlois and Dubois, *Autonomous Media,* 2005; Rodriguez, *Fissures in the Mediascape,* 2001.

9. Gramsci, *Selections from the Prison Notebooks,* 366.

10. Barney et al., *The Participatory Condition,* xviii–xxii.

11. Ibid., viii.

12. Arendt, *The Human Condition,* 2013.

13. Habermas and Habermas, *Structural Transformation of the Public Sphere,* 1991.

14. Bishop, *Artificial Hells,* 8.

15. Bowers, Ochs, and Jensen, *Rhetoric of Agitation,* 22–31.

16. Barney et al., *The Participatory Condition,* vii.

17. Jenkins, Ford, and Green, *Spreadable Media;* Jenkins, *Textual Poachers.*

18. Jenkins, Ito, and Boyd, *Networked Era,* 15.

19. Jenkins, Ford, and Green, *Spreadable Media.*

20. Ibid., 10.

21. I see participatory media culture as a relational process, functioning as a matter of degree. There is much to sort out about what might be considered productive participation, especially in a historical moment when there is a deep political divide in the United States and powerful economic disparity. In this context, I understand participatory culture as a mechanism of collectivity, with potential to operate around commercial and government institutions, collecting people around shared interests. Some participatory cultures can develop into activist media publics or social movements, in this context there exist the potential to turn the dial on social change. This research is developed in an effort to understand better cultural configurations for social justice.

22. Jenkins, Ito, and Boyd, *Networked Era,* 11.

23. Campbell, *Cinema Strikes Back.*

24. Waugh, *Show Us Life,* xiii.

25. Chanan, *The Politics of Documentary*, 7.
26. Kahana, *Intelligence Work*, 23.
27. Juhasz, *AIDS TV*.
28. Nisbet and Aufderheide, "Documentary Film: Towards a Research Agenda," 450–456.
29. Barney et al., *The Participatory Condition*, x.
30. Felski, *Beyond Feminist Aesthetics*, and Ebely, *Citizen Critic*.
31. Cloud, *Reality Bites*, 2–7.
32. Brownlow, *Behind the Mask of Innocence*, xvi.
33. Ross, *Working-Class Hollywood*, 43.
34. Robé, *Left of Hollywood*, 5.
35. Barnouw, *Documentary: History of the Non-Fiction Film*, 85–91.
36. Ruby, "Speaking for, Speaking About," 50–67.
37. Aitken, *The Documentary Film Movement*, 34.
38. Alexander, *Film on the Left*, 9.
39. Brownlow, *Behind the Mask of Innocence*, 498–508.
40. Ross, *Working-Class Hollywood*, 162.
41. Ibid., 221.
42. Ibid., 162.
43. Campbell, *Cinema Strikes Back*, 13; Ross, *Working-Class Hollywood*, 162.
44. Denning, *The Cultural Front*, xvi.
45. Ibid., xvi.
46. The cultural front was the expansion of social movement consciousness into popular mediums and texts that were not traditionally read as political, such as music and film. It was the encounter between a powerful democratic social movement and the modern cultural apparatuses of mass entertainment and education. Denning describes the laboring of cultural texts in the 1930s in four distinct ways: (1) the pervasive use of the critique of labor and its synonyms in the rhetoric of the period; (2) the increased participation of working-class Americans in the world of culture and the arts; (3) the new visibility of labor in cultural production through the organization of unions by the workers, including screenwriters and cartoonists; and (4) the Cultural Front, which led to a new rhetorical moment that acted as a second American Renaissance (xvi–xvii). In conclusion, Denning recognizes an important aspect of the interaction of cultural texts and social change; there is a significant relationship between activist cultural texts and the embodied organizations of people who are agitating on behalf of the issues emphasized in the text. The embodiment of activist work is a significant theoretical and practical connection that will be challenged, rechallenged, and emphasized in the history of activist documentary.
47. Barsam, *Nonfiction Film*, 42.
48. Barnouw, *Documentary: History of the Non-Fiction Film*, 85.
49. Ibid., 88.
50. Ibid., 90.
51. Ellis, *The Documentary Idea*, 78–79.
52. Campbell, 26.
53. Ibid., 27.
54. Barnouw, *History of the Non-Fiction Film*, 86.
55. With the emergence of "new social movements," Alberto Melucci argues, constitutive cultural strategies are the primary and most important acts of contemporary social movements: "Conflicts [of new social movements] do not chiefly express themselves through action designed to achieve outcomes in the political system. Rather, they raise a challenge that recasts the language and cultural codes that organize information. The ceaseless flow of messages only acquire meaning through the codes that order the flux and allow its meaning to be read. The forms of power now emerging in contemporary societies are grounded in an ability to 'inform' that is, to 'give form' " (102). As a result, the production

of cultural texts that challenge important language and cultural codes of the institutions of power, according to Melucci, is the primary political moment to be seized. Melucci's position, identified as New Social Movements theory, is indicative of most contemporary scholarship on social change.

56. Barnouw, *Documentary: History of the Non-Fiction Film*, 219.
57. Ibid., 234.
58. Couldry, *Why Voice Matters*, 130.
59. Ibid., 8.
60. Freedman, "Activist Television," 2005.
61. Boyle, *Subject to Change*, vi.
62. Ibid., 13.
63. Media Bus, *Radical Software*, 4.
64. Robé, *Left of Hollywood*, 4.
65. Freedman, "Activist Television," 2005.
66. Teasdale, "Lanesville TV," 2005.
67. Boyle, *Subject to Change*, 30.
68. Ibid., 6.
69. Barnouw, *Documentary: History of the Non-Fiction Film*, 289.
70. Winston, *A Handshake*, 35.
71. Abrash and Mertes, *In honor of George Stoney*, 6.
72. Winston, *A Handshake*, 37.
73. Stoney interview.
74. Ibid.
75. Boyle, *Subject to Change*, 4.
76. Ibid., 30.
77. Ibid., 72.
78. Teasdale, "Lanesville TV," 2005.
79. Robé, *Breaking the Spell*, 43.
80. Ibid., 45.
81. Freedman, "Activist Television," 2005.
82. Shamberg and Williams, "Top Value Television Coverage," 13.
83. Ibid.
84. Halleck, *Hand-Held Visions*, 274.
85. Robé, *Left of Hollywood*, 80–84.
86. Shamberg and Williams, "Top Value Television Coverage."
87. Boyle, *Subject to Change*, 31.
88. Ibid., 7.
89. Ibid., 11.
90. Halleck, *Hand-Held Visions*, 277.
91. Ibid.
92. Ibid., 191.
93. The guerrilla television movement asserted that "no alternative cultural vision could succeed without its own alternative information structure, not just alternative content pumped across the existing system . . . guerrilla television would coexist with broadcasting, restoring balance to the 'media ecology' of America." Boyle, *Subject to Change*, 33.
94. Robé, *Breaking the Spell*, 81.
95. Boyle, *Subject to Change*, 29.
96. Many early activist videotapes fell under the heading of street tapes, in which activist videotexts placed people in their living rooms, bedrooms, and the streets for the first time with the help of portable video equipment. The videos primarily addressed those who were part of the community and not those who resided outside. Images of massive protest mean very little to those not aligned with the commitments of those agitating for social change. Therefore, images that do not create a connection with an audience outside the activist

community are limited in their ability to create social change. The early activist-video movement inadvertently became a community in itself and not a community for itself.

97. Zimmermann, *States of Emergency*, 11.
98. Ibid., 13.
99. Ibid.
100. Ibid., xxi.
101. Ibid., 15.
102. Ibid., 23.
103. Paper Tiger TV began in the early 1980s and continues to exist as an open, nonprofit, volunteer, video collective, producing a wide range of alternative media. In the early 1980s, the organization was an almost solitary voice in media activism for a waning period of activist media in the public sphere. As Dee Dee Halleck explains in her book *Hand-Held Visions*, the 1980s became "a period of co-optation, or some might call it a 'sell-out' " (276). Paper Tiger Television produced cable programs analyzing and critiquing the media, culture, and politics (Paper Tiger). The Paper Tiger TV collective began to build a foundation for organizing media in the third wave of the activist documentary impulse. The structure of the collective was strictly nonhierarchical and committed to the process of community media making as a long-term goal for improving a communicative democracy.
104. As reported in *The New York Times* ten years later, much of the work produced by the movement was "emotionally searing, since so many of the demonstrators and the creators of these videos were fighting for their lives in a race against time" (Holden). Like much of the video activist work that preceded the AIDS documentary movement, "The video makers clearly positioned themselves in opposition to an unresponsive and often antagonistic government and mainstream media" (Hubbard, 2005).
105. Mann, Vargas, Foreman, and Moos, "Politics and Pop Culture," 2004.
106. In 2004, no film evoked more public deliberation and political discourse than *Fahrenheit 9/11* (Hays, Elam, Clarkin, and Rogers, 2004; Murray; Zahn, Meckler, and McIntyre). It became the essential event film. As one reporter noted, "It became a water-cooler subject, where everybody wanted to talk about it on talk radio and around the country" (Norville, 2004). The film was framed by the mainstream media, where it was most publicly discussed.
107. In his film and media interviews, Moore claims that mainstream news media outlets did not fulfill their civic function as the country geared up for a questionable war with Iraq. In Moore's interview with Katie Couric, he asks: "[T]he questions should be posed to NBC news and all other news agencies: Why didn't you show us that the people we are going to bomb in a few days are these people, human beings who are living normal lives, kids flying kites, people just trying to get by in their daily existence. . . . We killed civilians and we don't know how many thousands of civilians we killed . . . and nobody covered that" (Couric and Lauer, 2004). Moore's explicit condemnation of the mainstream media was present in the film and expressed more poignantly in his interviews with the press about the film.
108. McChesney, *Corporate Media*, 30.
109. Frank, "Why Johnny Can't Dissent," 38.
110. Ibid., 41.
111. Frank and Weiland, *Commodify Your Dissent*, 16. Advertising often uses this trend, deploying images of protest and liberation to sell products. Television shows like *Murphy Brown, Sex in the City,* and *Buffy the Vampire Slayer* coopt feminist themes to target a particular audience. The marketing of music is particularly guilty of this trend, and political expression and contestation are almost a requirement for hip rock stars. For example, Chris Martin from Coldplay routinely paints his hand with a symbol of equal rights for the gay community, and the Dixie Chicks spoke out against the Bush administration while arguing for free speech rights. The lines between commercial media, counterculture, and political dissent are blurred in the contemporary media environment.

112. As depicted in the second film, a group of viewers in Los Angeles began meeting on a regular basis to deliberate about the facts of the case after they watched the first film *Paradise Lost: The Child Murders at Robin Hood Hills*. This group in Los Angeles began to research the case, share information, and gather on a regular basis. The movie acted as a catalyst for social change by creating the environment for a public concerned with miscarriages of justice while creating rhetorical identification with the convicted, "The West Memphis Three." Without the film, counternarratives silenced in the official court hearings or by the mainstream media might never have proliferated in a significant way. Hence, *Paradise Lost: The Child Murders at Robin Hood Hills* (1996) and its sequel, *Paradise Lost Revisited* (2000), spurred counterpublics to create an instrumental identity and social change through the viewing of the texts.

113. Aguayo, "Paradise Lost and Found."

114. This social pattern is consistent with current studies on internet use and grassroots democracy. As reported by Jerry Berman and Deirdre Mulligan in the article "Digital Grass Roots," the internet is making an explosive impact on democratic practices: "Democracy is communicating to persuade. For these aspects of democracy, the internet is a powerful new tool for activism. It places in the hands of any individual with a computer and a phone line a previously unimaginable amount of information about government institutional process, and it allows that same individual to speak out—to be his or her own publisher—and to identify, communicate with, and to join others who share a similar viewpoint" (91–92).

115. Wolfson, *Digital Rebellion*, 183.

116. Wired.com.

117. *The Globe and Mail*.

118. Activist internet journalism set down its roots in 1999, during the World Trade Organization (WTO) meeting in Seattle. The meeting of the WTO spawned one of the largest and most cohesively organized instances of social protests in recent decades. Tens of thousands traveled to Seattle from around the world to protest the WTO's meeting, which was convened to discuss the possibility of further opening economic markets. While *The Seattle Times* invited guest columnists like U.S. Secretary of Commerce William Daley and Environmental Protection Agency Administrator Carol Browner to write for the paper, the internet-based Independent Media Center was reporting a far different story.

119. Such stories included a "man who said he had been hit in the face with rubber bullets fired by police. Another [story] showed police firing canisters of tear gas into a crowd" (salon.com). The images from the street reported by the IMA were reminiscent of a military invasion, while *The Seattle Times* published stories from the Clinton administration that justified the WTO meeting.

120. Berman and Mulligan, "Digital Grass Roots," 81–91.

121. Hand, *@ Is for Activism*, 68.

122. Ibid., 156.

123. Hall, "On Postmodernism and Articulation," 1986.

124. Palczewski, "Cyber-movements," 166.

125. Warner, *Publics and Counterpublics*, 2002.

126. Aguayo, "Paradise lost and found," 2005.

Chapter 3

1. Denning, *Cultural Front*, 38–50; Triece, *Protest and Popular Culture*, 25–48.

2. Hall, "Rediscovery of Ideology," 122–123.

3. Gramsci, "Hegemony Intellectuals," 2009.

4. Christensen, "Political Documentary," 22.

5. Nichols, *Speaking Truth*, 225.

6. Ibid., x.

7. Ibid., 228.
8. Benson and Snee, *New Political Documentary*, 3.
9. Ibid., 7.
10. Ibid., 9.
11. Gries, *Still Life with Rhetoric*, xiv.
12. Ibid., 86–87.
13. Edbauer, "Unframing Models of Public Distribution," 5–24.
14. Gries, *Still Life with Rhetoric*, 27.
15. Storey, *Cultural Theory and Popular Culture*, 226.
16. Box Office Mojo, *Roger and Me* Summary.
17. Box Office Mojo, *Hoop Dreams* Summary.
18. Mann, Vargas, Foreman, and Moss, "Politics and Pop Culture."
19. Box Office Mojo, *Bowling for Columbine* Summary.
20. Box Office Mojo, *Fahrenheit 9/11* Summary.
21. Corliss et al., "The World According to Michael," 2004.
22. Siegel, Norris, and Masters, "Surprising Box Office Success," 2004.
23. Norville et al., *Moore's Controversial New Film*.
24. Couric and Lauer, "*Fahrenheit 9/11* Gets Mixed Reviews."
25. Montagne, "Michael Moore's Controversial Documentary."
26. Parry-Giles and Parry-Giles, "Virtual Realism," 25.
27. Ibid., 26.
28. Gilgoff and Tobin, "Moore or Less"; Couric and Lauer, "*Fahrenheit 9/11* Gets Mixed Reviews"; Porton, "Weapon of Mass Instruction," 3; Smiley, "Michael Moore's *Fahrenheit 9/11*"; Wilshire, "Michael Moore's *Fahrenheit 9/11* and the US Election," 129–130; York, "The Passion of Michael Moore."
29. Shenon, "Michael Moore Is Ready for His Close-Up," 2004.
30. Moore, *Fahrenheit 9/11*.
31. Couric, "*Fahrenheit 9/11* Gets Mixed Reviews."
32. Couric and Lauer, "*Fahrenheit 9/11*."
33. Lauer, "Point."
34. Smiley, "Michael Moore's *Fahrenheit 9/11*."
35. Pennebaker interview.
36. Norville, "Drawing Crowds Overseas," 2004.
37. Dutka, "'*Celsius 41.11*'," 2004.
38. *Washington Post*-ABC News Poll.
39. Box Office Mojo, *Where to Invade Next* Summary.
40. Lynch, "Making a Murderer," *AdWeek*, 2016.
41. Helmore, "Making a Murderer Spurs 275,000 Viewers," *Guardian*, 2016.
42. Adams, "'Making a Murderer' and True Crime in the Binge-Viewing Era," 2018; Perks, *Media Marathoning*, 2014.
43. This documentary and the pressure for transparency continue to unfold. There have been new calls for the Baltimore Archdiocese to release documents about a controversial priest. https://www.cbsnews.com/news/netflix-the-keepers-series-controversy-catholic-church-baltimore-murder.
44. Aguayo, "Paradise Lost," 2013.
45. Dodd, "Beyond a Reasonable Doubt?"
46. King, "The Case of the West Memphis Three," King, "Damien Echols: Death Row Interview."
47. Panetta, *Worthy Fights*, 453.
48. Daniel, "Panetta, Dempsey Announce Initiatives," 2012.
49. Gillibrand, *Off the Sidelines: Raise Your Voice*, 2014.
50. Helfand is an accomplished filmmaker who has built and influenced many documentary institutions, contributing to the support of more diverse creative talent in the industry. I met

Helfand in a New York City park in the summer of 2010, where we talked about the documentary industry, diversity, and social change.

51. Ellison, "Panetta, Gates, Rumsfeld Face New Suit," 2012.
52. Rosenberg, "'The Invisible War'," 2013.
53. Risen, "Air Force Leaders Testify," 2013.
54. Rohter, "A Documentarian Focused on Trauma," 2013.
55. Box Office Mojo, *Invisible War* Summary.
56. Poland, "The Hunting Ground, Kirby Dick & Amy Ziering," 2015.
57. Ibid., 2015.
58. Allen, "Interview: Kirby Dick on 'The Hunting Ground'," 2015.
59. Ibid., 2015.
60. Cole and Briggs, *Culture on Campus*, 2016.
61. Kaufman, "Reality Checks," 2015.
62. Syckle, "'The Hunting Ground'," 2016.
63. Valenti, "Lady Gaga's New Song Has Leaked."
64. Ibid.
65. Felperin, "'The Hunting Ground."
66. "Talking to Documentarian Kirby Dick," 2016.
67. Ibid.
68. NcNary, *Holloywood Sexual Assault*, 2017.

Chapter 4

1. Kleinhans, Barbara Kopple interview.
2. Waugh, *"Show Us Life,"* xvi.
3. Polletta and Jasper, "Collective Identity," 285.
4. Ibid., 283–284.
5. Gerbaudo and Treré, "In Search of the "We"," 865.
6. Polletta and Jasper, "Collective Identity," 284.
7. Gerbaudo and Treré, "In Search of the "We"," 866.
8. Chávez, *Queer Migration Politics*, 27.
9. Burke, *Rhetoric of Motives*, 19–31.
10. Polletta, "Contending Stories," 1998.
11. Silverman, *Threshold of the Visible World*, 91.
12. Bennett and Segerberg, *Logic of Connective Action*, 2013.
13. Polletta and Jasper, "Collective Identity," 287.
14. Chavez, *Queer Migration Politics*, 27.
15. Cloud, "Reality Bites," 7.
16. Campbell, *Cinema Strikes Back*, 17.
17. Ibid.
18. Bowser, "Pioneers of Black Documentary," 6.
19. Ibid., 3.
20. Ibid., 7.
21. Ibid., 5.
22. Ibid., 8–11.
23. Ibid., 9.
24. Ibid., 19.
25. Campbell, "Radical Documentary in the United States," 69.
26. Ibid., 70.
27. Ibid., 71.
28. Ibid., 73.
29. Klotman and Cutler, *Struggles for Representation*, xvii.

30. Stoney, Helfand, and Rostock, *The Uprising of '34*, 1995.
31. https://hrmediaarchive.estuarypress.com
32. Quinn interview.
33. Kleinhans, Barbara Kopple interview.
34. Anne Lewis interview, 2007.
35. Henderson, *Struggle in Steel*, 1996.
36. Hollibaugh and Singh, 61.
37. Juhasz, *Women of Vision*, 126.
38. Reichert and Klein, *Union Maids*, 1979.
39. Couldry, *Why Voice Matters*, 12–13.
40. Gray, *With Babies and Banners*, 1979.
41. Ibid., 1979.
42. Ibid., 1979.
43. Shaffer, *Wobblies*, 1979.
44. Third Cinema is a film movement that begins in Latin America in the late 60s-70s. It is an approach to cinema that rejects colonialism, capitalism, and the Hollywood model of production.
45. Robé, Breaking the Spell, 407.
46. Zelzer interview.
47. Duncan interview.
48. Ibid.
49. Ibid.
50. Ibid.
51. Zelzer interview.
52. Combs, *From Selma to Montgomery*, 2013; Street, *Photographing Farmworkers*, 2004.
53. Street, "Poverty in the Valley of Plenty," 2007.
54. https://hrmediaarchive.estuarypress.com.
55. Ibid.
56. Abrash interview.
57. Process filmmaking is a mode of creative culture that is more interested in the relational and creative exchanges of production than the outcome of the final project.
58. Hoffman interview, 2009.
59. Ibid.
60. Gold interview, 2007.
61. Ibid.
62. Hoffman interview, 2009.
63. Ibid.
64. Gold interview, 2007.
65. Hoffman interview, 2009.
66. Gold interview, 2007.
67. Ibid.
68. Hoffman interview, 2009.
69. Kleinhans, Barbara Kopple interview.
70. Ibid.
71. Cloud, "Standpoint, Mediation," 7.
72. Negt and Kluge, 256.

Chapter 5

1. Gaines, *Political Mimesis*, 88.
2. Sisson and Kimport, "Telling Stories about Abortion."
3. Warren, "Abortion, Abortion, Abortion."

4. Renov, *Subject of Documentary*.
5. Smaill, The Documentary."
6. Juhasz, *Realist Feminist Documentary*, 191.
7. Lane interview.
8. Stasiulis, "Feminist Intersectional Theorizing."
9. Warren, "Abortion, Abortion, Abortion," 756.
10. Ibid., 756–757.
11. Gould, *Moving Politics*, 32.
12. Gaines, "Political Mimesis," 91.
13. Gould, *Moving Politics*, 35.
14. Condit, *Decoding Abortion Rhetoric*, 944.
15. Ibid., 44.
16. Ibid., 22–23.
17. Ibid., 22–23.
18. Ibid., 25–28.
19. Ibid., 31.
20. Ibid., 71–72.
21. Ibid., 46.
22. McGee, "The 'Ideograph'," 1.
23. Frank and Norman, "Reproductive Rights Films," 36.
24. Rich, *Chick Flicks*, 306.
25. Zimmerman interview.
26. Ibid.
27. Rich, *Chick Flicks*, 287.
28. Ibid., 301.
29. http://www.concentric.org/films/when_abortion_was_illegal.html
30. Lane, interview.
31. Rand, *Reclaiming Queer*, 132.
32. McCann, " 'Chrysler Pulled the Trigger'," 131–155.
33. Ahmed, *Cultural Politics of Emotion*, 30.
34. Cloud and Feyh, "Reason in Revolt," 4.
35. Gordon, *Ghostly Matters*, 195.
36. Cvetkovich, *Archive of Feelings*, 5.
37. Juhasz, *Realist Feminist Documentary*.
38. Lesage, "Political Aesthetics," 509.
39. Ibid., 515.
40. *Abortion Diaries*.
41. Ibid.
42. Ibid.
43. Aldrich and Baumgardner, *I Had an Abortion*. [Videorecording]..
44. Ibid.
45. Bell, *Cultural Contradictions of Capitalism*, 22.
46. Bowers, "Women," 16.
47. Dmedit, "Our Views Now," 2004; Eagle, "Stir up Controversy," 2004; Fleming, "T-shirt Sparks Backlash," 2012; Garfield, "Shirts Cause Rift," 2004; Thomas, "Promotion of 'I Had an Abortion' T-Shirts," 2004; Wise, "Planned Parenthood Selling," 2004.
48. *Abortion Diaries*.
49. Ibid.
50. Ibid.
51. Ibid.
52. *I Had an Abortion*.
53. Ibid.
54. Ahmed, 176.

55. Jennifer Baumgardner (author and activist) in an interview with Angela Aguayo, October 2009.

56. Abrash interview.

57. https://feminist.org/blog/index.php/2017/02/09/over-one-third-of-u-s-abortion-clinics-experience-severe-violence-and-harassment-according-to-new-feminist-majority-foundation-survey

58. http://www.pbs.org/independentlens/blog/dawn-porter-unlocks-story-of-laws-targeting-abortion-providers

59. *Soldiers in the Army of God* (2000).

Chapter 6

1. Vernacular communication has come to signify a variety of perspectives throughout cultural history. "[O]n one hand vernacular forms are those available to individuals or groups who are subordinated to institutions, and, on the other, they are a common resource made available to everyone through informal social interaction. Based on this dual meaning, the vernacular came to refer to discourse that coexists with dominant culture but is held separate from it." Howard, "Vernacular Web," 202.

2. Alexander, "Can You Be BLACK," 90.

3. DuVernay, *13th*, 2016.

4. Calafell and Delgado, "Reading Latina/o Images," 7.

5. Ibid., 107.

6. Lingel, *Digital Counter-Cultures*, 2.

7. Ibid., 4.

8. Gordon, *Ghostly Matters*, 190.

9. Ibid., 8.

10. Nichols, *Representing Reality*, 82–87.

11. Robé, *Breaking the Spell*, 37.

12. Ibid., 50.

13. Ibid., 47–50.

14. Horsfield, "Busing the Tube" and Hilderbrand, *Feedback*, 8.

15. Ibid., 8.

16. Ranucci interview.

17. Blumberg interview.

18. Halleck, *Hand Held Visions*, 2002.

19. During this time, ACT UP, a prominent gay activist group, created a video collective called DIVA TV (Damned Interfering Video Activist Television). Gregg Bordowitz, a DIVA TV member, produced some of the most influential AIDS activist videos, including *Voices from the Front* (Elgear, Hutt, and Meieran, 1992) and *Fast Trip, Long Drop* (Bordowitz, 1995). The videos present stirring portraits of the political struggle over the AIDS crisis in the public sphere and offers an intimate close-up as Bordowitz struggles with the effects of the disease on his body. As reported in the *New York Times* ten years later, much of the work produced by the movement is "emotionally searing, since so many of the demonstrators and the creators of these videos were fighting for their lives in a race against time" (Holden, "AIDS Activism"). Like much of the video activist work that preceded the AIDS documentary movement, "The videomakers clearly positioned themselves in opposition to an unresponsive and often antagonistic government and mainstream media" (Hubbard, "Fever in the Archive").

20. Asher, "NOPD in the Age of Mad Men," 2017.

21. Rodriguez, *Citizens' Media*, 234.

22. Drew, *Social History*, 59.

23. Alexander, "Can You Be BLACK," 79.

24. Ibid., 79.

25. Ibid., 91–92.
26. Drew, *Social History*, 59.
27. Hallin, *We Keep America on Top*, 1994; McChesney, *Rich Media, Poor Democracy*, 2015.
28. Atton, *Alternative Internet*, 495.
29. I understand digital rhetoric as a distinct form of communication, enabled by the advances in digital technology that allow easy media content creation and circulation. This process of digitization involves diverse forms of information, such as text, sound, image, or voice, converted into a single binary code. Information exists in coded signals of zeros and ones, an approximation of the information that it represents. This digitized information is easily edited, remixed, and shared, partly because of the coded signal and easy online networks. This includes official, commercial, and industry discourse but also vernacular forms of communication and stories seen through the eyes of the common people rather than politically privileged, economic elites or media professionals that typically control public content.
30. Atton, 2004.
31. Drew, *Social History*, 60.
32. Rodriguez, *Citizens' Media*, 22.
33. Gordon, *Ghostly Matters*, 2.
34. Rodriguez, *Citizens' Media*, 233.
35. Ibid., 237.
36. Gordon, *Ghostly Matters*, 8.
37. Rodriguez, *Citizens' Media*, 237–238.
38. Hoerl, "Remembering Black Dissent," 84.
39. Lenzner, "Emergence of Occupy Wall Street, 251.
40. Rodriguez, *Citizens' Media*, 24.
41. Ibid.
42. Durkin, "#EricGarner #ICantBreathe #NYC Protests."
43. McBride, "WATCH: Falcon Heights."
44. DeLong and Braunger, "Breaking down the Dashcam."
45. Jacobo and Francis, "Cops May Have Thought."
46. Peterson, "Why the Philando Castile Police-Shooting Video Disappeared."
47. Rodriguez, *Citizens' Media*, 265.
48. Masri, *Bassem*.
49. Rayford, "The Lost Voices" and "#Ferguson #fergusonshooting #MichaelBrown #mikebrown."
50. Giannachi, *Archive Everything*, xv.
51. Ibid., xviii.
52. Ibid., xvi.

Chapter 7

1. Grossberg, "On Postmodernism and Articulation," 1986.
2. Downing, "Social Movement Theories," 149.
3. Couldry, *Media, Society, World*, 208.
4. Greene, "Communicative Labor," 189.
5. Lewis and Miller, *Critical Cultural Policy Studies*, 2003.
6. Caldwell, *Production Culture*, 2008.
7. Miller, *Well-Tempered Self*, 1993.
8. Lewis and Miller, *Critical Cultural Policy Studies*, 2.
9. Ibid., 1.
10. Cunningham, *Framing Culture*, 2.
11. Hall, "Emergence of Cultural Studies," 17.
12. McRobbie, "All the World's a Stage," 335.
13. Lewis and Miller, *Critical Cultural Policy Studies*, 6.

14. Denning, *Cultural Front*.
15. Giannachi, x *Archive Everything*, v.
16. Ibid., xviii.
17. Ibid., xxi.
18. Couldry, *Media, Society, World*, 210.

References

Chapter 1

Aguayo, Angela J. "Paradise Lost and Found: Popular Documentary, Collective Identity and Participatory Media Culture." *Studies in Documentary Film* 7 (2013): 233–248.

Ahmed, Sara. *The Cultural Politics of Emotion*. 2 edition. New York: Routledge, 2014.

Alcoff, Linda. "The Problem of Speaking for Others." *Cultural Critique*, no. 20 (1991): 5–32.

Anderson, Benedict. *Imagined Communities: Reflections on the Origin and Spread of Nationalism*. New York: Verso, 2006.

Barney, Darin David, Jonathan Sterne, Tamar Tembeck, Christine Ross, and Gabriella Coleman (eds.). *The Participatory Condition in the Digital Age*. Minneapolis: University of Minnesota Press, 2016.

Barnouw, Eric. *Documentary: A History of the Non-Fiction Film*. New York: Oxford University Press, 1993.

Bennett, Jane. *Vibrant Matter: A Political Ecology of Things*. Durham, NC: Duke University Press, 2010.

Benson, Thomas W., and Carolyn Anderson. *Reality Fictions: The Films of Frederick Wiseman*. Carbondale: Southern Illinois University Press, 1989.

Bowers, John W., Donovan J. Ochs, and Richard J. Jenson. *The Rhetoric of Agitation and Control*. Prospect Heights, IL: Waveland Press, 1993.

Boyle, Deirdre. *Subject to Change: Guerrilla Television Revisited*. New York: Oxford University Press, 1997.

Burke, Kenneth. *A Rhetoric of Motives*. Berkeley: University of California Press, 1969.

Caldwell, John. *Production Culture: Industrial Reflexivity and Critical Practice in Film and Television*. Durham, NC: Duke University Press, 2007.

Campbell, Karlyn Kohrs. *Critiques of Contemporary Rhetoric*. Belmont, CA: Wadsworth, 1997.

Campbell, Russell. *Cinema Strikes Back: Radical Filmmaking in the United States, 1930–1942*. Ann Arbor, Michigan: UMI Research Press, 1982.

Chanan, Michael. *Politics of Documentary*. London: British Film Institute, 2008.

Chávez, Karma R., and Cindy L. Griffin. *Standing in the Intersection: Feminist Voices, Feminist Practices in Communication Studies*. Albany, NY: SUNY Press, 2012.

Chávez, Karma R. *Queer Migration Politics: Activist Rhetoric and Coalitional Possibilities*. Carbondale: University of Illinois Press, 2013.

Cloud, Dana L. "Fighting Words: Labor and the Limits of Communication at Staley, 1993 to 1996" *Management Communication Quarterly* 18, no. 4 (May 1, 2005): 509–542.

Conan, Neal. "Political Documentaries." June 24, 2004. *Talk of the Nation*. National Public Radio.

Daressa, Larry. "Is Social Change Media a Delusion?—California Newsreel at 30 and 2000." Accessed January 31, 2018. http://newsreel.org/articles/socialme.htm.

DeLuca, Kevin Michael. *Image Politics: The New Rhetoric of Environmental Activism*. New York: Routledge, 2012.

Downing, J. D. H. *Radical Media: Rebellious Communication and Social Movements*. Thousand Oaks, CA: SAGE, 2001.

Dutta, Mohan J. *Communicating Social Change: Structure, Culture, and Agency*. Boca Raton, FL: Taylor & Francis, 2011.

Edwards, Dustin. "On Circulatory Encounters: The Case for Tactical Rhetorics | Enculturation." *Enculturation: A Journal of Rhetoric, Writing and Culture*, October 4, 2017. http://enculturation.net/circulatory_encounters.

Foust, Christina R., Amy Pason, and Kate Zittlow Rogness. *What Democracy Looks Like: The Rhetoric of Social Movements and Counterpublics*. Tucaloosa: University of Alabama Press, 2017.

Fraser, Nancy. *Justice Interruptus*. New York: Routledge, 1997.

Gaines, Jane. "Political mimesis." From *Collecting Visible Evidence*, edited by J. M. Gaines and M. Renov, 84–102. Minneapolis: University of Minnesota Press, 1999.

Gamble, Christopher N., and Joshua S. Hanan. "Figures of Entanglement: Special Issue Introduction." *Review of Communication* 16, no. 4 (October 2016): 265–280.

Geiger, Jeffrey. *American Documentary Film: Projecting the Nation: Projecting the Nation*. Edinburgh: Edinburgh University Press, 2011.

Giannachi, Gabriella. *Archive Everything: Mapping the Everyday*. Cambridge, MA: MIT Press, 2016.

Gordon, Avery F. *Ghostly Matters: Haunting and the Sociological Imagination*. Minneapolis: University of Minnesota Press, 2008.

Greene, Ronald Walter. "Rhetoric and Capitalism: Rhetorical Agency as Communicative Labor." *Philosophy and Rhetoric* 37, no. 3 (2004): 188–206.

Greenwald, Robert (Dir.). *Wal-Mart: The High Cost of Low Prices*. 2005.

Gubrium, Aline, and Krista Harper. *Participatory Visual and Digital Methods*. Walnut Creek, CA: Left Coast Press, 2013.

Guggenheim, Davis (Dir.). *An Inconvenient Truth*. 2006.

Halleck, DeeDee. *Hand Held Visions: The Impossible Possibilities of Community Media*. New York: Fordham University Press, 2002.

Hands, Joss. *@ is for Activism: Dissent, Resistance and Rebellion in a Digital Culture*. New York: Pluto Books, 2011.

Hardt, Michael, and Antonio Negri. *Commonwealth*. Cambridge, MA: Harvard University Press, 2009.

Hill, Annie. "Breast Cancer's Rhetoricity: Bodily Border Crisis and Bridge to Corporeal Solidarity." *Review of Communication* 16, no. 4 (October 2016): 281–298.

hooks, bell. "Marginality as a Site of Resistance." In *Out There: Marginalization and Contemporary Cultures*, edited by R. Ferguson and T. Minh-ha, 241–243. Cambridge, MA: MIT Press, 1990.

Holling, Michelle A. "Centralizing Marginality, Marginalizing the Center in the WSCA 2018 Presidential Address." *Western Journal of Communication* 82, no. 5 (October 20, 2018): 529–536.

Juhasz, Alexandra. *AIDS TV: Identity, Community, and Alternative Video*. Durham, N.C: Duke University Press, 1995.

Kahana, Jonathan. *Intelligence Work: The Politics of American Documentary*. New York: Columbia University Press, 2008.

Kay, Jeremy. "Silverdocs Conference to Explore 'filmanthropy' Docs." *Screen*, April 20, 2007. https://www.screendaily.com/silverdocs-conference-to-explore-filmanthropy-docs/4032011.article.

Kellner, Douglas. *Media Culture: Cultural Studies, Identity and Politics Between the Modern and Postmodern*. New York: Routledge, 1995.

LaMarre, Heather L., and Kristen D. Landreville. "When Is Fiction as Good as Fact? Comparing the Influence of Documentary and Historical Reenactment Films on Engagement, Affect, Issue Interest, and Learning." *Mass Communication and Society* 12 (2009): 537–555.

Langlois, A., and Dubois, F. *Autonomous Media: Activating Resistance and Dissent*. Montreal: Cumulus Press, 2005.

Lewis, Anne, interview. 2007.

Lewis, Jon, and Eric Smoodin (eds.). *Looking Past the Screen*. Durham, NC: Duke University Press, 2007.

Lundberg, Christian, and Joshua Gunn. "'Ouija Board, Are There Any Communications?' Agency, Ontotheology, and the Death of the Humanist Subject, or, Continuing the ARS Conversation." *Rhetoric Society Quarterly* 35, no. 4 (2005): 83–105.

McKinnon, Sara L., Robert Asen, Karma R. Chavez, and Robert Glenn Howard (eds.). *Text + Field: Innovations in Rhetorical Method—Google Books*. University Park: Pennsylvania State University Press, 2016.

McLagan, Meg. "Imagining Impact: Documentary Film and the Production of Political Effects." In *Sensible Politics: The Visual Culture of Nongovernmental Politics*, edited by Meg McLagan and Yates McKee, 304–319. New York: Zone Books, 2012.

Manjoo, Farhad. "Welcome to the Post-Text Future." *The New York Times*, February 9, 2018, sec. Technology. https://www.nytimes.com/interactive/2018/02/09/technology/the-rise-of-a-visual-internet.html

Miller, Carolyn R. "What Can Automation Tell Us about Agency?" *Rhetoric Society Quarterly* 37 (2007): 137–157.

Moore, Michael (Dir.). *Fahrenheit 9/11*. 2004.

Morris, Errol (Dir.). *Thin Blue Line*. 1988.

Nichols, Bill. "Foreword." From *Introduction to Critical Cinema: Beyond Theory of Practice*, edited by Clive Myer, xiii–xvi. New York: Columbia University Press, 2011.

Nichols, Bill. *Representing Reality: Issues and Concepts in Documentary*. Bloomington: Indiana University Press, 1991.

Nisbet, Matthew C., and Patricia Aufderheide. "Documentary Film: Towards a Research Agenda on Forms, Functions and Impacts." *Mass Communication and Society* 12 (2009): 450–456.

Ono, Kent A., and John M. Sloop. "The Critique of Vernacular Discourse." *Communication Monographs* 62, no. 1 (1995): 19–46.

Pezzullo, Phaedra. *Toxic Tourism: Rhetorics of Pollution, Travel, and Environmental Justice*. Tuscaloosa: University of Alabama Press, 2009.

Polletta, F., and Jasper, J. M. "Collective Identity and Social Movements." *Annual Review of Sociology*, 27 (2001): 283–305.

Portillo, Lordes (Dir.). *Senorita Extraviada*. 2001.

Robé, Chris. *Breaking the Spell: A History of Anarchist Filmmakers, Videotape Guerrillas, and Digital Ninjas*. Oakland, CA: PM Press, 2017.

Rodriguez, Clemencia. *Fissures in the Mediascape: An International Study of Citizen's Media*. Cresskill, NJ: Hampton Press, 2001.

Sandoval, Chela. *Methodology of the Oppressed*. Minneapolis: University of Minnesota Press, 2000.

Schiller, Naomi. "Framing the Revolution: Circulation and Meaning of the Revolution Will Not Be Televised." *Mass Communication and Society* 12 (2009): 478–502.

Scott, A. O. "Documentaries (in Name Only) of Every Stripe." October 13, 2010. *New York Times*. http://www.nytimes.com/2010/10/17/movies/17scott.html?_r=0

Spivak, Gayatri Chakravorty. "Can the Subaltern Speak?" In *Can the Subaltern Speak? Reflections on the History of an Idea*, edited by R. Morris, 21–80. New York: Columbia University Press, 2010.

Spuclock, Morgan (Dir.). *Supersize Me*. 2000.

Tuck, Eve, and Wayne K. Yang. "R-Words Refusing Research." In *Humanizing Research: Decolonizing Qualitative Inquiry with Youth and Communities*, edited by D. Paris and M.T. Winn, 223–248. Thousand Oaks, CA: SAGE, 2014.

Waugh, Thomas, Ezra Winton, and Michael Brendan Baker, eds. *Challenge for Change: Activist Documentary at the National Film Board of Canada*. Montréal: McGill-Queen's University Press, 2010.

Waugh, Thomas. *Show Us Life: Toward a History and Aesthetics of the Committed Documentary.* Metuchen, NJ: Scarecrow Press, 1984.

Whiteman, David. "Documentary Film as Policy Analysis: The Impact of Yes, In My Backyard on Activists, Agendas, and Policy." *Mass Communication and Society* 12 (2009): 457–477.

Whiteman, David. "Out of the Theaters and into the Streets: A Coalition Model of the Political Impact of Documentary Film and Video." *Political Communication* 21 (2004): 51–69.

Zimmermann, Patricia R. *States of Emergency: Documentaries, Wars, Democracies.* Minneapolis: University of Minnesota Press, 2000.

Chapter 2

Abrash, Barbara, and Cara Mertes. "Introduction: A Festschrift in Honor of George Stoney." *Wide Angle* 21, no. 2 (1999): 3–7.

Aguayo, Angela J. "Paradise Lost and Found: Popular Documentary, Collective Identity and Participatory Media Culture." *Studies in Documentary Film* 7 (2013): 233–248.

Aitken, Ian. *The Documentary Film Movement: An Anthology.* Edinburgh: Edinburgh University Press, 1998.

Alexander, William. *Film on the Left: American Documentary Film from 1931 to 1942.* Princeton, NJ: Princeton University Press, 1981.

Anderson, Benedict. *Imagined Communities.* New York: Verso, 2006.

Arendt, Hannah. *The Human Condition: Second Edition.* Chicago: University of Chicago Press, 2013.

Barney, Darin David, Jonathan Sterne, Tamar Tembeck, Christine Ross, and Gabriella Coleman (eds.). *The Participatory Condition in the Digital Age.* Minneapolis: University of Minnesota Press, 2016.

Barnouw, Eric. *Documentary: A History of the Non-Fiction Film.* New York: Oxford University Press, 1993.

Barsam, Richard M. *Nonfiction Film: A Critical History.* Bloomington: Indiana University Press, 1992.

Berlinger, Joe, and Bruce Sinofsky (Dirs.). *Paradise Lost: The Child Murders at Robin Hood Hills.* 1996.

Berman, Jerry, and Deirdre K. Mulligan. "Digital Grass Roots: Issue Advocacy in the Age of the Internet." In *The Civic Web: Online Politics and Democratic Values*, edited by David M. Anderson and Michael Cornfield, 77–93. Lanham, MD: Rowman & Littlefield, 2003.

Bishop, Claire. *Artificial Hells: Participatory Art and the Politics of Spectatorship.* London: Verso Books, 2012.

Bowers, John W., Donovan J. Ochs, Richard J. Jensen, and David P. Schulz. *The Rhetoric of Agitation and Control: Third Edition.* Long Grove, IL: Waveland Press, 2009.

Boyle, Deirdre. *Subject to Change: Guerrilla Television Revisited.* New York: Oxford University Press, 1997.

Brownlow, Kevin. *Behind the Mask of Innocence.* Berkeley: University of California Press, 1990.

Burdowitz, Gregg (Dir.). *Fast Trip, Long Drop.* 1995.

Campbell, Russell. *Cinema Strikes Back: Radical Filmmaking in the United States, 1930–1942.* Ann Arbor, MI: UMI Research Press, 1982.

Chanan, Michael. *Politics of Documentary.* London: British Film Institute, 2008.

Campbell, Russell. "Leo Seltzer Interview 'A Total and Realistic Experience.'" *Jump Cut: A Review of Contemporary Media* 14 (1977): 25–27.

Cloud, Dana L. *Reality Bites: Rhetoric and the Circulation of Truth Claims in U.S. Political Culture.* Columbus: Ohio State University Press, 2018.

Couldry, Nick. *Why Voice Matters: Culture and Politics after Neoliberalism.* London: SAGE, 2010.

Couric, Katie, and Matt Lauer. "Michael Moore Discusses Fahrenheit 9/11." *Today Show, NBC.* 21 June 2004. Transcript.

Denning, Michael. *The Cultural Front.* New York: Verso, 2000.

Diani, Mario. "Social Movement Networks Virtual and Real." *Information Communication and Society* 3 (2003): 386–401.

Downing, J. D. H. *Radical Media: Rebellious Communication and Social Movements.* Thousand Oaks, CA: Sage, 2001.

Eberly, Rosa A. *Citizen Critics: Literary Public Spheres.* History of Communication. Urbana: University of Illinois Press, 2000.

Elgear, Sandra, Robyn Hutt, and David Meieran (Dirs.). *Voices from the Front.* 1992.

Ellis, Jack C. *The Documentary Idea: A Critical History of English-Language Documentary Film and Video.* Englewood Cliffs, NJ: Prentice Hall, 1989.

Felski, Rita. *Beyond Feminist Aesthetics: Feminist Literature and Social Change.* Cambridge, MA: Harvard University Press, 1989.

Fox, Josh (Dir.). *Gasland.* 2010.

Frank, Thomas. "Why Johnny Can't Dissent." In *Commodify Your Dissent,* edited by Thomas Frank and Matt Weiland, 31–45. New York: W. W. Norton, 1997.

Frank, Thomas, and Matt Weiland. *Commodify Your Dissent.* New York: W. W. Norton, 1997.

Freedman, Eric. "Activist Television." The Museum of Broadcast Communications. Accessed September 8, 2005. http://www.museum.tv/archives/etv/AhtmlA/activisttele/activisttele.htm.

Friedberg, Jill, and Rick Rowley (Dirs.). *This Is What Democracy Looks Like.* 2000.

Gramsci, Antonio. *Selections from the Prison Notebooks of Antonio Gramsci.* New York: International Publishers, 1971.

Grierson, John (Dir.). *Drifters.* 1929.

Habermas, Jurgen, and Jürgen Habermas. *The Structural Transformation of the Public Sphere: An Inquiry into a Category of Bourgeois Society.* Cambridge, MA: MIT Press, 1991.

Hall, Stuart. "On Postmodernism and Articulation: An Interview with Stuart Hall." *Journal of Communication Inquiry* 10, no. 2 (1986): 45–60.

Halleck, DeeDee. *Hand-Held Visions: The Impossible Possibilities of Community Media.* New York: Fordham University Press, 2002.

Hands, Joss. *@ Is for Activism: Dissent, Resistance and Rebellion in a Digital Culture.* New York: Pluto Books, 2011.

Hays, Kathleen, Stephanie Elam, Greg Clarkin, and Jen Rogers. "The Emergence of Documentary Film as Political Force." *The Flipside,* CNN Financial News. 25 June 2004. Transcript.

Holden, Stephen. "CRITIC'S NOTEBOOK; When and How AIDS Activism Finally Found Its Voice and Power." *New York Times,* December 1, 2000. https://nyti.ms/2Rk0CTP.

Hubbard, Jim. "Fever in the Archive: AIDS Activist Video." *ACT UP New York.* 7 September 2005. http://www.actupny.org/divatv/guggenheim.html.

IWA (Dir.). *Passaic Textile Strike.* 1926.

Jenkins, Henry, Mizuko Itō, and danah boyd. *Participatory Culture in a Networked Era: A Conversation on Youth, Learning, Commerce, and Politics.* Cambridge, UK; Malden, MA: Polity Press, 2015.

Jenkins, Henry, Sam Ford, and Joshua Green. *Spreadable Media: Creating Value and Meaning in a Networked Culture.* New York: New York University Press, 2013.

Jenkins, Henry. *Textual Poachers: Television Fans and Participatory Culture.* New York: Routledge, 2013.

Juhasz, Alexandra. *AIDS TV: Identity, Community, and Alternative Video.* Durham, N.C: Duke University Press, 1995.

Kahana, Jonathan. *Intelligence Work: The Politics of American Documentary.* New York: Columbia University Press, 2008.

Kellner, Douglas. *Media Culture: Cultural Studies, Identity and Politics Between the Modern and Postmodern.* New York: Routledge, 1995.

Kopple, Barbra (Dir.). *American Dream.* 1990.

Langlois, A., and F. Dubois. *Autonomous Media: Activating Resistance and Dissent.* Montreal: Cumulus Press, 2005.

Mann, Jonathan, Sibila Vargas, Tom Foreman, and Jeanne Moos. "Politics and Pop Culture." CNN International. 12 July 2004. Transcript.

McChesney, Robert W. *Corporate Media and the Threat to Democracy*. New York: Seven Stories Press, 1997.

"Media Bus." *Radical Software* 1, no. 3 (1971): 4.

Melucci, Alberto. "A Strange Kind of Newness: What's 'New' in New Social Movements." In *New Social Movements: From Ideology to Identity*, edited by Enrique Laraña, Hank Johnston, and Joseph R. Gusfield, 101–130. Philadelphia: Temple University Press, 1994.

Moore, Michael (Dir.). *Bowling for Columbine*. 2002.

Moore, Michael (Dir.). *Capitalism: A Love Story*. 2009.

Moore, Michael (Dir.). *Fahrenheit 9/11*. 2004.

Moore, Michael (Dir.). *Roger and Me*. 1989.

New York Newsreel (Dir.) Columbia Riots. 1968.

Nisbet, Matthew C., and Patricia Aufderheide. "Documentary Film: Towards a Research Agenda on Forms, Functions and Impacts." *Mass Communication and Society* 12 (2009): 450–456.

Palczewski, Catherine Helen. "Cyber-Movements, New Social Movements, and Counterpublics." In *Counterpublics and the State*, edited by Robert Asen and Daniel C. Brouwer, 161–186. Albany: State University of New York Press, 2001.

Paper Tiger Television. "About Paper Tiger." http://www.papertiger.org/index.php?name=about_copy.

Raindance Corporation and Michael Shamberg. *Guerrilla Television*. New York: Holt, Rinehart and Winston, 1971.

Robé, Chris. *Breaking the Spell: A History of Anarchist Filmmakers, Videotape Guerrillas, and Digital Ninjas*. Oakland, CA: PM Press, 2017.

Robé, Chris. *Left of Hollywood: Cinema, Modernism, and the Emergence of U.S. Radical Film Culture*. Austin: University of Texas Press, 2012.

Rodriguez, C. *Fissures in the Mediascape: An International Study of Citizen's Media*, Cresskill, NJ: Hampton Press, 2001.

Ross, Steven J. *Working-Class Hollywood: Silent Film and the Shaping of Class in America*. Princeton, NJ: Princeton University Press, 1999.

Ruby, Jay. "Speaking for, Speaking about, Speaking with, or Speaking alongside—An Anthropological and Documentary Dilemma." *Visual Anthropology Review* 7 (1991): 50–67.

Salon.com 1 December 1999. *Salon News*. Edited by Fiona Morgan www.salon.com/news/feature/1999/12/01/weblog/index.html.

Shamberg, Michael, and Megan Williams. "Top Value Television Coverage of 1972 Political Conventions." *Radical Software* 2 (1972): 11–14.

Sinofsky, Bruce, and Joe Berlinger (Dir.). *Paradise Lost, Vol. 2: Revelations*. 2000.

Spurlock, Morgan (Dir.). *Supersize Me*. 2000.

Stoney, George, interview. 2009.

Teasdale, Parry D. "Lanesville TV (aka Video Freex)." *Video History Project Website* 7 September 2005. http://www.experimentaltvcenter.org/history/groups/gtext.php3?id=43.

The Globe and Mail. 7 September 2001. The Globe. Ed. Roma Luciw.

TVTV (prod.). *Four More Years*. 1992.

Warner, Michael. *Publics and Counterpublics*. New York: Zone Books, 2002.

Winston, Brian. "'A Handshake or a Kiss': The Legacy of George Stoney (1916–2012)." *Film Quarterly* 67, no. 3 (March 2014): 35–49.

Wired News. August 5, 2000. *Wired.com*. Ed. Declan McCullagh. www.wired.com/news/politics/o.1283,38038,00.html.

Waugh, Thomas. *"Show Us Life": Toward a History and Aesthetics of the Committed Documentary*. Metuchen, NJ: Scarecrow Press, 1984.

Wolfson, Todd. *Digital Rebellion: The Birth of the Cyber Left*. Champaign: University of Illinois Press, 2004.

Zimmermann, Patricia R. *States of Emergency: Documentaries, Wars, Democracies*. Minneapolis: University of Minnesota Press, 2000.

Chapter 3

Adams, Sam. "'Making a Murderer' and True Crime in the Binge-Viewing Era." *Rolling Stone*, January 13, 2016. https://www.rollingstone.com/tv/news/making-a-murderer-and-true-crime-in-the-binge-viewing-era-20160113.

Aguayo, Angela J. "Paradise Lost and Found: Popular Documentary, Collective Identification and Participatory Media Culture." *Studies in Documentary Film* 7, no. 3 (2013): 233–248.

Allen, Nick. "Interview: Kirby Dick on 'The Hunting Ground.'" *The Interviews, Roger Ebert*, March 23, 2015. https://www.rogerebert.com/interviews/interview-kirby-dick-on-the-hunting-ground.

Bonanno, Mike, interview, 2010.

Benson, Thomas W., and Brian J. Snee (eds.). *The Rhetoric of the New Political Documentary*. Carbondale: Southern Illinois University Press, 2008.

Box Office Mojo. *Bowling for Columbine*. http://www.boxofficemojo.com/movies/?id=bowling-forcolumbine.htm.

Box Office Mojo. *Fahrenheit 9/11*. http://www.boxofficemojo.com/movies/?id=fahrenheit911.htm

Box Office Mojo. *Hoop Dreams*. http://www.boxofficemojo.com/movies/?id=hoopdreams.htm.

Box Office Mojo. *The Invisible War*. http://www.boxofficemojo.com/movies/?id=invisiblewar.htm

Box Office Mojo. *Roger and Me*. http://www.boxofficemojo.com/movies/?id=rogerandme.htm.

Box Office Mojo. *Where to Invade Next*. https://www.boxofficemojo.com/movies/?id=whereto-invadenext.htm

Christensen, Christian. "Political Documentary, Online Organization and Activist Synergies." *Studies in Documentary Film* 3, no. 2 (January 1, 2009): 77–94. https://doi.org/10.1386/sdf.3.2.77/1.

Cole, Maria Cuomo, and Jimmie Briggs. "The Hunting Ground Is Shifting the Culture on Campuses." *Huffington Post* (blog), January 19, 2016. https://www.huffingtonpost.com/maria-cuomo-cole/the-hunting-ground-shifting-culture_b_9008356.html.

Corliss, Richard, Desa Philadephia, Jeffrey Ressner, Jackson Baker, Betsy Rubiner, John F. Dickerson, and Adam Zagorin. "The World According to Michael." *Time Magazine*, July 12, 2004.

Couric, Katie. "Michael Moore Discusses Fahrenheit 9/11." *NBC News*, June 21, 2004.

Couric, Katie, and Matt Lauer. "Michael Moore's Documentary 'Fahrenheit 9/11' Gets Mixed Reviews and Lots of Attention at the Cannes Film Festival." *Today Show NBC News*, May 18, 2004.

Cowperthwaite, Gabriela (Dir.). *Black Fish*. 2013.

Daniel, Lisa. "Panetta, Dempsey Announce Initiatives to Stop Sexual Assault." U.S. Department of Defense, April 16, 2012. http://archive.defense.gov/news/newsarticle.aspx?id=67954.

Denning, Michael. *The Cultural Front: The Laboring of American Culture in the Twentieth Century*. Brooklyn, NY: Verso, 1998.

Dick, Kirby, interview. 2010.

Dodd, Johnny, "Beyond a Reasonable Doubt? Could Three Men, in Prison for a Ghastly Crime, Have Been Wrongly Convicted?" *People Magazine* (January 21, 2008): 69.

Dutka, Elaine. "'Celsius 41.11' Lacks '9/11' Heat." *Los Angeles Times*, October 27, 2004. http://articles.latimes.com/2004/oct/27/entertainment/et-celsius27.

Edbauer, Jenny. "Unframing Models of Public Distribution: From Rhetorical Situation to Rhetorical Ecologies." *Rhetoric Society Quarterly* 35, no. 4 (September 1, 2005): 5–24. https://doi.org/10.1080/02773940509391320.

Ellison, Jesse. "Panetta, Gates, Rumsfeld Face New Suit over U.S. Military Rape 'Epidemic.'" *Daily Beast*, March 6, 2012. https://www.thedailybeast.com/articles/2012/03/06/panetta-gates-rumsfeld-face-new-suit-over-u-s-military-rape-epidemic.

Felperin, Leslie. "'The Hunting Ground': Sundance Review | Hollywood Reporter." January 23, 2015. https://www.hollywoodreporter.com/review/hunting-ground-sundance-review-766461.

Gilgoff, Dan, and Michael Tobin. "Moore or Less." *US News & World Report*, July 12, 2004.

Gillibrand, Kirsten. "Off the Sidelines: Raise Your Voice, Change the World." *The Princeton Review*, 2014.

Gramsci, Antonio. "'Hegemony, Intellectuals, and the State.'" In *Cultural Theory and Popular Culture: A Reader*, edited by John Storey, 4th ed, 75–80. Harlow, UK: Pearson Education, 2009.

Gries, Laurie. *Still Life with Rhetoric: A New Materialist Approach for Visual Rhetorics*. 1st ed. Logan: Utah State University Press, 2015.

Hall, Stuart. "The Rediscovery of Ideology: The Return of the Repressed in Media Studies." In *Cultural Theory and Popular Culture: A Reader*, edited by John Storey, 4th ed, 111–141. Harlow, UK: Pearson Education, 2009.

Helmore, Edward. "Making a Murderer Spurs 275,000 Viewers to Demand Pardon for Central Character." *Guardian*, January 9, 2016. http://www.theguardian.com/world/2016/jan/09/netxflix-murder-whoddunit-petition.

Kaufman, Anthony. "Reality Checks: How 'The Hunting Ground' Can Change the Conversation about Campus Rape." *IndieWire*, March 6, 2015. http://www.indiewire.com/2015/03/reality-checks-how-the-hunting-ground-can-change-the-conversation-about-campus-rape-64407.

King, Larry. "The Case of the West Memphis Three." *The Larry King Live New York Cable News Network (CNN)*, September 1, 2010.

King, Larry. "Damien Echols: Death Row Interview." *Larry King Live*. CNN, December 19, 2007.

Lauer, Matt. "Moore to the Point, Michael Moore's Controversial New Film Fahrenheit 9/11." *Dateline NBC*. June 18, 2004.

Lynch, Jason. "Over 19 Million Viewers in the U.S. Watched Making a Murderer in Its First 35 Days." February 11, 2016. http://www.adweek.com/tv-video/over-8-million-viewers-us-watched-making-murderer-its-first-35-days-169602.

Mann, Jonathan, Sibila Vargas, Tom Foreman, and Jeanne Moos. "Politics and Pop Culture." CNN International Insight, July 12, 2004.

McNary, Dave. "'Hunting Ground' Filmmakers Working on Hollywood Sexual Assault Documentary." *Variety* (blog), October 23, 2017. http://variety.com/2017/film/news/hollywood-sexual-assault-documentary-1202597015.

Montagne, Renee. "Michael Moore's Controversial Documentary 'Fahrenheit 9/11.'" *Morning Edition*. National Public Radio, June 25, 2004.

Moore, Michael (Dir.). *Fahrenheit 9/11*. 2004.

Nichols, Bill. *Speaking Truths with Film: Evidence, Ethics, Politics in Documentary*. Oakland: University of California Press, 2016.

Norville, Deborah. "Michael Moore's Controversial New Film 'Fahrenheit 9/11' Is Drawing Crowds Overseas, as Well as in the U.S. Some Worry about Its Effect on the U.S. Elections in November." *Deborah Norville Tonight*, July 12, 2004.

Panetta, Leon. *Worthy Fights: A Memoir of Leadership in War and Peace*. New York: Penguin. 453.

Parry-Giles, J. Shawn, and Trevor Parry-Giles. "Virtual Realism and the Limits of Commodified Dissent in Fahrenheit 9/11." In *The Rhetoric of the New Political Documentary*, edited by Thomas W. Benson and Brian J. Snee. Carbondale: Southern Illinois University Press, 2008.

Pennebaker, DA, interview. 2009.

Perks, Lisa Glebatis. *Media Marathoning: Immersions in Morality*. Lanham, MD: Lexington Books, 2014.

Plantinga, Carl. *Rhetoric and Representation in Nonfiction Film*. Grand Rapids, MI: Schuler Books, 2015.

Poland, David. The Hunting Ground, Kirby Dick & Amy Ziering. Interview with David Poland on DP/30: The Oral History of Hollywood, February 26, 2015. https://www.youtube.com/watch?v=B6cmgwad2J4.

Porton, Richard. "Weapon of Mass Instruction." *Cineaste* (Fall 2004): 3–7.

Psihoyos, Louie (Dir.). *The Cove*. 2009.

Risen, James. "Air Force Leaders Testify on Culture That Led to Sexual Assaults of Recruits." *New York Times*, January 23, 2013. https://www.nytimes.com/2013/01/24/us/air-force-leaders-testify-on-culture-that-led-to-sexual-assaults-of-recruits.html.

Rohter, Larry. "A Documentarian Focused on Trauma in Its Many Forms." *The Carpetbagger* (blog), *New York Times*. https://carpetbagger.blogs.nytimes.com/2013/01/23/a-documentarian-focused-on-trauma-in-its-many-forms.

Rosenberg, Alyssa. "'The Invisible War': How Oscar's Military Rape Documentary Might Change Everything." *Daily Beast*, February 7, 2013. https://www.thedailybeast.com/articles/2013/02/07/the-invisible-war-how-oscar-s-military-rape-documentary-might-change-everything.

Shenon, Philip. "Michael Moore Is Ready for His Close-Up." *New York Times*, June 20, 2004. https://www.nytimes.com/2004/06/20/movies/michael-moore-is-ready-for-his-close-up.html.

Siegel, Robert, Michele Norris, and Kim Masters. "Surprising Box Office Success of Michael Moore's new film, 'Fahrenheit 9/11.'" National Public Radio, June 28, 2004.

Smiley, Tavis. "Michael Moore's *Fahrenheit 9/11*." National Public Radio. July 1, 2004.

Storey, John. *Cultural Theory and Popular Culture: An Introduction*, 7th ed. London: Routledge, 2015.

Syckle, Katie Van. "'The Hunting Ground' Subjects Talk New Book, Oscar Loss and the Netflix Factor." *Variety* (blog), April 11, 2016. http://variety.com/2016/film/news/the-hunting-ground-andrea-pino-book-we-believe-you-1201750547.

"Talking to Documentarian Kirby Dick about 'The Invisible War.'" *Notebook Interview*, November 1, 2016. https://mubi.com/notebook/posts/talking-to-documentarian-kirby-dick-about-the-invisible-war.

Triece, Mary Eleanor. *Protest and Popular Culture: Women in the U.S. Labor Movement, 1894–1917*. Boulder, CO: Westview Press, 2001.

Valenti, Lauren. "Lady Gaga's New Song Has Leaked, Proves Her Music Is Changing." *Marie Claire*, February 27, 2015. https://www.marieclaire.com/culture/news/a13522/lady-gaga-til-it-happens-to-you.

"Washington Post-ABC News Poll." *Washington Post*. Accessed January 20, 2018. https://www.washingtonpost.com/wp-srv/politics/polls/postpoll_021010.html.

Wilshire, Peter. "Michael Moore's *Fahrenheit 9/11* and the US Election: A Case of Missed Opportunity?" *Screen Education* 39 (Summer 2005): 129–134.

York, Byron. "The Passion of Michael Moore: Fun and Games with Fahrenheit 9/11." *National Review Online*, July 24, 2004.

Zimmermann, Patricia Rodden. *States of Emergency: Documentaries, Wars, Democracies*. Minneapolis: University of Minnesota Press, 2000.

Chapter 4

Abrash, Barbara, interview. 2009.

Anderson, Madeline (Dir.). *I Am Somebody*. New York: Carnegie Corporation, 1970. New York.

Aroy, Manongs, and Niall McKay (Dirs.). *Delano Manongs*. 2014.

Bennett, Professor W. Lance, and Dr. Alexandra Segerberg. *The Logic of Connective Action: Digital Media and the Personalization of Contentious Politics*. Cambridge, UK: Cambridge University Press, 2013.

Blumenthal, Jerry, and Gordon Quinn (Dirs.). *Taylor Chain I*. 1980.

Blumenthal, Jerry, and Gordon Quinn (Dirs.). *U.E. Wells*. 1975.

Bowser, Pearl. "Pioneers of Black Documentary Film." In *Struggles for Representation: African American Documentary Film and Video*, edited by Phyllis Rauch Klotman, 483. Bloomington: Indiana University Press, 1999.

Burke, Kenneth. *A Rhetoric of Motives*. Berkeley: University of California Press, 1969.

Campbell, Russell. *Cinema Strikes Back: Radical Filmmaking in the United States, 1930–1942*. UMI Research Press, 1982.

Campbell, Russell. "Radical Documentary in the United States: 1930–1942." In *Show Us Life: Toward a History and Aesthetics of the Committed Documentary*, edited by Thomas Waugh, 69–88. Metuchen, NJ: Scarecrow Press, n.d.

Carracedo, Almudena (Dir.). *Made in L.A.* 2007.

Chávez, Karma R. *Queer Migration Politics: Activist Rhetoric and Coalitional Possibilities*. Champaign, IL: University of Illinois Press, 2013.

Cloud, Dana L. *Reality Bites: Rhetoric and the Circulation of Truth Claims in U.S. Political Culture*, 2018.

Cloud, Dana L. "Standpoint, Mediation and the Working-Class Public Sphere." *Javnost—The Public* (January 3, 2018): 1–8.

Combs, Barbara Harris. *From Selma to Montgomery: The Long March to Freedom*. New York: Routledge, 2013.

Couldry, Nick. *Why Voice Matters: Culture and Politics after Neoliberalism*. Thousand Oaks, CA: SAGE, 2010.

Courtney, Heather (Dir.). *Los Trabajadores*. 2003.

Duncan, Larry, interview. November 10, 2010.

Fischler, Steven, and Joel Sucher (Dir.). *Anarchism in America*. 1983.

Friend, Andrew (Dir.). *Workers Republic*. 2010.

Funari, Vicky, and Sergio De La Torre (Dirs.). *Maquilapolis*. 2006.

Gerbaudo, Paolo, and Emiliano Treré. "In Search of the 'We' of Social Media Activism: Introduction to the Special Issue on Social Media and Protest Identities." *Information, Communication & Society* 18, no. 8 (August 3, 2015): 865–871. https://doi.org/10.1080/1369118X.2015.1043319.

Godfried, Nathan. "Labor-Sponsored Film and Working-Class History: The Inheritance (1964)." *Film History* 26, no. 4 (December 2014): 84–119. https://doi.org/10.2979/filmhistory.26.4.84.

Gold, Tami, interview. Summer 2007.

Gold, Tami, Dan Gordon, and Erik Lewis (Dirs.). *Signed, Sealed and Delivered: Labor Struggle in the Post Office*. 1980.

Grahm, Allison, David Appleby, and Steven Ross (Dirs.). *At the River I Stand*. 1993.

Gray, Lorraine (Dir.). *With Babies and Banners*. 1979.

Hanig, Josh, and David Davis (Dirs.). *Song of the Canary*. 1979.

Henderson, Ray, and Tony Buba (Dirs.). *Struggle in Steel*. 1996.

Hoffman, Judy, interview. November 14, 2009.

Hoffman, Judy (Dir.). *HSA Strike-75*. 1975.

Hoffman, Judy (Dir.). *What's Happening at Local 70*. 1975.

Hollibaugh, Amber, and Nikhil Pal Singh. "Sexuality, Labor, and the New Trade Unionism: A Conversation." In *Out at Work: Building a Gay-Labor Alliance*, edited by Kitty Krupat and Patrick McCreery, 60–77. Minneapolis: University of Minnesota Press, 2001.

James, Dante (Dir.). *Philip Randolph: For Jobs and Freedom*. 1996.

Juhasz, Alexandra (ed.). *Women of Vision: Histories in Feminist Film and Video*. Visible Evidence, vol. 9. Minneapolis: University of Minnesota Press, 2001.

Klein, Jim, and Julia Reichert (Dir.). *Seeing Red*. 1983.

Kleinhans, Chuck. "Barbara Kopple Interview: Making Harlan County, USA." *Jump Cut: Review of Contemporary Media*, no. 14 (1977): 4–6.

Klotman, Phyllis Rauch, and Janet K. Cutler. *Struggles for Representation: African American Documentary Film and Video*. Bloomington: Indiana University Press, 1999.

Kopple, Barbara (Dir.). *American Dream*. 1990.

Kopple, Barbara (Dir.). *Harlan County, USA*. 1976.

Rachel Lears and Robin Blotnick (Dirs.). *The Hand That Feeds*. 2015.

Leshne, Carla. "The Film & Photo League of San Francisco." *Film History* 18, no. 4 (December 2006): 361–373.

Lewis, Anne (Dir.). *Fast Food Women*. 1991.

Lewis, Anne (Dir.). *Morristown*. 2007.

Lewis, Anne, interview. 2007.

Lichtenstein, Brad (Dir.). *As Goes Jainsville*. 2012.

MacLory, Randall (Dir.). *Mine Wars*. 2016.

Mayer, Harold (Dir.). *The Inheritance*. 1964. Amalgamated Clothing Workers of America. Harold Mayer Production Company.

Mayfield, Sam (Dir.). *Wisconsin Rising*. 2014.

Negt, Oskar, and Alexander Kluge. *Public Sphere and Experience: Toward an Analysis of the Bourgeois and Proletarian Public Sphere*. Theory and History of Literature, v. 85. Minneapolis: University of Minnesota Press, 1993.

Occupational Safety and Health Administration, commissioned. *Worker to Worker*. 1980.

Pearcy, Glen (Dir.). *Fighting for Our Lives*. 1975.

Perez, Ray, and Lorena Parlee (Dirs.). *Caesar's Last Fast*. 2014.

Perry, Hart (Dir.). *Valley of Tears*. 2003.

Polletta, Francesca. "Contending Stories: Narrative in Social Movements." *Qualitative Sociology* 21, no. 4 (December 1998): 419–446.

Polletta, Francesca. "Participatory Democracy's Moment." *Journal of International Affairs* 68, no. 1 (Fall/Winter 2014): 79–92.

Polletta, Francesca, and James M. Jasper. "Collective Identity and Social Movement." *Annual Review of Sociology* 27 (2001).

Pomer, Judith (Dir.). *Pregnant but Equal*. 1982.

Prado, Anayansi (Dir.). *Maid in America*. 2005.

Public Broadcasting Service. *Joe Hill*. 2015.

Quinn, Gordon, interview, 2009.

Quinn, Gordon (Dir.). *Where's I.W. Abel?* 1975.

Quinn, Gordon, and Jerry Blumenthal (Dir.). *The Last Pullman Car*. 1983.

Reichert, Julia, and James Klein (Dirs.). *Union Maids*. 1979.

Reuther, Sasha (Dir.). *Brothers on the Line*. 2012. Porter Street Pictures.

Richards, Harvey (Dir.). *Perch of the Devil*. 1960. Kanopy.

Richards, Harvey (Dir.). *The Harvesters*. 1960. Kanopy.

Richards, Harvey (Dir.). *This Land is Rich*. 1966. Kanopy.

Richards, Paul. *Critical Focus: The Black and White Photographs of Harvey Wilson Richards*. Oakland, CA: Estuary Press, 1987.

Robé, Chris. *Breaking the Spell: A History of Anarchist Filmmakers, Videotape Guerrillas, and Digital Ninjas*. Oakland, CA: PM Press, 2017.

Shaffer, Deborah (Dir.). *The Wobblies*. 1979.

Silverman, Kaja. *The Threshold of the Visible World*. New York: Routledge, 1995.

Smith, William. *Heroic Negro Soldiers of World War*. 1919. Frederick Douglass Film Company.

Stoney, George, Judith Helfand, and Susanne Rostock (Dirs.). *The Uprising of '34*. 1995.

Street, Richard Steven. *Photographing Farmworkers in California*. Stanford, CA: Stanford University Press, 2004.

Street, Richard Steven. "Poverty in the Valley of Plenty: The National Farm Labor Union, DiGiorgio Farms, and Suppression of Documentary Photography in California, 1947–66." *Labor History* 48, no. 1 (February 1, 2007): 25–48. https://doi.org/10.1080/00236560601054116.

Telles, Ray, and Rick Tejada-Flores (Dirs.). *Fight in the Fields*. 1997.

Wagner, Paul (Dir.). *Miles of Smiles*. 1982.

Washington, Booker T. (commissioned). *A Day at Tuskegee*. 1909.

Waugh, Thomas. *"Show Us Life": Toward a History and Aesthetics of the Committed Documentary*. Metuchen, NJ: Scarecrow Press, 1984.

Williams, Amie (Dirs.). *We Are Wisconsin*. 2011.

Wilkerson, Travis (Dirs.). *Injury to One*. 2002.

Zelzer, Steve, interview, 2010.

Chapter 5

Abrash, Barbara, interview. 2009.

Ahmed, Sara. *The Cultural Politics of Emotion*, 2nd ed. New York: Routledge, 2014.

Aldrich, Gillian, and Jennifer Baumgardner (Dirs.). *I Had An Abortion*. 2005; New York: Women Make Movies, 2005. DVD.

Bell, Daniel. *The Cultural Contradictions of Capitalism.* New York: Basic Books, 1976.

Bilge, Sirma. "Recent Feminist Outlooks on Intersectionality." *Diogenes* 57, no. 1 (February 2010): 58–72.

Bowers, Mary. "Women: Getting It off Your Chest: Feminist Activist Jennifer Baumgardner Caused a Huge Stir with Her 'I Had an Abortion' T-Shirt, and Now She's Back with a Design That Reads 'I Was Raped'. She Tells Mary Bowers about Her Compulsion to Confront Taboo Subjects." *The Guardian* (London), April 23, 2008.

Cloud, Dana L., and Kathleen Eaton Feyh. "Reason in Revolt: Emotional Fidelity and Working Class Standpoint in the 'Internationale'." *Rhetoric Society Quarterly* 45, no. 4 (August 8, 2015): 300–323.

Condit, Celeste Michelle. *Decoding Abortion Rhetoric: Communicating Social Change.* Urbana: University of Illinois Press, 1990.

Cvetkovich, Ann. *An Archive of Feelings: Trauma, Sexuality, and Lesbian Public Cultures.* Durham, NC: Duke University Press, 2003.

Delgross, Savannah. "Abortion Diaries Exhibit Provides Space for Women to Share Stories." *The Denisonian.* Granville, OH: Denison University, March 29, 2016.

Dmedit. "Our Views Now There's a Bad Idea 'I Had an Abortion' T-Shirts Won't Do Women Any Credit." *Charleston Daily Mail (WV),* August 9, 2004.

Eagle, Amy. "'I Had an Abortion' T-Shirts Stir up Controversy: [Chicago Final Edition]." *Chicago Tribune; Chicago, Ill.* August 4, 2004, sec. Woman News.

Fleming, Olivia. "'I Had an Abortion' T-Shirt Sparks Backlash at College, Students Wear 'I Haven't Killed a Baby' in Protest." *Daily Mail,* April 19, 2012.

Frank, Aimee J., and Abigail Norman. "Reproductive Rights Films as Organizing Tools." *Jump Cut: Review of Contemporary Media,* no. 31 (1986): 36–38.

Gaines, Jane. "Political Mimesis." In *Collecting Visible Evidence,* edited by Michael Renov and Jane Gaines, 84–102. Minneapolis: University of Minnesota Press, 1999.

Garfield, Ken. "'I Had an Abortion' Shirts Cause Rift Within Planned Parenthood; Carolinas Affiliates Say Message Goes Beyond `pro-Choice' Values." *Charlotte Observer, The (NC),* July 28, 2004.

Gillooly, Jane. *Leona's Sister Gerri.* Docurama, 2007.

Gould, Deborah B. *Moving Politics: Emotion and ACT UP's Fight Against AIDS.* Chicago: University of Chicago Press, 2009.

Gordon, Avery F. *Ghostly Matters: Haunting and the Sociological Imagination.* Minneapolis: University of Minnesota Press, 1997.

Juhasz, Alex. "They Said We Were Trying to Show Reality—All I Want to Show Is My Video: The Politics of the Realist Documentary." In *Collecting Visible Evidence,* edited by Michael Renov and Jane Gaines, 190–215. Minneapolis: University of Minnesota Press, 1999.

Kaplan, E. Ann. "Women's Happytime Commune: New Departures in Women's Films." *Jump Cut: A Review of Contemporary Media* 9 (1975): 9–11.

Lane, Penny, interview. 2009.

Lane, Penny (Dir.). *The Abortion Diaries.* 2005. New York. [Online videorecording] Accessed August 29, 2017. http://pennylaneismyrealname.com/film/the-abortion-diaries-2005.

Lesage, Julia. "The Political Aesthetics of the Feminist Documentary Film." *Quarterly Review of Film and Video* 3, no. 4 (January 1, 1978): 507–523.

McCann, Bryan J. "'Chrysler Pulled the Trigger': The Affective Politics of Insanity and Black Rage at the Trial of James Johnson, Jr." *Rhetoric Society Quarterly* 46, no. 2 (March 14, 2016): 131–155.

McGee, Michael Calvin. "The 'Ideograph': A Link Between Rhetoric and Ideology." *Quarterly Journal of Speech* 66, no. 1 (February 1980): 1.

Nelligan, Marci. "Beyond Dinner and a Movie: The Abortion Diaries." *Off Our Backs,* no. 11/12 (2005): 31.

Rand, Erin. *Reclaiming Queer: Activist and Academic Rhetorics of Resistance.* Tuscaloosa: University of Alabama Press, 2014.

Renov, Michael. *Subject of Documentary.* Minneapolis: University of Minnesota Press, 2004.

Rich, B. Ruby. *Chick Flicks: Theories and Memories of the Feminist Film Movement*. Durham: Duke University Press, 1998.

Rottenberg, Catherine. "The Rise of Neoliberal Feminism." *Cultural Studies* 28, no. 3 (May 2014): 418–437.

Sisson, Gretchen, and Katrina Kimport. "After *After Tiller*: The Impact of a Documentary Film on Understandings of Third-Trimester Abortion." *Culture, Health and Sexuality* 18, no. 6 (June 2, 2016): 695–709.

Sisson, Gretchen, and Katrina Kimport. "Telling Stories about Abortion: Abortion-Related Plots in American Film and Television, 1916–2013." *Contraception* 89, no. 5 (May 2014): 413–418. http://dx.doi.org/10.1016/j.contraception.2013.12.015.

Smail, Belinda. *The Documentary: Politics, Emotion, Culture*. London: Palgrave Macmillan, 2010.

Stasiulis, D. "Feminist Intersectional Theorizing." In *Race and Ethnic Relations in Canada*, edited by P. Li, 347–397. Toronto: Oxford University Press, 1999.

Swift, Crystal Lane. "'I Had an Abortion.': The Rhetorical Situation of a Planned Parenthood T-Shirt." *Qualitative Research Reports in Communication* 8, no. 1 (October 2007): 57–63.

Thomas, Alice. "Promotion of 'I Had an Abortion' T-Shirts Not Wearing Well." *Columbus Dispatch, The (OH)*, July 29, 2004.

Trigg, Stephanie. "Introduction: Emotional Histories—Beyond the Personalization of the Past and the Abstraction of Affect Theory." *Exemplaria* 26, no. 1 (January 2014): 3–15.

Warren, Shilyh. "Abortion, Abortion, Abortion, Still: Documentary Show and Tell." *South Atlantic Quarterly* 114, no. 4 (October 2015): 755–779.

Warren, Shilyh. "Consciousness-raising and Difference in The Woman's Film (1971) and Self-Health (1974)." *Jump Cut*, no. 54 (Fall 2012), accessed August 27, 2017. https://womenandfilmproject.wordpress.com/2013/04/08/consciousness-raising-and-difference-in-the-womans-film-1971-and-self-health-1974-by-shilyh-warren.

Williams, Scott. "'I Had an Abortion' T-Shirt Stirs Debate; Some Offended, Others Empowered by Declaration." *Milwaukee Journal Sentinel (WI)*, August 3, 2004.

Wise, Kris. "Planned Parenthood Selling 'I Had an Abortion' T-Shirts Apparel Will Improve Dialogue, Group Says; Opponents Say the Item Makes Light of Issue." *Charleston Daily Mail (WV)*, August 5, 2004.

Zimmerman, Debra, interview. 2010.

Chapter 6

Alexander, Elizabeth. "'Can You Be BLACK and Look at This?': Reading the Rodney King Video (S)." *Public Culture* 7, no. 1 (1994): 77–94.

Atton, Chris. *An Alternative Internet: Radical Media, Politics and Creativity*. Edinburgh: Edinburgh University Press, 2004.

Asher, Jeff. "NOPD in the Age of Mad Men." *NOLA Crime News* (blog), January 10, 2017. https://nolacrimenews.com/2017/01/10/nopd-in-the-age-of-mad-men.

Borodowitz, Greg. *Fast Trip, Long Drop*, 1995.

Calafell, Bernadette Marie, and Fernando P. Delgado. "Reading Latina/o Images: Interrogating *Americanos*." *Critical Studies in Media Communication* 21, no. 1 (March 2004): 1–24. https://doi.org/10.1080/0739318042000184370.

DeLong, Matt, and Dave Braunger. "Breaking down the Dashcam: The Philando Castile Shooting Timeline—StarTribune.Com." *StarTribune*. Accessed March 1, 2018. http://www.startribune.com/castile-shooting-timeline/429678313.

Drew, Jesse. *A Social History of Contemporary Democratic Media*. New York: Routledge, 2013.

Durkin, Jeff. *#EricGarner #ICantBreathe #NYC Protests Part 1*. Accessed March 1, 2018. http://www.ustream.tv/recorded/56123992.

DuVernay, Ava. *13th*. Documentary, Crime, History, 2016. http://www.imdb.com/title/tt5895028/.

Giannachi, Gabriella. *Archive Everything: Mapping the Everyday*. Cambridge, MA: MIT Press, 2016.

Halleck, DeeDee. *Hand-Held Visions: The Impossible Possibilities of Community Media*. New York: Fordham Universoty Press, 2002.

Hallin, Daniel. *We Keep America on Top of the World: Television Journalism and the Public Sphere*. New York: Routledge, 2005.

Hoerl, Kristen. "Remembering Radical Black Dissent." In *Race and Hegemonic Struggle in the United States: Pop Culture, Politics, and Protest*, edited by Michael G. Lacey and Mary Eleanor Triece, 69–87. Madison: Fairleigh Dickinson University Press, 2014.

Holden, Stephen. "CRITIC'S NOTEBOOK; When and How AIDS Activism Finally Found Its Voice and Power." *New York Times*, December 1, 2000. https://nyti.ms/2Rk0CTP.

Horsfield, Kate. "Busting the Tube: A Brief History of Video Art." In *Feedback: The Video Data Bank Catalog of Video Art and Artist Interviews*, edited by Kate Horsfield and Lucas Hilderbrand, 7–16. Philadelphia: Temple University Press, 2006.

Howard, Robert Glenn. "The Vernacular Web of Participatory Media." *Critical Studies in Media Communication* 25, no. 5 (December 2008): 490–513.

Hubbard, Jim. "Fever in the Archive: AIDS Activist Video." *ACT UP New York*. 7 September 2005. http://www.actupny.org/divatv/guggenheim.html.

Jacobo, Julia, and Enjoli Francis. "Cops May Have Thought Philando Castile Was a Robbery Suspect." ABC News, July 12, 2016. http://abcnews.go.com/US/cops-thought-philando-castile-robbery-suspect-dispatch-audio/story?id=40439957.

Lenzner, Ben. "The Emergence of Occupy Wall Street and Digital Video Practices: Tim Pool, Live Streaming and Experimentations in Citizen Journalism." *Studies in Documentary Film* 8, no. 3 (September 2, 2014): 251–266. https://doi.org/10.1080/17503280.2014.961634.

Lingel, Jessa. *Digital Countercultures and the Struggle for Community: Digital Technologies and the Struggle for Community*. Cambridge, MA: MIT Press, 2017.

Masri, Bassem. *BassemMasri*. Accessed March 1, 2018. http://www.ustream.tv/recorded/53775071. http://www.ustream.tv/recorded/53812456.

McBride, Jessica. "WATCH: Falcon Heights, Minnesota Police Shooting Facebook Live Video [WARNING: GRAPHIC]." *Heavy.Com* (blog), July 7, 2016. https://heavy.com/news/2016/07/falcon-heights-minnesota-police-shooting-lavish-reynolds-facebook-live-video-watch-uncensored-shooting-youtube-shot-by-police.

McChesney, Robert W. *Rich Media, Poor Democracy: Communication Politics in Dubious Times*. New York: New Press, 2015.

Nichols, Bill. *Representing Reality: Issues and Concepts in Documentary*. Bloomington: Indiana University Press, 1991.

Peterson, Andrea. "Why the Philando Castile Police-Shooting Video Disappeared from Facebook—Then Came Back." *Washington Post*, July 7, 2016, sec. The Switch. https://www.washingtonpost.com/news/the-switch/wp/2016/07/07/why-facebook-took-down-the-philando-castile-shooting-video-then-put-it-back-up.

Ranucci, Karen, interview. 2009.

Rayford, Bradley J. "#Ferguson #fergusonshooting #MichaelBrown #mikebrown." Instagram, August 14, 2014. https://www.instagram.com/p/rsILXus8ei.

Rayford, Bradley J. "The Lost Voices Have Been Marching and Protesting Almost since Day One. This Is Definitely a Group That Is Committed to Their Cause. . . " Instagram, September 18, 2014. https://www.instagram.com/p/tG31LnM8Yv.

Robé, Chris. *Breaking the Spell: A History of Anarchist Filmmakers, Videotape Guerrillas, and Digital Ninjas*. Oakland, CA: PM Press, 2017.

Rodríguez, Clemencia. *Citizens' Media Against Armed Conflict: Disrupting Violence in Colombia*. Minneapolis: University of Minnesota Press, 2011.

Chapter 7

Caldwell, John Thornton. *Production Culture: Industrial Reflexivity and Critical Practice in Film and Television.* Durham, NC: Duke University Press, 2008.

Couldry, Nick. *Media, Society, World: Social Theory and Digital Media Practice.* Hoboken, NJ: John Wiley & Sons, 2013.

Cunningham, Stuart. *Framing Culture: Criticism and Policy in Australia.* Crows Nest, Australia: Allen & Unwin, 1992.

Denning, Michael. *The Cultural Front: The Laboring of American Culture in the Twentieth Century.* New York: Verso, 1998.

Downing, John D. H. "Activist Media, Civil Society and Social Movements." In *Global Activism, Global Media,* edited by Wilma de Jong, Martin Shaw, and Neil Stammers 149–164. London: Pluto Press, 2005.

Fraser, Nancy. *Justice Interruptus.* New York: Routledge, 1997.

Giannachi, Gabriella. *Archive Everything: Mapping the Everyday.* Cambridge, MA: MIT Press, 2016.

Greene, Ronald Walter. "Rhetoric and Capitalism: Rhetorical Agency as Communicative Labor." *Philosophy and Rhetoric* 37, no. 3 (2004): 188–206.

Grossberg, Lawrence. "On Postmodernism and Articulation: An Interview with Stuart Hall." *Journal of Communication Inquiry* 10, no. 2 (June 1986): 45–60.

Hall, Stuart. "The Emergence of Cultural Studies and the Crisis of the Humanities." *The Humanities as Social Technology* 53 (Summer 1990): 11–23.

Lewis, Justin, and Toby Miller (eds.). *Critical Cultural Policy Studies: A Reader.* Malden, MA: Blackwell Pub, 2003.

McRobbie, Angela. "All the World's a Stage, Screen or Magazine: When Culture Is the Logic of Late Capitalism." *Media, Culture and Society* 18, no. 2 (April 1, 1996): 335–342.

Miller, Toby. *The Well-Tempered Self: Citizenship, Culture, and the Postmodern Subject.* Baltimore, MD: Johns Hopkins University Press, 1993.

Index

For the benefit of digital users, indexed terms that span two pages (e.g., 52–53) may, on occasion, appear on only one of those pages.

A. Philip Randolph: For Jobs and Freedom, 122–23
abortion
  access, 149, 158
  affect, 149, 156–58, 171–72
  documentary, 149–74
  history, 1–2, 4, 149–53, 156–62, 172–73,
    174, 180–81
  representation, 149–53, 162–70, 171,
    175–80, 181
  rhetoric, 149, 152–53, 156–57
  speaking out, 37–38, 156
Abortion: Desperate Choices, 160
Abortion Diaries, The, 154, 156, 160–61, 162–64,
  170–71, 172–73
Abortion: Stories Women Tell, 179–80
Abrash, Barbara, 141, 174
Academy Awards, 95–97, 103, 128, 160
Act of Killing, The, 59
ACT UP, 51–52
activism, 1, 9, 16, 24, 30–31, 40, 46, 47–48, 49, 55–
  56, 59, 73, 106, 145–46, 152–53, 161, 186–
  87, 207–9, 212, 219, 222, 228–29, 233
activist documentary, 4, 18–19, 29–30, 36, 40,
  50–52, 53–55, 57–58, 62–63, 67, 68, 85–86,
  98, 111, 233
advocacy documentary, 4
aesthetic
  articulation, 6
  choices, 12, 46–47
  counterculture, 47–48, 57, 116, 117–20, 153,
    154, 187–88
  entertainment, 16
  interests, 10, 166–68
  mainstream, 142, 155, 229
  production, 45–46
  revolutionary, 149

affect
  abortion, 156–58, 161
  activism, 24, 97, 152–53, 156, 160–61, 181
  affinity, 54
  body, 18–19, 156–57
  communication, 21, 22, 89–90, 149, 152, 155–
    56, 164, 181
After Tiller, 175–77, 179–80
agency
  circulation, 98–99
  contingent, 19–20
  embodied, 21, 107, 126–27, 184
  function, 19
  identification, 22, 59, 67–68, 88–89, 105, 147–
    48, 181, 189, 238–39
  instrumental, 107, 142, 230–31
  kinetic energy, 21, 58, 230–31
  limited, 16–17
  political, 106, 110, 156, 196, 227–28, 234–35
  power, 23–24, 99–100, 237
  public, 141, 142–43, 146, 219
  reflexive, 37–38
  representations of, 125, 127, 186,
    210–12, 222–23
  rhetorical, 19–21, 66, 67, 152–53, 157, 168–70
  social change, 16–17, 71, 232
agit-prop documentary, 4
Ahmed, Sarah, 22, 161, 172
Alcoff, Linda, 17–18
Aldrich, Gillian, 154, 165–66, 173–74
All My Babies, 42–43
Alpert, Jon, 41
Alternative Media Center, 44
American Dream, 51, 120
analog, 4–5, 21, 29–30, 31, 47–48, 186–87,
  189, 190

Anarchism in America, 127–28
anarchist-inflected practices, 39
Anderson, Benedict, 27
antagonism, 3, 27
archives, 12, 13–15, 31–32, 99, 107–8, 110, 114–
    15, 129, 130, 137, 152, 159–60, 223, 224,
    231, 236–37
*Arresting Power: Resisting Police Violence in
    Oregon,* 206–7
As Goes Jainsville, 137–38
At the River I Stand, 122–23
audience
    agency of, 21
    commercial, 62
    diverse, 14, 115
    engagement, 7–9, 10, 19–20, 21, 28–29, 34–35,
        36, 53, 54, 55, 57–58, 59–60, 62–63, 67, 73,
        77, 85–86, 87, 97, 99–100, 107–8, 111, 127,
        142–43, 147, 185, 230–31
    global, 5
    identification, 21–22, 34–35, 49, 57, 80–82, 87,
        105–7, 114, 115, 120, 125, 126–27, 132–34,
        149, 153, 160–61, 162, 164, 171, 188, 209,
        219, 232, 239–40
    interests, 11
    mainstream, 54
    mass, 1, 52, 62, 71, 73, 88–89, 111, 113,
        146–47, 155–56
    target, 8
    witness, 41, 79–80
Axiographics, 10–11

Back-Alley Detroit, 4
Balog, Lester, 1–2, 111–12
Baltimore Rising, 210–12
Banzhuf, Marion, 171
Barad, Karen, 19–20
Barnouw, Eric, 35, 107–8
Baumgardner, Jennifer, 149, 154, 165–66,
    170, 173–74
Bennett, Jane, 19–20
Benson, Thomas, 65–66
Berkeley in the Sixties, 136–37
Berlinger, Joe, 55, 59
Bishop, Claire, 28
black documentary, 108–10
Black Lives Matter, 55–56, 178, 219, 220
Black Panther Party, 41, 67–68, 200–1,
    203, 206–7
Blackfish, 61
Bland, Sandra, 185–86
Blumberg, Skip, 189
Bonanno, Mike, 86
Booked for Safekeeping, 190–91
border, 5, 9–10, 59–60, 131–37

Bordowitz, Gregg, 51–52
Bowling for Columbine, 54, 68–69
Boyle, Deidre, 4, 38–39, 44–45
Brody, Samuel, 111
Brothers on the Line, 114
Brown, Michael, 24, 184–86, 195, 212, 220, 222,
    223, 224
*Burn Motherf*cker, Burn!* 210

Caldwell, John, 13
California Newsreel, 11, 223–24
Campbell, Russell, 35–36
Canon, George E., 110
capitalism, 24, 30, 53–54, 73, 105, 114, 122–23,
    124, 125, 128, 131, 137, 147–48, 168–70
Capitalism: A Love Story, 54, 73
Carnegie Corporation of New York, 122–23
Castile, Philando, 24, 221–22
Celsius 41.11, 74–75
Cesar's Last Fast, 136
Chain Camera, 91–92
Chanan, Michael, 15, 29–30
Chavez, Cesar, 134–35, 136
Chavez, Karma, 22, 106–7
*Chicano! History of the Mexican American Civil
    Rights Movement,* 136–37
cinema
    history of, 1, 13–14, 45, 103, 108, 153
    politics of, 19, 32, 45–46, 56–57, 65, 98, 106,
        110, 114–15, 162
    studies, 12–13, 31–32, 66–67
    working class, 33–34, 35–36, 228–29
Cinéma Vérité, 38, 153, 158–59
circulation, 19–20
    agency in, 66, 98–99, 222–23, 230
    asynchronous, 12
    automated, 12
    networks of, 6, 28–30, 31, 53, 65, 66–68, 85–
        86, 89–90, 99–101, 159, 189–90, 212, 229,
        230–31, 236
    productive, 8
    publics arising from, 13, 20, 29–30, 58, 59–60,
        66, 67, 85–86, 99
    shifts in, 15
    theory, 22–23, 66
    uptake, 13, 24–25, 67
Citizens United, 74–77
civic engagement. *Also see* engagement
Cloud, Dana, 31, 107
coalition building, 5, 29–30, 65, 67–68, 85–86,
    106, 239
collective
    action, 6–7, 18–19, 29–30, 80–82, 106–7, 202,
        228, 237–38
    agitation, 23–24, 31, 134–35

conjuring, 3
  engagement, 131
  field of vision, 8–9
  formations, 100, 106, 147
  imaginary, 104, 234
  interests, 125, 147
  memory, 92–94
  organizing, 56–57, 58, 59, 104
  power, 125, 166–68
  processes, 4–5
  social practices, 3
collective identification
  affect, 152–53, 181
  agency, 22–23, 59, 105, 147–48, 201,
    227–28, 238–39
  audiences, 6, 12, 80–82, 87, 88–89,
    105–6, 140–41
  circulation, 22–23
  coalitions, 21–22, 27, 86, 147
  connection, 21, 100, 114
  discursive, 21–22, 43–44
  fluidity, 22
  interests, 107, 145
  long-lasting, 22
  publics, 12, 21
colonialism, 11–12, 13–14, 17–18, 49, 239
Columbia Revolt, 46
commercial culture, 2, 7–8, 16, 24, 27, 41–42,
    44–45, 47, 50–51, 52–54, 62–63, 65,
    68–69, 73, 74–75, 90–91, 97–98, 108,
    110, 112, 153, 199, 209–10, 212, 228, 229,
    232–33, 235–36
committed documentary, 4, 18, 29
Committee on Un-American Activities, 114–15
commons
  documentary, 6–7, 24, 51, 58, 59, 100–1, 227,
    228, 237–38, 239–40
  inclusive, 1, 6–7, 147, 231
  participatory, 3, 40, 58, 100, 106
complex personhood, 8–9
Condit, Celeste, 156–57
Cop Watch, 203–4
Copwatch: These Streets Are Watching,
    203–4
Cottonpicker's Strike, 111
Couldry Nick, 232
Cove, The, 97
critical media production practice, 236, 237
Cry for Help, The, 190–92
cultural policy studies, 235, 236

Daressa, Larry, 11
Day at Tuskegee, A, 109–10
de Antonio, Emile, 15
Deep Dish TV, 134–35

Deferred Action for Childhood Arrivals
    (DACA), 238
Delano Manongs, 136
Deliberation, 6–7, 22, 83, 152–53
Democracy, 1–2, 4, 34, 35, 36, 75–77, 114, 228–29,
    234, 239–40
Denning, Michael, 34
DiAnna's Hair Ego, 123
Dick, Kirby, 59, 86–87, 88–89, 91–92,
    95–99, 232–33
digital
  archive, 224, 236, 237
  culture, 2–5, 12, 13–14, 15, 24, 28–30, 31, 55,
    58, 62, 66–67, 106–7, 184–87, 189, 200, 212,
    221–22, 225, 229–30, 236, 239–40
  democracy, 42, 186–87
  environment, 12–13
  formats, 21, 190
  media, 7
  methodology, 13–14
  rhetoric, 200, 224
  technologies, 7–8, 12, 24, 51–52, 55–56,
    184–86, 220–21
  video, 30–31
Direct Cinema, 37, 38, 42–43, 70, 74, 155
discrimination, 1–2, 123–24
dissent, 16–17, 38, 54, 62–63, 69–70, 73, 143,
    146, 237
DIVA TV, 51–52
documentary
  access, 2, 9, 13–14, 24, 31–32, 39, 41, 44, 45, 48,
    62, 160, 186–88, 200, 202–3, 219, 220–21,
    224, 227, 228–29, 236, 237
  agency, 6, 16–17, 19, 21, 43–44, 59, 83–85,
    88–89, 90–91, 98, 104, 105, 147–48,
    152–53, 156, 181, 189, 222–23, 228,
    230–31, 238–39
  audiences, 1, 2, 3–4, 5–6, 8, 11–12, 32, 34–35,
    53, 55, 59–60, 61–62, 64, 105–7, 127, 147,
    155–56, 162, 212, 231, 239–40
  circulation, 4–5, 12–13, 19–21, 22–23, 59–60,
    66–67, 99, 230–31
  civic, 4–5, 12–13, 23, 50, 59–60, 63, 65–66,
    107–8, 146
  codes of conduct, 10–11
  consent for, 10–11
  culture, 5, 40, 61–62, 100, 228–29
  engagement, 3–4, 6, 7–8, 15–16, 17, 19–20, 21,
    38–39, 55, 57–58, 59, 63–64, 65–66, 85–86,
    98, 99, 100, 106–7, 131, 142–43, 160–61,
    229, 234, 235
  ethics of, 10–11, 14, 17–18
  event, 4, 6–7, 20, 21, 23, 55, 67–68, 69–70, 85–
    86, 98, 120
  global, 5–6, 24, 35–36, 65, 97, 100,
    185–86, 231

documentary (*cont.*)
  history, 5–6, 12, 13–15, 17–18, 29–30, 31–32,
    50, 53–54, 56–58, 61–62, 64–66, 67, 90–91,
    103, 104, 105, 107–8, 114–15, 122–23, 124,
    131, 141–42, 144, 146–47, 155, 183, 236,
    237, 238, 239
  industry, 8, 9, 11–12, 64–65, 90–91,
    105, 142–43
  infrastructure, 5, 7–8, 42, 48, 49–50,
    129–30, 234
  institutions, 5–6, 7–9, 11, 12, 15, 23–24, 42–43,
    50–51, 53, 59, 61–63, 64–65, 67–68, 87,
    90–91, 153, 159–60, 173, 191, 232–33, 234,
    235, 236, 239
  intervention, 6–7, 8–9, 11–14, 18–19, 30, 42–43,
    46, 56–57, 62–63, 86, 89–90, 111, 114–15,
    117–20, 122, 131, 145, 153, 162, 172–74,
    200–1, 202–3, 209–10, 219, 222–23, 227–28,
    236, 237–39
  methods, 11–12, 14–16, 17–18, 25, 56–57
  nation-state, 5–6, 49–50
  networks, 6–7, 12, 20, 22–23, 28–30, 42, 46, 53,
    57–58, 59–60, 62, 64, 66–67, 89, 97, 98–100,
    105, 122, 159, 173–74, 185, 189–90, 212,
    220–21, 227, 230–31, 239–40
  performance, 14, 20, 21, 97, 105–6, 220, 238–40
  political, 2, 3, 6, 11–13, 21, 27, 62, 65–66, 68–69,
    75–77, 100–1, 153
  popular, 24, 61–63, 65, 67, 69, 75–77, 80–82,
    85–86, 98, 99–101
  practitioners, 11–12, 13, 14–15, 57–58, 59–60,
    64–65, 74, 237, 239
  production, 1–2, 3, 5, 9–10, 13, 30–31, 33, 37,
    50–51, 55, 62, 64, 65, 67–68, 86, 90–92, 105,
    122, 147, 185–86, 228–29, 233, 234, 236, 239
  protest, 2, 3, 16–17, 53–54, 55–56, 62–63, 65,
    104, 116, 146, 187, 232
  reception, 4–5, 13, 18–19, 31, 32, 53
  representation, 10–11, 16–17, 37, 46, 80–82,
    161–62, 179–80, 185–87, 195–96, 198,
    200–1, 209
  rhetoric, 6, 17, 18–20, 21–23, 37–38, 54, 57, 65–
    67, 69, 83–85, 106–7, 127, 147, 166–68, 200
  screen, 6, 10, 14, 77, 98, 107, 186, 237, 238–39
  social change, 1–2, 3–6, 7–10, 11–12, 13–14,
    15–17, 18–19, 21, 23, 28–29, 31–32, 35, 37,
    43–44, 50, 54, 57, 58, 59–60, 104, 146, 147–
    48, 228, 233, 237
  studies, 3, 4–5, 6, 7–8, 11–13, 14, 23–24, 57, 65–
    66, 100–1, 104, 107–8, 132, 228
  theory, 15, 16–17, 29–30
Downing, John, 12
Downtown Community Television Center
    (DCTV), 41, 45, 142
Drew, Robert, 37–38
Drifters, The, 35
Duncan, Larry, 129–30
Durst, Robert, 77–79, 233

Eberly, Rosa, 29–30
Eisenstein, Sergei, 15, 142–43
emotion. *Also see* affect
End of the Line, 63
engagement
  activist, 27, 38–39, 42, 100, 142–43, 173–74,
    234, 235–36
  audience, 7–8, 239–40
  circulation, 99, 223–24
  civic, 3–4, 23, 72
  documentary, 7–8, 17, 58–59, 62–63, 64, 65, 98,
    100, 229, 234, 238
  industry, 63
  instrumental, 48
  media, 2–3, 57–58
  online, 55, 184–85, 229
  participatory, 15–16, 19, 55, 57–58, 83–85, 91–
    92, 106–7, 131, 234
  political, 3, 13–14, 16–17, 19–20, 48, 99–100,
    142–43, 155–56, 160–61, 173–74, 181, 229,
    236, 239
  popular, 100
  production, 91–92, 145
  public, 2–3, 7–8, 9, 235
  rhetorical, 28–29, 38–39, 230–31
Engels, Friedrich, 73
Every Mother's Son, 201, 202, 207–9
exploitation, 10, 11, 16–17, 32, 49, 52, 54,
    105, 122–23, 126, 128, 131, 135–36,
    147–48, 158–59
Eyes on the Prize, 136–37

Factory Farms, 132–34
Fadiman, Dorothy, 160
Fahrenheit 11/9, 54
Fahrenheit 9/11, 4, 52–53, 54, 61, 68–72, 74–77,
    99, 100
Fast Food Women, 121–22
Fast Trip, Long Drop, 51–52
Federal Election Commission (FEC), 74–75
Felski, Rita, 29–30
feminism, 21, 37–38, 105, 124–25, 126–27, 153–
    55, 156, 158–59, 160, 168–70, 173–74, 181
field-based research, 14, 64
*Fight in the Fields: Cesar Chavez and the Farmer
    Struggle,* 136–37
Fighting for Our Lives, 134–35
Filmanthropist, 7–8
Finally Got the News, 187–88
Ford Foundation, 63
Four More Years, 47
Fox, Josh, 54
Frank, Aimee, 158
Fraser, Nancy, 10, 48, 232
Frederick Douglass Film Company, 110
Fresno, CA-Multi-Ethnic Community Policing,
    192–95, 196

Friedberg, Jill, 56
From Danger to Dignity, 4, 149, 160
Frontier Films, 111

Gaga, Lady, 95–97
Gaines, Jane, 3–4, 18–19, 155–56, 160–61, 209
Gardner, Eric, 24, 185–86, 195–96, 220
Garvey, Marcus, 109–10, 125–26
Gasland, 61
Gillette, Frank, 48
Global Village, 40
Gold, Tami, 121, 123–24, 137, 142–43, 144, 145,
    146, 201
Gordon, Avery, 8–9, 186, 201
Gould, Deborah, 155–56
Grant, Oscar, 203
Gray, Freddie, 224
Green, Ronald, 234–35
Grid of Intelligibility, 6, 74, 98, 105–6
Grierson, John, 15, 34–35, 36, 42, 107–8,
    109–10, 146
Gries, Laurie E., 67
guerilla television, 47–48

Hall, Stuart, 59, 234–35, 236
Halleck, DeeDee, 4, 47, 48
Hampton, Fred, 41
Hand That Feeds, The, 141
Hardt Michael, 6–7
Harlan County, USA, 103, 120, 145
Harvest, The, 135–36
Harvest of Shame, 134
Harvesters, The, 134
HBO (Home Box Office), 124
Healthcaring: From Our End of the Speculum, 159
Hegedus, Chris, 37–38
Helfand, Judith, 89, 113
Heroic Negro Soldiers of World War, 110
Hill, Annie, 18
Hillary: The Movie, 74–75
Hoffman, Judy, 116, 117–20, 142–43, 144–45, 146
Hoop Dreams, 68
Horsfield, Kate, 188
How to Survive a Plague, 97
HSA Strike-75, 115–16, 120
Hunting Ground, The, 59, 90–99

I Am Somebody, 122–23
I Had an Abortion, 154, 156, 162, 165–66, 168, 170,
    171, 172–73
Icarus, 97
identification
    audience, 21–22, 80–82
    complex, 22–23
    cultural, 21
    political, 18
    process, 22, 34–35, 160–61, 162
    psychoanalytic, 21
    sensory, 21
    shared, 6, 21–22, 30–31, 33–34, 88–89, 106–7
    substance, 21–22
    working-class, 33–34, 50, 109–10, 114, 124–25,
        126–27, 140–41, 145, 147–48
identity
    collective, 21–22, 68, 104, 105–7, 110, 120,
        147–48, 231
    dominate, 21
    formation, 21, 127, 136, 189
    national, 5–6, 222
imagined communities, 5–6, 27, 30–31
impact, 4–5, 7–8, 29–30, 37, 43–44, 46, 58, 63–
    64, 90–91, 99, 153, 173–74, 180, 222–23,
    229, 232
Impact Partners, 97
Inconvenient Truth, An, 4, 61, 63
Independent Media Center (IMC), 55–56
Indigenous Cultural Theory, 13
Industrial Workers of the World (IWW), 127–28
Inheritance, The, 113
Injury to One, An, 127–28
injustice, 1, 8, 9–10, 11–12, 17, 28, 53, 57, 59–60,
    80–82, 85–86, 127, 185–86, 222–23, 227–28,
    232, 233, 239–40
instrumentality, 18, 27, 29, 35, 36, 48, 54, 59–60,
    80–82, 107, 142
interests
    activist, 59, 161
    capitalist, 50–51, 105
    civic, 64–65, 239
    commercial, 54, 64–65, 90–91, 229
    corporate, 37, 61, 62–63
    countercultural, 49
    institutional, 65
    intersectional, 18, 154–55
    production, 10, 11–12, 16–17, 30–31, 33
    shared, 8–9, 15–16, 22, 27, 29–30, 40, 55, 86,
        106, 107, 120, 147, 168–70
    worker, 121, 125, 129, 131, 146–48
International Documentary Association, 64
intervention, 10–11, 19, 21, 22–23, 232
    documentary, 11–12, 13–14, 31, 46, 56–59, 62,
        64–65, 77, 80, 86, 131, 159, 200–1, 222–23
    participatory, 43–44, 89–90, 190, 237–38
    political, 6–7, 28–29, 30, 56–57, 106, 111, 112,
        114–15, 117–20, 153, 156, 162, 172–73,
        179–80, 202–3, 209–10, 222–23, 224–25,
        232, 235–36
    radical, 127–29
    rhetorical, 18–19, 20
    social change, 17–18, 230
Invisible War, The, 86–87, 88, 89, 90–91,
    97–99, 232–33
It Happens to Us, 149, 158–60

James, Steve, 68
Jane: An Abortion Referral Service, 160
Jarecki, Andrew, 77–78
Jenkins, Henry, 28–29, 229–30
Jinx, The, 77–79, 233
Joe Hill, 127–28
Juhasz, Alexandra, 21–22, 29–30, 124–25, 153
July '64: Unrest in Rochester New York, 196–97
Justice Interruptus, 10

Kahana, Jonathan, 3–4, 29–30
Kaplan, E. Ann, 153
Kartemquin Film Collective, 115–16, 120, 142–43
Keepers, The, 78–79
King, Rodney, 24, 185–87, 198–200, 209, 210
Klein, James, 124–26, 128
Kopple, Barbara, 51, 103, 120, 145–46

LA 92, 199–200
LA Burning, 199–200
labor
    contingent, 121–22
    deliberative, 22–23
    documentary, 105, 107–8, 112–13, 114, 122,
        128–29, 146–48, 184, 196
    movement, 36, 104, 105, 112, 122–23, 124, 125,
        126, 127–28, 129–31, 137, 141, 187–88
    participatory, 19
    protections, 1–2
    representation, 104, 115–16, 120, 123, 124–25,
        126–27, 132–34, 137, 147–48, 188
Labor Beat, 129–30
Labor Video Project, 129
Lane, Penny, 153–54, 160–61, 162, 171, 173
Last Pullman Car, The, 115–16
Latour, Bruno, 19–20
Lazarus, Margaret, 158–59
League of Revolutionary Black Workers, 187–88
Leona's Sister Gerri, 149, 160–61
Lesage, Julia, 162
Let It Fall: Los Angeles 1982–1992, 199–200
Let the Fire Burn, 197–98
Lewis, Anne, 11, 121–22, 135–36
Live Nude Girls Unite, 123
Lorenz, Pare, 42
Los Trabajadores, 135–36
Lost Tapes: LA Riots, The, 199–200

McCann, Brian, 161
McCarthyism, 112–13, 131
Made in L.A., 135–36
Maid in America, 135–36
Making a Murderer, 77
Man in the Middle, 190–91

*Manufacturing Dissent: Uncovering Michael
    Moore,* 74
Maquilapolis, 135
March of the Penguins, 68
marginalization, 1–2, 3, 16–18, 48, 52, 105, 124
Mask, The, 190–91
Martin, Trayvon, 203–4
Marx, Karl, 73
Masri, Bassem, 223
Materialism, 19–20, 67, 160
matter, 19–20, 67
Maysles, Albert and David, 145
media publics. *See* documentary publics
Melucci, Albert, 36
memory, 12, 15–16, 22–23, 58, 62, 92–94, 113,
    125, 127, 141, 146–47, 203, 209–10, 230
Miles of Smiles, 122–23
Miller, Carolyn, 20
Miller, Toby, 234–36
Mine Wars, 114
mobile media, 2–3, 30–31, 55, 56, 58, 62, 114–15,
    152, 181, 184–85, 186–87, 190, 202–4
Moore, Cornelius, 223–24
Moore, Michael, 53, 54, 68–72, 73, 74, 75–77, 85–
    86, 88–89, 97–98, 100
Morris, Errol, 4
Morristown, 135–36
Mother Is a Mother, A, 159–60
Motherhood by Choice, Not Chance, 160
Murrow, Edward R., 134

National Endowment for the Arts, 64
National Endowment for the Humanities, 128
National Negro Business League (NNBL), 109
Negri, Antonio, 6–7
Neoliberalism, 24, 52, 105, 135–36, 153–55
Netflix, 77, 78–79
networks
    activist, 42, 55–56, 97, 122, 173–74, 220–21
    alternative, 46, 159, 189–90, 227
    automation, 12, 20
    broadcast, 51
    communication, 28–29, 42, 59–60, 67
    distribution, 185
    influence, 22–23, 28–29, 57–58, 66–67, 89,
        98–100, 230–31
    institutional, 53
    online, 62, 230, 239–40
    participatory, 29–30, 57, 189, 239–40
    popular, 61, 212
    professional, 64, 173
    public, 98
    shared interests, of, 22
    social change, 22
New Day Films, 158–59
New York Newsreel, 45–46, 142–43, 189–90

Nichols, Bill, 10–11, 24–25, 63, 65–66, 186
No Justice No Peace: California's Battle Against Police Brutality and Racist Violence, 204–5
Norman, Abigail, 158

objects, 7, 12, 19–20, 22, 29, 39, 57–58, 66–68, 90, 92–94, 99–100, 122, 156, 161, 172, 230–31
Occupy Wall Street, 55–56, 137, 141, 219
Operation Small Axe, 203
Oppenheimer, Joshua, 59
oral
    history, 14–15, 31–32, 46, 224, 237
    traditions, 12, 65–66, 69, 185–86
organizing
    community-based, 3–4, 5, 18, 22, 36, 45–46, 59, 62, 86, 105, 147, 203–4, 223–24
    needs, 11
    participatory, 22–23, 28–30, 36, 39, 40, 54, 55–56, 58, 59–60, 80–82, 83–86, 100, 225, 233, 236, 239
Our Lives on the Line, 159–60
Out at Work, 123–24

pain narratives, 17–18
Paper Tiger TV, 51–52
Paradise Lost, 59, 61, 78–79, 80–82, 83–86, 99, 100
Paradise Lost Revisited, 54, 79
Parlee, Lorena, 136
Parry-Giles, Shawn J., 69
Parry-Giles, Trevor, 69
participatory
    activity, 23–24, 91–92
    actors, 20, 83–85
    commons, 3, 40
    condition, 28, 29, 30–31
    culture, 6–7, 29, 30–31, 56–57, 77, 209
    intervention, 28, 89–90
    labor, 22–23
    methodology, 13–14
    mode, 61
    networks, 57
    research, 64
    turn, 14
participatory media culture
    collective, 6–7, 106
    digital, 2, 152
    networks, 29–30, 189
    publics, 2–3, 4–6, 12–13, 15–16, 19, 23, 24, 83, 99, 227–28, 239
    social cement, 22, 27
    social change, 5, 23–24, 30, 78–79, 233–34
Passaic Textile Strike, The, 33–34
PBS, 124

Pearcy, Glen, 134–35
Pennebaker, D. A., 28, 73–74
People's Video Theater, 4, 40, 49
Perch of the Devil, 115
performance, 14, 20, 21, 105–6, 220, 238–40
Perry, Hart, 135–36
petition, 3, 28, 37–38, 58, 62, 110, 127, 146
Pezzullo, Phaedra, 9
Planned Parenthood, 170, 172–73
Plantinga, Carl, 65–66
polarization, 3, 28–29, 33–34, 72, 88–89
police brutality, 24, 52, 56, 104, 111, 134–35, 183–84, 185–86, 196, 198, 200–1, 202, 203, 204–5, 206, 210, 212, 222, 224
Police Officer, 205–6
Policing the Police, 206
political engagement. *See* engagement
popular culture, 1, 2, 53, 61–63, 68–69, 95–96, 97–100, 154–55
Porter, Dawn, 175, 177–78
Portillo, Lourdes, 9–10, 142–43
power, 18
    agency, 6–7, 23–24, 125
    agitation, 134–35
    archive, 13–14, 237
    communication, 16–18, 22, 28–29, 37–38, 62–63, 184, 222
    documentary, 15–16, 21, 30–31, 33–34, 65, 136–37, 146, 190, 199, 203, 212, 227–28, 232–33, 239–40
    institutional, 19
    media, 2–3
    radical, 144
    relationships, 109–10, 203–4, 232
    social change, 13, 49, 115–16
    structures, 8–9, 18–19, 183–84
    thing, of the, 19–20, 99–100
practitioners, 11–12, 13, 14–15, 57–58, 59–60, 63, 64–65, 74, 239
Pregnant but Equal, 120–21
Primary, 37–38
privilege, 9–10, 16–17, 41, 46, 49, 107–8, 126, 128–29, 166–68, 224
production
    activist, 49, 50, 62, 142–44, 202–3, 219, 220–21, 222–23
    collaborations, 59, 86, 91–92
    documentary, 5, 12, 27, 33, 37, 42, 67–68
    interests, 10–11, 30–31
    media, 10, 19
    practice, 7–8, 9–12, 14, 15–16, 19–20, 31, 41, 43–44, 45–46, 47, 89, 149, 184, 187, 200, 229, 234, 235, 236, 237
    process, 8–9, 13, 17, 23, 40, 46, 48, 91–92, 122, 145, 147
Production Culture, 13
promulgation, 3, 28–29

protest, 3, 16–17, 53–54, 55–56, 65, 83, 104, 115,
        137, 146, 160–61, 190, 202, 203–4, 219–20,
        222, 223, 232
public imaginaries, 8–9, 18–19
public speech, 19–20, 28, 37, 120, 238

Quinn, Gordon, 115–16

radical
        documentary, 29, 30, 32, 33–34, 45, 50–51, 65,
                111, 124–29, 142–43, 146, 220
        history, 126
        images, 19
        movements, 34, 125, 127, 128–29, 233
        politics, 28–29, 41, 115, 141
Raindance Corporation, 40, 47–48
Ranucci, Karen, 179–80, 188, 189
Rayford, Bradley, 223
reception, 4–5, 13–14, 18–19, 31, 32
recognition, 1–2, 10, 13–14, 17–18, 22, 37–38, 48,
        83, 90, 105, 123–24, 127, 170–71, 184–85,
        186, 201, 209, 225, 232
redistribution, 10, 11, 17, 48, 209
Reichert, Julia, 124–26, 128, 146
representation
        affect, 152, 155, 203
        cinematic, 1, 108
        documentary, 10–11, 16–17, 18, 31, 37, 38–39,
                80–82, 126–27, 161–62, 179–80, 185–87,
                195–96, 198, 200–1, 209
        ethics, 10–11
        feminist, 154–55, 161–62
        political, 33–34, 45–46
        power, 62–63, 109–10
        social change, 19, 33–34, 36, 48, 109–10, 112,
                181, 188–89, 203–4, 209–12, 224
        social patterns, 1, 10, 32–33, 46, 122–23,
                202–3, 223–24
        working class, 50, 117–20, 122, 124, 125, 126–
                28, 137, 140–41, 146–47
reproductive
        capacity, 155, 158–59
        choice, 157, 172–73
        health care, 149, 153–54, 155, 158–59, 168–70,
                172–73, 174, 177–78
        justice, 149, 157–58, 159, 171, 180, 181
        outcomes, 172
        rights, 158, 176
resistance, 1–2, 6–7, 22, 24, 62–63, 127, 161, 184,
        200, 202, 209–10, 222, 228, 232, 238–39
Revolution '67, 197
rhetoric, 17
        agency, 20
        circulation theory, 22–23, 66–67, 99–100

digital, 185–86, 200, 224
documentary theory, 65–66
doxa, 31
identification, 106–7, 147
invention, 18–19, 21
materialism, 21
performance, 20
social change, 17, 18, 28–29, 57, 168
stasis, 205, 206, 228
Rice, Tamir, 185–86
Rich, B. Ruby, 160
Richards, Harvey, 114–15, 131–32, 134–37
River, The, 42
Road to Life, 111
Robé, Chris, 46, 48, 128–29
Rodriguez, Clemencia, 202, 219, 222, 224–25
Roe vs. Wade, 160, 174, 180
Roger and Me, 51, 68–69
Rothschild, Amalie, 158–59
Rouch, Jean, 142

Salesman, 145
Sandoval, Chela, 22
Schiller, Herbert, 51
Scott, A. O., 4, 233
Seeing Red, 128
Seltzer, Leo, 35–36
Senorita Extraviada, 9–10, 135
Serial, 77, 78–79
778 Bullets, 67–68
Shaffer, Deborah, 127–28
shared identification. See collective identification
Signed, Sealed and Delivered: Labor Struggle in the
        Post Office, 121, 137
Sinofsky, Bruce, 55, 59
Snee, Brian, 65–66
Sobchack, Vivian, 186
social change
        cultural, 10
        documentary, 1–2, 4–6, 7–8, 9, 10, 11–12,
                13–14, 15–16, 18, 19, 21, 23–25, 50,
                54, 147–48
        evaluation, 8, 11–12, 56–57, 67
        frameworks, 12–13, 17, 58–59, 231–34
        function, 16–17, 43–44, 56–57, 104, 174
        grassroots, 30, 33–34
        instrumental, 27, 29, 48
        market-based, 7–8, 63–65
        material, 14, 17
        media, 10
        metrics, 8
        outcomes, 8
        process, 3–4, 13, 17, 59–60, 65, 106, 174,
                179–80, 231–32
        recognition, 17–18

redistribution, 10
representation, 9, 48, 82–83, 200
socio-economic, 10
stakeholders, 8
theory, 16–19
social influence. *Also see* social change
social movements, 12–13, 22, 27–28, 34, 36, 54,
    59–60, 80–82, 83–86, 104, 107, 174, 219, 232
social networks, 22–23, 185
social transformation, 3, 4–5, 10, 16–17, 18–19,
    59–60, 232, 237
solidarity
    corporeal, 18
    documentary, 4, 112–13, 115, 117, 122–23, 127,
        132, 134–35
    radical, 105, 124, 146
    social change, 85–86, 147–48, 170
    social movements, 27, 36, 83–85, 146, 171,
        188, 220
Soldiers in the Army of God, 175–77, 179
solidification, 3, 28, 168–70
Song of the Canary, 120–21
speaking out, 37–38, 147, 156, 165–66, 168–70,
    171, 181, 210
Spiro, Ellen, 123
Steinem, Gloria, 168
Stoney, George, 42–44, 45, 57–58, 82–83, 88–89,
    91–92, 113, 142, 190–92
*Stop Challenging NYPD's "Stop and Frisk"
    Policies,* 207–9
streaming, 20, 55, 56, 61, 152, 155, 185, 209–10,
    219, 220, 221, 223, 224–25, 238
street tapes, 4, 55–56, 184–85, 187–88, 190, 200,
    212, 233
Struggle in Steel, 122
Subjectivity, 6, 22, 29–30, 106, 110, 125, 126, 147,
    155, 158–59, 179–80, 235, 236
Supersize Me, 4, 54

*Taking Our Bodies Back: The Women's Health
    Movement,* 158–60
Taylor Chain I, 115–16
Thigpen, Dorothy, 189–90
tourism
    arm chair, 10, 19, 63
    engagement, 9
    exploitation, 11
    political, 9, 16–18
    problematic, 9, 49
trauma, 9, 15–16, 149, 156–57, 160–61, 162, 199,
    212, 233

U.E. Wells, 115–16
UnAmerican Activities Committee Hearings, 115

Under Pressure, 190–91
Union Maids, 125, 126, 127, 128
United Farm Workers, 134–35, 136
United Negro Improvement Association
    (UNIA), 109–10
Uprising: Hip Hop and the LA Riots, 199–200
Uprising of '34, The, 113
Use of Force: The Death of Eric Garner,
    195, 219–20

Valley of Tears, 135–36
Van Der Zee, James, 109
Vassi, Marco, 48, 49
vernacular cinematic discourse, 116, 117–20, 186–
    87, 198, 220–21
Vertov, Dziga, 15, 50–51
Video Freex, 4, 39, 40–41, 45, 48, 189
Videopolis, 142
Voices from the Front, 51–52

Waiting for Superman, 63
Wal-Mart: The High Cost of Low Prices, 4
Warner, Michael, 59–60
Warren, Shilyh, 149–52, 155
Washington, Booker T., 1–2, 109–10, 232–33
Waugh, Thomas, 18, 29, 104–5
Weather Underground, The, 58
We Are Wisconsin, 137
West Memphis Three, 54, 79–82, 83, 233
What If You Had No Choice, 149, 159–60
What's Happening at Local 70, 116–17, 120
When Abortion Was Illegal, 160–61
When Justice Isn't Just, 205
Where Is Hope—The Art of Murder, 205
Where to Invade Next, 75–77
Where's I.W. Abel? 115–16
Whose Streets, 212
Williams, Linda, 7, 186
Winged Migration, 68
Wisconsin Rising, 137–38
Wiseman, Fredrick, 4
With Babies and Banners, 126, 127
witnessing, 2–3, 15–16, 18–19, 23, 24, 62, 185–86,
    199, 200–1, 203–5, 220, 228, 238–39
Wobblies, The, 127–28
Women Make Movies, 159
Worker to Worker, 120–21
Workers Film and Photo League, 27, 35–36,
    50, 112
Workers International Relief (WIR), 36, 111
Workers Republic, 135–36

X, Malcolm, 210

Yes Men, The, 86
Young Lords, 49
*Youth Pride and Achievement of Colored People of
    Atlanta, Georgia,* 108
YouTube, 77

Zelzer, Steve, 129, 130–31
Ziering, Amy, 59, 86–87, 89, 90–92, 95–96,
    97–99, 232–33
Zimmerman, Debra, 158, 159
Zimmermann, Patricia, 49–50, 62

CPSIA information can be obtained
at www.ICGtesting.com
Printed in the USA
BVHW040431150121
597809BV00003B/10